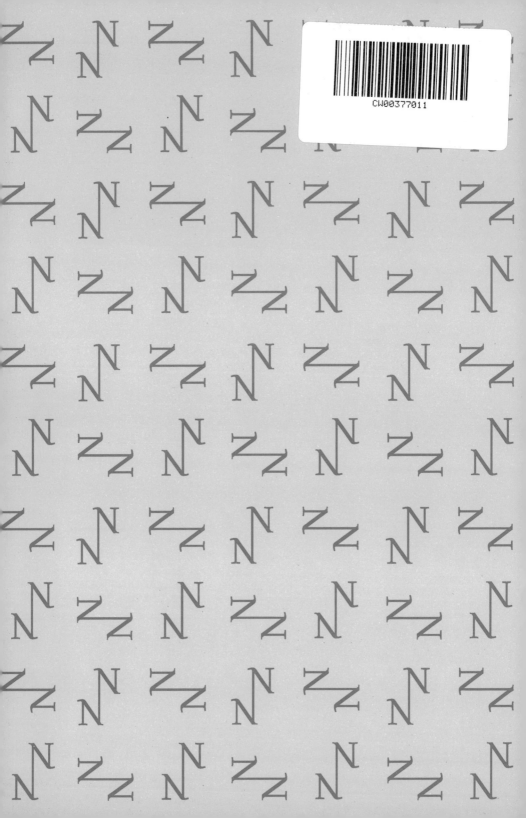

THE NEW NATURALIST LIBRARY

A SURVEY OF BRITISH NATURAL HISTORY

ISLANDS

THE NEW NATURALIST LIBRARY

The Natural History of
ISLANDS

R. J. BERRY

Collins

This edition published in 2009 by Collins,
an imprint of HarperCollins Publishers

HarperCollins Publishers
77–85 Fulham Palace Road
London W6 8JB
www.collins.co.uk

First published 2009

A CIP catalogue record for this book is
available from the British Library.

Edited and designed
by D & N Publishing
Lambourn Woodlands,
Hungerford, Berkshire

Printed in Hong Kong by Printing Express

Hardback
ISBN 978-0-00-726737-8

Paperback
ISBN 978-0-00-726738-5

Contents

Editor's Preface

THE NEW NATURALIST LIBRARY covered *The Highlands and Islands* in the sixth volume in the series, followed by *Shetland, Orkney* (both previous volumes in the series authored by Professor R. J. Berry), then *Hebrides*, and more recently *The Isles of Scilly*. We have thus touched on the fascinating subject of the islands that lie off the shores of Britain and Ireland – the islands off the Isles – but not looked at them together. Professor Berry's new volume in the series takes a holistic view of islands – from what constitutes an island, how they are formed and what can be found on them. What he reveals is that the islands found around our coasts are some of the most intensively studied islands in the world, with flora, fauna and histories equal to, arguably exceeding, more famous groups such as the Galapagos or Hawaiis. Each group has specialists – both human, and fauna and flora – that warrant more of our attention. The islands on the edge of Britain have also been at the forefront of changes in the coastline of Britain over the last 10,000 years – the Island of Doggerland was completely submerged 8,000 years BP and the Isles of Scilly were actually a single island until about 1,000 years ago, with the Isle of Thanet only becoming part of the mainland in the 1800s. Their past thus gives us some indication of changes we can expect in the future and the effects that these changes may have on all their inhabitants.

FIG 1. Satellite image of Great Britain and Ireland. (Science Photo Library)

Author's Foreword
and Acknowledgements

T HIS IS A BOOK about the biology of the islands around Great Britain and Ireland. I have tried to write it in the appropriately sober style and tradition of the New Naturalist series. But islands have an ethos of their own; my difficulty has been that the excitement and magic of real islands kept interrupting me as I wrote. I hope I have managed to transmit a sensible scientific message. But I hope also that the infection of 'islomania' (*see* page 1) has not completely disappeared.

My first islands were fictional – although mythical in the sense that theologians use the word might be better: Daniel Defoe's *Crusoe*, Robert Louis Stevenson's *Treasure Island*, Arthur Ransome's Wild Cat, Crab and Mastodon Islands. Then I ventured onto real islands, walking and climbing on Arran and Skye. Soon after that, I married an islander – from Jersey – and was introduced to a very different sort of island habitat and culture.

Early in our married life, I began a professional involvement with islands, at first as a welcome diversion from laboratory-based biology, then as a more serious and focused series of studies on the genetic consequences of island life. Some of these are described in my first New Naturalist, *Inheritance and Natural History* (1977). My seduction by island natural history came by way of melanic moths in Shetland, working with Bernard Kettlewell in a continuation of his now-classic unravelling of industrial melanism in peppered moths. I followed this with a ten-year study of mice on the small Welsh island of Skokholm, a place described by Julian Huxley in his autobiography as where he felt,

> perhaps even more than in Africa, the power and independence of nature – nature that helps things make themselves, as Charles Kingsley wrote in the Water Babies.

The swarms of puffins flying down from the cliffs and resting on the sea, the screeching of guillemots, the great black-backed gulls screaming and devouring the plump young shearwaters as they stumbled to the cliff-edge before attempting their first flight, yet (if they survived the predatory gull's attack) immediately at home and knowing what to do when they reached the water; the occasional gannets soaring on their wide white wings: all these manifestations of the vast interrelated web of life never ceased to provoke my interest and wonder.

Skokholm remains a special place for me, even though it is many years since I was last there. It wraps one in the powerful peace of isolation, linked to the invaluable realisation that many of the apparent necessities of modern existence are irrelevant distractions from a true quality of life.

Skokholm also introduced me to island literary legend, because it will always be associated with one of the best-known island characters, Ronald Lockley. As a young man, Lockley (like many another youngster) was bewitched with the idea of island life. In 1927, aged 24, he took on the tenancy of the uninhabited (apart from lighthouse keepers) 98-ha Skokholm. Like many others before and since,

FIG 2. Skokholm, Pembrokeshire, made famous by Ronald Lockley. (Sid Howells)

Lockley was defeated by the economics of island farming, but survived and achieved fame for himself and his island with his pioneering bird studies (*Shearwaters*, 1942; *Puffins*, 1953), together with a series of widely read descriptions of life on the island (*Dream Island*, 1930; *Island Days*, 1934; *The Way to an Island*, 1941; *Letters from Skokholm*, 1947), never mind the New Naturalist on *Sea Birds* (1954), co-authored with James Fisher. He increasingly depended on visitors to Skokholm for his living, establishing it as a place of pilgrimage for both bird and island lovers. In 1933 Skokholm became the first formal bird observatory in Britain.

In 1970, my mouse research took me on to the Isle of May, an island at the mouth of the Firth of Forth. It is in many ways ecologically similar to Skokholm – and it was also a site for pioneering ornithologists, identified as a key bird migration site by Eagle Clarke in his pioneering *Studies in Bird Migration* (1912), and another place of ornithological pilgrimage, recorded in visits by the Misses Rintoul and Baxter beginning in 1907 and leading to the establishment of a bird observatory there in 1934. I extended my studies of natural populations to Orkney and Shetland, which led to two more New Naturalists: *The Natural History of Shetland*, 1980 (written jointly with Laughton Johnston, and originally conceived as a need to record the islands' biology before the advent of North Sea oil) and *The Natural History of Orkney*, 1985. I then travelled more widely – to St Kilda to explore why its distinctive house mice had become extinct, to other Hebridean islands, and for comparison of the effects of climate on mice, to the Faroes and various sub-Antarctic and tropical islands. I have been fortunate to visit the Galapagos and Hawaiian archipelagos, which have stimulated – indeed, driven – some of the most basic research into the mechanisms of evolution. All this means that for most of my professional life I have been involved with islands. It has been an enormous privilege to have had such an expanded laboratory, and it has been tremendous fun.

This background will show that I was delighted to be asked by Crispin Fisher on behalf of the New Naturalist Board to write a New Naturalist on the natural history of the islands around Britain and Ireland, both of them islands in their own right as well as 'having' islands. This invitation came soon after the publication of *The Natural History of Orkney*. I accepted with alacrity and said that I looked forward to writing the book, but that it would have to wait until I retired and had time to visit and collate what is known about the various islands. I am now retired, and the Leverhulme Trust awarded me an Emeritus Fellowship, part of whose purpose was to write this book. The New Naturalist Board has generously waited. So, more than 20 years after its inception, herewith *The Natural History of Islands*.

It seems right to survey all our islands, but much more is recorded about some than about others. The result is that a minority of recorded and well-studied islands takes a disproportionate amount of space in what follows. I make no apology for this. The principles of island natural history apply to them all, although every island has its own specialities and unique excitements. Another decision I have had to make concerns how much referencing I should do to the voluminous literature on our islands. Much of the published work is scattered, and one of my surprises has been coming across quite important studies apparently only known locally. Hence it seems sensible to list key references, both to island biology in general and also to local biota, topography and history, without attempting completeness. I have inserted the author and date for more important sources in the text and listed the appropriate references in the References and Further Reading section. The detailed reference list is at the end of the book. I hope that the usefulness of the references in the text will outweigh the annoyance that their intrusion will certainly cause to some. I have included a number of local faunas but only the more substantial local floras, because the publication in 2002 of the *New Atlas of the British and Irish Flora* (edited by C. D. Preston, D. A. Pearman & T. D. Dines) has meant that the botanical data of every locality are available in one volume (and on CD). I hope that the various compromises involved in this selectiveness will allow readers to follow up topics that interest them, whilst not frustrating them by omitting key leads. For ease of reading, the scientific names of most species have been omitted from the text. They can all be found in the index.

My thanks are due to the late Crispin Fisher and to Myles Archibald of Collins for their patience and support, and to a multitude of people who have excited and incited me about islands, beginning with John Barrett of Dale Fort who introduced me to Skokholm and to New Naturalist authorship. I reproduced his letter to me in my preface to *Inheritance and Natural History* (New Naturalist 61). Other people who have helped me, most of them far better naturalists than I will ever be, include:

Stewart Angus (Scottish Natural Heritage), the late John Morton Boyd (Nature Conservancy Council, Scotland) and his son Ian (Director of the NERC Sea Mammal Research Unit) (joint authors of the New Naturalist on the *Hebrides*), Don Brothwell (University of York), Elaine Bullard (great dame of Orkney botanists), David Cabot (author of the New Naturalist on *Ireland*), James Cadbury (RSPB), Steve Compton (University of Leeds) and Roger Key (Natural England), Bob Crawford (University of St Andrews), John Crothers (Field Studies Council), Gina Douglas (Librarian, Linnean Society of London), Pehr Enckell and Sven-Axel

Bengtson (Lund University), Paul Harding and his colleagues at the Biological Records Centre, Monks Wood, Kate Hawkins (Manx Museum), Peter Hope Jones (formerly of the Nature Conservancy Council), Nigel Jee and Paul Veron (Guernsey), Laughton Johnston (formerly of Scottish Natural Heritage), David Lees (University of Cardiff), Adrian Lister (University College London), Mike Majerus (University of Cambridge, author of *Ladybirds* and the second New Naturalist on *Moths*), Eric Meek (RSPB, Orkney), Trevor Norton and John Thorpe (Port Erin Marine Station, Isle of Man), Michael O'Connell of the Aran Islands, Josephine Pemberton (University of Edinburgh), the late Frank Perring (doyen of botanical recording in the modern era, and much else), Mike Romeril, Mike Freeman, John Renouf, Roger and Margaret Long (Jersey), Stephen Royle, Ian Montgomery and Thomas Bodey (Queen's University of Belfast), Jeremy Searle (University of York), Willie Wagstaff (Isles of Scilly), Bob White (University of Cambridge), Max Whitby of Lindisfarne, Rob Whittaker (University of Oxford), Derek Yalden (University of Manchester). Many of these have read and commented on particular sections of the book and saved me from some embarrassing mistakes. I am in their debt. I apologise to anyone misquoted, misunderstood or neglected.

I have tried to illustrate both topography and biology; many people have helped me with pictures. I hope I have correctly attributed all of them. I am particularly grateful to John Baxter of Scottish Natural Heritage and Fergus MacTaggart of the British Geological Survey for their generosity and care in providing photographs for me. I was glad to discover the Geograph British Isles Project, which aims to collect representative photographs for each square kilometre of Great Britain and Ireland. My thanks are due to members of this project for allowing me to publish pictures of places that I had despaired of being able to illustrate.

I am very grateful to Jim Bacon for his meticulous drawings, and to Hugh Brazier for correcting many of my internal errors and contradictions. There must be many remaining. I apologise for any mistakes; ultimately they are my fault.

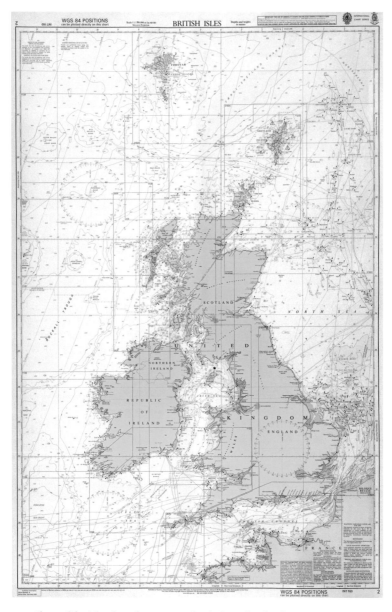

FIG 3. Chart of the islands and seas around Britain and Ireland.
(Crown Copyright. Reproduced by permission of the Controller of Her Majesty's
Stationery Office and the UK Hydrographic Office, www.ukho.gov.uk)

CHAPTER 1

What is an Island?

I SLANDS INCITE PASSION and commitment. Frank Fraser Darling, pioneer conservationist, author of the New Naturalist on *Natural History in the Highlands and Islands*, and serial island dweller, commented towards the end of his life that 'the sea subtly detaches one from immediate, practical reality and casts one into a kind of mystic reverie linking one's life and nature, fusing visible stimuli with meditation.' Lawrence Durrell began his book *Reflections on a Marine Venus* with the words:

> *I once found a list of diseases as yet unclassified by medical science, and among these there occurred the word Islomania, which was described as a rare but by no means unknown affliction of spirit. There are people, Gideon used to say by way of explanation, that find islands somehow irresistible. The mere knowledge that they are on an island fills them with an indescribable intoxication.*

Islomania certainly exists. Although it is a chronic and recurring disease, for most it is a non-threatening malady and rarely fatal. In one form or another it has been about for centuries. The challenge is to understand something about islands and their natural history without diluting their seductive 'intoxication'.

Pliny the Elder was being nothing more than prosaic when he wrote in the first century AD that 'opposite the Rhine delta lie the Britannia islands; they lie to the north-west [of Europe], separated from Germany, Gaul and Spain and the greatest part of Europe by a wide channel.' He recorded that the largest island was called Albion by the natives; he says they referred to themselves as *Pretani* (painted ones), a word which somehow mutated into *Bretani* (Britons). He listed the other islands that make up what he called the Britannias as 40 Orcades

(Orkney), seven Haemodes (Shetland?), 30 Hebudes (Hebrides), Mona (Anglesey), Monopia (Isle of Man), Riginia (Rathlin Island), Vectis (Isle of Wight) and Silumnus (Scilly – which formed a single landmass until around AD 1000).

Pliny never visited the Britannias. He and other early writers got their knowledge of British geography from a voyage around 320 BC by Pytheas the Greek of Massalia (Marseilles). Pytheas had followed the route of the tin traders from Brittany to Cornwall and thence sailed in a series of stages up the west coast of England and Scotland to Orkney (and possibly as far as Shetland or even Iceland: Cunliffe, 2001). From the north isles of Orkney it is possible to see three points of land further north: Fair Isle, halfway between Orkney and Shetland; Fitful Head, on the main Shetland island (always known in Shetland as the Mainland); and most distant, the island of Foula. Pytheas believed he had seen the edge of the world (*Ultima thule*). He returned south down the east coast of Great Britain, completing its first known circumnavigation. He described Britain as triangular, 'like Sicily', with its nearest point (Kantion – or Kent) 19 km from mainland Europe. He estimated that the shortest side of the island was 1,400 km long, the other sides being 2,800 km and 3,700 km, giving a total of 7,900 km – remarkably close to the true figure of 7,580 km.

The next historical record of the British islands – if historical is the right word – tells of an Irish saint, Brendan (c.484–577) of Clonfert (a place on Lough

FIG 4. John o' Groats, looking north across the Pentland Firth towards Orkney. (R. J. Berry)

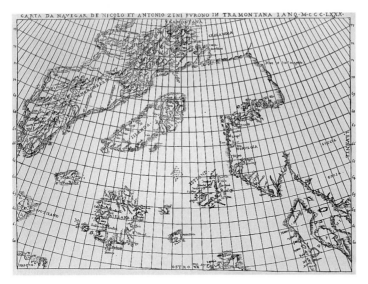

FIG 5. The 'Zeno map' (1558), probably produced when Nicolò Zeno was associated with Henry Sinclair, appointed Earl of Orkney in 1379. 'Friesland' seems to be the Faroe Islands (Ramsey, 1972). (Reproduced by permission of the Royal Geographical Society)

FIG 6. The North Atlantic as shown in *Theatrum Orbis Terrarum* (1570) by Abraham Ortelius (1527–98). This was the first reasonably accurate map of such an extensive area. (Reproduced by permission of the Royal Geographical Society)

Derg in Galway) who is supposed to have made several fantastic voyages. Between 520 and 530 he went to Brittany and perhaps the Mediterranean. Then in 545 he built a curragh in Kerry and set sail on a five-year voyage which took him to St Kilda, Shetland, the Faroes and the Westman Islands off Iceland. Finally he travelled in a larger wooden ship from the Aran Islands to North America, where he allegedly found Irish monks already settled.

Three centuries after Brendan, another Irish holy man, Dicuil, wrote the *Liber de Mensura Orbis Terrae* (825), apparently drawing on first-hand knowledge. He tells us:

> All round our island of Hibernia [Ireland] there are islands, some big, some small, some middling; some lie in the sea to the south of Britain, others to the west; but they are most numerous in the northwestern sphere and in the north. On some of these islands I have lived, on others set foot, of some had a sight, of others read … These islands are for the most part small with narrow sounds between them. In these islands hermits coming from Ireland have lived for almost a hundred years.

Dicuil is generally believed to have been describing the Faroes. The *Færeyinga Saga* (dating from the twelfth or thirteenth century) tells us that the Irish were there from about 700 until the first Norse coloniser (Grim Kamban) arrived on Suðuroy in 820 and dispossessed them. Further north in southeastern Iceland there are place names suggesting that Irish Christians (*papar*) were resident when the Norse arrived about 860; there is written testimony that these *papar* refused to live with the heathen incomers. They took themselves off leaving behind bells, crosiers and devotional books written in Irish script.

A recurring problem in all these early accounts is separating fact from over-imaginative interpretation or sheer fiction. For example, the *Navigatio Sancti Brendani*, a widely circulated account that appeared four centuries after Brendan's death, tells of Brendan sailing on one of his journeys westward from Ireland for 15 days with a crew of 60 men, becoming becalmed for a month, and then landing on the 'Fortunate Islands', which the *Mappa Mundi* hanging in Hereford Cathedral (completed c.1275) places at the site of the Canaries; it labels them *Fortunate Insulae sex sunt Insulae Sct Brendani*. Several decades later Brendan's islands appeared at the site of Madeira on a map made by Alelino Dulcert in 1339. Then in 1544 Sebastian Cabot sited them at the latitude of Newfoundland in mid-Atlantic. They lingered on in subsequent maps until finally disappearing in the mid seventeenth century.

St Brendan's islands probably relate to real discoveries, although it is impossible to be certain which islands were being described and whether he was really their discoverer. The same cannot be said of the island of Buss or Brasil, which first appeared on an Anglo-Saxon map of about 993 as a huge island west of Ireland. Its name may be derived from the Irish Gaelic, meaning 'the great and wonderful island'; it certainly had nothing to do with the country we call Brazil. In 1625 a man in County Monaghan secured a royal grant to own the island. Then in 1674 an Irish sea captain, John Nisbet, claimed to have landed on it and rescued several Scottish castaways. Not to be outdone, one Morrogh O'Ley of Galway declared he had lived there for six or seven years in the 1680s. He had not been idle. Whilst there he learnt to practise medicine.

Then there was Friesland, first reported by a Venetian adventurer, Nicolò Zeno, in 1392 (although his account was not published until 1558) on a voyage sponsored by Henry Sinclair, Earl of Orkney, who wanted to extend his influence. Friesland occurs on all maps of the area from 1558 to 1660, usually plotted southeast of Greenland and southwest of Iceland; it may possibly have been based on an early landing in North America.

Friesland did not survive long in the cartographic record. In contrast, Buss died hard: although it dwindled in size on successive maps from a large island to a small rock, it was only finally removed from British Admiralty charts in 1873. And it was not unique: nineteenth-century charts included around 200 islands now known not to exist. Many of these must have been simple optical illusions, wistfully imagined from ships but perhaps no more than a low cloud bank or iceberg. Or they may have been wrongly positioned. Or perhaps fraudulently described to satisfy financial backers – this certainly happened in the case of French claims to a fertile and mineral rich landmass south of Africa.

Another problem is that islands may actually erode away and disappear. Well-authenticated examples of this are the volcanic islands of Gunnbjörn's Skerries between Iceland and Greenland, and Nyer and Geirfuglaskir (where great auks once nested) off Iceland. They are obviously not the same as another sort of disappearing island familiar in Celtic lore, ones visible only to the elect. Once upon a time it was said that nine islands to the west of Ireland rose out of the sea every seven years, plainly visible from the coast of Galway, but that they vanish if anyone attempts to reach them. The Orkney island of Eynhallow was similar: it was claimed to emerge periodically but sink again unless someone could sail to it with steel in his hand and without looking away. Once this was achieved, the island has stayed put. Is is still there. The fascinating saga of disentangling myth from reality for the North Atlantic islands is set out by William Babcock (*Imaginary Islands of the Atlantic*, 1922) and Raymond Ramsay (*No Longer on the Map*, 1972).

The first reasonably accurate map of the British Isles was produced by Mercator in 1564, but the outlying parts were very vague. Even though St Kilda is visible from

Lewis, the proprietor, Rory Mor MacLeod of Dunvegan, could be no more precise in 1615 than that it was 'a day and a night sailing from the rest of the North Isles [Outer Hebrides], far out on the ocean sea'. The first detailed map of St Kilda was prepared by Martin Martin in 1697. The first systematic survey of the British coasts was begun in 1748 on the west coast of Scotland by Murdoch Mackenzie, an Orcadian who was Hydrographer to the Admiralty. He was commissioned because of the frustrations of the Hanoverian forces in tracking down Bonnie Prince Charlie among the many Scottish islands after the 1745 uprising. MacKenzie's charts were a monumental achievement and infinitely superior to the rough sketches then in use. By 1776 he had produced charts of the west coast of Britain from Orkney to the Bristol Channel, plus the entire Irish coast. He was elected to the Royal Society, nominated by Joseph Banks and Thomas Pennant. Although the Ordnance Survey was set up in 1791, it did not survey St Kilda for itself until 1967. The first good map of Fair Isle appeared in 1752.

BRITISH ISLANDS

How many British islands are there (Figs 8 & 9)? (To avoid confusion I will call the largest British island 'Britain' or 'Great Britain', and reserve the term 'British Isles' for Britain plus Ireland and all the other islands round the two big ones). One guesstimate is about 5,000, but many of these are little more than isolated rocks. The Scottish Tourist Board claims there are 790 Scottish islands. They probably got this figure from Bill Murray (1973), who wrote that there are 787, with 589 of them off the west coast. He was clearly more generous (and certainly more accurate) than the figure of 453 for all the islands round the British Isles – based on the saying that there are as many islands round England as hours in the day, as many round Wales as months in the year, as many around Ireland as weeks in the year, and as many round Scotland as days in the year. This is too glib. David Walsh has visited most of the islands round Ireland in his kayak, and lists 'over 300' in his book *Oileáin*. But what is an island? Does one count reefs and skerries like the Eddystone, Wolf, Fastnet and Bishop Rocks, which project about high tide but are little more than wave-washed humps? Trinity House (which looks after lighthouses in England, Wales and the Isle of Man) has 20 'rock lighthouses', the Northern Lighthouse Board has 26, and the Commissioners of Irish Lights another ten, but these vary between towers on virtually submerged reefs to lights on substantial pieces of land such as Lundy, Skokholm and the Isle of May.

Apparently the modern sense of an island as land completely surrounded by water only came with the tentative offshore explorations of the fifteenth and sixteenth centuries, when the 'ocean' ceased to be regarded as an impassable barrier and became a connecting sea (Gillis, 2003). Gillian Beer has pointed out that the word *island* is made up of two elements, *isle* and *land*. *Isle* was derived from a word for water; it meant 'watery' or 'watered'. In the fifteenth century, *land* was added to it, making *is-land*, 'water-surrounded land'. She says, 'The idea of water is thus intrinsic to the word, as essential as that of earth.' Confusingly for us, the Latin word *insula* was used to describe peninsulas, land surrounded by marsh, wooded copses, blocks of buildings, even people living remote from others (Beer, 1990: 271).

A more familiar understanding of an island is reflected in a Scottish saying cited by Michael Shea in his book *Britain's Offshore Islands*: 'If a piece of land will

FIG 7.
Copinsay, an
Orkney island
that is dedicated
to the memory of
James Fisher.
(Richard Welsby)

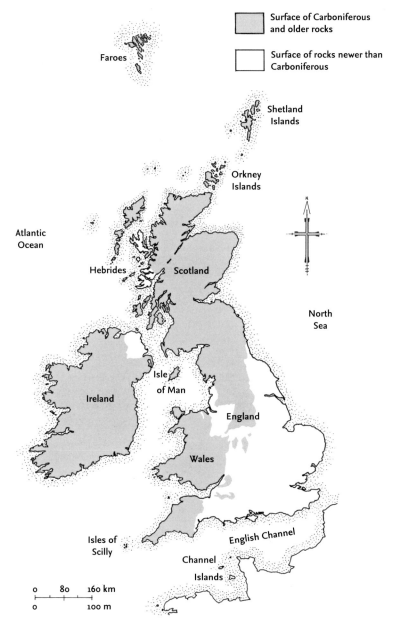

Surface of Carboniferous
and older rocks

Surface of rocks newer than
Carboniferous

Faroes

Shetland
Islands

Orkney
Islands

Atlantic
Ocean

Hebrides   Scotland

North
Sea

Ireland

Isle
of Man

England

Wales

Isles of
Scilly

English Channel

Channel
Islands

0   80   160 km

0   100 m

FIG 8. Most of the islands around the British Isles lie to the north and west, where the
rocks are hard.

Depths in metres

FIG 9. The British Isles lie on the edge of the continental shelf. Many of the surrounding seas are shallow and indicate recent (on the geological time-scale) introgressions.

support a sheep, it is an island; if it will not, it is a rock.' Whoever said this first, it has become a formally recognised definition: the 1861 Census decreed that an island is 'any piece of solid land surrounded by water which affords sufficient vegetation to support one or two sheep, or is inhabited by man'.

But that is not enough for purists. For them, to qualify for island status the area concerned must not by connected by a bridge or permanent causeway. This would exclude Achill, Sheppey, Foulness, Anglesey and (since 1995 and 2001, respectively) Skye and Eriskay. A study by the European Union was even more restrictive, coming up with a definition that, to qualify for island status, an island must have more than 50 residents, be more than 1 km from the mainland and have no rigid link to it, and not be home to the capital of an EU state. This caused political ripples: it would exclude many of the British islands from EU funding. However, the EU denied that all they intended was to remove support from smaller tracts and formally confirmed that 'increased funding can be made available to all areas with a geographical or natural handicap'.

The Vikings were less fussy. For them, an island was one if the passage between it and the mainland was navigable by a ship with its rudder in place. This would allow Lindisfarne (Holy Island) to be recognised as an island, because its causeway is flooded for two hours each side of high water.

And should the Isle of Portland be on the list? It probably became a 'proper' island when the sea level rose in the eighth millennium BC, but a baymouth bar progressively extended from its western end, becoming a tombolo and eventually linking to the mainland of Dorset, the feature we know as the Chesil Bank (Fig. 10). The bank is occasionally breached – or certainly overtopped by wave action. In 1546, Henry VIII's antiquarian, John Leland, wrote:

> *The nature of this bank of Chisil is such, that as often as the wind bloweth strene at South Est so often the se betithit, and losith the bank and breakith through it. So that if this might continually blow there, this bank should soon be beaten away and the se fully enter and devide Portland, making it an isle, as surely it must in tymes past have beene … Portland has been of auncient tyme, by all likelihod environid with the se, and yet berith the name of an isle.*

Did Portland forfeit its island status when the Chesil Bank attained its present extent, or should it be regarded as an island until 1896 when a causeway was built connecting it to Weymouth? For that matter, its neighbour the Isle of Purbeck, which is now merely a tract of land around the southern side of Poole Harbour, was more like a 'proper' island in the past, but nowadays only retains a courtesy title of island – notwithstanding it qualifies as an 'isle' in the pre-modern sense

FIG 10. Chesil Bank, a 13-km-long storm beach linking the Isle of Portland to the Dorset mainland at Abbotsbury. (Unit for Landscape Modelling, University of Cambridge)

FIG 11.
The island of
Seil, south of
Oban, has been
linked to the
mainland of
Scotland by this
'Bridge over the
Atlantic' since
1792. (R. J. Berry)

FIG 12. Causeway and bridge linking Eriskay to South Uist. (R. J. Berry)

FIG 13. The Skye Bridge, connecting Skye to the mainland across Loch Alsh. (Martyn Gorman)

(i.e. as a promontory). Similar considerations apply to Thanet and Foulness. It seems reasonable to demote them to non-islands because they are really little more than promontories with a tidal channel on one side, but it seems over-pedantic to disallow Skye, which is virtually the archetype of many people's perception of an island, on the grounds that it has been connected to the mainland by a bridge since 1995 (Fig. 13). And what about the Uists and Benbecula, connected by causeways built in 1960 (the North Ford) and 1983 (South Ford, replacing a bridge built in 1942), or Dursey, which has had a cable-car link to mainland Ireland since 1969, or Seil, which claims to be reached by a 'bridge across the Atlantic' (albeit only about 50 m long) built in 1792?

Another definition of an island is that it must be big enough to sustain a freshwater supply, which raises the lower limit of size to around 10 ha. This would exclude Grace Darling's Longstone (4ha), Coquet Island (6ha) with most of the British (as distinct from Irish) roseate terns, and Round Island (6ha) in the Scillies. And what about Grassholm (8ha), which is home to nearly a fifth of Britain's gannets and certainly big enough to have a freshwater supply, but doesn't?

A negative definition arises from the Convention on the Law of the Sea, which disallows 'rocks that cannot sustain habitation' for the purpose of establishing exclusive economic zones. This caused a problem for the British Government when it wanted to extend its 'exclusive economic zone' further into the Atlantic in case oil was discovered there. It got over the difficulty by passing the Rockall

FIG 14. Old and new bridges over the Swale, connecting Sheppey to north Kent. (Geograph: Penny Moyes)

FIG 15. Causeway to Lindisfarne (Holy Island), Northumberland. (Geograph: Phil Catterall)

FIG 16. Bridge from Portmagee to Valentia, County Kerry. (Geograph: Jonathan Billinger)

FIG 17. Causeway to Baleshare from North Uist. (Stewart Angus)

Act of 1972, 'to make provision for the incorporation of that part of Her Majesty's Dominions known as the island of Rockall into that part of the United Kingdom known as Scotland'. In other words, it created an island by law rather than geography. Rockall is a bare outcrop of granite, 19 m high and a mere 74 m² in area, 461 km from mainland Scotland and 430 km north of northwest Ireland.

In practice it seems unhelpful to be too rigorous in defining an island. For Eileen Molony (1951), 'a true islander should live within half a day's walk of the sea coast on all sides.' My pragmatic solution has been to use the listings given by Donald McCormick in his three volumes on the islands of England and Wales, of Scotland and of Ireland (McCormick, 1974a, 1974b, 1974c), in which he tabulates 138, 247 and 110 islands, respectively. He is not wholly consistent. For example, he has entries for island groups (such as Shetland, St Kilda or the Isles of Scilly) but then includes also the individual islands within each group. Nevertheless, McCormick's total of nearly 500 is as reasonable an estimate as any. In his comprehensive description of *The Scottish Islands*, Hamish Haswell-Smith (1996) includes all islands over 40 ha (i.e. about 100 acres). Whilst this is bigger than 'a piece of land able to support one or two sheep', in practice it identifies what most of us would call 'an island'. For the record, he lists 165 islands, ranging in size from the 'Long Island' of Lewis and Harris at 220,020 ha down to Flodday (east of Barra) and Brother Isle (in Yell Sound, Shetland) at his cut-off point of 40 ha.

In fact, the debate about which islands to include and which to leave out is largely academic from the point of view of this book because natural-history information is available for only a small minority of McCormick's 500. Species distributions have been published for the main animal and plant groups for the whole of the British Isles (although usually on a 10 km square grid basis which pays no attention to the limits of particular islands), but detailed studies are available for only a few island sites – and often only for particular groups (such as the serpentine flora of Unst, the orchids of Jersey, red deer on Rum, Soay sheep on St Kilda, gannets on the Bass Rock, hen harriers on Orkney and the Isle of Man, migrant birds on Fair Isle, the Isle of May, Cape Clear and the Isles of Scilly, etc.). Few islands have had comprehensive studies of their natural history (outstanding exceptions being St Kilda, Rum, Fair Isle, Clare Island, Lundy and Skokholm). The islands included in the following chapters (some with no more than a brief mention) are listed in Table 1. Eccentrically, I have included the Faroes group in some of the descriptions and comparisons. They are not – and never have been – British islands, but they are major insular neighbours of ours and are more isolated than we are, thus exhibiting some island traits more dramatically than the strictly British islands.

TABLE 1. The islands around Great Britain and Ireland.

The British Isles comprise two large islands (Great Britain and Ireland), a number that are so large that they are almost a scaled-down version of their large neighbour (Anglesey, Man, Sheppey, Wight), several discrete archipelagos (Channel Isles, Farnes, Outer and Inner Hebrides, Orkney, the Isles of Scilly, Shetland – also the Faroes, although these are not, and never have been, British islands), and hundreds of smaller islands ranging in size from several hundred hectares to mere rocks or skerries, often marked by nothing more than a lighthouse or buoy (e.g. Bell Rock, Eddystone, Fastnet, Skerryvore, the Smalls, Wolf).

The more significant and better known islands are listed in approximately anticlockwise order from the point where Great Britain finally separated from the continent, c.7000 BP.

The commonest derivation of the names of individual islands is given, although it should be recognised that many are disputed. They are mainly taken from Haswell-Smith (1996) and Ritsema (1999).

Island areas should be regarded as approximate. Population numbers are largely from the 2001 UK census and the 2002 Irish census.

	AREA (ha)	MAXIMUM HEIGHT (m)	POPULATION
North Foreland			
Sheppey (Sceapige or Island of Sheep)	9,404	50	3,7852
Thames Estuary			
Canvey (Cana's Island)	1,845	5	37,479
Foulness (Bird Promontory)	13,200	4	212
Osea	136	< 10	7
Ray	41	< 10	0
Hamford Water islands, including Pewit, Skipper's, Hedge-end and Horsey	3	< 10	
Mersea (Isle in the Mere)		21	7,182
Havergate	108	< 10	0
Scolt Head	740	< 10	0
Coquet	6		0
Farnes (15 islands at HW, 28 at LW), Megstone group to the west, Crumstone to the east	32	19	0
Lindisfarne (Holy Isle)		19	162

(*continued*)

TABLE 1. (*continued*)

	AREA (ha)	MAXIMUM HEIGHT (m)	POPULATION
England/Scotland border			
Bass Rock	7.5	107	0
Inchcolm (Columba's Is)	9	34	0
Inchkeith (Robert de Keith's Island)	28	66	0
May Island (Gull Is)	45	50	0
Pentland Firth			
ORKNEY			
Stroma (Island in the Tide)	375	53	0 since 1961
Swona (Pig Isle)	92	41	0 since 1974
Flotta (Flat Grassy Is)	876	58	110
South Ronaldsay (Rognvald's Is)	4,980	11	854
Burray (Broch Is)	903	80	262
Hoy (High Island) & Walls	35,380	479	392
Graemsay (Grim's Is)	409	62	27
Mainland (or Pomona)	13,413	225	15,339
Copinsay (Seal-pup Island)	152	64	0 since 1930s
Gairsay (Gárekr's Is)	240	102	3
Shapinsay (Helpful Island)	2,948	64	300
Wyre (Spear's Head)	311	32	18
Egilsay (Church Is)	650	35	37
Eynhallow (Holy Isle)	75	30	0 since 1851
Rousay (Hrolf's Is)	4,860	250	267
Auskerry (East Skerry)	85	18	0 since 1891
Stronsay (Prosperous Is)	3,275	44	358
Sanday (Sandy Is)	5,043	65	478
Eday (Isle of the Isthmus)	2,745	101	131
Faray (Sheep Isle)	180	32	0 (since 1947)
Papa Westray (Priest's Is)	918	48	65
Westray (West Is)	4,713	169	563
North Ronaldsay (Ringa's Is)	690	20	70
Sule Stack and Skerry	19	108	0
SHETLAND			
Fair Isle (Far-off Is)	830	217	86

(*continued*)

TABLE 1. (*continued*)

	AREA (ha)	MAXIMUM HEIGHT (m)	POPULATION
Mainland	97,902	450	17,575
Mousa (Mossy Is)	180	55	0 since 1840s
Burra (Broch Is) and Trondra	1,554	81	1,038
Bressay (Bruse's Is)	2,805	226	357
Noss (Nose)	313	181	0
Foula (Bird Is)	1,380	518	31
Papa Stour (Big Priests' Is)	828	87	23
Whalsay (Whale Is)	1,970	119	1,034
Out Skerries	218	53	76
Muckle Roe	1,813	169	104
Fetlar (Fat Land)	4,078	158	81
Yell (Barren)	21,211	205	957
Unst	12,068	284	720

FAROES

(an independent nation, allied to Denmark, but an important
island group beyond and adjacent to the British Islands)

	AREA (ha)	MAXIMUM HEIGHT (m)	POPULATION
Suðuroy	16,600	610	5,064
Stóra and Lítla Dímun	265	396	5
Skuvoy	1,000	392	90
Sandoy	11,210	479	1,700
Nólsoy	1,028	371	320
Vágar	17,790	722	2,937
Mykines	1,028	560	30
Streymoy	37,347	790	20,000
Eysturoy	28,633	882	10,405
Kalsoy	3,087	787	130
Kunoy	3,546	831	100
Borðoy	9,490	755	4,900
Viðoy	4,100	841	600
Svinoy	2,735	587	60
Fugloy	1,118	620	60

Cape Wrath

	AREA (ha)	MAXIMUM HEIGHT (m)	POPULATION
Sula Sgeir (Solan Goose Rock)	21	68	0

(*continued*)

TABLE 1. (*continued*)

	AREA (ha)	MAXIMUM HEIGHT (m)	POPULATION
Rockall (Sea Rock of Roaring)	0.1	19	0
North Rona (Isle of Seals)	109	108	0 since 1840s
St Kilda	846	430	0 since 1930
Handa (Dog Island)	363	123	0 since 1851
OUTER HEBRIDES			
(Havbredey, isles on the edge of the sea)			
Lewis (Marshy) & Harris (Hilly)	220,020	799	19,918
Scalpay (Scallop Island)	653	104	322
Scarp (Sharp Island)	1,045	308	0 since 1971
Taransay (Taran's Island)	1,475	267	0 since 1974
Shiants (Enchanted Isles)	225	160	0 since 1901
Flannans (St Flannan's Is)	92	8	0
Pabbay (Priest Island)	820	196	0 since 1970s
Sound of Harris			
Berneray (Björn's Island)	1,010	93	136
North Uist	29,875	348	1,320
Benbecula (Small Mount of the Fords)	8,203	124	1,249
Monachs or Heisker (Monk Islands)	577	19	0 since 1931
South Uist	36,519	606	1,818
Eriskay (Eric's Isle)	703	185	69
Barra (St Barr's Isle) and Vatersay	6,835	383	1,172
Mingulay (Big Island)	635	273	0 since 1912
Berneray or Barra Head (Bjorn's Isle)	185	193	0 since 1931
INNER HEBRIDES			
Skye (Cloudy or Misty Isle)	16,562	993	9,251
Raasay (Roe-deer Island)	6,405	443	194
Soay (Sheep Is)	1,063	141	7
Scalpay (Scallop Is)	2,483	392	7
Rum (Wide Is)	10,864	812	22
Muck (Isle of Pigs)	559	137	20
Eigg (Notched Is)	3,049	393	133
Canna (Porpoise Is)	1,314	210	20

(*continued*)

TABLE 1. (*continued*)

	AREA (ha)	MAXIMUM HEIGHT (m)	POPULATION
Tiree (Land of Corn)	7,834	141	770
Coll	7,685	104	113
Summer Isles	473	122	0
Treshnish Isles	208	103	0 since 1824
Kerrera (Kjarbar's Is)	1,214	189	42
Mull (Rounded Hill)	87,794	966	2,696
Iona	870	100	125
Staffa (Stave or Pillar Island)	33	42	0 since 1800
Lismore (Great Garden)	2,351	127	146
Seil	1,329	146	560
Luing (Heather Isle)	1,543	94	220
Colonsay (Columba's Isle) & Oronsay	4,617	143	58
Jura (Deer Isle)	36,692	785	188
Islay (Green Isle)	61,956	491	3,457
Gigha (God's Is)	1,395	100	233
Bute (Corn Island)	12,217	278	7,228
Cumbrae (Island of the Welsh-speakers)	1,168	127	1,434
Arran (High Place)	43,201	874	5,058
Ailsa Craig (Fairy Rock)	104	338	0

North Channel between Scotland and Ireland

	AREA (ha)	MAXIMUM HEIGHT (m)	POPULATION
Rathlin	1,400	136	113
Sheep	4		0
Skerries (Reefs)	200		0
Inishtrahull (Island of the Distant Shore)	46	36	0 since 1928
Tory (Place of Towers)			133
Inishsirrer (Eastern Island)	97		
Gola (Forked)	203		0 since 1966
Owey (Caves)	124		0 since 1970s
Arranmore (Ridged Is)	2,599	228	543
Rutland (from the Duke of Rutland)			0 since 1960s
Inishfree (Is of Heather)			0 since 1951
Inishmurray (St Murray's Is)	85	20	0 since 1948
Coney (Rabbit Is)		13	6
Bartagh	149		0 since 1950s

(*continued*)

TABLE 1. (*continued*)

	AREA (ha)	MAXIMUM HEIGHT (m)	POPULATION
Inishkeas (St Ciath's Islands)	381		0 since 1930
Achill	14,760	671	2,620
Westport (or Clew) Bay islands	10		27
Clare (after St Clare)	1,555	462	127
Inishturk		191	70
Inishbofin (Island of the White Cow)	971	81	178
Inishark		100	0 since 1960
Omey (St Feichin's Seat)	216	26	4
Mweenish	248	23	146
Annaghvaan	126	15	121
Lettermore	907	117	497
Gorumna	4,144	53	1,015
Lettermullen	324	36	219
Furnace (Outer Is)		27	56
Inishtravin	78		1
Inisherk	29		24
Mutton			0
ARAN ISLANDS (Ridged Islands):			
Inisheer (East Is)	583	61	262
Inishmaan (Middle Is)	907	75	187
Inishmore (Large Is)	3,108	123	831
Blaskets	735	292	0 since 1953
Valentia	2,590	266	690
Skellig Michael (Splintered Is)	40	218	0
Little Skellig	7	136	0
Dursey			6
Fastnet		30	0
Roaringwater Bay Islands			
Sherkin	518		129
Cape Clear (St Kiernan's Is)	162	159	129
Saltees (Salt Is)	127		0
Bull Island	3		17
Lambay (Lamb Is)	250	127	6
Ireland's Eye			

(*continued*)

TABLE 1. (*continued*)

	AREA (ha)	MAXIMUM HEIGHT (m)	POPULATION
Strangford Lough Islands	71		
Copeland	202		0 since 1940
Irish Sea			
Isle of Man (a Celtic sea god)	58,793	621	76,315
Calf of Man	249	128	
Walney	1,299		11,388
Hilbre Islands	10	0	
Puffin Island	27	55	0
Anglesey (Isle of the Angles, or Strait Island)	71,500	178	69,149
Bardsey (Bardr's Island)	180	168	58
Cardigan Island	16	52	0
Ramsey (Raven's Isle)	265	136	3
Skomer (Cloven Island)	293	79	2
Skokholm (Island in the Sound)	98	50	2
Grassholm (Grass Island)	8	42	0
The Smalls	2		0
Caldey	183	183	60
Severn Estuary			
Lundy (Puffin Island)	405	142	142
Steepholm	60	78	0
Flatholm	20	25	0
ISLES OF SCILLY: one Island (Ennor) until *c.* AD 1000			
St Mary's	650	49	1,666
Tresco	298	37	180
St Martin's	223	47	142
Bryher	143	42	100?
Samson	49	42	0
Tean	16	33	0
White Isle	15	29	0
Annet	20	15	0
St Agnes and Gugh	175	24	165

(*continued*)

TABLE 1. (*continued*)

	AREA (ha)	MAXIMUM HEIGHT (m)	POPULATION
Land's End			
Drake's Island	3		0
Poole Harbour islands (7 islands)	248		
Brownsea (Bruno's Island)	203		211
Wight	38,100	241	124,577
English Channel			
CHANNEL ISLANDS			
(Guernsey becomes island *c.*9200 BP; Jersey separates from France *c.*5800 BP)			
Jersey	11,630	143	87,186
Guernsey (Green Island)	6,505	110	59,807
Herm and Jethou	182	98	97
Sark	520	105	591
Alderney	1,554	90	2,294

FIG 18. Rough island seas. (Richard Welsby)

On the other hand, I have resisted the temptation to include Heligoland (or
Holy Island, allegedly named by St Willibrod when he was shipwrecked there in
699 while on an evangelistic expedition from the Lindisfarne [Holy Island]
monastery), which lies in the Heligoland (or German) Bight 70km from the
mouth of the rivers Weser and Elbe and about 500 km east of Great Yarmouth. It
was a British colony from 1807 until 1890, when Prime Minister Lord Salisbury
exchanged it for German East Africa to the displeasure of Queen Victoria
(Drower, 2002). It is a 60ha sandstone outcrop with 60 m cliffs. The population
is around 1,700; it is the only German 'high sea' island.

However, the case for including Heligoland would not be imperial or
colonial, but that it has had a significant place in the history of British natural
history. From 1843 to 1887 an amateur birdwatcher, Heinrich Gätke, kept daily
records of the birds, especially migrant numbers on the island, revealing much
new and unexpected information about bird biology and making the island a
mecca for ornithologists from all over the world (Gätke, 1895). In the nineteenth
century, little was known about the distribution and movements of birds around
Britain and Ireland. In an attempt to remedy this, John Harvie-Brown (*see* page
318) and John Cordeaux wrote in 1869 to the keepers on 100 lighthouses to ask for
information about birds attracted to the lights. Two-thirds replied. Encouraged
by this, Harvie-Brown and Cordeaux persuaded the father-figure of British
ornithology, Alfred Newton, to chair a group under the auspices of the British
Association for the Advancement of Science, consisting of themselves, Alexander
More and R. M. Barrington from Ireland, James Hardy from Berwickshire, and P.
M. C. Kermode from the Isle of Man to enquire more comprehensively. Kermode
was soon replaced by William Eagle Clarke, a young museum curator from Leeds,

FIG 19. William Eagle Clarke (1853–1938). (Fair Isle
Bird Observatory)

soon to move to the Royal Scottish Museum in Edinburgh. Eagle Clarke increasingly took on the work of collation and analysis for the committee, with Barrington dealing with the Irish birds. This work reached its climax with Eagle Clarke's two-volume *Studies in Bird Migration* (1912), which laid the basis for systematic recording of migrants around our islands.

Meanwhile a permanent observatory had been established on Heligoland in 1909, building on Gätke's dedicated and regular censuses. Eagle Clarke (Fig. 19) identified Fair Isle as 'the British Heligoland'; he was a frequent visitor to Fair Isle from 1905 until 1921. Inspired by his example, the Misses Rintoul and Baxter began in 1907 to record on the Isle of May every spring and autumn (and, incidentally, to question the then assumption that migration was channelled along well-defined routes, leading them to work towards the modern idea of weather-dependent 'drift migration'). Then, in 1933, W. B. Alexander, appointed three years earlier as Director of the Oxford Bird Census (which became the British Trust for Ornithology), took a group to Heligoland to learn about the techniques used there, which included the large funnel trap familiar to all modern bird-observatory visitors as the 'Heligoland trap'; it was a development of traps used by the islanders to catch birds for food. One of Alexander's party was Ronald Lockley, who, on his return to Skokholm, erected his own version of a Heligoland trap in his vegetable garden. The following autumn he shipped his flock of sheep and farming equipment off the island, sealing his shift from struggling farmer to founder of the first British bird observatory. He visited Heligoland again in October 1936, and on his first day there he ringed 752 migrants (see *I Know an Island*, 1938).

ISLANDS AND BIOLOGY

Islands have enormous benefits for biological research because of their relatively uncomplicated ecology (usually fewer species than in mainland situations and hence fewer competitors or predators, little immigration or emigration – meaning that the fate of all individuals can in principle be determined), often extreme environments, and even the possibility of 'replicates' on different islands. In the context of the British and Irish islands, we can ignore the more extreme isolation of oceanic islands (like Ascension, Tristan da Cunha, Easter Island, Hawaii, etc.) and some of the longer-term effects of island life, since biological life on our islands dates almost entirely from post-Pleistocene times. (For a review of these wider problems, *see* Whittaker, 1998.) Notwithstanding, to describe the factors that determine and limit the animals and plants on the 500

British islands (never mind their parent islands of Great Britain and Ireland), we have to draw together a host of factors – geology, history, isolation and situation, climate and oceanicity, human impact, genetic chance and adaptation. We can generalise about the effects of these factors, but we are still left with many uncertainties and surprises – which provide many of the lures and importance of the islands.

The recognition of the potential of islands for science can be said to have started with Thomas Wollaston's (1822–78) work on Madeira, quickly followed by Alfred Russel Wallace (1823–1913) and Joseph Hooker (1817–1911), but modern studies were really begun by Charles Elton (1900–91). Whilst still an undergraduate at Oxford University, Elton went as an assistant to Julian Huxley on expeditions to Spitsbergen and Bear Island (1921, 1923, 1924). He was captivated by the simplicity of the food web(s) there. At the behest of Huxley, he wrote in 1927 (allegedly in 85 days) the book *Animal Ecology*, which became one of the founding texts of ecology (and a seminal document for 'new naturalists'). Years later, he expounded some of his ideas relevant to islands in a series of broadcast talks and then expanded them into a book, *The Ecology of Invasions by Animals and Plants* (1958). Meanwhile, following Elton's lead, many islands have become sites for classic studies of ecology. Some of these are described in this book: grey seals on North Rona, Soay sheep on St Kilda, red deer on Rum, meadow brown butterflies in the Scillies, and others.

In this treatment, I have confined myself to salt-water islands, not because islands in fresh or brackish water (such as those in the Lake District or Lough Neagh) or biological isolates (on mountain tops or inner-city parks) lack biological interest, nor because their characteristics and study are different to those of islands in the sea. My restriction is arbitrary, because the biological consequences of non-marine islands are not markedly different to marine ones. However, it is for the experts of the Cairngorm plateau, the Shropshire meres, the sewage beds on the outskirts of many towns, ancient churchyards, or Buckingham Palace gardens to insert their own examples into the description and results of islandisation as described in the chapters which follow.

References and Further Reading for Chapter 1 are listed on page 341.

CHAPTER 2

Island-Making

A T THE END of the seventeenth century, three Cambridge University contemporaries produced books within ten years of each other – books that can perhaps be regarded as proto-New Naturalist volumes. Most famous was Isaac Newton (1642–1727), whose *Principia Mathematica* set out the bases of modern physics and the interactions between bodies (and therefore, by extension, ecology); it was published in 1687. Of more direct relevance to biologists was the work of John Ray (1627–1705), rightly called the father of natural historians, who produced the first ever local flora (of Cambridgeshire) and sensible classifications of much of the animal kingdom a century before Linnaeus; his *The Wisdom of God Manifested in the Works of Creation* came out in 1691 and was reprinted many times in the next century and a half. Thirdly, *The Sacred Theory of the Earth*, by Thomas Burnet (1635–1715), appeared in parts in English between 1684 and 1690.

Burnet's *Sacred Theory* (Fig. 20) was the most idiosyncratic; it was said that Burnet would have become Archbishop of Canterbury if he had not written it. It has been the least enduring of the three, but it was highly influential in its time. Its relevance here lies in its attempt to explain why the surface of the earth is so uneven in terms of mountains, seas and landmasses, including islands. Burnet began with the almost unquestioned assumption of his time that God had created the world as a series of concentric layers, with a crust lying over water, and 'no Rocks or Mountains, no hollow caves, nor gaping Channels, but even and uniform all Over'. Rivers ran from the poles to the tropics, where they dissipated. This primitive order was devastated by the biblical Flood. For Burnet, the earth is now a ruin of the 'perfect' pre-Flood situation. The oceans are gaping holes and the mountains upturned fragments of the old Edenic crust. Burnet was

THE SACRED

THEORY

OF THE

EARTH:

Containing an Account of the

Original of the Earth,

And of all the

GENERAL CHANGES which it hath already undergone, or is to undergo, till the
CONSUMMATION of all Things.

IN FOUR BOOKS.

I. *Concerning* the *DELUGE*,
II. *Concerning* *PARADISE*,
III. *The* Burning *of the* *WORLD*.
IV. *The* New Heavens *and* New Earth.

WITH

A REVIEW of the THEORY, and of its
Proofs; efpecially in reference to Scripture.

As alfo

The AUTHOR's *Defence of the* WORK, *from
the Exceptions of* Mr. Warren, *and the Examination of* Mr. Keil,

AND

An ODE to the Author by Mr. *Addifon*.

VOL. I.

LONDON:

Printed for H. LINTOT, at the *Crofs-Keys* againft St. *Dun-
ftans-Church* in *Fleet-ftreet*.

FIG 20. Title page of Thomas Burnet's *Sacred Theory of the Earth* (1684–90), in which he argued that all unevennesses on the earth's surface (such as mountains and islands) are the result of Noah's flood.

particularly offended by mountains: 'If you look upon a heap of them together they are the greatest examples of confusion that we know in Nature; no tempest or earthquake puts things into more disorder' (Nicolson, 1959).

Burnet's ideas were widely criticised by his contemporaries as 'poetic fiction', but his recognition that earthquakes and other phenomena as well as the Flood could 'contribute something to the increase of rudeness and inequalities of the earth in certain places' led eventually to the science of what is now called geomorphology.

WHENCE THE BRITISH ISLES?

The geological history of our islands is almost as improbable as Burnet's ideas. It has only become credible with the recognition, over the past half-century or so, that the surface of our globe is composed of a series of tectonic plates, which move in response to convection currents generated by the internal heat of the planet. A thousand million years ago (1,000 Ma), there was a single 'supercontinent' that geologists refer to as Rodinia. Around 750 Ma, Rodinia broke up, but 150 Ma later the fragments reassembled to form another supercontinent, Pannotia. This soon (in terms of geological time scales) split into two large plates called Laurentia and Gondwana, which moved away from each other over 570–430 Ma, creating the Iapetus Ocean in the gap between them (Fig. 21). The rocks which were to form the British Isles were partly on Gondwana, partly on Laurentia. About 540 Ma, Gondwana in turn began to break up – albeit over a period of 100 million years. The Avalonian plate (including what would become southern Britain) drifted northward towards Laurentia, closing the Iapetus Ocean, which at one stage was 5,000 km wide (Fig. 22). In due course the two plates collided and fused to give rise over the next 100 million years to the Caledonian (or Acadian) mountain chain extending from Svalbard through western Greenland to the Appalachians, represented now in Britain by the higher parts of western Wales and Scotland. At the time this happened, the land which was going to become Britain was around 20°S of the Equator. We have no means of knowing how high the young Caledonian mountains were – perhaps of the same order as the Alps nowadays, around 5,000 m.

England, Wales and southeast Ireland were part of Avalonia (itself a part of Gondwana); a strip of northwest Scotland, together with Skye and the Outer Hebrides, plus northwest Ireland and the tip of western Cornwall, were part of Laurentia. When the plates came together, they formed a geologically complex zone of continental margin and oceanic slivers running northeastwards from Clew Bay in County Mayo to Fair Head in Antrim and thence through Arran and

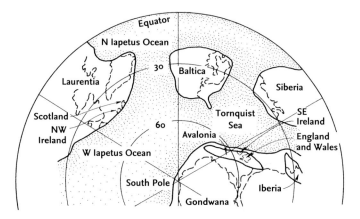

FIG 21. The tectonic plates resulting from the break-up of an original supercontinent and carrying the land that would eventually form Britain and Ireland, moved first towards the South Pole, but then travelled northwards towards their present position.

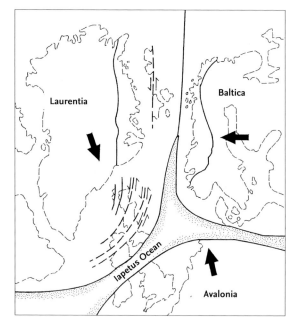

FIG 22. Laurentia and Avalonia collided around 420 million years ago, with the consequent westward thrusting leading to the Caledonian mountains – now mere remnants of their former majesty.

along the southern edge of the Scottish Highlands. Its southern margin in Britain is the Solway Firth, which marks the place where the Iapetus Ocean finally disappeared. The Iapetus existed for something like 180 million years, from near the end of the Precambrian, 542 million years ago, to the middle of the Silurian, 420 million years ago.

The remnants of Laurentia form the Lewisian complex of orthogneisses. They are the oldest rocks in Britain and Ireland and among the oldest in the world; they are most extensively seen at the surface in the Outer Hebrides. But the islands at their birth were far from their present shape and extent: since Laurentia and Avalonia came together, both sea and land have repeatedly risen and fallen. During the Devonian (416–359 Ma), much of Scotland was near the equator and was a desert with little vegetation. The mountains eroded quickly and the valleys filled with alluvial material, which became compressed into boulder conglomerates and sandstones. In the northeast of Britain a large shallow lake, Lake Orcadie, appeared, extending over much of what is now the Moray Firth, Caithness and Orkney.

In the late Cretaceous period (80 Ma), most of our present land was under water, with only the Scottish Highlands and perhaps the Southern Uplands, central Wales and central Ireland appearing as islands. Break-up between Britain and Greenland started around 60 Ma, leading to the formation of the North Atlantic. During this time the British Isles drifted north at a rate of about 8 cm a year to their present position. The boundary between the Cretaceous and Palaeogene periods (65 Ma) was a particularly active time geologically. Never mind the extinction of the dinosaurs, which took place at this time, the events that led to the formation of the North Atlantic also resulted in a short period (geologically speaking) of explosive volcanic activity in the northwest of our islands between 62 and 54 Ma, with a peak at 59–58 Ma. Between 1 and 2 million km^3 of basalt lavas

FIG 24. Staffa, showing its spectacular vertical columns, produced as the result of slow cooling of the basalt rock. (Scottish Natural Heritage)

FIG 23. Lewisian gneiss on Haskeir. (Geograph: George Brown)

FIG 25. Hexagonal pattern of basalt columns on Staffa, formed as the original lava outflow cooled and then shrank. The same pattern occurs on the Giant's Causeway of Antrim, parts of Mull and Skye, and Suðuroy in the Faroes. (Andrew Berry)

were extruded around 55 Ma, extending from Norway to the southern tip of the Rockall Bank. Lavas extend underwater across much of the continental shelf, currently exposed as the spectacular hexagonal basalt columns of the Giant's Causeway in Antrim, and in Staffa (Figs 24 & 25) and Mull. The worn-down remnants of the volcanoes formed at this time are now represented by the Mountains of Mourne, Arran, Mull, the Ardnamurchan headland, Rum and Skye. St Kilda emerged in the same period, although all the lavas that originally covered it have eroded away. The Faroe Islands were also above the sea by 55 Ma, leaving coal seams and plant remains in the lavas as indications of its history. Rockall, the last fragment of land before the edge of the continental shelf, is composed of a rare form of granite from about the same time, apparently intruded into older lava and gabbro.

Sea-floor spreading separated Greenland from Europe; the British Isles were a promontory of western Europe. In quiet periods between eruptions, forests were able to establish themselves. Some of the rocks of the west coast of Mull contain fossils of temperate-climate trees – hazel, oak, plane, together with magnolia and sequioa. The most famous of these is 'MacCulloch's tree' discovered by Dr John MacCulloch in 1811. It is the remains of a cypress standing 12 m high, which had been overwhelmed by molten basalt lavas.

FIG 26. 'MacCulloch's Tree' on the Ardmeanach coast of the Isle of Mull, first identified by John MacCulloch in 1811 and described in his book *A Description of the Western Isles of Scotland* (1819). It is a 12 m-high fossilised *Cupressinoxylon* conifer, surrounded by magma-type lavas similar to those found on Staffa. It is a remnant of a forest covered by a volcanic eruption c.60 million years ago. (British Geological Survey)

FIG 27. Hutton's Unconformity at Siccar Point, near Cockburnspath on the east coast of the Scottish Borders. Sedimentary Devonian rocks lie above almost vertical hard Silurian rocks, with an enormous time gap in their ages. This was visited in 1788 by James Hutton (1726–97) and is one of the sites that led to his ideas of uniformitarianism and about the age of the earth. (British Geological Survey)

The Sgurr of Eigg is formed of pitchstone, an acidic lava, remaining after weaker basalt lavas around it have eroded away. Hugh Miller – geologist extraordinaire and unrelenting anti-evolutionist – wrote an eloquent description of it in *The Cruise of the Betsey* (1858): he found a fossil tree at the base of the pitchstone as well as a plesiosaur (a fish-eating dinosaur) in Jurassic shales in the north of Eigg.

By this time in the late Cretaceous, some familiar features were beginning to appear. For example, the eastern coast of the Outer Hebrides was clear: it borders a channel 100–150 m deep, which probably represents the valley of a river that once drained southwestwards into the Atlantic.

These massive rearrangements of the Earth's crust form the starting point for the events that eventually shaped our islands and provided the framework for the processes that much later have given us our fauna and flora: colonisation, establishment and competition; isolation and adaptation; survival and extinction. But much was still to change. Our islands attained the shape familiar to us about two million years ago, at the beginning of the Quaternary period or Ice Ages (Table 2). The warm phase in which we are living began 11,500 years ago and is really no more than the latest in the cyclical climate sequence of the Ice Ages, during which there have been repeated warmer and cooler phases, each lasting around 100,000 years, thought to be the result of repeated and predictable patterns of solar radiation from changes in the earth's orbit round the sun, initially recognised by a self-taught Scotsman, James Croll in the nineteenth century and analysed in detail by a Serbian geophysicist, Milutin Milkanovitch (1879–1958).

During the cooler periods, continental ice sheets extended over much of the British Isles. Cores extracted from the bed of the Atlantic Ocean show 17 cycles of cold temperature, ten of them in the last million years. The earlier episodes are difficult to explore in detail, because subsequent events have obscured them. It is only during the last 300,000 years that we have clear knowledge of our climate. During this period there have been three cold phases, when ice has covered much of Britain (the Anglian, reaching its maximum 460,000 years ago; the Wolstonian, peaking at 135,000 years ago; and the Devensian, at about 30,000 years ago). The last ice sheet (Fig. 28) began to retreat about 18,000 years before the present. This was accelerated by a period of rapid warming about 14,700 years ago, but there was a brief flurry of cold again between 12,900 and 11,500 years ago (Loch Lomond Re-advance). The present interglacial period (the Flandrian) started after this. It is the time when the history of our current fauna and flora begins to make sense, and when our islands gained more or less their present shapes.

TABLE 2. Divisions of the Quaternary period.

EPOCH	CONTINENTAL SHELF STAGE	BRITISH ONSHORE STAGE	IRISH STAGE	YEARS BEFORE PRESENT AT ONSET
Holocene	Flandrian	Flandrian	Littletonian	10,000
Upper Pleistocene	Weichselian	Devensian	Midlandian	80,000
	Eemian	Ipswichian		130,000
	Saalian	Wolstonian	Munsterian	300,000
	Holsteinian	Hoxnian	Gortian	430,000
Middle Pleistocene	Elsterian	Anglian		480,000
	Cromerian	Cromerian		630,000
		Beestonian (part)		
	Bavelian	(hiatus)		
	Menapian	(hiatus)		
	Waalian	(hiatus)		
	Eburonian	Beestonian (part)		1,650,000
	Tiglian C5–6	Pastonian		
Lower Pleistocene	Tiglian 4c	Pre-Pastonian/ Baventian		
	Tiglian C1–4b	Bramertonian/ Antian		
	Tiglian B	Thurnian		
	Tiglian A	Ludhamian		
	Praetiglian	Pre-Ludhamain		2,600,000
Pliocene	Reuverian	Waltonian		

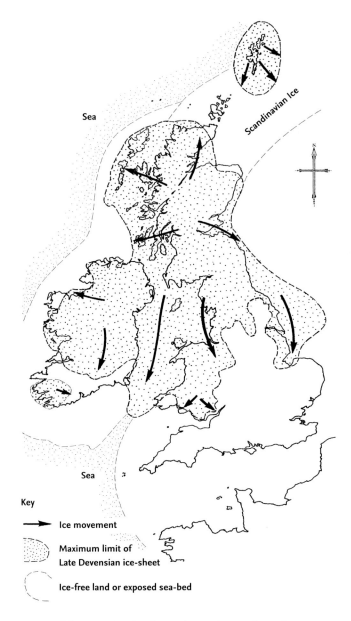

Key

→ Ice movement

Maximum limit of
Late Devensian ice-sheet

Ice-free land or exposed sea-bed

FIG 28. Extent of the Devensian ice sheet at its maximum, about 18,000 years ago, showing the direction of the flow of ice from the major ice caps.

HUMANS AND OTHER MAMMALS

The first signs of humans in Britain – indeed in northern Europe – are from Pakefield, on the Suffolk cost near Lowestoft, around 700,000 years ago. Further evidence has been unearthed at Boxgrove near Chichester in Sussex and from eroded cliffs at Happisburgh in Norfolk, dating from about 500,000 years ago. Skeletal fragments have been found at Swanscombe on the Thames Estuary, the remains of people who lived in the Hoxnian interglacial about 300,000 years ago. Hoxnian man (and woman) shared Britain with many animals familiar to us – voles, common shrews, red, roe and fallow deer, rabbits; but also lions, straight-tusked elephants, cave bears and giant elks. During the subsequent Wolstonian, these animals disappeared and reindeer, mastodons and woolly mammoths ranged over the tundra below the ice sheet, which extended as far south as Birmingham and Coventry. This was followed by the Ipswichian interstadial, when temperatures were higher than today, and when hippos swam in the Thames and lions and hyenas roamed where Trafalgar Square is now.

An enormous collection of stone tools, plus mammoth and rhinoceros bones, has been found in the chasm of La Cotte de St Brelade in Jersey, showing human occupation over a period of a quarter of a million years until around 150,000 years ago. After this, humans apparently disappeared from Britain for tens of thousands of years until about 40,000 BP, when New Stone Age tools begin to appear. During this time Britain was little more than a peninsula of northern Europe, and there is plentiful evidence of human life in southern Europe. However, *Homo sapiens* was certainly present in Britain in later Devensian times from 15,000 BP, with stone tools characteristic of the upper Late Palaeolithic found in Kent's Cavern, Torquay, and they (we) have been an increasingly dominant part of our fauna ever since. Nevertheless, there were only an estimated 2000 people in Britain in 10,000 BC, leaving traces of their presence but having little impact on the land or its creatures. By 3000 BC the population had grown to around 20,000, and it then began to increase rapidly. There were an estimated 250,000 in the Iron Age (500 BC) and around a million when the Romans came.

ISLAND BRITAIN

Britain was intermittently cut off from continental Europe during the Pleistocene. It was an island at a time of high sea levels in the Ipswichian, about 100,000 years ago, but the land connection with the continent was re-established

FIG 29. Weisdale Voe, Shetland, an ice-scoured valley flooded when the sea level rose at the end of the last Ice Age, leaving a series of rounded islands. (Scottish Natural Heritage)

FIG 30. Raised beaches at Dougarie, on the west coast of Arran. The sea level at the end of the last Ice Age was c.30 m higher than at present, leaving a level beach above the road, which is on another raised beach, c.6 m above the present beach. (Scottish Natural Heritage)

during the Devensian. However, brackish water began to appear in the formerly estuarine southern North Sea c.9560 BP, as shown by deposits containing cockle shells; the Dogger Bank was submerged around 8700 BP. Organic material below marine deposits in the Straits of Dover has been dated to 8770±300 BP. Britain became finally isolated soon after this when the English Channel as we know it today finally broke through between France and England. The sea continued to rise after this, as shown by freshwater peats found intertidally in eastern England and the existence of estuarine sediments on the seabed up to 6km offshore from the present-day Suffolk coast.

There is no simple way of calculating absolute rises in sea levels. The extent of the sea relative to the land can vary through vertical changes of either sea or land. Alteration of sea level may result from a change in the volume of water (which may come from the addition or subtraction of water by freezing or melting, or from expansion through a change in temperature) and will be global; such alteration is termed *eustatic*. But we also have to take into account vertical land movements, which may be long-continued and due to tectonic plate shifts, or shorter-term and more local – often associated with depression or release of the crust from changes in a load of sediment, ice, etc. These are *isostatic*. The maximum depth of the Straits of Dover between England and France is 55 m, but it would be naive to assume that this represents the absolute rise in sea level since the strait was formed: we have to separate the effects of isostasy and eustasy for every region, usually from information gleaned from estuarine sediments and coastal lakes. In places, raised beaches show a relative fall in sea level, particularly striking in Mull and other parts of the Hebrides. In others places, underwater peat beds indicate a

FIG 31. The Eastern Isles of Scilly, looking towards St Martin's and Tresco – a drowned landscape with shallow channels visible between many of the islands. (Blom Aerofilms)

relative rise. The Isles of Scilly exhibit many evidences of a drowned landscape, as do the tombolos and ayres of Orkney and Shetland.

Even then we have not finished, because the earth's crust does not behave as a solid block but may suffer differential warping and subsidence: crustal movement in one place must be compensated elsewhere, sometimes leading to a 'forebulge' beyond the stressed section. It has been suggested that dry land between Britain and Ireland may have been produced by such forebulging in post-Pleistocene

FIG 32. Approximate locations of postulated Late Quaternary land bridges between Britain and Ireland (after Devoy, 1995).

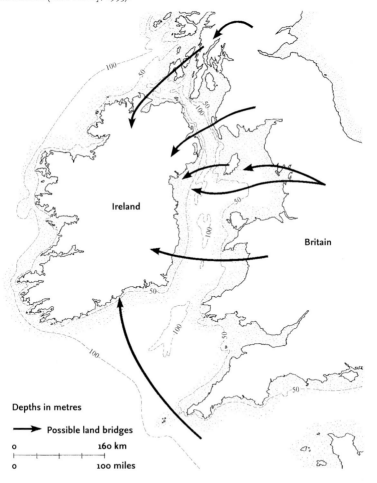

Ireland

Britain

Depths in metres

→ Possible land bridges

0   160 km

0   100 miles

times. Lambeck and Purcell (2001) have brought together all the relevant geological evidence and argued that there may have been 'a tenuous land bridge at about 16,000 years ago' in the general area of Waterford (Fig. 32). If they are right, this might have allowed some animals and plants to cross, although it would have been too soon after the retreat of the ice sheet for most of the present fauna and flora.

As we shall see, the existence (or not) of land bridges is an important element in understanding the biota of islands. If, when or where land bridges existed continues to excite considerable controversy. Biogeographers tend to be fond of invoking land bridges to account for unusual distributions of particular species. Geologists are impressed by the biogeographers' assertions and suggest reasons for these hypothetical stretches of land – and biologists take this as confirmation of their speculation.

In most cases it is impossible to state exactly when a particular island or island group came into existence purely from channel depths. Every locality has to be evaluated from a combination of largely local evidence. To take one example, at Fawley in Hampshire there has been a eustatic rise in sea level of c.3 m and a crustal depression of more than 4.5 m since 6500 BP: southeast England is sinking at around 0.85 mm per year. The northwest of Britain, on the other hand, is rising 2–3 mm a year: raised beaches in the west of Ireland (around Clew, Galway and Bantry Bays) contain marine molluscs around 5 m above the current sea level. Mark Williamson (1981: 15) summarises the situation well:

> In the temperate and Arctic zones many islands would have been connected to the neighbouring mainland within the last 20,000 years, but with a climate appreciably colder than at present. The unravelling of the movements of plants and animals northwards as the ice retreated, and a determination of whether any particular species could reach certain islands before the sea level cut them off, is difficult and controversial. Even if there were good fossil evidence of the time at which a particular species had reached what is now an island, it would still be difficult to know whether it had reached there across the sea or over a land bridge when the climate was colder than at present.

There is no doubt that many – perhaps most – temperate species survived the Pleistocene cold in what is now the Balkans, and spread northwards, following a route either to the south or to the east of the Alps, when the temperature increased. The 'south' and 'east' streams often remained relatively distinct when they met in western Europe, with the formation of a hybrid zone (Hewitt, 1999, 2000, 2004). But the post-Pleistocene recolonisation of Britain is not a simple reoccupation of territory following the retreat of the ice. It has to be dealt with species by species, and is turning out to be highly complicated (Davis & Shaw, 2001).

GEOLOGY VERSUS BIOLOGY: THE IRISH SEA AND PYGMY SHREWS, AND SUCH-LIKE

Islands have fewer species than mainlands, and our two large islands of Ireland and Great Britain show this very clearly. Western Europe has 134 species of native terrestrial mammals, Britain has 43 species, Ireland has 18 (Table 3). Ireland has about 65% of the terrestrial and freshwater insect fauna of Britain (2,131 species as compared with 3,297). There are 1,591 native flowering plant species in Britain but only 1,073 (67%) in Ireland.

By their very nature, islands are difficult for non-flying creatures to reach. We shall return to this in detail, because missing terrestrial species may indicate either local extinction or, conversely, give clues to when the island was cut off from its next-door land. However, the presence of a terrestrial species on an island does not necessarily mean that it arrived by a conventional route. In this context, the pygmy shrew is important (Fig. 33). It is the only native small mammal in Ireland, the Isle of Man, Orkney and probably the Outer Hebrides. The traditional assumption has been that the islands were cut off at a time when the pygmy shrew had managed to cross a declining land bridge, but before its close relative the common shrew could follow.

FIG 33. Pygmy shrew – a small mammal found on many islands, and the subject of much speculation as to how it managed to colonise. (Stewart Angus)

TABLE 3. Numbers of 'native' species on different islands and island groups. The numbers in this table are likely to vary slightly with new records or local extinctions.

	FAROE	SHETLAND	ORKNEY	OUTER HEBRIDES	TIREE	SKYE	ISLE OF MAN	LUNDY	ISLES OF SCILLY	CHANNEL ISLANDS	GREAT BRITAIN	CLARE ISLAND	ARAN ISLANDS	IRELAND
Vascular plants	340	495	570	606	432	663	679	338	528	824	1,591		437	1,073
Mammals (excl. bats)	4	9	12	14	5	22	13	6	10	15	43	6	5	18
Birds	41	66	92			85		38	45	76	204		58	137
Reptiles	0	0	0	0	0	1	1	0	2	2	8	0	1	1
Amphibians	0	1	1	0	0	0	2		1	3	6	0	0	0
Butterflies	0	5	9	17	10	18		23	20	47	56		19	28
Bumblebees	0	4	7	7	2	6		1	6	10	18		6	13
Dragonflies	0	1	3	0	2	4	3	3		23	43	0		22
Grasshoppers	0	2	2	3			3	3	7	23	30		1	5

Much ingenuity has been expended on speculating about the minimal conditions that would allow a passage for the pygmy shrew. For example, common shrews depend on earthworms and these are not found in waterlogged ground. This could have been a reason why they were excluded from a partly flooded land bridge (*see* Yalden, 1981). However, the energy spent on possible scenarios seems to have been wasted. The young science of molecular phylogenetics shows several lineages of pygmy shrews in Europe. Comparisons of DNA from mitochondria show that British shrews belong to a 'northern family' extending from Britain to Lake Baikal while Irish shrews have a very different sequence found only in southern Europe (Mascheretti *et al.*, 2003). The Irish and British shrews have separate origins, and presumably arrived by different routes.

Intriguingly, molecular studies on the pine marten in Ireland show a similar pattern: the Irish martens are more closely related to populations in southwest Europe than to ones in Britain (Davison *et al.*, 2001). It has been generally assumed that martens were intentionally introduced to Ireland for their fur, but the genetic link raises the possibility that trade links with southern Europe may have been important in an early colonisation of Ireland by temperate species.

The situation with the mountain hare and the stoat is not dissimilar, but more complicated. The Irish hare is distinguished as a subspecies (*hibernicus*), being slightly larger than its Scottish cousin and turning only partly white in winter. There are fossil hare remains in Ireland dated at 34,000, 12,000 and 8700 BP, but no convincing evidence that the species survived in Ireland during the last glaciation. If they were absent in the cold phase, they must have been an early member of the postglacial fauna. Irish hares are genetically distinct from Scottish ones, but the evidence does not yet exist to indicate their closest relatives (Hamill *et al.*, 2006). The situation with the stoat is comparable. The Irish form has an irregular dividing line between its dorsal russet brown and its ventral white, leaving only a narrow white stripe. Largely on this basis, the Irish and Isle of Man stoats are regarded as a subspecies (*hibernica*) of the British and continental European race. However, the British form has much less variability in its mitochondrial DNA than either the Irish or the continental European ones (Martínková *et al.*, 2007), implying that it is likely to have been a more recent coloniser. Making assumptions about the rate of molecular change, Martínková *et al.* calculate that the Irish race is around 24,000 years old, while the British one is only about less than half that. They argue that this suggests that stoats survived in Ireland and the Isle of Man through the last Ice Age, but that a less cold-tolerant form invaded and replaced the British race after Ireland and Man were isolated. They support this interpretation of different waves of immigration by pointing out that Scottish water voles are genetically distinct from English and

Welsh ones, a fact that has been interpreted to mean that the northern race (the original post-Pleistocene colonisers from Iberia) was replaced by later immigrants (Piertney *et al.*, 2005).

REFUGES AND LAND BRIDGES

These possibilities about survival of species through a glacial period – either *in situ* or in a refuge elsewhere – raise questions about the origins of the Irish biota overall (Woodman *et al.*, 1997). The more we have learnt about the submarine contours around Ireland, the less likely it becomes that there has been a post-Pleistocene land bridge to Britain, although it is impossible to exclude completely the existence of a low-lying and transitory strait formed by a deformation of the seabed behind a depression caused by the weight of the ice cap (the *forebulging* mentioned above). It is a theoretical possibility, but remains no more than a hypothesis (Wingfield, 1995).

What about the Isle of Man? The sea between it and the Cumbrian coast around St Bees Head is only about 20m deep, and may have persisted as dry ground after 8000 BP, long after Ireland was apparently cut off. Nevertheless, Man is like Ireland in having no native small mammals except the pygmy shrew (it also has the long-tailed field mouse, but this cannot be assumed to be a true native), and biodiversity is relatively low compared to Ireland and Britain (Table 4). David Allen (1984 – *see* page 254) has argued that the limited range of available habitats and soil types can account for the poverty of the island's flora, but there is no dissent that 'the island has formed a distinct biogeographical unit from the late Glacial period onwards' (Innes *et al.*, 2004).

If shrews did not walk to Ireland, the pressure is off to find the land bridge for them to walk over, although we are still faced with the problem of how they got there. But shrews are not the only unexpected species in Ireland, and many biologists have identified 'Lusitanian' species that have a Mediterranean distribution beyond Ireland and southwest Britain. In their influential study *Reading the Irish Landscape*, Frank Mitchell and Michael Ryan (1997) give weight to a shore-living bug, *Aepophilus bonnairei*, which can neither swim nor fly, but which occurs along the Atlantic coast from Morocco to Portugal, and then in southwestern Britain, western Ireland and the Isle of Man; and to the Irish orchid, *Neotinea intacta*, which is found in western Ireland and the Isle of Man. Indeed there are 15 plant species which have a restricted distribution in Ireland and do not occur in Britain – but eight of them are found also in the northwest of the Iberian peninsula. Such species form the basis of claims for a 'Lusitanian' biota.

Could they have survived in a temperate refuge during the coldest parts of the Ice Age? Whilst the evidence for land bridges is meagre and disputed, we cannot entirely exclude the possibility of such refugia where temperate organisms may have survived. It now seems likely that small stands of trees existed much further north than previously thought (Cruzan & Templeton, 2000; Stewart & Lister, 2001; Willis & van Andel, 2004). Oak charcoal dated at 13,000 years BP has been found in Belgium at a time when pollen and beetle studies seemed to indicate

TABLE 4. Biodiversity of the Isle of Man (after Allen, 1962).

	SPECIES RECORDED ON THE ISLE OF MAN	MANX RECORDS AS % OF TOTAL FOR	
		IRELAND	GREAT BRITAIN
PLANTS			
Flowering plants and vascular cryptograms	675	68	45
Mosses	273	62	44
Lichens	345	40	25
Liverworts	85	44	31
Mammals	11	62	26
ANIMALS			
Birds	96	70	47
Macrolepidoptera	370	65	44
Microlepidoptera	157	30	20
Hymenoptera	81	47	15
Land and freshwater bugs	59	23	12
Caddis flies	23	20	12
Harvestmen	9	60	43
Stone flies	10	56	31
Lacewings	13	45	24
Mayflies	11	46	24
Dragonflies	11	41	26
Grasshoppers and crickets	7	70	21
Spiders	92	29	17

The numbers of species recorded on the Isle of Man must be regarded as minima, dependent on the intensity of collecting. In the best-studied groups, about two-thirds of the Irish species and between one-third and two-fifths of the British species have been found on the island.

that northern Europe was treeless; fossil oak, elm, hazel and alder dated between 8500 and 8000 years BP has been found in the Scandes Mountains of Sweden, immediately after deglaciation; the late-glacial vegetation of Skye in 12,000 BP was as diverse as it is today. Molecular studies on Scots pine on Arran shows that it is genetically different from other north European stands; it seems possible that it is derived from a comparatively northern refuge, perhaps in Ireland (Sinclair *et al.*, 1999). Such island refuges may account for the existence of red deer remains in the hilly site of Kent Cavern 25,000 years BP, even though they are absent from other, non-wooded sites during the same period. Such unexpected survivals could have provided colonisers for postglacial spread. This would remove the need to assume the otherwise surprisingly rapid spread of some tree species from their traditional restriction to southern Europe (Iberia, Italy and the Balkans) at the end of the Pleistocene. They could also have provided a haven for a number of animal species.

The possibility is therefore that there may have been a mosaic of relict vegetation patches around the edge of the main ice front, rather than a uniformly treeless steppe tundra. Such refugia are clearly very different from the major land corridors hypothesised by early workers – but support the assumption that some at least of our post-Pleistocene recolonisation was from 'island refuges' rather than continental area.

FIG 34. Low tide at Jersey reveals peat and tree roots from a time when the sea level was lower than at present. (Roger & Margaret Long)

To the north of Britain, we are on more certain ground. The Faroes and Shetland lie along a volcanic ridge. Although this was once continuous, the Faroes broke away in the Cretaceous and is now separated by the deep Faroe–Shetland trough. Shetland has never had any land link with Scotland since well before the Pleistocene. Orkney is geologically a part of the Caithness plain. Although it may have had a short-lived land connection with northern Scotland as the post-Pleistocene sea rose, there is no evidence that it persisted long enough for biological life to spread over it.

The reality is that species distribution data can only poorly differentiate between hypotheses of relict survival, colonisation via land, or introduction at a later time. We have to be extremely careful in extrapolating from current plant and animal distributions to assumptions about how these distributions have arisen. There are too many examples of species 'hitch-hiking' (on the feathers or feet of birds, on floating timber, in high-altitude air currents, or other unlikely routes) to make credible any hypothetical land bridges for colonisers to walk over. This is an area where molecular phylogenetics is going to be an increasingly important tool in determining the sources of island biota.

References and Further Reading for Chapter 2 are listed on page 341.

CHAPTER 3

Island Pressures

A N OUTSTANDING FEATURE *of islands is their strangeness; many of them are downright weird. Naturalists of the last three centuries, Darwin and Wallace among them, brought back to civilisation accounts of strange and unimagined creatures found only on remote islands. Dodos. Sphenodon. The Komodo dragon. Daisies as tall as trees ... A second feature is replicated evolution: numerous organisms of very different origins have gone down the same or very similar evolutionary paths under similar insular conditions ... A third feature is the apparent rapidity of diversifying evolution on islands.*

Peter Grant, *Evolution on Islands*, 1998a

The two defining traits of islands are 'boundedness' and isolation. Isolation is, of course, relative: Hawaii is more isolated than the Hebrides; Sula Sgeir is more isolated than the Isle of Wight. But isolation, allied to size and topography (both of which affect the range of habitat variability), is the factor above all which defines an island. It has a variety of consequences, both biological and physical. Islands have fewer species than continental areas. They also have some that are unique (or endemic), species that are found nowhere else. Indeed, very isolated islands have a high proportion of such species, and this immediately raises questions about how this has come about. One contributing factor could be that an island dweller has fewer (and less variety of) relatives available to breed with. This may lead to inbreeding and a possible reduction in vigour, but it also has an important positive result, in that it allows specialisation (or *adaptation*) to local conditions. This is not possible when immigrants from other parts of the species' range are continually arriving and contributing their genes: unless local selection pressures are very strong, this influx of migrants limits adaptation to an environment averaged over the whole species' range. Are island endemics local ecotypes, or is there more to it than that?

Are there environmental features common to islands? The British and Irish islands share the major climatic influence of the Gulf Stream and the succession of cyclonic frontal systems that roll in from the Atlantic, but within this frame are many local effects. Islands often generate their own environments, as witness the clouds which frequently obscure their upper parts. This can lead to an increased rainfall, particularly on the windward side, with a 'rain shadow' on the lee side. The annual rainfall on the eastern side of Hawaii Island is about 2,000 mm; 50 km away on the opposite side of the islands it is around 200 mm. Closer to home, Skye is justly called the 'misty island'.

CONTINENTALITY AND OCEANICITY

An important way of characterising island environments – or at least those of small islands – makes use of the fact that island land temperatures are buffered by the temperature of their surrounding sea and consequently vary much less than those in continental areas. This fact can be quantified in terms of temperature extremes or 'oceanicity'.

FIG 35. Navelwort or pennywort, a species common in western areas, where it is strongly associated with oceanicity. (Robert Crawford)

Oceanicity can be expressed in various ways, but one of the commonest measures is Conrad's Index of Continentality (K), defined as:

$$1.7A / [\sin (Ç + 10)] - 14$$

where A is the average annual temperature range and $Ç$ is latitude.
K varies from nearly zero for Tórshavn in the Faroes to almost 100 for Verkoyansk in central Russia. In the British Isles, K is 12.5 for Heathrow in central southern England, while the whole of Ireland and most of Scotland have values below 8 (Fig. 37).

Oceanicity measures give a useful indication of the extent to which maritime influences modify the environment of an area, although they inevitably oversimplify because a single figure cannot give a complete picture of ecological influences.

Similar oceanicities are, of course, found both on islands and on their nearby mainlands, but the idea of oceanicity is useful for understanding island biotas because all islands have high values. High oceanicity (or its converse, low continentality) tends to be associated with prolonged soil saturation, partly as a result of reduced evaporation and partly due to increased rainfall (particularly on west-facing coasts). These factors reduce soil fertility as leaching accelerates the removal of nutrients and waterlogging impedes mineralisation and nitrogen fixation. Blanket bog is strongly correlated with high oceanicity. Cool summers and winters, plus wetter winters with strong winds, further impoverish natural habitats – as well as giving problems for farmers and foresters. A general increase in cloudiness tends to depress the altitudinal tree line and leads to a relative lack of woody shrub species. Cowberry and bog bilberry, and the *hermaphroditum*

FIG 36. Ward Hill (479 m) of Hoy, Orkney: a land surface scoured by wind and ice. (Peter Reynolds)

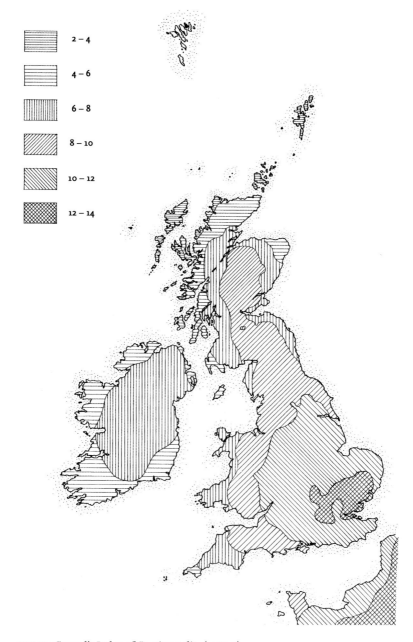

FIG 37. Conrad's Index of Continentality (*see* text).

FIG 38. Looking from Ward Hill on Hoy, Orkney, towards Bay of Quoys. (Robert Crawford)

subspecies of the crowberry, are major components of the vegetation in such situations.

Somewhat counter-intuitively, warm, wet winters do not unequivocally favour plant growth. They may lead to over-consumption of carbohydrate reserves, flooding (encouraging bog development and competition from flood-tolerant species), wind-throw, or soil leaching. On the other hand the rarity of frost benefits many species. The 'Lusitanian' element in the flora (particularly of Ireland and some of the western islands: e.g. the pale butterwort, St Dabeoc's heath, and the Dorset, Cornish and Irish heaths) is dependent on the absence of frost and drought.

Figure 40 shows climate recording stations on a range of island and mainland sites around the British Isles, and Tables 5–8 summarise climatological data from these stations.

FIG 39. Keen of Hamar, Unst. The soil is mineral-rich serpentine debris with a characteristic flora adapted to life on the debris, including the endemic Edmondston's chickweed, first described by Thomas Edmondston, a local man who went on to be Professor of Botany in Glasgow (*see* Chapter 15). (Scottish Natural Heritage)

FIG 40. Climate recording stations (*see* Tables 5–8).

TABLE 5. Average monthly temperatures (°C): mean of daily minimum and maximum.

	JANUARY	FEBRUARY	MARCH	APRIL	MAY	JUNE	JULY	AUGUST	SEPTEMBER	OCTOBER	NOVEMBER	DECEMBER	ANNUAL
Tórshavn, Faroes	3.3	3.5	3.7	5.0	7.0	9.1	10.3	10.5	9.1	7.4	4.6	3.7	6.5
Lerwick, Shetland	3.0	2.8	3.8	5.4	7.6	10.1	12.7	12.9	10.6	8.5	5.8	4.0	7.1
Fair Isle	4.5	4.3	4.5	5.6	7.5	9.7	11.4	11.9	10.5	8.8	6.7	5.3	7.6
Kirkwall, Orkney	3.7	3.6	4.7	6.1	8.5	10.7	12.5	12.7	11.1	9.0	6.4	4.4	7.7
Cape Wrath, Sutherland	4.3	3.9	5.1	6.3	8.3	10.7	11.8	12.3	11.3	9.5	6.7	5.3	8.0
Stornoway, Hebrides	4.3	4.4	5.7	6.9	9.3	11.6	13.2	13.3	11.7	9.3	6.9	5.4	8.5
Tiree	5.1	4.7	5.8	7.3	9.7	12.9	13.3	13.4	12.2	10.3	7.2	6.0	8.8
Lairg, Sutherland	1.1	1.7	4.1	6.5	8.9	12.3	12.7	12.7	11.4	8.1	3.9	1.9	7.1
Braemar	0.8	0.6	2.7	4.9	8.2	11.4	12.0	11.5	10.2	7.3	3.7	1.8	5.3
Ronaldsway, Isle of Man	5.3	4.9	6.0	7.6	10.0	12.8	14.5	14.5	13.1	11.1	8.2	6.3	9.5
Valley, Anglesey	5.5	5.1	6.5	8.3	11.0	13.6	15.3	15.4	13.4	11.6	8.1	6.4	10.0
Aldergrove, Belfast	3.8	4.0	5.4	7.5	10.0	13.2	14.7	15.0	12.5	9.5	6.0	4.7	8.6
Belmullet, Co. Mayo	5.7	5.6	6.8	8.2	10.0	12.6	14.0	14.1	12.8	10.8	7.7	6.6	9.6
Birr, Co. Offaly	4.6	4.8	6.1	7.9	10.0	13.2	14.9	14.6	12.6	10.1	6.4	5.4	9.3
Valentia	6.8	6.6	7.6	8.9	11.0	13.3	14.8	14.8	13.5	11.5	8.7	7.6	10.4
Dale, Pembrokeshire	6.2	5.6	6.6	8.1	11.0	13.8	15.6	15.9	14.4	12.1	8.8	7.3	10.5
Isles of Scilly	6.0	6.0	6.1	7.0	9.0	11.5	13.4	13.7	12.6	10.8	8.2	7.0	9.3
Wisley, Surrey	4.1	4.3	6.3	12.0	12.0	14.8	15.8	16.4	14.2	11.1	6.8	4.9	11.4
Guernsey, Channel Islands	6.6	6.3	7.4	8.7	12.0	14.0	16.2	16.6	15.1	12.6	9.5	7.8	11.1

In Tables 5–8, means are for the period 1961–90, except for Fair Isle (1974–98). Data from the Meteorological Office, Royal Meteorological Society (Fair Isle), Guernsey Meteorological Service, Irish Meteorological Service and the Danish Meteorological Institute (Cappelen & Laursen, 1998).

TABLE 6. Mean rainfall (mm).

	JANUARY	FEBRUARY	MARCH	APRIL	MAY	JUNE	JULY	AUGUST	SEPTEMBER	OCTOBER	NOVEMBER	DECEMBER	TOTAL
Tórshavn, Faroes	133	95	132	88	70	61	70	83	128	155	127	142	1,284
Lerwick, Shetland	131	91	113	72	62	60	63	77	118	136	143	139	1,202
Fair Isle	100	69	85	50	39	43	52	61	89	108	117	104	916
Kirkwall, Orkney	106	73	84	56	50	53	56	78	102	116	123	112	1,009
Stornoway, Hebrides	122	85	105	65	61	63	73	83	116	138	133	128	1,171
Tiree	127	79	96	59	59	61	77	95	129	140	122	120	1,162
Braemar	107	63	72	48	66	58	54	71	81	93	86	89	888
Ronaldsway, Isle of Man	89	61	67	56	46	56	53	71	81	99	93	93	862
Valley, Anglesey	83	56	65	53	49	52	53	74	74	91	101	94	844
Aldergrove, Belfast	88	59	68	54	59	63	66	81	84	88	79	78	867
Belmullet, Co. Mayo	124	80	96	58	68	67	68	94	108	132	128	120	1,143
Birr, Co. Offaly	76	54	61	53	62	55	59	78	71	84	74	79	804
Valentia, Co. Kerry	167	123	123	76	90	79	74	111	124	156	148	159	1,430
Dale, Pembrokeshire	86	93	66	50	46	52	44	67	71	93	95	96	829
Isles of Scilly	102	82	76	50	55	48	43	62	68	88	96	100	869
Wisley, Surrey	61	40	51	47	54	49	45	55	58	64	62	63	648

TABLE 7. Mean hours of sunshine.

	JANUARY	FEBRUARY	MARCH	APRIL	MAY	JUNE	JULY	AUGUST	SEPTEMBER	OCTOBER	NOVEMBER	DECEMBER	TOTAL
Tórshavn, Faroes	14	36	71	107	124	125	111	97	79	48	20	7	840
Lerwick, Shetland	22.6	52.3	85.6	129.9	168.3	148.2	120.0	124.6	100.8	65.4	33.0	14.9	1,066
Fair Isle	26.8	57.7	95.0	148.2	197.7	169.9	137.0	145.6	116.7	71.9	36.9	17.6	1,218
Kirkwall, Orkney	28.5	59.9	96.7	134.7	161.5	156.3	128.7	129.0	95.7	73.2	35.7	19.5	1,119
Stornoway, Hebrides	34.4	68.4	106.0	154.8	184.5	168.9	129.0	133.0	102.0	80.3	43.5	24.8	1,230
Tiree	39.4	66.4	108.5	170.1	213.6	195.0	158.7	156.2	111.0	78.4	48.0	30.1	1,375
Braemar	24.8	56.5	94.9	139.1	162.1	168.5	159.3	146.9	103.5	67.9	36.0	18.6	1,179
Ronaldsway, Isle of Man	51.8	71.2	113.5	169.8	215.9	208.0	193.8	179.8	130.8	95.2	64.2	42.8	1,536
Valley, Anglesey	56.9	83.4	122.5	177.4	223.2	208.9	197.5	185.7	141.0	103.5	66.3	49.6	1,614
Aldergrove, Belfast	45.4	66.5	97.6	154.0	183.7	170.1	147.7	139.5	108.9	85.3	59.1	38.8	1,296
Belmullet, Co. Mayo	45.6	67.5	102.0	158.1	190.3	160.8	133.0	143.5	109.5	81.5	52.2	33.9	1,068
Birr, Co. Offaly	49.6	64.7	98.6	139.2	164.9	144.0	131.4	129.0	111.0	82.8	60.9	43.7	1,016
Valentia	43.7	60.5	94.6	150.0	180.1	153.6	140.4	139.5	108.3	78.4	51.6	36.3	1,220
Dale, Pembrokeshire	59.8	78.9	131.2	190.3	228.5	215.2	224.0	206.8	153.7	104.9	72.6	52.0	1,718
Isles of Scilly	57.7	76.2	128.3	188.4	223.2	209.7	216.1	203.7	161.1	108.8	75.9	50.2	1,699
Wisley, Surrey	50.8	68.4	109.8	147.1	194.4	197.0	197.2	187.2	145.8	107.9	64.5	40.9	1,511
Guernsey, Channel Islands	57.9	78.4	126.1	183.2	233.8	238.2	248.1	235.0	174.0	118.3	74.9	52.2	1,820

TABLE 8. Number of days with frost.

	JANUARY	FEBRUARY	MARCH	APRIL	MAY	JUNE	JULY	AUGUST	SEPTEMBER	OCTOBER	NOVEMBER	DECEMBER	TOTAL
Tórshavn, Faroes	13.0	10.0	10.0	7.0	2.2	0	0	0	0	0.7	4.2	6.7	38.0
Lerwick, Shetland	9.3	9.1	7.4	4.9	0.5	0	0	0	0	0.6	4.7	8.0	44.4
Fair Isle	4.7	3.7	3.4	1.9	0.3	0	0	0	0	0	1.0	3.1	18.1
Kirkwall, Orkney	7.7	7.6	5.5	3.5	0.6	0	0	0	0	0.2	3.0	5.5	32.9
Stornoway, Hebrides	8.2	8.1	6.3	4.1	0.7	0	0	0	0.1	0.5	5.0	7.0	40.1
Tiree	4.5	4.8	2.9	1.6	0	0	0	0	0	0	1.2	2.8	17.9
Braemar	19.1	18.7	16.9	11.7	4.5	0.5	0	0.4	1.5	5.0	12.8	15.8	106.9
Ronaldsway, Isle of Man	5.4	5.4	3.3	1.5	0.1	0	0	0	0	0.3	2.3	4.2	22.3
Valley, Anglesey	5.7	6.5	2.8	0.8	0	0	0	0	0	0.1	1.4	4.2	21.7
Aldergrove, Belfast	10.6	9.2	6.6	3.9	0.8	0	0	0	0	0.6	6.0	8.4	46.2
Belmullet, Co. Mayo	5.0	4.3	2.1	0.9	0	0	0	0	0	0.1	1.3	3.1	16.7
Birr, Co. Offaly	9.0	7.7	7.0	4.2	1.0	0.1	0	0	0.3	1.5	7.1	7.8	45.7
Valentia, Co. Kerry	3.4	3.3	2.2	0.6	0	0	0	0	0	0.1	1.3	3.0	13.9
Dale, Pembrokeshire	3.8	3.9	1.2	0.2	0	0	0	0	0	0	0.3	2.0	11.4
Isles of Scilly	0.9	0.6	0.3	0.03	0	0	0	0	0	0.01	0	0.1	1.93
Wisley, Surrey	10.5	10.5	7.4	3.7	0.6	0	0	0	0	1.4	6.4	9.9	50.5

SEX, NON-SEX AND DISPERSAL

Island species are often unique. On Madagascar 50% of the birds, 70% of the plants and 95% of the reptiles and land snails are endemic to the island; likewise 80% of the plant species of New Guinea, New Zealand and St Helena. This involves an irony that although island species must have had good dispersal ability to colonise in the first place, once there their dispersal powers are a disadvantage. The American botanist Sherwin Carlquist (1974), who studied the plants of Hawaii and other Polynesian islands for many years, commented: 'I observed types of fruits and seeds that seemed incongruously poor at dispersal. The floras of these islands must have arrived by long-distance dispersal, yet during evolution on the island areas various groups of plants have lost dispersability' (*see also* Cody & Overton, 1996; Grant, 1998b).

Charles Darwin was excited when he realised this link between endemism and low dispersal ability. He got it from reading a book by Thomas Wollaston on the insects of the island of Madeira and immediately wrote (7 March 1855) to his friend, the botanist Joseph Hooker:

> It is an admirable work. There is a very curious point in the astounding proportion of *Coleoptera* that are Apterous & I think I have grasped the reason, viz that powers of flight wd be injurious to insects inhabiting a confined locality & expose them to be blown to the sea; to test this, I find that the insects inhabiting the Dezerta Grande, a quite small islet, would be still more exposed to this danger, & here the proportion of apterous insects is even considerably greater than on Madeira proper.

Such loss of flight ability is widespread. For example, Tristan da Cunha has 20 endemic species of beetles, 18 with reduced wings; on Hawaii 184 of the 200 endemic species of carabid beetles are flightless, as are representatives of another six arthropod orders.

For any species to establish itself on an island (as opposed to merely getting there), it must be able to reproduce itself and achieve a population sufficient in size to maintain itself (Hengeveld, 1989). This places a premium on asexual methods of reproduction. *Ischnura hastata* is common in the Americas, but is always a traditional sexual breeder there. On the Azores it forms the only known population of parthenogenetic damselflies. In plants, hermaphroditism and self-compatibility are valuable after long-term dispersal because they enable successful reproduction even when animal pollinators are absent (as they may well be if the island is sufficiently isolated). For example, only 15% of insect orders are

FIG 41. Great auk, from *A Natural History of Uncommon Birds* by George Edwards (1743–51), where it was labelled the 'Northern penguin'. The last British great auk was killed in 1813 on Papa Westray in Orkney. (Linnean Society)

present in the Hawaiian islands and few species seem to be pollinators; there are only six native species of hawkmoths, two species of butterflies, and no bumble bees. In New Zealand, long-tongued bees and hawkmoths are entirely absent; the main pollinators are flies. In general, oceanic islands have many more plants with small white or green flowers than brightly coloured ones with tubular corollas (Barrett, 1998). Such differences are more pronounced in more distant islands than on the inshore islands we are concerned with in this book, but they well illustrate the pressures that island colonisers face.

Flightless birds are common on islands. Many of these are rails (the family that includes coots and moorhens) – at least 23 species are flightless on islands, while another eight species are poor fliers. In fact all rails, including those on mainlands, are poor or reluctant fliers. A better example – probably the best known – is the dodo, one of a group of flightless birds related to pigeons once found on the Indian Ocean islands of Mauritius, Réunion and Rodriguez. All are now extinct.

A flightless bird only slightly less famous than the dodo is the great auk of the North Atlantic, described by the early travellers to St Kilda and last seen (and killed) on land on a British island (Papa Westray in Orkney) in 1813, although one was handled by William Fleming on board the Northern Lighthouse Board ship off Scalpay (near Harris) in 1821 (Gaskell, 2000). The species probably became extinct in the 1840s. The great auk was not confined to islands, but like all the auks it was probably largely limited to islands for its breeding.

Darwin was right in concluding that flight may be 'injurious' to island birds or insects. The problem is not wings as such, but the energy needed for their growth and maintenance, which may be more usefully invested in (say) longer and stronger legs. The only completely flightless rail on Tasmania (the Tasmanian native hen) can run at 50 km/h, much faster than its partially flighted relatives. In some flightless species (such as the Galapagos cormorant and the New Caledonian kagu), wings still exist and are waved around, perhaps for cooling or courtship display. Presumably on the same principle of trading survival against unnecessary flight, the great majority of insect species on the sub-Antarctic islands are flightless.

SIZE EFFECTS

Island species may have to 'make do' with a niche different to their normal one. Many of the British and Irish islands are treeless, and tree-nesting birds have to find somewhere else to raise their young (Table 9). There is no evidence that these 'niche shifts' are other than pragmatic. Indeed, there is no evidence of any inherited dispersal or breeding adaptations in the organisms living on our islands (although the flight habit of the autumnal rustic moth in Shetland may be one: see page 177). An effect that does occur in the British islands is size differences in animals. This is well documented elsewhere. For example, the largest earwig in the world is found on St Helena: it is 78 mm long. The clearest instances are in mammals, where small mammals become bigger on islands and big ones smaller (Table 10).

The probable reason for these size differences is that food is limiting for larger species, while smaller species are not constrained by having to escape from predators and so can increase to a more physiologically efficient size by reducing their relative surface area. For example, the body size of the long-tailed field mouse on European islands is not affected by climate, island size or distance from the mainland but is greater in the absence of its usual competitors (the yellow-necked mouse or the bank vole) or ground predators (stoat, weasel, ferret, adder). At the other end of the spectrum, there were red deer on Jersey in the last interglacial that were only the size of a dog – 125–130 cm high at the shoulder and weighing c.200–250 kg. Some of the Mediterranean islands had similarly dwarfed hippos and elephants. This was so marked that it must have been a genetic

TABLE 9. Unusual nesting sites on Orkney noted by David Lack (after Williamson, 1981).

SPECIES	NORMAL MODE	ORKNEY MODE
Fulmar	Cliffs	Flat ground and sand dunes
Woodpigeon	Trees	Heather moorland
Song thrush	Bushes and trees	Walls and ditches
Blackbird	Woods and bushes	Rocky and wet moorland
Rock pipit	Sea cliffs	Out of sight of sea
Linnet	Bushes and scrub	Cultivated land, reedy marshes
Kestrel	Holes or ledges	Open ground

TABLE 10. Change in size of island mammal species when compared with their mainland relatives (after Foster, 1964).

	NUMBER OF SPECIES		
	SMALLER	SAME	LARGER
Marsupials	0	1	3
Insectivores	4	4	1
Lagomorphs	6	1	1
Rodents	6	3	60
Carnivores	13	1	1
Artiodactyls	9	2	0

FIG 42. The Irish elk, or giant deer, had the largest antlers of any known deer, up to 3.65 m from tip to tip. Fossils have been found across Eurasia, but the species has come to be associated particularly with Ireland and the Isle of Man. (Grant Museum at University College London. Photo by Adrian Lister)

reduction rather than a simple shortage of food. However, some size differences seem to have been wholly phenotypic. Large stags were repeatedly imported to Rum in Edwardian times in attempts to increase the size of the deer on the island, but to no effect: the high density of deer on the island meant that they were chronically undernourished.

ECOLOGICAL FRAGILITY

Islands tend to have fewer species than mainlands. Because of the relatively small size of the sorts of islands considered here (i.e. ignoring larger islands like Madagascar or even Great Britain), the number of individuals of any one species may also be fairly small. In addition, some island species are rare in their mainland range, implying that they may have special requirements and limitations (Kay & John, 1997). This may be compensated for when they get to an island, because they are likely to leave many of their parasites behind when they come into a new habitat, and hence improve their fitness (Southwood & Kennedy,

1983; Clay, 2003). The down side is that island biotas are more susceptible than mainland ones to invasion by predators or competitors. Charles Elton (1958) turned this into an 'ecological resistance hypothesis', arguing that in long-established biotas (i.e. those on mainland areas), competition keeps invaders in check, while 'ecological resistance' is less on species-poor islands. An intriguing example of this is that interspecific competition from introduced hares is more effective in controlling rabbits on islands than either myxomatosis or cat predation (Flux, 1993). Whilst hares are primarily released as game, Flux found that they had replaced rabbits completely on 27% of the 607 islands he reviewed from round the world. In contrast, the introduction of cats removed rabbits from 11% of islands and myxomatosis removed them from 10%. In general, predators, parasites and other checks to survival are often absent on islands, with the result that a new coloniser may lead to the extinction of an island race or the destabilisation of habitats unprotected by the interactions present in a continental situation (Elton, 1958; Fosberg, 1963). Holdgate (1967) lists the current condition and damage from introduced species on more than 30 south temperate islands.

Species may be introduced for a variety of reasons. Colonial settlers often took familiar species with them for food, sport, transport, companionship, or even to remind them of home. Flux and Fullagar (1992) list 800 islands where the European rabbit has been released. Most artificial introductions never manage to become established, but a few have done incredibly well when taken out of their native environment. Such incomers may be intentionally introduced (like rabbits in Australia, grey squirrels in Britain, the goats released on many oceanic islands by sailors to provide a self-renewing source of meat, or the carnivorous snails taken to control previously introduced edible snails in Hawaii but which have caused the extinction of many indigenous molluscs) or they may be entrepreneurial hitch-hikers – seeds on the feet of a bird or commensals travelling with human travellers. They may be transient, like the 'boat cough' suffered by many remote island communities after an unwonted pathogen arrives, but they are more dangerous when they establish permanent residence.

Globally, islands have been damaged enormously by introductions. The worst culprits are four rodent species, which have hitched their way across the world as commensals: the ship or black rat (very uncommon in Britain now, although it flourishes in many other parts of the world), the common or brown rat, the house mouse and the Pacific rat. The last was intentionally spread to many Pacific islands by Polynesian voyagers as a food source (and may have played a critical part in the ecological decline of Easter Island through its predation on the nuts of trees – *see* page 74), but the others have been accidentally introduced throughout the world, most commonly as a result of shipwrecks.

All these rodents take the eggs and young of small vertebrates, and have a particularly devastating effect on colonies of burrowing or ground-nesting birds. They are generalist feeders with an ability to survive and rapidly increase in number in a variety of habitats. The black and common rats are the worst offenders, but house mice on the uninhabited Gough Island in the South Atlantic (a large form, not unlike those on Foula or the Faroes), probably introduced by sealers in the mid nineteenth century, are apparently killing tens of thousands of Tristan albatross and Atlantic petrel chicks every year.

The converse of extinction is colonisation. Ascension Island is a cautionary tale of the serial problems that introductions may cause. The island was occupied by the British in 1815 to deter possible attempts to free Napoleon from St Helena. Rats were common, allegedly coming from the ship of the pirate William Dampier, which foundered at Ascension in 1701). Cats were introduced by the Navy to deal with them. However, by 1824 the island was overrun by cats, and dogs were released to control the cats. Notwithstanding, a few decades later, the gannets, boobies, terns and frigate birds that had previously nested on the lower slopes of Ascension were gone – driven to cliff ledges or an offshore islet which remained cat-free. The plants were threatened by goat grazing (from animals left by early sailors; at one time there were several hundred goats, but they have now

FIG 43. Raft of Manx shearwaters at dusk, off the Pembrokeshire coast. (David Boyle)

been eliminated) and by introduced alien plant species (around 300 have been recorded) – such as the Mexican thorn, which is spreading rapidly and has the potential to cover 90% of the island's surface.

Another island where cats were intentionally released to catch rats was the sub-Antarctic Marion Island. Two adults and three kittens were introduced in 1949, and by 1977 there were more than 3,400 cats, killing half a million ground-nesting birds every year. A few animals infected with feline panleucopenia were then set free, and by 1982 the cat population had declined to an estimated 605. The population was finally eradicated by 1991 by a combination of shooting and trapping.

The fragility of island biology is shown by the fact that 75% of all known extinctions (i.e. where an identifiable species has become extinct, as distinct from calculated extinction rates based on loss of habitat) have occurred on islands. Forty-three bird species are represented only by subfossil bones on the Hawaiian islands alone, having disappeared in the centuries between the appearance of the Polynesians and the visit of Captain Cook in 1778. Every native bird species on Guam has been lost since the introduction of the brown snake in the Second World War. Overall, 42% of recorded historical bird extinctions and the local decline of many others are the consequence of introduced mammal predators.

An alarming statistic about Gough Island, which is one of the most isolated islands in the world (the first recorded landing was in 1675, and probably fewer than a thousand humans have ever set foot there), is that 71 of the 99 insects recorded thereon are introductions.

As far as the British Isles are concerned, the estimates of non-native species present are:

23 mammals
24 birds
3 reptiles
7 amphibians
14 fish
170 insects
12 molluscs
1,380 plants

This is a significant proportion of the total number of species present in the British Isles (see Table 3). Probably about 10% of the introduced species can be regarded as pests, although their impact has not been so devastating as in some other places. Notwithstanding, there are certainly enough examples of damage to serve as a warning (Manchester & Bullock, 2000). For example, the Manx shearwater is so called because of the vast numbers that used to nest on the Calf of Man, a teardrop of an island below the Isle of Man proper. According to *Njáls Saga*, a Viking fleet anchored off the Calf in 1014 prior to a battle near Dublin was 'attacked' by shearwaters to the extent that the sailors had to protect themselves with swords and shields. In the seventeenth century, around 10,000 plump young birds were harvested each year from the Calf for human food. But in 1780 or thereabouts brown rats reached the island, and the colony had disappeared within 20 years.

Puffins are probably even more susceptible, and many islands have been completely cleared by rats. The puffins on Puffin Island (Fig. 44) off Anglesey were likened to 'swarms of bees' in 1774, but rats colonised the island and the colony had disappeared by 1835. In 1892 it was said of Lundy (which is literally 'Puffin Isle' in Old Norse) that 'there would not be room for another puffin'.

FIG 44. Puffin Island, off the east coast of Anglesey. Puffins no longer breed on the island, following its invasion by rats after a shipwreck. (Peter Hope Jones)

Black rats were on the island by 1630 and brown rats some time before 1877. Puffins no longer nest on Lundy. In the Faroes by far the largest colonies of puffins are on the rat-free island of Mykines. Surprisingly, the Shiants still have an apparently stable puffin population of 65,000 pairs, said to be the next largest British colony after St Kilda and Foula, although black rats reached there about 1900 and notoriously flourish (Brooke *et al.*, 2002).

The commonest way for rats to reach an island is from a shipwreck (Fig. 45). In some cases the wreck is known, because of the rapid impact that rats have on the human population. A tragic example was on North Rona, the most isolated British island (apart from the exposed stack of Rockall). It is 109 ha in extent and

FIG 45. A Spanish trawler, *Spinningdale*, wrecked on Hirta, St Kilda, on 1 February 2008, raising fears that rats might invade the island. (Andrew Berry)

lies at 59° N, 70 km northeast of Lewis and 72 km northwest of Cape Wrath. The island had a reputation for fertility and was apparently inhabited from the eighth century. In the early eighteenth century the Lord Registrar of Scotland, Robert Sibbald, reported that it

> had for many generations been inhabited by five families, which seldom exceeded thirty souls in all; they had a kind of commonwealth among them, in so far as if any of them have more children than another, he that had fewer took from the other what his number equalled, and the excrescence of above thirty souls was taken with the summer boat to the Lewis to the Earl of Seaforth, their master, to whom they paid yearly some quantities of meal stitched up in sheep's skins, and feather of sea fowls.

Around 1680 'a swarm of rats came into the island [presumably from a ship] and in a short time had consumed all the corn. A few months later, some seamen landed and robbed the people of their one bull.' An expected supply boat from Lewis never arrived. Martin Martin, writing in 1716, records that 'the steward of St Kilda being by a storm driven in there, found a woman dead, and a child with his mouth set on his dead Mother's Breast – a melancholy scene indeed; and by farther progress on this island the Husband of this woman, they found dead also

FIG 46. Grey seals on North Rona. (Stewart Angus)

... those deceased persons aforesaid died of want; none was surviving.' The island was soon resettled from Lewis, although it was finally abandoned in 1844. There are no rats there now. In 1850, Rona was offered by its owner (Sir James Matheson of Lewis) as a gift to the government for a penal settlement, but it was not accepted. Frank Fraser Darling spent several months studying grey seals on the island in 1938; his account was published in *Island Years* (1940), and his work has been continued and greatly extended in recent years. Around a quarter of the 13,000 pups born each year in the Outer Hebrides are produced on the shores of Rona.

A number of islands have now been cleared of rats by persistent poisoning programmes (Table 11). These have been successful on Lundy, the Calf of Man, Ailsa Craig, Handa, Puffin Island (Anglesey), Cardigan Island and Sheep Island (Co. Antrim). The National Trust cleared an estimated rat population of 10,000 from Canna by widespread poisoning, having previously removed 300 long-tailed field mice for care elsewhere and subsequent return. There are now indications that puffins are beginning to return to some of these islands (page 252), and there has been a very rapid increase in razorbill numbers on Canna.

Feral goat herds are found on Rum, Mull, Colonsay, Islay, Jura, Man, Calf of Man, Lundy, Achill and Rathlin. Whilst goats have been a major pest on many oceanic islands, browsing rather than grazing on the vegetation, on the British islands they are in small numbers and do not seem to do significant damage.

TABLE 11. Islands with brown rats (after Arnold, 1993).

FAROES	Suðuroy, Vágar, Streymoy, Eysturoy, Kunoy, Borðoy, Viðoy
SHETLAND	Mainland, Unst, Out Skerries
ORKNEY	Mainland, Hoy, Shapinsay, Egilsay, Rousay, Stronsay, South Ronaldsay, Wyre, Westray, Sanday, Flotta, Eday, South Faray, Graemsay, Inner Holm, Burray
OUTER HEBRIDES	Lewis, North Uist, Benbecula, South Uist, Grimsay, Barra, [Handa]
INNER HEBRIDES	Skye, Iona, Coll, Lismore, Jura, Rum, Canna, Cara, Islay, Jura
CLYDE ISLANDS	Great Cumbrae, Arran, Holy Island (Arran), [Ailsa Craig], Bute
IRISH SEA	Isle of Man, [Calf of Man], Anglesey, [Puffin Island, Anglesey], [Cardigan Island], Ramsey, [Lundy]
ISLES OF SCILLY	St Mary's, St Agnes
SOUTH COAST	Brownsea, Wight
CHANNEL ISLANDS	Alderney, Jersey, Herm, Guernsey, Lihou
EAST COAST	Lindisfarne

FIG 47. Feral goats on Lundy. (Roger Key)

In contrast, mink are serious pests. They have escaped or been released from fur farms on Lewis and Harris, the Uists, Bute and Arran, and throughout mainland Ireland. They are certainly responsible for significant predation on ground-nesting birds (Nordström *et al.*, 2003) and a determined attempt is being

FIG 48. American mink on the Outer Hebrides. (Stewart Angus)

FIG 49.
Hedgehogs pose
a serious threat
to ground-
nesting birds in
the Outer
Hebrides.
(Stewart Angus)

made to exterminate them. Over 400 animals have been killed in the Outer Hebrides alone.

Hedgehogs are a rather more unlikely menace. They are frequently transported to islands as pets. In most situations they are harmless, but they have become a serious predator of birds on machair in the Outer Hebrides, where there are few trees and thus a high proportion of ground-nesting birds. In recent years dunlin numbers there have fallen by 65%, ringed plover by 57%, redshank by 40%, snipe by 43% and lapwings by 43%. There are an estimated 5,000 hedgehogs on the Uists and Benbecula, all descended from four individuals released on South Uist in 1974. In one study, excluding hedgehogs from an area led to a 2.5 times increase in breeding success in wader species within a couple of years (Jackson & Green, 2000; Jackson, 2001). Efforts to reduce their numbers have not been very successful. Some enterprising locals are said to have earned hundreds of pounds from the bounty of £20 per animal offered by a consortium of animal-welfare organisations.

Faced with the damage from invasions by exotic species of many sorts, we naturally think of any exotic as a potential and unmitigated disaster to be eliminated as quickly as possible. However, an invasion also gives serendipitous opportunities for studying interactions, rates of ecological processes, and concepts of community organisation. It may show that a native species is not optimally adapted to its environment, that species distribution is limited by dispersal rather than physiology, that adaptive genetic change can take place

rapidly and that population bottlenecks do not preclude colonisation success (Sax
et al., 2007). The antibiotic revolution and its consequences for modern medicine
stem from the fortuitous infection of one of Alexander Fleming's bacterial
cultures. It is proper to see species invasions as possibilities to learn from, as well
as problems to protect against.

A notorious and unusual example of the intentional introduction of a serious
pest to an island was on Gruinard Island (211 ha), 1,200 m from the Scottish
mainland of Wester Ross. In 1942 it was intentionally sown with spores of
anthrax as a test of biological warfare, prompted by reports that Germany and
Japan might be developing biological weapons. Anthrax can survive for long
periods in soil, and the island was quarantined. However, following a programme
in the 1980s of repeatedly dousing the contaminated area with weak formalin
solution and then testing soil samples and antibodies in the blood of the island
rabbits, and finally by allowing sheep to graze over the previously infected area, it
was declared safe in 1990 and handed back to its original owner as 'fit for
habitation by man and beast'.

Island frailty of still another sort was shown in 1810 on the Monachs, a group
of four islands (three of them linked by sand bars) 13 km west of North Uist. The

FIG 50. Erosion on the Monach Islands, Outer Hebrides. (Geograph: Bob Jones)

land was overgrazed and the unstable sward that resulted was destroyed in a storm. The disappearance of grazing land meant the human population had to be evacuated. Marram grass was planted to stabilise the land surface, and by 1841 39 people were living there. Twenty years later, the population had increased to 127, with ten crofts. But numbers then declined again, and only two families of lighthouse keepers were left by 1931. Another, albeit less well-attested, story about the Monachs was that there used to be a sand bar linking the islands to North Uist, which was exposed at low water, but which was swept away by an enormous wave in the seventeenth century. There is a tradition that the last crossing was made about 1650 by a girl taking a heifer to a bull. The Monachs are now uninhabited, and are the site of an even bigger grey seal colony than North Rona (page 242). They also have a very productive machair: Perring and Randall (1972) found 257 species of plants there.

Although far from Britain, a disaster from human mismanagement, which dwarfs those on North Rona and the Monachs, and which serves as a cautionary tale of islands everywhere, has been the fate of Easter Island in the central Pacific (27° S, 109° W), said to be the most isolated inhabited land in the world. Its pollen record extends back 37,000 years and shows that until fairly recent times the island was well wooded. The earliest human inhabitants were Polynesians who arrived around 1,500 years ago. Within 400 years, trees were showing a significant decline, presumably from clearance for crops and from the use of timber for canoes and houses, but perhaps even more from predation of fruits by rats. This caused a spiral of catastrophe: leaching and soil erosion, a reduction of water retention and hence a drying-up of streams and springs; a loss of deep-sea fishing capability because boats could no longer be built; over-harvesting of palm fruits compounded by competition from rats (introduced for food) and other grazing animals. All of this sparked fighting and reduction in human population numbers (from around 1680). At one time there were 22 species of birds; now only one nests on the main island, although another six survive on offshore islets. Stretching the island's resources beyond their limits has led to a disaster of the sort predicted in the nineteenth century by Thomas Malthus, never mind more recent environmental pessimists.

References and Further Reading for Chapter 3 are listed on pages 341–2.

CHAPTER 4

The Inhabitants of the British and Irish Islands: Distribution

THERE ARE MANY fewer species of plants and animals in Britain and Ireland than on continental Europe, and even fewer on the islands around our coasts. Some of this is our fault: we have removed most of our trees and many of our hedges, and with them the habitat of many bird and butterfly species; the Scottish Highlands are well described as a man-made wet desert. However, whilst it is true that we lack many species found at similar latitudes on the continent and have only a few endemics, we have species and habitats that are rare elsewhere. The British islands are globally important both botanically and zoologically. Our bird islands are especially notable. Eighty per cent of the world's Manx shearwaters, 60% of the world's gannets, 60% of its great skuas and 40% of its lesser black-backed gulls nest around our shores, mostly on islands. Thirty per cent of Europe's guillemots, 20% of her razorbills and 10% of her puffins are on our coasts. Half of the 320,000 grey seals in the North Atlantic are in the eastern Atlantic, and around 85% of these breed around Britain, three-quarters in the Outer Hebrides or Orkney. We also have over 40% of the European population of the much less rare common or harbour seal.

High humidity coupled with an oceanic climate means that Britain is the European headquarters for many Atlantic species of ferns, bryophytes and lichens. Maritime heath, machair, blanket mire and other associations are much commoner here than elsewhere. The complex geology and steep climatic gradients found in many parts of our islands have produced an intricate and unique mosaic of ecosystems. Some of our islands – even some close inshore – combine wilderness, biological interest and mystery in ways almost impossible to find anywhere else in the world.

STOCKTAKING

What plants and animals will we find on any particular island? The complete answer to that question would be a largely indigestible series of lists – triumphs for those who compiled them and perhaps useful for visitors, but out of date even before they are published, because new records continually appear and local populations commonly go extinct. The avifauna illustrates this well (Table 12). Compared to many parts of the world, we have relatively few bird species but an enormous host of experienced birdwatchers. The presence or absence of a particular bird is more likely to be noted than for any other group; local lists are continually being revised. This is especially true for places where birdwatchers congregate.

FIG 51. Guillemot breeding ledges. (Richard Welsby)

TABLE 12. Breeding birds. r, regular; o, occasional (*see* page 81 for further explanation).

	FAROE	SHETLAND	ORKNEY	ST KILDA	OUTER HEBRIDES	SKYE	MULL	ISLAY	ISLE OF MAN	ARAN ISLANDS	CAPE CLEAR	SALTEES	ANGLESEY	LUNDY	SCILLIES	WIGHT	CHANNEL ISLANDS	FARNES	MAY
Red-throated diver	r	r	r		r	r	r	r											
Black-throated diver					r	o	o	o											
Little grebe			r		r	r	r	r	o		r		r			r	r		
Fulmar	r	r	r	r	r	r	r	r	r		r	r	r	r	r	r	r	r	r
Manx shearwater	r	r	r	r								r		r	r		r		
Storm petrel	r	r	r	r	r		r		r?	r	r				r		r		
Leach's petrel	r	r		r	r														
Cormorant	r	r	r		r	r	r	r	r				r	r	r	r	r	r	
Shag	r	r	r	r	r	r	r	r	r		r	r	r	r	r	r	r	r	r
Heron		o			r	r	r	r	r				r		o	r	o		
Mute swan		r	r		o		r	r	r				r		r	r	r		
Whooper swan		r		r															
Greylag goose	r		r		r	o	r		o				r		r				
Canada goose	r					o	r	r	r				r		r	r			
Shelduck		r	r		r	r	r	r	r	r	r	r	r		r	r		r	r
Mandarin duck																r	r		
Wigeon	o	r	r		o	o	o	r					o		o				
Gadwall		r			r			o			r	r	r		r	r			
Teal	r	r	r		r	r	r	r	r				r		o	r			
Mallard	r	r	r		r	r	r	r	r	r	r	r	r	r	r	r	r	r	
Pintail	o		r					r											
Shoveler	o	r	r		r		o	o					r		o	r	r		
Pochard		r	o					o					r		r				
Tufted duck	o	r	r		r	r		r	r				r	r	r	r	r		
Eider	r	r	r	r	r	r	r		r										r
Common scoter		r				o		r											
Goldeneye		o			o	o		o											
Red-breasted merganser	r	r	r		r	r	r	r	r	o	o		r					r	
Goosander						o	o						r						
White-tailed eagle					r	r													
Hen harrier		r			r	r	r	r	r										
Sparrowhawk		r			r	o	r	r	r		r		r			r	r		
Buzzard		r			r	r	r	r					r			r			
Golden eagle					r	r	r	r											
Kestrel		o	r		r	r	r	r	r	r	r		r		r	r	r		
Merlin	r	r	r		r	o	r	r	o										
Peregrine		r	r		r	r	r	r	r	r	r	r	r	r	o	r			o

(continued)

TABLE 12. (*continued*)

	FAROE	SHETLAND	ORKNEY	ST KILDA	OUTER HEBRIDES	SKYE	MULL	ISLAY	ISLE OF MAN	ARAN ISLANDS	CAPE CLEAR	SALTEES	ANGLESEY	LUNDY	SCILLIES	WIGHT	CHANNEL ISLANDS	FARNES	MAY
Red grouse		r	r		r	r	r	r	r										
Ptarmigan						r	r												
Black grouse							o	r											
Red-legged partridge			o					r	r				r		o	r			
Grey partridge						o		r	r				r		r	r	r		
Quail	o	o	o		o	o		o					o	o	o	o			
Pheasant		r				o		r	r	r	r	r	r		r	r	r		
Water rail		o	r				o	r	r				r		o	r	o		
Corncrake	o	o	r		r	r	r	r	r	o			r						
Moorhen		r	r		r		o	r	r	r			r		r	r	r		
Coot		r	r		r		o	r					r		r	r	r		
Oystercatcher	r	r	r	r	r	r	r	r	r	r	r	r	r	r	r	r		r	r
Ringed plover	r	r	r		r	r	r	r	r	r	r	o	r		r	r	r	r	
Golden plover	r	r	r		r	r	r	r	o										
Lapwing	r	r	r		r	r	r	r	r	r	r	r	r	r		r	r		
Dunlin	r	r	r		r	r	r	r	o						o	o			
Snipe	r	r	r	r	r	r	r	r	r	o	r		r		o	r			
Woodcock			o			r	r	r	r					o		r			
Black-tailed godwit	r	r	r		o												o		
Whimbrel	r	r	r	o	r	o													
Curlew	r	r	r		r	r	r	r	r	o	o		r		o	r			
Redshank	r	r	r		r	r	r	r	r				r		o	r			
Greenshank		r			r	r	r												
Common sandpiper		r	r		r	r	r	r	r	o	r		r		o	r			
Red-necked phalarope	r	r																	
Arctic skua	r	r	r		r			r											
Great skua	r	r	r	r	r														
Black-headed gull	r	r	r		r	r	r	r	r		r		r			r		r	
Common gull	r	r	r		r	r	r	r	o						r				
Lesser black-backed gull	r	r	r	r	r	r	r	r	r			r	r	r	r	r	r		r
Herring gull	r	r	r	r	r	r	r	r	r	r	r	r	r	r	r	r	r	r	r
Great black-backed gull	r	r	r	r	r	r	r	r	r	r	r	r	r	r	r	r	r	r	r
Kittiwake	r	r	r	r	r	r	r	r	r	r	r	r	r	r	r		r	r	r
Sandwich tern		r			r								r		r	r	r	r	o
Common tern	o	r	r		r	r	r	r	r		r		r		r	r	r	r	r
Arctic tern	r	r	r		r	r	r	r	r	r	r		r					r	r
Little tern		r			r				r	r	r					r			

(*continued*)

TABLE 12. (*continued*)

	FAROE	SHETLAND	ORKNEY	ST KILDA	OUTER HEBRIDES	SKYE	MULL	ISLAY	ISLE OF MAN	ARAN ISLANDS	CAPE CLEAR	SALTEES	ANGLESEY	LUNDY	SCILLIES	WIGHT	CHANNEL ISLANDS	FARNES	MAY
Guillemot	r	r	r	r	r	r	r	r	r	r	r	r	r	r	r	r	r	r	r
Razorbill	r	r	r	r	r	r	r	r	r	r	r	r	r	r	r	r	r	r	r
Black guillemot	r	r	r	r	r	r	r	r	r	r			r						
Puffin	r	r	r	r	r	r			r		r	r	r		r			r	r
Rock dove	r	r	r		r	r	r	r	r	r	r	r	r		r	r			
Stock dove								r	r				r		r	r			
Woodpigeon	o	r	r		r	r	r	r	r	r	r	r	r	r	r	r	r		
Collared dove	r	r	r		r	r	r	r	r	o	r		r	o	r	r	r		
Turtle dove															o	r	r		
Cuckoo		r	o		r	r	r	r	r	r	r		r		r	r	r		
Barn owl						r	o	r	r				r			r	r		
Tawny owl						r	r	r					r			r			
Long-eared owl			o		r		r		r							r	r		
Short-eared owl		r			r	r	r	r	r										
Swift					o	o	o	o	o	r	o		r		o	r	r		
Kingfisher													o			r	r		
Great spotted woodpecker						o	r						r			r	r		
Lesser spotted woodpecker														o		o	r		
Skylark	o	r	r		r	r	r	r	r	r	r	o	r	r	r	r	r		
Sand martin			o			r	r	r	r	o			r		o	r	r		
Swallow	o	r	r		r	r	r	r	r	r	r	r	r	r	r	r	r		o
House martin	o	r	r		o	r	r	r	r			r	r	r	r	r	r		
Tree pipit						r	r	r	r							r			
Meadow pipit	r	r	r	r	r	r	r	r	r	r	r	r	r	r	o	r	r		
Rock pipit	r	r	r		r	r	r	r	r	r	r	r	r	r	r	r	r	r	r
Grey wagtail		r	o		r	r	r	r	r		r		r			r	r		
Pied wagtail	r	r	r		r	r	r	r	r	r	r		r		r	o	r	r	r
Dipper			o		r	r	r	r	r	o			r						
Wren	r	r	r	r	r	r	r	r	r	r	r	r	r	r	r	r	r		o
Dunnock		r			r	r	r	r	r	r	r	r	r	r	r	r	r		
Robin	r	r	r		r	r	r	r	r	r	r	r	r	r	r	r	r		
Redstart						r	r	r	o				o			r			
Whinchat			o		r	r	r	r	r	r			r			o			
Stonechat		r			r	r	r	r	r	r	r	o	r		r	r	r		
Wheatear	r	r	r	r	r	r	r	r	r	r	r		o	r	r	r	r		o

(*continued*)

TABLE 12. (continued)

	FAROE	SHETLAND	ORKNEY	ST KILDA	OUTER HEBRIDES	SKYE	MULL	ISLAY	ISLE OF MAN	ARAN ISLANDS	CAPE CLEAR	SALTEES	ANGLESEY	LUNDY	SCILLIES	WIGHT	CHANNEL ISLANDS	FARNES	MAY
Ring ouzel	o		r		o	r	o	r											
Blackbird	r	r	r		r	r	r	r	r	r	r	r	r	r	r	r	r		
Fieldfare	o		o				o	o											
Song thrush		r	r		r	r	r	r	r	r	r	r	r	r	r	r	r		
Redwing	r	r	o		o	o		o											
Mistle thrush						r	r	r	r	r	r		r			r	r		
Ceti's warbler																r	r		
Grasshopper warbler					o	r	r	r	r		o		r			r			
Sedge warbler			r		r	r	r	r	r		r	r	r		r	r	r		
Reed warbler													r		r	r	r		
Dartford warbler																r	r		
Lesser whitethroat	o												r			r	r		
Whitethroat			o		o	r	r	r	r	o	r		r	o	o	r	r		
Garden warbler	o		o		o		r	o	o				r		o	r	r		
Blackcap	o	r	o			o	r	r	r	o			r		r	r	r		
Chiffchaff	o		o		r	r	r	r	r			o	r	r	r	r	r		
Willow warbler	o	r			r	r	r	r	r	o	r		r	r	r	r	r		
Goldcrest	r	r	r		r	r	r	r	r		r		r		r	r	r		
Spotted flycatcher			o		r	r	r	r	r	o			r	r	r	r	r		
Pied flycatcher						o							o						
Long-tailed tit						r	r	r	r				r			r	r		
Marsh tit																r			
Willow tit													r						
Blue tit						r	r	r	r	r	o		r		r	r	r		
Great tit						r	r	r	r		r		r		r	r	r		
Nuthatch													r			r			
Treecreeper						r	r	r	r				r			r			
Jay													r			r	r		
Magpie								o	r	r	r	o	r			r	r		
Chough									r	r	r	r	r						
Jackdaw		o	r		r	r	r	r	r	r	r	r	r				r	r	
Rook		r	r		r	r	r	r	r				r			r			
Crow (carrion/hooded)	r	r	r	o	r	r	r	r	r	r	r	r	r	r	r	r	r		o
Raven	r	r	r	r	r	r	r	r	r	o	r	r	r	r	r	r	r		
Starling	r	r	r	r	r	r	r	r	r	r	r	o	r	r	r	r	r		o
House sparrow	r	r	r		r	r	r	r	r	r	r		r	r	r	r	r		
Tree sparrow	o				r	r		o	r				r						

(continued)

TABLE 12. (*continued*)

	FAROE	SHETLAND	ORKNEY	ST KILDA	OUTER HEBRIDES	SKYE	MULL	ISLAY	ISLE OF MAN	ARAN ISLANDS	CAPE CLEAR	SALTEES	ANGLESEY	LUNDY	SCILLIES	WIGHT	CHANNEL ISLANDS	FARNES	MAY
Chaffinch	o	r	r		r	r	r	r	r	r	r		r	r	r	r	r		
Greenfinch			r		r	r	r	r	r	o	r		r		r	r	r		
Goldfinch					r	r	r	r	r				r	r	r	r	r		
Siskin	o		o		r	r	r	r					r						
Linnet			r		o	r	r	r	r	r	r	r	r	r	r	r	r		
Twite	o	r	r		r	r	r	r		o									
Redpoll			o		r	r	r	r	r				r						
Crossbill		o			r	r	r	r					r						
Bullfinch					o	r	r	r					r		r	r	r		
Snow bunting	o																		
Yellowhammer						r	r	r	r	o	r		r		r	r	r		
Cirl bunting																	r		
Reed bunting	o	r	r		r	r	r	r	r	o	r	r	r			r	r		
Corn bunting					r	o					o					r			

A table like this can be only be a snapshot in time. It does not include information about species that may have been regular breeders at some time in the past but have become locally extinct or irregular, while breeders recorded as 'occasional' may really be vagrants. Information about past breeding is often available for birds but not for most other groups. Data from Gibbons *et al.* (1993), with additional information from Sven-Axel Bengtson (Faroes), Stewart Angus (Hebrides), Eric Meek (Orkney and Shetland), Michael Harris (St Kilda and the Isle of May), Oscar Merne (Irish islands), Roger Long (Channel Islands) and John Walton (Farnes).

A pioneer in the study of island birds was David Lack. In the Second World War he became a 'civilian technical adviser' on radio equipment used for gun-laying. He volunteered for service in Orkney, where he spent March to August 1941 (and, a mild-mannered teacher at an independent school, 'found the beer-drinking Manchester territorials excellent company') (Thorpe, 1974). Whilst there he collected a mass of information on the birds of Orkney, which was published in two long papers in *Ibis* (Lack, 1942a, 1943). This inspired him to develop more general ideas, first set out in a paper on 'Ecological features of the bird faunas of

British small islands' (Lack, 1942b). In this he listed the breeding birds of Caithness (at the northeastern corner of Scotland), Orkney, Shetland and the Faroes, and compared them with previously published lists. He noted that at the time of his survey 26 species had established themselves on Orkney since 1800, while at least another eight species (and perhaps as many as 20) bred occasionally. Thirteen of the 26 'new' species could be attributed to the planting of woods, gardens, trees and bushes in the nineteenth century, assisted by an increase in the land under cultivation. A further eight species resident in Orkney in 1800 had extended their range to other islands; in contrast, six species no longer bred on Orkney. Local extinction is, of course, the result of a fluctuation in numbers to zero: Lack found that 61 (84%) of the inland breeders and 15 (60%) of the sea and shore birds changed significantly in density over his study period. This turnover in the avifauna is one of the most striking features of his survey.

Widening the focus: Ireland has only three-fifths the number of bird species of Britain although it is only 80 km from Wales, which might be thought too short a distance to be a barrier for most birds. Indeed, all but six of the regular British breeders have been recorded in Ireland on one or more occasions; the great spotted woodpecker, the British race of which is sedentary, has been recorded over 50 times. However, most of the missing Irish breeders do not breed in western Britain. Lack (1969a) recorded 122 regular breeders in Wales compared to 171 in Britain as a whole. Most of the species not found in Ireland are ones that breed only in south or southeast England or the Scottish Highlands. Lack concluded that their absence from Wales and Ireland must be due to ecological factors rather than mere isolation. The same phenomenon occurs in flowering plants: nearly all those widespread in Britain occur in Ireland, but those least well represented are the ones restricted to eastern England (Praeger, 1950).

Sometimes colonisation and spread has been documented. James Fisher (1952) has recorded how the fulmar spread from Iceland to the Faroes around 1820 and thence to Shetland, being first proved to breed on the cliffs of Foula in 1878. Thereafter the species exploded around the coasts of Britain and Ireland, 'probably the most remarkable change in the numbers and distribution of a wild animal in Britain that has ever been carefully examined by man' (Fisher, 1952: 145). The story of the spread of the house sparrow to the Faroes has been told by Bengtson et al. (2004). Before 1935, the species had only been recorded in the islands once (in 1900). Four birds arrived at Vágur on the southernmost island of Suðuroy – perhaps from a ship. The first birds bred in the island capital of Tórshavn in 1946, and thence they spread to Eysturoy in 1948, finally reaching the northern islands of Viðoy and Fugloy in the early 1960s. There are probably more than 2,500 pairs breeding in the Faroes nowadays.

Taking into account all the data he could find on the populations of small islands, Lack (1969a) concluded that they showed:

- Frequent and unusual habitat adaptations (Table 9);
- Small population sizes (e.g. on St Kilda five out of ten regularly breeding inland species were represented by less than ten pairs each, on Coll 20 out of 42, on Bardsey 14 out of 19, on Lundy 17–18 out of 24);
- Numerous erratic breeders (12 out of 25 species on Fair Isle, 11 out of 30 on Bardsey, 10–12 out of 18 on Steepholm);
- Frequent colonisations (in Shetland five of the 38 regular breeding species had become established since 1800, in the Outer Hebrides 19 out of 75, in the Isle of Man 17–20 out of 87–89, in the Isles of Scilly nine out of 31);
- Extreme fluctuations in numbers (in Orkney at least 61 of the 73 regular breeding land and freshwater species showed marked fluctuations, in Shetland 15 out of 38, in the Outer Hebrides at least 35 out of 75, in the Scillies 15 out of 31);
- Irregular distributions (Lack noted the common gull breeding on Fair Isle but not Foula or St Kilda; tree sparrow, whitethroat, scaup, greenshank and little tern were regular breeders on the Outer Hebrides but not Orkney; jackdaw was absent on Skokholm and Lundy but breeding on Bardsey; starling but not jackdaw was breeding on the Isles of Scilly).

The details of these findings have changed since Lack's surveys, but the general conclusions stand. Lack's own summary was that they 'demonstrate the remarkably large amount of change going on in island bird populations'. He reinforced this with a study (Lack, 1969b) of all the records of birds observed and breeding on the 98 ha island of Skokholm from 1928 (when Ronald Lockley began systematically recording there) to 1967; Mark Williamson (1983) extended this to

FIG 52. Two species common in Shetland: (*left*) gannets at Hermaness, Unst; (*right*) great skuas (*bonxies*) on the island of Noss. (Scottish Natural Heritage)

FIG 53. Skokholm from West Dale, Pembrokeshire. (R. J. Berry)

1979. There were nine land birds that bred regularly throughout the period (oystercatcher, lapwing, skylark, meadow pipit, dunnock, wheatear, carrion crow, raven, starling); Lack regarded the rock pipit, which has 30–40 pairs a year, as a seabird. Skylarks failed to breed in 1938; dunnocks were extinct for 1946–64; starlings only started to breed in 1940; other species came and went. In 2002 there were 17 breeding species (plus rock pipits) – lapwing and dunnock did not breed, but buzzards, peregrine falcons, moorhens, swallows, pied wagtails, wrens, blackbirds, sedge warblers, choughs and jackdaws were successful. Notwithstanding, buzzard, peregrine, chough and raven were represented by only one breeding pair each.

Tim Reed (1980, 1981) enormously extended Lack's work, with data for 73 of the British islands, which he collected from a range of sources – local societies, bird-observatory reports, etc. He found that the best predictor of species number on any island was the number of habitats on the island, which usually (but not inevitably) increased with the land area of the island (hilly islands will have more area for colonisation than 'flat' ones). This conclusion held up in a more intensive study of the birds of the Inner Hebrides (Reed *et al.*, 1983), with an additional recognition that any factors that affect habitats on a small island (such as marsh drainage or tree planting) may have a marked effect on the number of breeding species. On the Small Isles (Rum, Muck, Eigg and Canna), the number of woodland species (tits, finches and warblers) was significantly greater in larger and more diverse woods than in smaller, more uniform ones. Stuart Pimm and his colleagues have further expanded these findings, showing from data collected on 67 species at 16 observatories on islands around the British and Irish coasts that the likelihood of extinction is linked to both population size (and therefore island area), and body size: large birds (which have a longer life span than small ones) are less susceptible to extinction at low numbers, but are at greater risk at high ones (above seven pairs) – presumably because of their demand for resources (Pimm *et al.*, 1988).

Area is also important in another and more indirect way: larger islands have a greater area of suitable habitat for any particular species. A species may reach an island, but if there is too little suitable habitat it is unlikely to breed successfully. In practice there must be enough habitat to support a population greater than a threshold size, which will differ for each species. Peregrines need a large area for their hunting and therefore always occur at a relatively low density; they disappeared from all but a few islands in the late 1950s as their numbers fell nationally. Chaffinches are infrequent breeders on Bardsey because woody cover there is restricted to small clumps of elder, willows and blackthorn; annual recruitment is always low and periodic extinctions occur, often with a break of several years before a population is re-established. Species with simple habitat requirements (such as oystercatchers or rock pipits) are found on almost all islands (although they are absent on Hilbre, presumably because of the extent of human disturbance there), whilst wood warblers (dependent on tall broad-leaved cover) occur rarely.

Persistence of a species on an island is affected by its distance from the nearest mainland, in part because immigrants 'top up' the population, but, as Lack found, persistence depends on more than physical distance. Species near the edge of their range will be relatively rare immigrants, even if apparently suitable habitat is available; small changes in any of the factors affecting breeding are likely to affect such species in particular. O'Connor (1986) distinguished between sporadic breeders, recolonising species and invaders. He pointed out that the number of bird species breeding in woodland decreases from southeast to northwest Britain, perhaps linked to the availability of invertebrate food. For example, Scotland has 19 species that breed nowhere else in Britain; most of them are probably periodically 'topped up' by incomers from Scandinavia. These are all factors to be taken into account when assessing the likelihood of new recruits to any area.

Beetle populations are affected in other ways. We know more about their past distributions than for most animal groups, because their presence or absence can be traced reasonably accurately in subfossil deposits. A few species are found for the first time in archaeological sites and can be regarded as human introductions, but many Atlantic species have a wide range, from the British islands to the Faroes, Iceland and Greenland. Their presence on the last three (at least) could not possibly be explained by survival in refugia or travelling across land bridges. Geoffrey Coope (1986) has argued that most of the present beetle fauna of the North Atlantic dispersed through being carried westward by fresh meltwater and ocean surface currents in a fairly short period after the ice sheets finally retreated. Part of the reason for this conclusion is that of all the species that could tolerate the climate on each island group, only 54% occur in Shetland, 26% in the Faroes, 19% in Iceland, and a mere 4% in Greenland. Coope concludes that 'The only satisfactory explanation of these figures is that the faunas were derived from the east and that there were progressive losses in the transatlantic "sweepstake".'

Spiders are different again. They are more uniformly distributed than virtually any other animal group. Their eggs are so light that they are swept into high altitudes and may come to land anywhere. This means that individual species are limited by climate or habitat, but not by the opportunity to colonise. The Faroes have only two-thirds of the spider species found in Shetland, but a third of the species in the Faroes are absent from Shetland. The difference is probably due to the higher latitude and higher hills of the Faroes. Iceland has almost as many species as Shetland, but more than half of them are different. Since over 80% of the Iceland species are found in mainland Scotland, their absence in Shetland probably reflects the greater range of habitats in Iceland. Spiders found in Iceland but not Britain are mainly Arctic forms. Notwithstanding, the spiders of the eastern North Atlantic form a common faunal area and are not very useful markers for island faunas (Ashmole, 1979).

In general, the colonisation and extinction patterns of flying insects are not unlike those of birds, with the same principles of dispersal and settlement applying. Notwithstanding, successful colonisation may be exceedingly rare. One of the most studied cases of inter-island movement of animals is that of the 'picture-winged' *Drosophila* of the Hawaiian archipelago, which has been worked out using chromosome markers. Even between islands mainly in sight of each other, only one successful colonisation takes place on average every 25,000 years (Williamson, 1981: 219).

Tables 13 and 14 show the occurrence of mammals, reptiles and amphibians on British and Irish islands (plus the Faroes). Table 15 shows the percentage of flowering plant species in different biomes on different groups of islands.

TABLE 13. Mammal species on islands.

	FAROE	SHETLAND	ORKNEY	ST KILDA	OUTER HEBRIDES	INNER HEBRIDES	CLYDE ISLANDS	MAN	ANGLESEY	BARDSEY	SKOKHOLM	SKOMER	LUNDY	SCILLY	WIGHT	CHANNEL ISLANDS	IRELAND	RATHLIN	TORY	CLARE	ARAN	SHERKIN	CLEAR	SALTEES	LAMBAY
INSECTIVORA																									
Hedgehog *Erinaceus europaeus*		+	+		+	+	+	+	+					+	+	+	+								
Mole *Talpa europaeus*						+	+		+					+	+	+									
Common shrew *Sorex araneus*			+		+	+	+	+	+						+										
Pygmy shrew *Sorex minutus*			+		+	+	+	+	+	+			+				+	+	+	+	+	+	+	+	
Water shrew *Neomys fodiens*						+	+		+																
Lesser white-toothed shrew *Crocidura suaveolens*														+		+									
Greater white-toothed shrew *Crocidura russula*																+	+								
CHIROPTERA																									
Greater horseshoe bat *Rhinolophus ferrumequinum*															+	+									
Natterer's bat *Myotis nattereri*							+	+	+						+		+								
Daubenton's bat *Myotis daubentonii*								+	+						+		+								

(continued)

TABLE 13. (continued)

	FAROE	SHETLAND	ORKNEY	ST KILDA	OUTER HEBRIDES	INNER HEBRIDES	CLYDE ISLANDS	MAN	ANGLESEY	BARDSEY	SKOKHOLM	SKOMER	LUNDY	SCILLY	WIGHT	CHANNEL ISLANDS	IRELAND	RATHLIN	TORY	CLARE	ARAN	SHERKIN	CLEAR	SALTEES	LAMBAY
Noctule *Nyctalus noctula*		+	+						+						+										
Pipistrelle *Pipistrellus pipistrellus*		+	+			+	+	+	+					+	+	+	+								
Brown long-eared bat *Plecotus auritus*					+	+	+	+	+						+	+	+								
Grey long-eared bat *Plecotus austriacus*															+	+									
LAGOMORPHA																									
Rabbit *Oryctolagus cuniculus*		+	+		+	+	+	+	+	+	+	+	+	+	+	+	+	+	+	+	+		+	+	+
Brown hare *Lepus europaeus*		+	+		+	+	+	+	+						+		+							+	
Arctic hare *Lepus timidus*	+	+	+			+	+	+									+			+					
RODENTIA																									
Red squirrel *Sciurus vulgaris*							+		+					+	+	+	+								
Grey squirrel *Sciurus carolinensis*									+								+								
Bank vole *Clethrionomys glareolus*						+			+			+			+	+	+								
Field vole *Microtus agrestis*					+	+		+	+						+										
Common vole *Microtus arvalis*			+													+									

(continued)

TABLE 13. (continued)

	LAMBAY	SALTEES	CLEAR	SHERKIN	ARAN	CLARE	TORY	RATHLIN	IRELAND	CHANNEL ISLANDS	WIGHT	SCILLY	LUNDY	SKOMER	SKOKHOLM	BARDSEY	ANGLESEY	MAN	CLYDE ISLANDS	INNER HEBRIDES	OUTER HEBRIDES	ST KILDA	ORKNEY	SHETLAND	FAROE
Water vole *Arvicola terrestris*										+	+						+		+	+				+	
Long-tailed field mouse *Apodemus sylvaticus*	+	+	+	+	+	+	+	+	+	+	+	+		+		+	+	+	+	+	+	+	+	+	+
House mouse *Mus domesticus*			+	+	+	+	+	+	+	+	+	+			+		+	+	+	+	+	+	+	+	+
Brown rat *Rattus norvegicus*	+				+			+	+	+	+	+	+				+	+	+	+	+	+	+	+	+
Black rat *Rattus rattus*									+	+			+				+	+	+		+				
CARNIVORA																									
Fox *Vulpes vulpes*											+						+	+	+	+					
Pine marten *Martes martes*																			+	+					
Stoat *Mustela erminea*								+			+						+	+	+	+					
Weasel *Mustela nivalis*																	+			+					
Polecat *Mustela putorius*																	+	+	+						
Ferret *Mustela furo*											+										+				
Mink *Mustela vison*																			+		+				
Badger *Meles meles*											+								+	+					
Otter *Lutra lutra*						+		+	+	+	+	+					+		+	+	+			+	

(continued)

TABLE 13. (*continued*)

	FAROE	SHETLAND	ORKNEY	ST KILDA	OUTER HEBRIDES	INNER HEBRIDES	CLYDE ISLANDS	MAN	ANGLESEY	BARDSEY	SKOKHOLM	SKOMER	LUNDY	SCILLY	WIGHT	CHANNEL ISLANDS	IRELAND	RATHLIN	TORY	CLARE	ARAN	SHERKIN	CLEAR	SALTEES	LAMBAY
ARTIODACTYLA																									
Red deer *Cervus elaphus*					+	+																			
Sika deer *Cervus nippon*						+							+												
Fallow deer *Dama dama*									+																
Roe deer *Capreolus capreolus*						+	+	+	+		+				+										
Goat *Capra hircus*						+	+	+					+												+
	4	10	14	3	15	25	28	17	28	3	3	3	6	10	27	18	18	7	4	6	5	3	4	3	4

Note: The greater white-toothed shrew has occurred in Ireland since 2001 – almost certainly intentionally introduced (Tosh *et al.*, 2008).

TABLE 14. Reptile and amphibian species on islands.

	INNER HEBRIDES	ISLE OF MAN	ANGLESEY	SCILLY	WIGHT	CHANNEL ISLANDS
REPTILES						
Common lizard *Lacerta vivipara*	+	+	+		+	
Sand lizard *Lacerta agilis*						
Slow worm *Anguilis fragilis*	+		+		+	+
Grass snake *Natrix natrix*					+	+
Adder *Vipera berus*	+		+		+	
AMPHIBIANS						
Common frog *Rana temporaria*	+	+	+	+	+	+
Toad *Bufo bufo*	+		+		+	+
Natterjack toad *Bufo calamito*						
Smooth newt *Triturus vulgaris*	+		+		+	+
Palmate newt *Triturus helveticus*	+		+		+	
Great crested newt *Triturus cristatus*	+		+			

FIG 54. The wall lizard is widespread in western continental Europe. It may be native in Jersey, but elsewhere in the British Isles only introduced populations occur. (States of Jersey Planning Department)

TABLE 15. Percentage of native (plus long-established alien) flowering plant species in different biomes.

	SHETLAND	ORKNEY	OUTER HEBRIDES	INNER HEBRIDES	WEST IRISH SEA COAST	FORTH – TAY	SCILLY	WIGHT	CHANNEL ISLANDS	TOTAL GB & IRELAND
Arctic-montane	3.6	3.0	2.8	4.7	0.5	0.0	0.0	0.0	0.1	5.3
Boreo-arctic montane	3.4	3.2	2.3	3.0	1.5	1.0	0.2	0.2	0.5	2.6
Wide-boreal	2.4	2.1	2.0	1.5	1.5	1.6	2.0	1.3	1.2	1.3
Boreo-montane	7.3	7.5	8.3	8.2	2.6	3.4	0.0	0.8	0.5	7.0
Boreo-temperate	27.9	26.5	26.6	21.8	20.1	22.5	15.1	17.5	15.7	15.7
Wide-temperate	5.5	4.7	4.5	3.5	3.2	3.6	4.3	2.9	3.2	2.3
Temperate	31.3	32.6	33.0	36.7	41.8	43.0	38.8	44.8	40.7	37.6
Southern temperate	17.8	18.8	19.1	17.8	22.4	21.6	28.9	23.3	26.4	20.0
Mediterranean	0.8	1.6	1.5	2.7	6.4	3.1	10.8	9.2	11.7	8.2
Total species	495	570	606	790	802	670	557	957	886	
Percentage of total flora	33	39	41	53	54	45	38	65	60	

(RE)COLONISATION FOLLOWING
VOLCANIC ERUPTIONS

Colonisation is easier and turnover more rapid when empty habitats are available. Some wide-ranging species quickly establish themselves whenever a possibility occurs; they have been described as 'super-tramps' – good colonisers but usually poor competitors. In ecological terminology, they are r-selected as opposed to K-selected species (Southwood, 1988), although this is certainly not the only criterion for a successful invader (Lawton & Brown, 1986). We can follow colonisation experimentally (e.g. Bob Paine's clearance studies, page 96, or Dan Simberloff's artificial islands, page 127), but wonderful natural opportunities occur after volcanic eruptions (Schoener, 1988). The island of Krakatau in Indonesia exploded in 1883. In the first phase of re-establishment of biological life most of the colonisers away from the shore (an average of two species a year) were wind-borne, although there were also nearly as many species (1.64 per year) that colonised the shoreline. In the early years, only an average of one animal species every seven years penetrated into the interior. During the next phase (1897–1919), wind-borne pioneers lost ground and animal penetration of the interior increased ten-fold (to an average of 1.32 species per year) as fruit-bearing plants grew up and provided food for immigrants.

Then, in 1930, further volcanic activity produced a new island, Anak Krakatau ('Child of Krakatau'), which has experienced sporadic eruptions ever since. W. S. Bristowe landed on it six months after its appearance. He commented (Bristowe, 1969):

> Its virgin shore [was] composed entirely of dark grey ash, black cinders and white pumice stone. No plants would grow here until weathering and bacteria had had time to create soil in a year or two, but seeds, along with debris like banana stems and other vegetable matter, were awaiting their time to establish themselves … The only abundant insects were scavengers which could feed on whatever plant life the sea brought them – a springtail, a beetle, a species of ants, a tiny leaf-mining moth and a mosquito.

The process of colonisation on Anak Krakatau has been studied in detail by Ian Thornton of La Trobe University, Melbourne. The first birds seen were a Pacific reef-egret and beach thick-knee, together with migrants like the common sandpiper, grey wagtail, Pacific golden plover, Mongolian plover, whimbrel and great knot. Thornton placed plastic containers filled with sea water in places where the lava had flowed and found a constant rain of arthropods – in ten days in 1985 he collected 72 species. A great increase in bird species occurred in the same

FIG 55. Surtsey – an island in the Westmann group off the south coast of Iceland formed in 1963 as a result of an undersea volcanic explosion. (Sturla Fridriksson)

FIG 56. Pioneer shore community of lyme grass and sea sandwort on sandy lava, eastern Surtsey. These species are likely to have colonised from the neighbouring island or the mainland of Iceland (seen in the background). (Borgthor Magnusson)

FIG 57. Barren ropy lava on southern Surtsey in 2005. Nesting gulls have greatly enhanced plant colonisation in recent years. (Borgthor Magnusson)

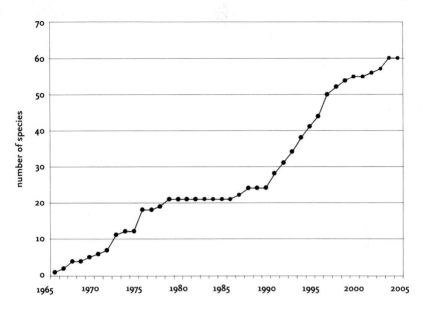

FIG 58. Cumulative increase of vascular plant species on Surtsey (after Fridriksson, 2005).

year, coinciding with the first fruiting of the island's figs and the consequent opening of a 'habitat window'. As these new species established themselves, some of the earlier-arrived ground nesting species disappeared. Then raptors came to feed on the fruit-eating species. About 150 plant species now inhabit the island (Thornton, 1996). The same process has been occurring on Surtsey (Fig. 58), an island produced by a volcanic eruption off the southwest corner of Iceland in 1963, although here the land surface has been eroding so quickly that the succession has not been as marked as for Krakatau (Fridriksson, 1975, 2005).

OLD AND NEW ARRIVALS

Volcanoes illustrate the dynamic of species arrival and replacement in a particularly vivid way, but in fact the species composition of all communities is affected in similar ways – by turnover resulting from colonisation and extinction. These processes must have been especially marked in Britain as the Pleistocene ice receded and gave way to sub-Arctic tundra and then temperate conditions, a procession involving considerable flux and opportunism. This sequence has been beautifully demonstrated by Bob Paine (1980) in situations that are intuitively stable – mature forest or rocky seashore. Paine followed the sequence of events after an old tree falls or a patch of shore is artificially cleared of its animals and plants. The dynamics of the re-establishment of the fauna and flora are the same as in the more spectacular circumstances of Krakatau and Surtsey, albeit in a less obvious manner.

Such dynamic processes are implicitly recorded in most species distribution atlases, where species not found since a particular date are usually distinguished from those only recorded since that date. The *New Atlas of the British & Irish Flora* (Preston *et al.*, 2002) differentiates between native species (endemics, or arriving without human intervention from an area where it is also native) and introduced ones, which may be archaeophytes (naturalised before 1500) or neophytes (introduced since 1500, or present only as casuals before 1500 but then naturalised as a result of subsequent reintroduction). Casuals are defined as plants whose populations fail to survive for more than five years or so and are therefore dependent on constant reintroduction. Sometimes fossils reveal the history of a particular species or group. One example of the use of time series is the conclusion of Mark Dinnin (1996) that all the Outer Hebridean insects can be regarded as postglacial colonisers, and that some species have disappeared as woodland declined on the islands.

Such firm information is relatively rare for most groups; in most cases, it is usually impossible to know whether a new record is a fresh arrival or merely the result of a more intense search – or perhaps simply the chance arrival of an expert taxonomist. Good data are sometimes available for birds, at least in recent decades (*see* above). In the case of plants, the *New Atlas* distinguishes in its maps only between 'native' and 'alien' populations. A further problem is that an 'extinct' species may truly have disappeared or may simply have been missed. An area has to be particularly well known for this to be resolved. For example, Hirons (1994) lists 115 plant species recorded on the Farne Islands since the first modern account in 1857, but notes that 36 of these are apparently no longer extant. Twelve of these had disappeared from the island of Inner Farne, which has become much drier in recent years. An earlier survey (in 1951) claimed that 16 species had disappeared, but six of these were found subsequently. Problems of this nature are one reason why it has not seemed worthwhile to include in this book detailed species lists for all the islands for which they are available. It seems more useful to record general patterns of distribution, noting something about more spectacular or unexpected presences or absences.

Some occurrences – and changes in distribution – are surprising. Red deer are (or were) present on the Outer Hebrides, the Isles of Scilly and the Channel

Islands. There are archaeological records from Neolithic sites of badgers on Harris, South Uist and Iona, and of pine martens and foxes in Orkney, well outside their current range (Fairnell & Barrett, 2007). It is possible these species were intentionally introduced – perhaps for their fur – but it is just conceivable that they managed to reach these islands by swimming. There were foxes on the Isle of Man in the nineteenth century. They became extinct, almost certainly before the end of the century. Then four foxes were released in the Santon Valley in 1986. By the early 1990s there were an estimated 120–300 animals on the island, but there were no signs of the species in 1999 (Reynolds & Short, 2003).

Whilst local changes in distribution are continually taking place for 'biological' reasons (through agricultural practices, escapes or deliberate introductions, climate change), the greatest barrier to complete understanding is unevenness of taxonomic cover. Birds and flowering plants have been – and are – recorded in great detail over most of the surface area of Britain and Ireland and their associated islands, but this is not true for almost all invertebrate groups and cryptogams. For many – indeed most – of the offshore islands, the availability of published data tends to depend on either casual observations or the serendipitous visit of an expert in a particular group. For example, it is possible to give a reasonably good picture of the fauna and flora of Orkney and Shetland, but knowledge of the fauna and flora of the Hebrides is much more patchy. It is fairly comprehensive for Rum and Mull because of the efforts of experts from the Natural History Museum and Nature Conservancy (and their successors in Scottish Natural Heritage) and for the Lepidoptera of Canna because of the long-term residence and interests of John Lorne Campbell, but is much less complete for (say) Skye or Eigg. Data for the Irish islands are much sparser than for the British islands. In their comprehensive and valuable *Bibliography of the Entomology of the Smaller British Offshore Islands*, Ken and Vera Smith (1983) collate the published information from the islands but found little from the islands around Ireland. Indeed, they list specifically only the Aran Islands, Cape Clear and Clare Island. This paucity of data is being attacked by the Dublin-based Irish Biogeographical Society, but there is much ground to be made up.

CLARE ISLAND SURVEYS, 1909–11, 1991–8

One outstanding exception to the lack of Irish data is Clare Island, 462 m high and 1,555 ha in extent, at the mouth of Clew Bay, County Mayo. The reason for this is a saga in its own right. The story began on the opposite coast of Ireland in 1904 when Cecil Baring (later the third Lord Revelstoke) of Barings Bank bought

FIG 59. Lambay, the largest island off the east coast of Ireland, where Cecil Baring commissioned Robert Praeger to carry out a survey in 1905–6. The Lambay study was the forerunner of the Clare Island survey of 1909–11. (Blom Aerofilms)

Lambay Island, a small (250 ha) volcanic remnant 5 km from the Dublin coast north of Howth. Baring introduced mountain sheep from Corsica, chamois (which worried the sheep), kinkajous (which teased the chamois), rheas, bustards, peacocks and (in defiance of St Patrick) snakes. Most of these exotics quickly disappeared, and Baring became more interested in the native fauna and flora. This led to him getting in touch with Robert Praeger (1865–1953), one of the heroic figures of Irish natural history.

FIG 60. Clare Island, at the mouth of Clew Bay, Co Mayo, as seen from Roonah Quay. (Geograph: Charles Nelson)

Praeger suggested that 'a detailed survey of the island's natural productions – animal, vegetable and mineral – would be interesting and might have important scientific results.' Baring warmed to this idea, and a succession of specialists visited Lambay (Fig. 59) in 1905 and 1906. They found nearly 90 species of animals and plants hitherto unrecorded in Ireland, 17 not previously recorded from Britain, and five completely new to science (Praeger, 1907).

Excited by these successes, and spurred by results from such esoteric places as Christmas Island, Krakatau, the Faroes and the sub-Antarctic islands of New Zealand, Praeger felt that an even more intensive study of the dispersal of animals and plants across a comparatively narrow stretch of sea might throw light on how species made the passage over wider barriers. He identified Clare Island as an ideal site (Fig. 60). He hoped it might be possible to demonstrate the beginnings of population differentiation, and perhaps even show on a large scale that Ireland possessed plants and animals found nowhere else in the world. Wallace and Hooker had found very high rates of endemism in the islands they

FIG 61. Clouds clearing from Croaghmore, Clare Island. The photograph was taken in the early twentieth century by R. J. Welch, official photographer to the original Survey, and a keen conchologist. (Welch Collection, Ulster Museum)

had studied: could the same apply to Ireland? He planned a Clare Island Survey, writing that 'comparison between the island's fauna and flora with those of the mainland was of special importance, in so far as it will bear on variation produced by isolation and with success and extinction amid the peculiar conditions of insular life' (quoted by Lysaght, 1998).

The selection of Clare Island was influenced by its suitable size and varied topography. The work on Lambay provided a 'dry run' for Clare. Between 1909 and 1911, nearly 80 naturalists worked on Clare. The results were published in 67 parts of the *Proceedings of the Royal Irish Academy*. Three hundred and ninety-three species of native plants and 20 introduced ones were recorded, increasing the number of known plant species in Ireland by 18%; 5,269 animal species were found, increasing the Irish list by 24%, 109 of them new to science (Collins, 1999). But there was nothing 'extraordinary' about the fauna and flora of the island. Its biological inhabitants were those that might be expected on any small island off the west coast of Ireland. Praeger (1915) had to acknowledge that 'the proximity of Clare Island to the mainland proved a factor which much lessened its value for the investigation of insular problems.'

Notwithstanding, the Clare Island Survey is significant because it provides a record of the biota of a small island probably unparalleled in its depth. And its value is even greater because it has now (1991–8) been repeated. The results of the New Survey of Clare Island are being published by the Royal Irish Academy in a

FIG 62. Naturalists on the western cliffs of Clare Island in 1910. Robert Praeger is in the centre. On the right is Arthur Stelfox – mainly an entomologist, but an all-round naturalist and largely responsible for setting up the *Irish Naturalists' Journal*. (Praeger Collection, Royal Irish Academy)

series of 11 volumes; when they are all available, it will be possible to compare
changes in the fauna and flora of the island over nearly a century. Hopefully it will
be possible to identify – at least partially – the influence of anthropogenic effects
(the population of the island has declined by almost three-quarters between the
two surveys – from 460 in 1911 [down from over 1,600 in 1841] to 127 in 2002).
Compared with the 393 native and 20 introduced higher plant species found in the
1909–11 survey, only 307 natives plus 22 introduced or garden escapes were
recorded in 1984 (Doyle & Foss, 1986). The most notable losses were of weed
species associated with grain and root crops, suggesting that the major shift from
arable to sheep-grazing has been largely responsible: in 1925, 104 ha of the island
was under arable crops, but by 1960 this was down to 23 ha. The former heather
community had disappeared, and had been almost entirely replaced by a severely
grazed and eroded grassland dominated by common bent and sheep's fescue.

HOW NATIVE IS NATIVE?

A major problem in getting to grips with the animals and plants of an island is
knowing how 'significant' any particular species is for the local situation. Mobile
species like birds come and go, and their presence or absence can be attributed
to ecological factors or mere chance. Less mobile forms may say something
about the history of the fauna and flora. We have to be discerning in our choice
of species.

This distinction may seem unnecessarily pedantic, but its importance for
island biotas is highlighted by a discussion about the indigenous races of moths
in Shetland by E. B. Ford in his New Naturalist, *Moths* (1955a). He dated their

FIG 63.
Strake townland,
Clare Island.
(Geograph: Aiden
Clark)

antiquity to about half a million years ago, from the time that the field mouse reached the islands in 'the early part of the interglacial phase which followed the second [cold stage] within the fourth main Pleistocene glaciation', since its arrival must have meant that 'there was a land connection to the islands at this time, for the long-tailed field mouse *Apodemus fridariensis* which inhabits them could not have survived [the relatively severe second cold phase].' But this assumes that the field mice must have arrived over a bridge. In fact, there has never been a land bridge between Shetland and Scotland. The mice are almost certainly a relatively recent introduction – perhaps as late as the eighth century AD (page 147). Ford was wrong to assume that the differentiation of the mice – and therefore the moths – must have taken place over hundreds of thousands of years and that they are truly natives in the islands.

As we have seen, the *New Atlas of the British and Irish Flora* distinguishes native species (1,363 in total, plus another 44 which may by native) from aliens, which are divided between archaeophytes (149 species), neophytes (1,155 species) and casuals (240 species). The non-native species may have come as associates of intentionally introduced forms or simply as garden 'escapes' indicating nothing more than the habitats of plant hunters or the popularity of garden centres. Aliens are commoner around major towns – which means they are less common on islands. But there are fewer species on islands than on the mainland.

Only a few groups of invertebrate animals are sufficiently well recorded to give useful information about island occurrence. Dragonflies and damselflies are large and distinctive enough for good data to exist, coupled with the fact that there are only 40 species in Britain and Ireland and that we have proportionately more of the species found on the European mainland than for most groups (Table 16). However, they give no surprises (Hammond, 1983). Intraspecific variation seems to have been little studied. Melanism is frequently noted and may occur anywhere, although it is most common in the north and west of the British islands, particularly in isolated populations. There is a Scottish form of the common hawker with a darker abdomen than further south; the common blue-tailed damselfly has a number of minor colour forms, but there is no obvious geographical pattern to them; there is a 'blue' form of the azure damselfly. Three species (*Sympecma fusca*, *Crocothemis erythraea* and *Lestes viridis*) are recorded only from Jersey; *Lestes barbarus* occurs on Jersey and Alderney. There is much work awaiting an island odonatologist.

There are 56 species of butterflies in Britain and Ireland, but few on the islands (Table 17) with the exception of the Isle of Wight, where 50 of the 56 occur. Only five species are recorded in Shetland and nine from Orkney, 14 from Rathlin, 16 from Great Saltee – but 36 from Jersey.

TABLE 16. Number of resident or formerly resident Odonata species (after Merritt *et al.*, 1996).

	ZYGOPTERA	ANISOPTERA	TOTAL
Norway	15	26	41
Great Britain	17	23	40
Ireland	11	11	22
Channel Islands	10	13	23
France (excluding Corsica)	30	51	81
Holland	25	39	64
Europe (Total)	37	77	114

TABLE 17. Butterflies on islands (omitting the Isle of Wight, where occurrence largely reflects that in mainland Hampshire) (based on Dennis & Shreeve, 1996; Fox *et al.*, 2006).

Essex skipper	*T. lineola*	Channel Islands
Large skipper	*Ochlodes sylvanus*	Channel Islands
Dingy skipper	*Erynnis tages*	Anglesey, Channel Islands
Swallowtail	*Papilio machaon*	Channel Islands
Clouded yellow	*Colias croceus*	Widely distributed
Brimstone	*Gonepteryx rhamni*	Anglesey, Arans, Channel Islands
Large white	*Pieris brassicae*	Widely distributed, incl. Orkney, Shetland
Small white	*P. rapae*	Widely distributed
Green-veined white	*P. napi*	Widely distributed, incl. Orkney
Orangetip	*Anthocharis cardamines*	Widely distributed
Green hairstreak	*Callophrys rubi*	Widely distributed
Purple hairstreak	*Neozephyrus quercus*	Channel Islands
Small copper	*Lycaena phlaeas*	Widely distributed
Silver-studded blue	*Plebeius argus*	Anglesey, Channel Islands
Brown argus	*P. (Aricia) agestis*	Anglesey, Channel Islands
Common blue	*Polyommatus icarus*	Widely distributed, incl. Orkney
Holly blue	*Celastrina argiolus*	Widely distributed (not Scotland)
Red admiral	*Vanessa atalanta*	Widely distributed, incl. Orkney, Shetland

(*continued*)

TABLE 17. (*continued*)

Painted lady	*V. cardui*	Widely distributed, incl. Orkney, Shetland
Small tortoiseshell	*Aglais urticae*	Widely distributed, incl. Orkney, Shetland
Peacock	*Inachis io*	Widely distributed
Comma	*Polygonia c-album*	Widely distributed in E&W, Channel Islands
Small pearl-bordered fritillary	*Boloria selene*	Widely distributed (not Ireland, Channel Islands)
Dark green fritillary	*Argynnis aglaja*	Widely distributed
Marsh fritillary	*Euphydryas aurinia*	Western distribution only
Glanville fritillary	*Melitaea cinxia*	Channel Islands
Speckled wood	*Pararge aegeria*	Widely distributed
Wall	*Lasiommata megera*	Widely distributed (S Scotland only)
Scotch argus	*Erebia aethiops*	Western Scotland only
Grayling	*Hipparchia semele*	Widely distributed coastally
Gatekeeper	*Pyronia tithonus*	Anglesey southward (incl. Ireland)
Meadow brown	*Maniola jurtina*	Widely distributed, incl. Orkney
Ringlet	*Aphantopus hyperantus*	Widely distributed, incl. Orkney
Small heath	*Coenonympha pamphilus*	Widely distributed
Large heath	*C. tullia*	Widely distributed in north, incl. Orkney

FIG 64. Common blue butterflies. (Richard Welsby)

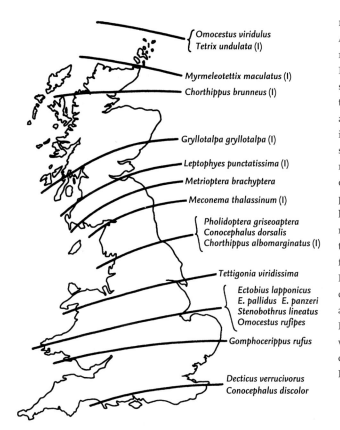

{ Omocestus viridulus
Tetrix undulata (I)

Myrmeleotettix maculatus (I)
Chorthippus brunneus (I)

Gryllotalpa gryllotalpa (I)

Leptophyes punctatissima (I)
Metrioptera brachyptera
Meconema thalassinum (I)

{ Pholidoptera griseoaptera
Conocephalus dorsalis
Chorthippus albomarginatus (I)

Tettigonia viridissima

{ Ectobius lapponicus
E. pallidus E. panzeri
Stenobothrus lineatus
Omocestus rufipes

Gomphocerippus rufus

Decticus verrucivorus
Conocephalus discolor

FIG 65. Approximate northern limits of British grasshopper species. (I) means that the species has also been recorded in Ireland. Such species are the most northerly in occurrence – presumably the hardier ones, which might be assumed to have been the first to enter Britain from continental Europe and colonised Ireland whist there was still a land connection (after Ragge, 1963).

Non-flying animals tend to be more informative for unravelling the history of colonisation. For example, grasshoppers and crickets require warmth and are much commoner and more diverse in southern England than further north. Ragge (in Marshall & Haes, 1988) argued that the distribution of the grasshopper fauna could be accounted for largely in terms of migration over the land bridge from continental Europe following the final retreat of the Pleistocene ice sheet. Different species extended northwards to different extents, presumably indicating the availability of suitable habitats and tolerance to adverse conditions. Only the most northerly British species occur in Ireland (Fig. 65). This suggests that they may have managed to arrive there before the land connection between Britain and Ireland disappeared, because there is suitable habitat for many of the other species. The occurrences of grasshoppers and their relatives on the smaller islands supports this interpretation in general (Table 18).

TABLE 18A. Offshore island records of crickets, grasshoppers and other insects – England, Wales, Ireland & Channel Islands (from Marshall & Haes, 1988). P, present in 1961 or later; (P), indicates no record since before 1961.

	ENGLAND AND WALES									IRELAND						CHANNEL ISLANDS				
	ISLE OF WIGHT	SCILLY	LUNDY	SKOKHOLM	SKOMER	RAMSEY	BARDSEY	ANGLESEY	ISLE OF MAN	CLEAR ISLAND	ARAN ISLANDS	GORUMNA	CLARE ISLAND	ARAN ISLAND	TORY ISLAND	JERSEY	GUERNSEY	HERM	SARK	ALDERNEY
CRICKETS																				
Meconema thalassinum	P															P				
Tettigonia viridissima	P	P														P	P	P	P	P
Decticus verrucivorus	(P)																			
Pholidoptera griseoaptera	P								P							P				
Platycleis albopunctata	P	P														P	P	P	P	P
Metrioptera roeselii	P																			
Conocephalus discolor	P															P	P	P	P	P
C. dorsalis	P							P								P				
Leptophyes punctatissima	P		P		P				P	P						P	P			
Acheta domesticus	P							P	P							P	(P)			
Gryllus campestris	(P)															P				(P)
Nemobius sylvestris	P															P				
Pseudomogoplistes squamiger																(P)				
Gryllotalpa gryllotalpa	P															(P)	P			

(continued)

TABLE 18A. (*continued*)

	ENGLAND AND WALES									IRELAND						CHANNEL ISLANDS				
	ISLE OF WIGHT	SCILLY	LUNDY	SKOKHOLM	SKOMER	RAMSEY	BARDSEY	ANGLESEY	ISLE OF MAN	CLEAR ISLAND	ARAN ISLANDS	GORUMNA	CLARE ISLAND	ARAN ISLAND	TORY ISLAND	JERSEY	GUERNSEY	HERM	SARK	ALDERNEY
GROUND- AND GRASSHOPPERS																				
Tetrix ceperoi	P															P	(P)			
T. subulata	P															P				
T. undulata	P	P						P	P							P				
Oedipoda caerulescens																P	P			
Stenobothrus lineatus	P																			
S. stigmaticus									P											
Omocestus viridulus	P			P	P	P		P	P			P								
Chorthippus brunneus	P	P	P	P	P	P	P	P	P			P				P	P	(P)	P	P
C. vagans																P				
C. parallelus	P				P			P								P				
C. albomarginatus	P															P				
Euchorthippus pulvinatus elegantulus																P				
Myrmeleotettix maculatus	P		(P)							P	P					P				

(continued)

TABLE 18A. (*continued*)

	England and Wales									Ireland						Channel Islands				
	Isle of Wight	Scilly	Lundy	Skokholm	Skomer	Ramsey	Bardsey	Anglesey	Isle of Man	Clear Island	Aran Islands	Gorumna	Clare Island	Aran Island	Tory Island	Jersey	Guernsey	Herm	Sark	Alderney
COCKROACHES																				
Pycnoscelus surinamensis	P	P														P	P			
Blatta orientalis	P	P						(P)	P							(P)	(P)			
Blatella germanica	P															P	P			P
Ectobius lapponicus	P															P	P			
E. pallidus	P																			
E. panzeri	P	P	P					P								P	P			(P)
EARWIGS																				
Euborellia annulipes	(P)															(P)	(P)			
Labia minor								(P)	P											
Forficula auricularia	P	P	P	P	P	P	P	P	P	(P)	(P)		(P)	(P)	(P)	P	P		(P)	P
STICK INSECTS																				
Acanthoxyla geisovii	P																			
Clitarchus hookeri	P																			

TABLE 18B. Offshore island records of crickets, grasshoppers and other insects – Scotland (from Marshall & Haes, 1988). P, present in 1961 or later; (P), pre-1961 records.

	SCOTLAND	ARRAN	ISLAY	JURA	COLONSAY	MULL	TIREE	EIGG	RUM	CANNA	SKYE	RAASAY	BARRA	S UIST	N UIST	BERNERAY	ST KILDA	HARRIS & LEWIS	ORKNEY	FAIR ISLE	SHETLAND	ISLE OF MAY	BASSROCK
GROUNDHOPPERS AND GRASSHOPPERS																							
Tetrix ceperoi	P																						
T. subulata	P																						
T. undulata	(P)		P	P	P	P		(P)	P	P	P			(P)									
Oedipoda caerulescens																			(P)				
Stenobothrus lineatus																							
S. stigmaticus																							
Omocestus viridulus	(P)		P	P	P	P	P	(P)	P	P	P		P	(P)						(P)			
Chorthippus brunneus	(P)		(P)			P		(P)		P	P	P											
C. vagans																							
C. parallelus	(P)		P	P		P		(P)	P	P	P												
C. albomarginatus																							
Euchorthippus pulvinatus elegantulus																							
Myrmeleotettix maculatus	P				P	P	P	(P)	P	P	P		P	P	P	P							

(continued)

TABLE 18B. (*continued*)

	SCOTLAND	ARRAN	ISLAY	JURA	COLONSAY	MULL	TIREE	EIGG	RUM	CANNA	SKYE	RAASAY	BARRA	S UIST	N UIST	BERNERAY	ST KILDA	HARRIS & LEWIS	ORKNEY	FAIR ISLE	SHETLAND	ISLE OF MAY	BASSROCK
COCKROACHES																							
Pycnoscelus surinamensis																							
Blatta orientalis																		(P)		(P)			
Blatella germanica																							
Ectobius lapponicus																							
E. pallidus																							
E. panzeri																							
EARWIGS																							
Euborellia annulipes																							
Labia minor						P		(P)															
Forficula auricularia		(P)	P								P		P	P	P	P	(P)	P	P	(P)	P	(P)	(P)

But even this simple explanation has complications. For example, the lesser mottled grasshopper occurs on the Isle of Man but nowhere else in the British Isles. The Man specimens are smaller than those from continental Europe, which implies that they may not be recent colonisers. Perhaps the species was once present in England but has become extinct through competition with the more successful meadow grasshopper.

Most bumblebees (Table 19) have a wide distribution in the British islands (Benton, 2006). They are of particular interest here because of the fairly common occurrence of local races or subspecies (Alford, 1975). The white-tailed bumblebee is abundant throughout most of Britain and Ireland, although it is replaced by the buff-tailed bumblebee in Orkney, Shetland and the Outer Hebrides. The heath

TABLE 19. Bumblebees on islands.

	SHETLAND	ORKNEY	OUTER HEBRIDES	INNER HEBRIDES	ISLES OF SCILLY	WIGHT	CHANNEL ISLANDS	IRELAND (NORTH)	IRELAND (WEST)	IRELAND (SOUTH)	IRELAND (EAST)
Bombus soroeensis				+		+					
B. lucorum				+	+	+	+	+	+	+	+
B. magnus	+	+	+	+		+		+	+	+	+
B. terrestris				+	+	+	+	+	+	+	+
B. jonellus	+	+	+	+	+	+		+	+	+	+
B. lapponicus											
B. pratorum				+		+		+	+	+	+
B. lapidarius		+		+	+	+	+	+	+	+	+
B. hortorum	+	+	+	+	+	+	+	+	+	+	+
B. ruderatus				+		+	+				
B. humilis						+					
B. muscorum	+	+	+	+	+	+	+	+	+	+	+
B. m. agricolae	+		+	+	+				+		
B. pascuorum		+		+		+	+	+	+	+	+
B. ruderarius			+			+	+	+	+	+	+
B. sylvarum						+	+				+
B. distinguendus	+	+	+	+					+		
Total	6	7	7	13	7	14	9	10	12	10	11

bumblebee has a number of colour forms. In Orkney, the corbicular hairs (which form the pollen basket on the hind legs) are black rather than reddish. More extreme forms (or subspecies) occur in Shetland (*vogtii*) and the Outer Hebrides (*hebridensis*). The moss carder bee has a generally 'fringing' distribution. The typical English form is *sladeni*, replaced in Scotland and Ireland by the redder *pallidus*. On Shetland and in the Hebrides (Outer and Inner), a form with a rich chestnut dorsal thorax and a black underside is found (ssp. *agricolae*); the Orkney form is identical to that found in the north of Scotland. The *agricolae* subspecies of moss carder bee occasionally invades western mainland Scotland, but is not established there. A particularly striking form (*allenellus*), darker than *smithianus*, occurs on the Aran Islands. A form (*scyllonius*), similarly coloured to *agricolae* but with pale hairs intermixed with the black ones, is found in the Isles of Scilly (where it is very rare) and the Channel Islands. The common carder bee is a widespread and very variable species; it seems to be spreading at the expense of the moss carder. A subspecies (*floralis*) not very different to the southern and central English form is found in Ireland; another subspecies (*flavidus*) occurs only in the Channel Islands. The great yellow bumblebee now survives only in the west of Ireland, the Outer Hebrides and Orkney, plus a few relict populations in Caithness and Sutherland.

INTRODUCTIONS OR RELICS?

We do not always know for certain the reason why many island forms are distinct from their relatives. A common explanation is that island races are relics of previously more widely distributed species. This is a hangover from pioneering proposals made by the marine biologist and Manxman, Edward Forbes (1815–54), in a work 'On the connexion between the distribution of the existing fauna and flora of the British Isles, and the geological changes which have affected their area, especially during the epoch of the northern drift', published in the first volume of the *Memoirs of the Geological Survey of Great Britain* (1846).

Forbes pointed out that there are three modes by which an isolated area may acquire its biota:

1. By special creation within that area – which he rejected because 'with very few, mostly doubtful exceptions, the terrestrial animals and flowering plants of the British Isles are identical with continental species.'
2. By transport to it – which he rejected as insufficient, since 'after making full allowances for all likely means of transport at present in action, there remains

a residue of animals and plants which we cannot suppose to have been transported, since either their bodily characters or certain phenomena presented by their present distribution, prevent our entertaining such an idea.'

3. By migration before isolation – which had to be the mechanism, if the other two modes are rejected. 'The greater part of the terrestrial animals and flowering plants now inhabiting the British Islands ... have migrated to it over continuous land before, during, or after the Glacial epoch.'

This immediately raises the question of where the recolonisers came from when the ice retreated. Forbes believed that all the species currently found in Britain originated in neighbouring countries and migrated here over land bridges. He suggested that our fauna and flora has five 'elements':

1.	Iberian or Asturian	originating in	Northern Spain
2.	Armorican or Norman		Channel Islands and western France
3.	Kentish		Northern and northeastern France
4.	Scandinavian or Boreal		Northern and sub-Arctic
5.	Germanic		Central and west central Europe

A strong advocate of this conclusion was the Irish entomologist, Bryan Beirne, who set out the case at length in his book *The Origin and History of the British Fauna* (1952). He believed that 'more than 95% of the British species of animals' arrived by overland migration, many of them from four interconnected areas represented approximately by the current inshore seas down to 50 m (25 fathoms) where temperate species survived the ice sheets: a Celtic Land from southern Ireland to northwest France; a Cambrian Land between western Ireland and northwest England; a Channel Land between southeast England and France; and Dogger Land, across the North Sea. The most important of these was the Celtic Land:

> *west and south-west of the British ice sheets ... broadened in the south to include a large area of low-lying land between the present west coast of Ireland and north-west coast of France. Most of the Celtic Land is now covered by sea, but it included some of the present land area of southern and western Ireland and of the Hebrides. As most of it is now covered by the sea, geological evidence of its fauna and flora and consequently of its climate, is lacking.*

Beirne suggested that temperate survivors from such areas colonised much of the currently existing land area before postglacial rises in sea level isolated them from their relatives and led in an unspecified way to subsequent differentiation (in this he anticipated the model used by MacArthur and Wilson – *see* page 127). For example, he regarded the 'Celtic Land' population of bank voles as being divided into smaller populations by sea-level rise, followed by independent development on islands where distinct subspecies have been described: Raasay, Mull, Skomer and Jersey. Likewise, he speculated that there were two Celtic Land populations of the field vole. The older one survives on Guernsey and Orkney but was replaced on the mainland of Great Britain by waves of another form, which spread northwards and colonised Bute, Islay and Eigg, followed by yet another form now occupying Britain south of the Highlands.

Beirne's scheme of glacial survival and progressive replacements and differentiation is little more than an extrapolation of Forbes' proposals and their development by Martin Hinton of the Natural History Museum (page 155). Notwithstanding, recent data from hares and stoats in Ireland and water voles in Scotland could be regarded as supporting it (page 44). He certainly pressed his ideas hard. Leo Harrison Matthews expressed doubt about them as they apply to small mammals in his New Naturalist on *British Mammals* (1952). Notwithstanding, this sort of explanation repeatedly recurs in discussions about island colonisations. A fierce proponent was John Heslop Harrison of Newcastle University. At a British Ecological Society symposium in 1946, he 'admitted' that he approached the present Hebridean biota with a bias towards a 100% survival of relict flora and fauna (Tallantire & Walters, 1947). He repeated this insistence at a Linnean Society meeting in 1955, where there was a sharp division of opinion about how wingless water beetles reached the Outer Hebrides. He was so convinced that he was right that there is little doubt that he went to the extent of manufacturing evidence to support his claim (Sabbagh, 1999; *see* page 174).

However, the death knell of routine colonisation from hypothetical refuges came in a short paper on island small mammals by Gordon Corbet, a successor of Hinton at the Natural History Museum. Corbet (1961) demolished all the evidence claimed in support – geological, palaeontological, archaeological and ecological.

Corbet pointed out that most of the islands that have mice or voles recognised as 'different' by taxonomists had never been connected to their nearby mainland at times when the species concerned might survive there (Table 20). He judged 'the Irish fauna as a whole to be of such an erratic composition as to suggest a series of chance introductions rather than an orderly sequence of arctic, followed by more temperate, faunas, until at some stage the supply suddenly stopped due to severance of the land connexion.' Corbet believed that the animals were most likely introduced to islands by human agency – either as commensals or in crops or fodder transported by early human populations. This does not mean that there are no Ice Age survivors on our offshore islands, but that they are likely to be the exception rather than the rule. Probable candidates for Ice Age survival are the 'French shrew'

TABLE 20. Distribution of small mammals on islands (after Yalden, 1999).

	COMMON VOLE Microtus arvalis	FIELD VOLE Microtus agrestis	BANK VOLE Clethrionomys glareolus*	LONG-TAILED FIELD MOUSE Apodemus sylvaticus	COMMON SHREW Sorex araneus	PYGMY SHREW Sorex minutus	LESSER WHITE-TOOTHED SHREW Crocidura suaveolens	GREATER WHITE-TOOTHED SHREW Crocidura russula
Shetland, St Kilda	–	–	–	+	–	–	–	–
Orkney	+	–	–	+	–	+	–	–
Isle of Man	–	–	–	+	–	+	–	–
Ireland	–	–	–	+	–	+	–	+
Lewis, Barra	–	–	–	+	–	+	–	–
North and South Uist	–	+	–	+	–	+	–	–
Eigg, Muck	–	+	–	+	–	+	–	–
Raasay	–	–	+	+	+	+	–	–
Mull	–	+	+	+	+	+	–	–
Skye, Islay, Jura, Gigha, Arran	–	+	–	+	+	+	–	–
Skomer	–	–	+	+	+	+	–	–
Isles of Scilly	–	–	–	+	–	–	+	–
Jersey	–	–	+	+	(+)**	–	+	–
Sark	–	–	–	+	–	–	+	–
Alderney, Herm	–	–	–	+	–	–	–	+
Guernsey	+	–	–	+	–	–	–	+

* Taxonomic purists have changed the name of Clethrionomys to Myodes, but it will be a long time before this change becomes common usage.
** The common shrew on Jersey is the French shrew, Sorex coronatus.

which replaces the common shrew in Jersey, and the greater white-toothed shrew in the Channel Islands, where it occurs on Alderney, Guernsey and Sark. The latter is a species distributed throughout southwest Europe, and has been found in interglacial-period cave deposits in Britain. Its close relative, the lesser white-toothed shrew, has a wider continental distribution; in Britain it occurs only on Jersey and the Isles of Scilly. It may be a relict on Jersey; the likelihood is that it is a human introduction to the Isles of Scilly, perhaps brought there by Iron Age tin traders sailing from Brittany, although there is no firm evidence of its origins.

All this has not inhibited speculation. We will be able to give more definite answers to the sources of the island races when molecular studies develop further. The realisation that the pygmy shrews of Ireland are not closely related to those of northern Europe (page 44) has meant that much fanciful theorising should disappear. But another problem is that many islands have distinct island forms, showing the operation of forces other than simple colonisation and establishment (*see* Chapter 6).

References and Further Reading for Chapter 4 are listed on page 342.

FIG 66. Bardsey (Enys Enlli), owned and managed by the Bardsey Trust. (Blom Aerofilms)

CHAPTER 5

Survivors and Non-Survivors: the Consequences of Island Life

I SLANDS POSSESS MANY *advantages for the study of the laws and phenomena of distribution. As compared with continents they have a restricted area and definite boundaries, and in most cases their biological and geographical boundaries coincide. The number of species and of genera they contain is always much smaller than in the case of continents, and their peculiar species and groups are usually well defined and strictly limited in range. Again their relations with other lands are often direct and simple and even when more complex are far easier to comprehend than those of continents; and they exhibit besides certain influences on the forms of life and certain peculiarities in their distribution which continents do not present, and whose study offers many points of interest.*

Alfred Russel Wallace, *Island Life*, 1880

Islands have been especially instructive because their limited area and their inherent isolation combine to make patterns of evolution stand out starkly.

David Quammen, *The Song of the Dodo*, 1996.

We are now in a position to be able to link together some of the consequences of life on islands. The key questions are apparently simple. How and (approximately) when did the inhabitants of a particular island get there? Are they just managing to hang on or are they a significant part of the biota? And what happens to a species when it settles on an island?

Once a population is isolated, population-level changes take place. These have been studied most intensively in small mammals. Often, island populations of small mammals show an increase in average size (page 62); frequently they have higher and more stable densities than on mainlands; they may show behavioural differences.

Because these changes tend to occur together and in different species, they have been characterised as an 'island syndrome' (Adler & Levins, 1994). Although not universal, such a syndrome is found commonly in small-island rodents. The key factors seem to be isolation and area. The 'island syndrome' is not found in large islands, perhaps because predators are more likely to be established in such situations and dispersal may allow an escape from interspecific competition.

The first extensive review of island animals and plants was by Alfred Russel Wallace in a book *Island Life* (Fig. 67), first published in 1880. He identified the 'best examples of recent continental islands' (in contrast to oceanic islands) as

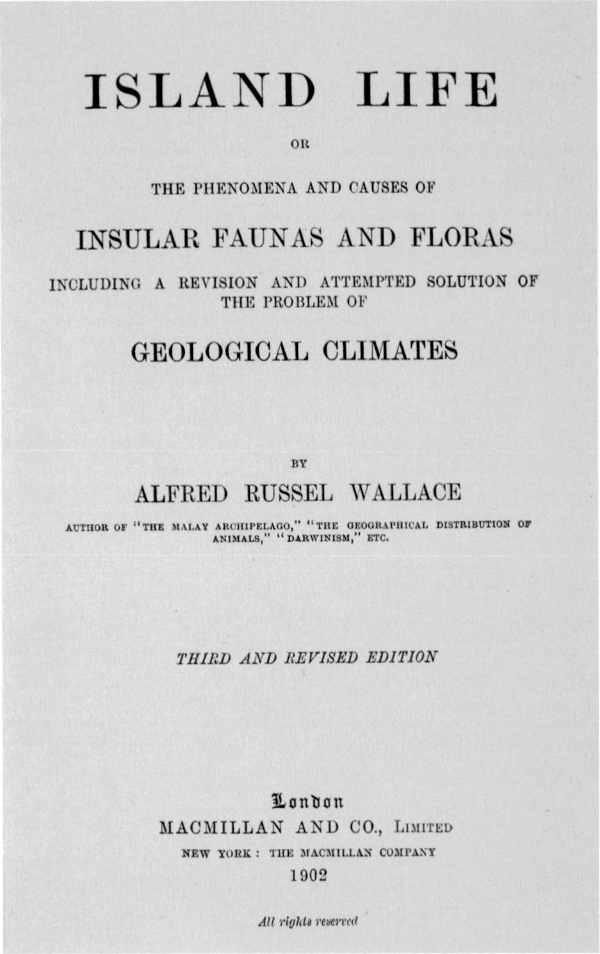

ISLAND LIFE

OR

THE PHENOMENA AND CAUSES OF

INSULAR FAUNAS AND FLORAS

INCLUDING A REVISION AND ATTEMPTED SOLUTION OF
THE PROBLEM OF

GEOLOGICAL CLIMATES

BY

ALFRED RUSSEL WALLACE

AUTHOR OF "THE MALAY ARCHIPELAGO," "THE GEOGRAPHICAL DISTRIBUTION OF
ANIMALS," "DARWINISM," ETC.

THIRD AND REVISED EDITION

London
MACMILLAN AND CO., Limited
NEW YORK : THE MACMILLAN COMPANY
1902

All rights reserved

FIG 67. Title page of Alfred Russel Wallace's *Island Life* (first published in 1880). The book was a sequel to Wallace's *The Geographical Distribution of Animals* (1876), and represented a major advance in the understanding of island biology.

Great Britain and Ireland, Japan, Formosa (Taiwan) and the larger Malay islands. He described them as having all being

> *separated ... at a period which, geologically speaking, must be considered recent [and]*
> *... always connected with their parent land by a shallow sea; they always possess*
> *mammalia and reptiles either wholly or in large proportion identical with those of the*
> *mainland; while their entire flora and fauna is characterised either by the total absence*
> *or comparative scarcity of those endemic or peculiar species and genera which are so*
> *striking a feature of almost all oceanic islands.*

As far as the British flora is concerned, he quoted H. C. Watson (1804–81, doyen of nineteenth-century British field botany) as telling him, 'It may be stated pretty confidently that there is no "species" peculiar to the British Isles.' This did not deter Wallace from listing 72 'species, sub-species and varieties of flowering plants found in Great Britain or Ireland, but not at present known in Continental Europe', plus 27 mosses and liverworts. He gave parallel lists of 179 Lepidoptera, 71 beetles and 122 molluscs. These lists would have to be severely revised nowadays, but they indicate a scale of differences between the fauna and flora of Britain and continental Europe.

Max Walters (1978) identified 23 plant species endemic to the British Isles, plus microspecies of apomictic forms of *Rubus, Sorbus, Hieracium* and *Taraxacum*; Chris Preston and Mark Hill (1997) have extended this to 48 species. And to take just one island example, Jermy and Crabbe (1978) list as endemics on Mull alone, two species of scurvy-grass not included by Walters in his list (*Cochlearia scotica* and *C. atlantica*), 19 (micro)species of *Hieracium* and four species of lichens (*Licanactis homalotropa, Ocellularia subtilis, Microglaena larbalestiere* and *Toninia pulvinata*). Notwithstanding, the amount of endemism in the British flora is small compared with c.66% in the Balearics and over 90% in Hawaii.

How have these forms arisen? From at least the time of the careful listings of Linnaeus, there has been a recognition that different species live in different habitats, straining the assumption that all forms have spread from a single site of creation in Iraq, as implied by a literal reading of the second chapter of Genesis. In his *British Zoology* (1761–6), Thomas Pennant described strictly regional associations of animals. Then in 1832 H. C. Watson published *Outlines of the Geographical Distribution of British Plants*, classifying the vegetation into six zones characterised by one or more indicator species; he followed this by a four-volume *Cybele Britannica; or British Plants and their Geographical Relationships* (1847–59), in which he set out his division of Britain into 112 recording areas (or vice-counties) – which in due course led to the formalising of plant distribution throughout the country, and hence the need for hypotheses to explain it.

FIG 68. HMS *Beagle* off James Island (now known as Isla Santiago or Isla San Salvador), Galapagos, on 17 October 1835, with Charles Darwin on board. (Painting by John Chancellor, reproduced by permission of Gordon Chancellor)

Islands have played a major role in making sense of all this taxonomic diversity, although the widely held myth that Charles Darwin was converted to a belief in descent with modification (i.e. evolution) as a result of studying the animals and plants on the islands of the Galapagos archipelago during the voyage of HMS *Beagle*, is not true (Fig. 68). He wrote before he got there that 'I look forward to the Galapagos with more interest than any other part of the voyage', but his anticipation was largely geological: he was fascinated by the thought of seeing active volcanoes. In fact Darwin seems to have been rather bored during the five weeks that the *Beagle* spent surveying around the islands. His host Robert FitzRoy, captain of the *Beagle*, was being particularly tiresome; Darwin himself had got fed up with the deserts of northern Chile and being flea-bitten whenever he slept ashore. He was becoming homesick, and his diary entries for the places he visited on the concluding part of the voyage (Tahiti, New Zealand, Australia, South Africa) are little more than perfunctory. As was his wont, he collected specimens of many groups, including the finches, which later showed much about the operation of natural selection and species differentiation (Weiner, 1994), but he did not even bother to label from which island they came. On his return to London, he merely recorded of the finches that 'their general resemblance in character and the circumstance of their indiscriminately associating in large flocks rendered it almost impossible to study the habits of particular species.'

This is not to suggest that Darwin had no idea that the Galapagos fauna might yield important secrets. In his 'ornithological notes' written on the final leg of the *Beagle*'s voyage, he commented about the indigenous mockingbirds of the Galapagos:

> *When I see these Islands in sight of each other & possessed of but a scanty stock of animals, tenanted by these birds but slightly differing in structure & filling the same place in Nature, I must suspect they are only varieties … If there is the slightest foundation for these remarks the zoology of Archipelagoes will be worth examining; for such facts would undermine the stability of Species.*

He had to face the full impact of this in March 1837, 18 months after his return to England, when John Gould, the ornithologist at the Zoological Society of London, told him that he (Darwin) had collected 13 different species of finch in the Galapagos, and that there were '26 true land birds [on the islands], all new except one'. In the original edition (1839) of his *Journal of Researches* on the *Beagle*, Darwin made only a passing reference to the finches; in the revised edition, published in 1845, he wrote:

> *Seeing this gradation and diversity in one small, intimately related group of birds, one might really fancy that from an original paucity of birds in this archipelago, one species might have been taken and modified for different ends.*

HOOKER ON ISLANDS

One of Darwin's closest friends was Joseph Dalton Hooker, a plant collector on a global scale and for many years director of the Royal Botanic Gardens at Kew. Darwin handed him the botanical material collected on the Galapagos (Table 21). Hooker was the final speaker in the infamous debate at the British Association for the Advancement of Science meeting in 1860 between Thomas Henry Huxley and the Bishop of Oxford. He claimed to have carried the day for the Darwinians, not least because 'Huxley had talked so fast that he could not be understood.' As a young man, Hooker had served as a naturalist in the Antarctic under Sir James Clark Ross; later in life he travelled widely in the Himalayas. He knew as much about the world's flora as anyone, and was the first to describe the characteristics and peculiarities of island floras.

TABLE 21. Joseph Hooker's data on endemic flowering plants in the Galapagos, based on specimens collected by Charles Darwin.

	NUMBER OF SPECIES	NUMBER OF SPECIES IN OTHER PARTS OF THE WORLD	NUMBER OF SPECIES CONFINED TO GALAPAGOS	NUMBER CONFINED TO ONE ISLAND	NUMBER CONFINED TO GALAPAGOS BUT ON MORE THAN ONE ISLAND
James (Santiago)	71	33	38	30	8
Albemarle (Isabella)	46	18	26	22	4
Chatham (San Cristóbal)	32	16	16	12	4
Charles (Floreana)	68	39	29	21	8

Darwin was particularly impressed by the frequency with which many endemic Galapagos genera such as *Scalesia* and *Euphorbia* are also endemic as distinct species on separate islands.

In one of the earliest public defences of Darwin's evolutionary ideas, at the British Association meeting in Nottingham in 1866, Hooker spoke on 'insular floras', comparing the plant communities of Britain, Madeira, the Canaries, the Azores, the Cape Verde Islands, St Helena, Ascension and Kerguelen (Williamson, 1984) (Fig. 69).

Hooker's 1866 address was the first detailed statement of the importance of islands for evolutionary studies. His identification of the main characteristics of island biotas still stands:

- They contain a high proportion of forms found nowhere else (endemics), although these endemics are usually similar to those found on the nearest continental mass;
- They are impoverished in comparison with comparable continental areas, i.e. there are fewer species on islands than on mainlands;
- Dispersal must play a part in the colonisation and establishment of islands, unless the island has been cut off from a neighbouring area and therefore carries a relict of a former continuous fauna and flora; and
- The relative proportions of different taxonomic groups on islands tends to be different from non-island biota, i.e. there is taxonomic 'disharmony'.

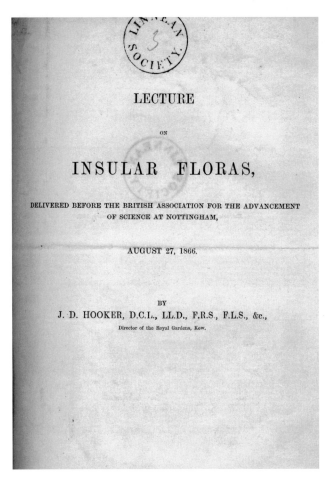

FIG 69.
Joseph Hooker's lecture on 'insular floras', given on 27 August 1866 at the meeting of the British Association for the Advancement in Science in Nottingham. (Linnean Society)

These points are well illustrated by the fauna and flora of the Outer Hebrides. In his inaugural lecture as Regius Professor of Zoology at Aberdeen University, James Ritchie (1930) suggested that:

> *In the fauna of St Kilda and in the thirty-two distinctive birds and thirty distinctive mammals of Scotland, we are looking upon the modelling from old species of new species and of geographical races, which we regard as the incipient stages of new species. In short, in the changes taking place in the balance of life, in the plasticity of animal form, not in the distant past of the geologists but in recent times, we are looking in Scotland upon Evolution in its course.*

Ritchie knew virtually nothing of the mechanisms of genetic change and species differentiation; these have been unravelled since his time. We can now be much more precise about the factors that 'model' new forms.

BIOGEOGRAPHY

Take a step back. For centuries it was believed that the world's animals were the descendants of those rescued by Noah from the Biblical deluge. Geological features were the result of the disruptions of the Flood. Erratic boulders were supposed to have been deposited by the Flood waters. But by the end of the eighteenth century, suggestions were being made that they had been transported on formerly widespread ice sheets. James Hutton (1726–97), the Scottish 'Father of Modern Geology', was converted to this view following a visit to the Jura mountains. But it was a Swiss naturalist, Louis Agassiz (1807–73), who emerged as the major proponent of the notion that moving sheets of ice had once covered large areas of the globe.

Agassiz's (Fig. 70) ideas were first presented in the 'Discourse of Neuchâtel' in 1837. Three years later he visited Britain, primarily to study fossil fish but also to lecture at the British Association meeting in Glasgow, where he argued that

FIG 70. Louis Agassiz (1807–73), ice-age advocate. (Harvard University)

FIG 71. Edward Forbes (1815–54), an early speculator about the origins of the British and Irish fauna and flora. (Linnean Society)

'At a certain epoch all of the north of Europe and also the north of Asia and America were covered by a mass of ice.' He converted William Buckland, Professor of Geology at Oxford and a leading diluvialist (i.e. a believer in the effects of the Flood), although it was another 20 years before the concept of 'ice ages' was generally accepted. Agassiz also visited Ireland (in 1840), but his arguments were received very sceptically there.

The effect of widespread and long-lasting ice sheets is to extinguish virtually all life. This immediately raises the question of where the recolonisers come from when the ice retreats, which was the question asked by Edward Forbes (Fig. 71). Some of Forbes' suggestions seem somewhat quixotic to us. For example, to account for the 'Lusitanian biota', the group of species found mainly in southwest Ireland and northern Spain (page 113), he proposed a Miocene land (called 'Atlantis') stretching 1,500 km from Spain to the Azores and then another 1,500 km to Ireland.

Forbes was criticised from many quarters. H. C. Watson considered that Forbes' theory 'absolutely teems with errors in its botany – inconclusive arguments, inconsequent logic, inept illustrations, and the guesswork of imagination put forward ostensibly as the ascertained facts of science'. However, Watson was notoriously cantankerous and his opposition did not convince many. Indeed, Forbes' ideas proved to be a major stimulus to biogeography. The infant science was dominated at the time by the notion of 'centres of creation'. Forbes' emphasis on the importance of migration impressed Lyell and J. D. Hooker. Darwin had already arrived at similar conclusions to Forbes (he carried out a series of experiments to investigate how long seeds could survive in sea water, to test if marine currents could be a major source of colonisers); when he wrote his *Autobiography* 30 years later, he was still ruing not having published these ideas himself.

A significant difference between Darwin and Forbes was the latter's claim for species' survival through the last stage of the Pleistocene on a subsequently drowned Atlantis continent. Were there refugia where some temperate species survived the last glaciation? It is a notion that endures. A century after Forbes, the Aberdeen botanist Jack Matthews argued that 'botanists most conversant with the flora of Ireland, among whom must be mentioned Lloyd Praeger, have given unqualified support to the thesis' (*Origin and Distribution of the British Flora*, 1955). Belief in refugia probably reached an extreme with Bryan Beirne (page 113). There is no evidence that any such vast ice-free refugia ever existed.

Notwithstanding, the possibility of more restricted land bridges and of the survival of animals and plants in refuges through the time when most of the current land surface of the British islands was biologically sterilised by massive ice sheets remains an important and still unsettled problem.

A major advance in the understanding of island biotas has been the theory of island biogeography, put forward by Robert MacArthur and Ed Wilson in 1963 and expanded into a book in 1967. It was the integration of ideas that had been around for a long time. H. C. Watson had pointed out that one square mile of Surrey holds half the plant species found in Surrey as a whole. In 1922 Henry Gleason generalised this in a paper 'On the relation between species and area', and Philip Darlington (1957) anchored it for islands by pointing out that in a range of islands a ten-fold increase in area led to a mere doubling in the number of species. But the species present in any one place are not fixed: as we have seen for birds (page 83), any animal or plant community has turnover in its composition – some species disappear and others appear. Michael Soulé (1983) listed 18 reasons why a population may go extinct. How can it be replaced? Isolated communities (and, by definition, all islands are to some extent isolated) will have fewer potential colonisers – both fewer species and fewer individuals of any species – and increased potentialities for unique interactions or exploitation of unusual habitats.

These ideas seem to have occurred in outline to many people. Alfred Russel Wallace had examined the principle long before in *Island Life* (1880: 532):

> *The distribution of the various species and groups of living things over the earth's surface and their aggregation in definite assemblages in certain areas is the direct result and outcome of ... firstly the constant tendency of all organisms to increase in numbers and to occupy a wider area, and their various powers of dispersion and migration through which, when unchecked, they are enabled to spread widely over the globe; and secondly, those laws of evolution and extinction which determine the manner in which groups of organisms arise and grow, reach their maximum, and then dwindle away.*

It was left to MacArthur and Wilson to give formal expression to these ideas.

THE THEORY OF ISLAND BIOGEOGRAPHY

The core of MacArthur and Wilson's thesis was that there is a balance between immigration to an island determined by its distance from the mainland and extinction thereon of local populations, which will vary with the island area. In other words, the number of species on an island will be the difference between those continually reaching it and those which are being lost (Fig. 72). The insight of MacArthur and Wilson was that this is a present dynamic rather than a simple historical hangover: species are *continually* going extinct locally; species are *continually* appearing and establishing themselves. As we have seen, species turnover on islands is normal. MacArthur and Wilson suggested that recurrent colonisations and extinctions create an equilibrium in which the number of species remains relatively constant although the species concerned will vary over time. They used data from the recolonisation of Krakatau to support their thesis. Wilson and Simberloff went on to test the theory by fumigating four small mangrove islands off the coast of Florida so as to kill all the resident animals and then monitoring their recolonisation over a period of years (Simberloff, 1969, 1976; Simberloff & Wilson, 1969, 1970).

FIG 72. The number of species (S) on an island is the result of a turnover (T) between rates of immigration (I) and extinction (E). Immigration will be affected by the proximity of an island to its source of immigrants (*n* = near, *f* = far) and the size of the island (*s* = small, *l* = large) (based on MacArthur & Wilson, 1967).

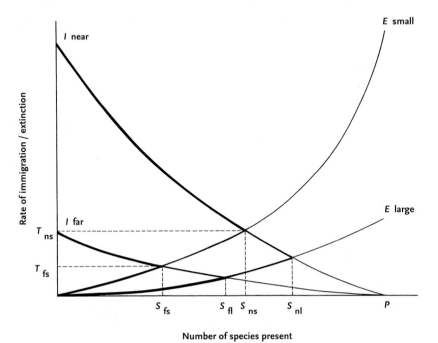

Number of species present

A test of the hypothesis for flowering plants on the British islands (using data from the original *Atlas of Flowering Plants*) showed that the best predictor of species number was the number of soil types (which can be regarded as a surrogate for island area). However, the pattern for Great Britain as a whole was closer to that of a continent than that of an island (Johnson & Simberloff, 1974). More stringent tests have come from studies on birds, and British birds have been particularly significant here – the amount of ornithological data from British islands is unique in the number of species and the length of time for which it is available. Tim Reed has collaborated with US biologists (Manne *et al.*, 1998) to test the generality of his earlier conclusions (page 126) and the relevance of the MacArthur & Wilson theory, using data collected from bird observatories all around the coast. Sufficiently complete data were available from 13 islands (Table 22). As expected, both immigration and local extinction rates increased with the number of breeding species on each island; they also declined, but not significantly, with island size and distance from the mainland pool of breeders.

Extinction and recolonisation data are probably more accurate for birds than for any other group, because it is usually easy to record a species failing to breed. Such failures may occur because numbers are generally declining, or they may be due to local factors like competition, change in habitat, or even pure chance.

TABLE 22. Total number of bird species recorded as breeding on islands with bird observatories (after Manne *et al.*, 1998).

ISLAND	NO. OF SPECIES BREEDING EVER RECORDED	TOTAL NO. OF SPECIES RECORDED BREEDING
Bardsey	45	132
Calf of Man	36	132
Copeland	25	132
Fair Isle	32	147
Farne	12	123
Handa	26	130
Hilbre	10	132
Isle of May	21	123
Lundy	49	164
Scolt Head	24	164
Skokholm	29	164
Skomer	42	164
Steepholm	25	164

A complication is that different species have different mobility, whatever their potential powers of flight. For example, woodpeckers rarely cross water, although obviously they may be involuntary colonisers through accidents of weather or other rare events. The ancestors of the finches on the Galapagos or the honey-creepers on Hawaii cannot be said to have 'intended' to settle on the respective islands, and their successful establishment and breeding represent extremely unlikely events. It is impossible to know how many of their relatives perished at sea, although some indication is given by the occurrence of twitchers' delights – 'vagrant' birds from distant parts of the world that appear on our shores, mostly to die a lonely death.

MacArthur and Wilson described the balance between immigration and extinction as an 'equilibrium', although as Mark Williamson (1981) has pointed out, it is really nothing more than a logical necessity. The number of species on an island can only be increased by two processes: immigration, which in turn will depend on the distance of the island from the source of potential colonisers, and the availability of ecological space for them; and it can be decreased only by those that fail to survive, i.e. by extinction. For David Lack, 'most species turnover is ecologically trivial.' Certainly the theory needs supplementing with ecological information. For birds, Russell et al. (2006) found that ideas of optimal foraging improved its predictions, since organisms will stay longer in an area if the distance to a neighbouring island is large. Another criticism of the theory is that immigration and extinction are not independent, since a high immigration rate may 'rescue' an island population of the same species, and hence reduce the likelihood of its extinction (Brown & Kodric-Brown, 1977).

Notwithstanding, the MacArthur and Wilson theory has proved useful: there is a turnover of species on any island over a period of years, and the total number of species tends to remain fairly stable. Examples of its testing are given by David Quammen in *The Song of the Dodo* (1996). However:

1. The theory deals only with the number of species, not with the number of individuals of a particular species. For example, the number of breeding bird species in Great Britain varies little from year to year (Gibbons et al., 1993). Most species have been present as long as records exist. A few pairs of species at the edge of their range, like the hoopoe or snowy owl, may breed for a short time and then disappear; other species, like the collared dove and avocet, seem to be extending their range and have become permanent members of our fauna. However, these changes have only marginal relevance to the state of bird communities in Britain as a whole.

2. The theory considers all species together, and tells us nothing about the biological community. It does not tell us, for example, why there are no rabbits on Tiree or snakes in Ireland.

3. It does not tell us anything about historical factors – why, for example, the common European vole (*Microtus arvalis*) is found only on Guernsey and Orkney whilst its close relative *M. agrestis* (the short-tailed or field vole) occurs widely in Great Britain and many of the smaller islands – but not in Ireland. The two species coexist over much of continental western Europe.

4. Most importantly, it tells us nothing about the evolution of endemic island forms. Indeed, the *Theory of Island Biogeography* is misleading in its discussion of the origins of island endemicity. Chapter 7 of the book is entitled 'Evolutionary changes following colonisation', but the authors omit any mention of genetic changes that may occur as a result of a colonising event. Part of the reason for this is historical. MacArthur and Wilson's book was published in 1967. In the previous year, however, two scientific papers had been published that forced a radical rethinking of population biology.

ENDEMICITY

A major change in population biology took place in the 1970s and 80s, which has radically affected our thinking on the way endemics originate. Traditionally biologists thought of individual animals or plants as genetically rather uniform. Clearly, inherited variation occurs (such as bridled guillemots, black rabbits, pin

FIG 73. The Inner Hebridean island of Rum, where human artefacts dated to 8,500 years ago have been found – the earliest human site so far identified in Scotland. (From William Daniell's *Voyage Round Great Britain*, 1814–25)

versus thrum primroses, mammalian blood groups, etc.) but the proportion of variable gene loci was thought to be very small. Indeed, there was a simple calculation showing that too much genetic variation could not be tolerated: it produced a 'genetic load', which reduced fitness and the reproductive potential of the population. This theory has now been shown to be too simplistic. It has had to be revisited because of experimental results. The assumption of genetic homogeneity was wrong: it has to be ditched following the demonstration by Harry Harris, working in London on human material, and Jack Hubby and Dick Lewontin, working in Chicago on *Drosophila pseudoobscura*, that heterozygosity (i.e. different alleles inherited from the two parents) occurs in 10% or more of genes (Harris, 1966; Lewontin & Hubby, 1966). This finding was rapidly extended to a wide range of organisms.

Two consequences of this high heterozygosity are extremely important in understanding the differentiation of island forms: (1) a small group of individuals drawn from a large population will almost certainly differ from its parental group in the frequency of alleles at a large number of loci; and (2) some alleles will be absent or relatively over-represented in the smaller group. If the small group is isolated (or is a colonising propagule), the daughter group will be immediately different from the source population. This only became evident after the time that MacArthur and Wilson were developing their ideas, and could well explain why they confined themselves to discussing evolutionary changes *following* colonisation.

Wilson and MacArthur were not particularly interested in the processes of speciation (for a discussion of these as they occur on islands, *see* Grant, 1998a). However, they have a chapter in their book on evolutionary changes, in which they state that as 'we believe that evolution through natural selection has produced the biotic differences which characterise islands, it is appropriate for us to study how natural selection works on islands.' They continue (MacArthur & Wilson, 1967: 154):

> We can think of the evolution of the new population as passing through three overlapping phases. First the population is liable to respond to the effects of its initial small size. This change, if it occurs at all, will take place quickly, perhaps only in a few generations. The second phase, which can begin immediately and must continue indefinitely, is an adjustment to the novel features of the invaded environment. The third phase, an occasional outgrowth of the first two, consists of speciation, secondary emigration and radiation.

MacArthur and Wilson explicitly equate their first phase with 'the founder effect', a concept put forward by the Harvard biologist Ernst Mayr in one of the defining works of the neo-Darwinian synthesis, *Systematics and the Origin of Species* (1942) and described more fully in a 1954 essay, 'Change of genetic environment and evolution'. The two biogeographers regard the founder effect as 'an omnipresent possibility but one easily reduced to insignificance by small increases in propagule size, immigration rate, or selection pressure ... The founder principle is actually no more than the observation that a [founding] propagule should contain fewer genes [alleles] than the entire mother population.'

This is not true. It would have been a reasonable assumption before the discovery of high levels of heterozygosity, but the post-1966 revolution showing the enormous genetic variability in any group of organisms means that the founder effect will almost certainly change allele frequencies as well as reducing variability to some extent (Fig. 74). The geneticist Sewall Wright, one of the founders of modern population genetics, pointed out the error. He referred to Mayr's emphasis of the founder effect as leading to gene (or allele) loss and a reduction in variability, but for Wright (in Provine, 1989: 57):

FIG 74. Effect on the frequencies and numbers of alleles at a single gene locus as the result of a bottleneck in numbers of a population. This will be especially marked when a new population is founded by a small number of individuals. Similar loss of alleles and changes in frequency will occur at every locus in the genome, resulting in the founded population being genetically different from the ancestral one.

frequencies of allelomorphs at one locus in population

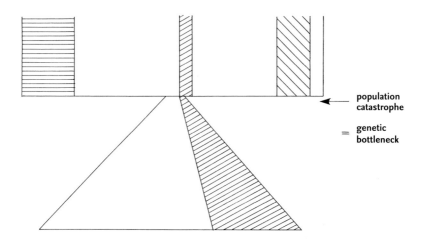

population catastrophe

= genetic bottleneck

I attribute most significance to the wide random variability of gene frequencies (not fixation or loss) expected to occur simultaneously in tens of thousands of loci at which the leading alleles are nearly neutral, leading to unique combinations of gene frequencies in each of innumerable different local populations ... The effects attributed to the 'founder effect' by Mayr [and also by MacArthur and Wilson] are the most obvious but the least important of the three.

In other words, the main effect of the colonisation of an island by a small number of individuals will be a population differing from its parent at a large number of loci, producing instant differentiation. Every colonising event will be a new experiment, exposing to the environment a set of reaction systems determined by the alleles carried by the founding group. It is these that represent its ability to respond (or not – most colonisations result in rapid extinction because of the failure of the animals or plants to cope in their new situation) to natural selection. This response is phase 2 in the MacArthur and Wilson scheme; it will necessarily be limited by the chance collection of alleles present in the founders. We shall see the effect of these genetic mechanisms in producing differentiation in the next chapter.

This 'instant' effect of a founding event seems obvious once the association of taking a small number of individuals from a genetically heterogeneous source is realised. Peter Grant has described it as 'perhaps the most novel and influential contribution of the century to ideas about how evolution occurs on islands' (Grant, 2001: 389). Notwithstanding, some theoreticians regard the founder effect as having only a minor role in speciation (e.g. Barton, 1989), and its importance remains unproven to others (Clegg *et al.*, 2002). Notwithstanding, there are a growing number of studies showing the influence of founder effects in establishing local genetic heterogeneity and hence the possibility of further differentiation (e.g. Haag *et al.*, 2006, on waterfleas on islands in the archipelago of southern Finland). There seems no reason to doubt that it is the main determinant of the distinct island races described here.

Surprisingly, the low heterozygosity which is expected in populations that have gone through a founder effect is much less than expected (Table 23). Only if the founder bottleneck persists for a long period, or if it is repeated, does genetic variability remain low (Bryant *et al.*, 1990). Kaneshiro (1995) has suggested that the disruption of a few individuals entering a new habitat may lead to the breakdown of sexual selection and thus involve a higher proportion of males breeding than usual, so increasing the effective gene pool.

Populations with little genetic variation are exposed to an increased hazard because of their difficulty in adjusting to environmental hazards; whilst captive

TABLE 23. Inherited biochemical variation in island and mainland populations of the same species (after Frankham, 1997).

	MEAN HETEROZYGOSITY PER LOCUS		% REDUCTION IN
	MAINLAND	ISLAND	HETEROZYGOSITY
Red deer *Cervus elaphus*	0.033	0.026	21.2
Japanese macaque *Macaca fuscata*	0.019	0.013	31.6
Deer mice			
Peromyscus eremicus	0.040	0.009	77.5
Peromyscus leucopus	0.080	0.071	11.3
Peromyscus maniculatus	0.088	0.068	22.7
Peromyscus polionotus	0.063	0.052	17.5
Voles *Microtus pennsylvanicus*	0.142	0.056	60.6
House mouse *Mus domesticus*	0.091	0.041	55.0
Bush rat *Rattus fuscipes*	0.047	0.011	76.6
Black rat *Rattus rattus*	0.031	0.026	16.1
Masked shrew *Sorex cinereus*	0.078	0.054	30.8
Chaffinch *Fringilla coelebs*	0.052	0.043	27.3
Red grouse *Lagopus lagopus*	0.080	0.069	13.7
Fruit fly *Drosophila simulans*	0.162	0.073	54.9
Spittlebug *Philaenus spumarius*	0.087	0.062	28.7

breeding programmes (such as endangered species maintained in zoos) properly make great efforts to avoid inbreeding and the potential loss of inherited variation (Soulé, 1987). This experimental finding suggests that this risk may be over-emphasised in field (i.e. non-managed) situations. The concept of a minimum viable population, widely used in conservation planning, is usually more important ecologically than genetically, although clearly the two cannot be entirely separated (*see* Primack, 1993, for a detailed description of the genetics involved).

However, the reduction in genetic variability as a result of a founding event must not be ignored. Inbreeding depression leading to reductions in fertility, fecundity and longevity has been found in a range of plants and animals (Keller & Waller, 2002), but it is less clear how important this is in natural populations, particularly on islands, where competitive pressures may be less than on mainlands. Saccheri *et al.* (1998) record the extinction of an inbred population of the Glanville fritillary on the Åland islands, but in contrast Gage *et al.* (2006) found no effect at the population level despite an increased proportion of abnormal sperm in inbred rabbits, including animals from the Uists, the Isle of May and Inner Farne.

FOUNDER EFFECT: IS THERE A GENETIC REVOLUTION?

At the same time that Robert MacArthur and Ed Wilson were exploring island biogeography, a group of evolutionary geneticists were speculating about the genetics of colonising species at a pioneering conference at Asilomar, California (Baker & Stebbins, 1965). The discussions were summed up by Ernst Mayr, who emphasised the need of ecologists to know something about the genetics of the organisms they studied, and for geneticists to become familiar with the ecology of their organisms. This is what he had attempted to do in describing the 'founder effect'. Although his original proposal about the origin of differentiation was similar to that of Wilson and MacArthur – on changes *following* colonisation – in his 1954 paper a decade earlier, Mayr extended his idea by proposing that animals and plants are faced with a new 'genetic environment' when they are isolated and as a consequence undergo a 'genetic revolution'.

As a young man Mayr had worked on the birds on the islands north of Australia. Time and time again he found that species that differentiated little on larger land masses were represented on the smaller islands by very different forms – and by forms that differed from those on other islands. He wrote, 'that mutation, recombination, selection and isolation are the four cornerstones of evolution is now generally acknowledged ... [However,] the role of a sudden change in the genetic environment seems never to have been properly considered.' He did not believe the two factors usually cited for 'the striking dissimilarity' of peripherally isolated populations, differences of physical and biotic environment (MacArthur and Wilson's explanation) or genetic drift (random changes in a small population), were a sufficient explanation. He focused on the importance of 'gene-flow or immigration'. He pointed out that genetic experiments in laboratories go to great lengths to avoid immigrants, which are regarded as 'genetic contaminants'.

Mayr argued that in a widely distributed population continually exposed to individuals moving in from elsewhere, there will be selection for genes that will tolerate combination with 'alien' genes. He cited populations of plants subjected to powerful stresses due to high salinity or desiccation, which may develop locally adapted races (or 'ecotypes') but which tend to be very variable due to the inflow of genes from nearby populations. If we think of single genes, we can measure their effects on physiology and reproductive success. But all the genes carried by an individual work together to produce a functioning whole; it is wrong to think of them behaving as independent entities like beans in a bean bag.

Gene is (perhaps surprisingly) rather a loose term. Generally speaking, it refers to the length of DNA at a particular point (or *locus*) on a chromosome. However there can be different forms (or *alleles*) of a gene at any locus, arising by mutation from the original gene. All species have their own genetic architecture, so that the loss or gain of a particular allele may affect other genes than the one at its locus. Such genetic architecture is often referred to as a *coadapted* system. The effect of this is seen when two varieties (or subspecies) breed together. Very often the two forms remain distinct, despite the occurrence of obvious hybrids between them.

One of the clearest British examples of this situation is in the carrion and hooded crows, which hybridise freely in northern Scotland but retain their separate identities away from the hybrid zone. For Mayr, 'the selective value or viability of a gene (allele) is not an intrinsic property but is the total of its viabilities on all the genetic backgrounds that occur in a population.' In other words, there is an internal genetic environment as well as an external one. The implication is that any disharmonious gene or gene combination introduced into a coadapted complex will be discriminated against by selection. There is plenty of evidence for this, such as the occurrence of 'recombinational lethals' produced by crossing over between two chromosomes, which may exhibit hybrid vigour in the normal form but which lead to inviability when the genes on them are disrupted by recombination (*see* Chapter 5 in my New Naturalist *Inheritance and Natural History*, 1977). Importantly, as Brakefield (1991) has commented,

> the existence of coadaptation between genes and of forms of non-additive genetic contributions to quantitative variation are likely to make variability within populations more resistant to loss than would be expected on the basis of theory developed largely from the perspectives of genes acting independently from each other and in a purely additive manner.

All this led Mayr to suggest that a group isolated on an island will undergo a 'genetic revolution' because they will not have to cope with a constant influx of new alleles and can therefore adapt to the circumstances on the island without the need to compromise due to the disrupting effect of immigrants. However, the power of genetic cohesion or coadaptation remains unknown, although evidences of its occurrence are common (e.g. epistasis and other specific gene interactions; complex traits being controlled by many loci; selection favouring the formation of 'balanced' chromosomes with positive and negative traits intermingled, etc.: Berry, 1997). Recent findings from gene-mapping show that higher organisms have fewer genes than previously supposed. This implies that many genes act together in development and behaviour, and strengthens the idea of the importance of genetic architecture. However, for the moment, the effect of Mayr's 'genetic revolution' remains unproven.

Whatever the ultimate fate of the genetic revolution concept, it is certainly not as important for island differentiation as was originally believed by Mayr. He effectively assumed that the genetic changes that take place in the process of colonisation and isolation are negligible and can be neglected. As we have seen, this is not so. This does not negate the fact that environmental factors are likely to be different on islands and therefore may act selectively. It may be helpful to distinguish the *founder principle* that occurs through the chance collection of genes carried by founders from *founder selection*, which occurs following isolation. The *founder effect* is the result of both processes.

It is usually impossible to separate the founder principle from the subsequent effects of founder selection, because we rarely know the frequencies of the alleles carried by the founding group. However, it has been possible to reconstruct the genetic constitution of the founders in some human isolates. For example, the population of Tristan da Cunha has by far the highest frequency in the world of a recessively inherited progressive blindness, retinitis pigmentosa. The Tristan population was effectively founded by 15 individuals, and we know the pedigree of them all from the time the community was established in 1817 (when the military garrison intended to prevent the escape of Napoleon from the sister island of St Helena was withdrawn) to the time when the population was evacuated in 1961 following the eruption of the island volcano. One of the original founders must have been heterozygous for the retinitis pigmentosa mutation, which meant that its frequency was one in 30 – about 3%. The population increased 17-fold during its period of isolation, but the frequency of the allele remained constant: there were 17 copies of the allele in 1961 – four homozygotes with two copies each of the gene and nine heterozygotes, each with a single copy.

An example of founder selection apparently in action is porphyria variegata in South Africa. This is an inherited defect of porphyrin, part of the haemoglobin molecule. The porphyria allele causes extreme sensitivity to sunburn, so its occurrence is easily recognised. In South Africa it is carried by about 8,000 individuals, three in every 1,000 of the white population, but it is very rare outside the country. All the present-day sufferers in South Africa are in 32 family groups, and they can all trace their ancestry back to one of the original 40 pairs of white settlers, an immigrant family from Holland that arrived in 1688. One million of the current population have the same surnames as the original 40 – implying an increase of 12,500 times in three centuries. However, the porphyria allele is present in only two-thirds of these. Presumably its deleterious effects (particularly in the sunny climate of South Africa) have led to selection against porphyria carriers.

A disease where it is impossible to separate pre- and post-colonisation frequencies is the severe demyelinating disease multiple sclerosis. This is not inherited in a simple way like retinitis pigmentosa or porphyria; it is often precipitated by a viral disease, while diet and climate seem to protect against it. However, it undoubtedly has a significant genetic element in its causation. The highest prevalence of multiple sclerosis in the world is in Shetland (1.3 per 1,000), closely followed by Orkney. The prevalence in the Faroes is only a third of this (0.5 per 1,000), while in Iceland it is even less (0.4 per 1,000). In the specialist medical literature, it has been said that these population differences rule out a significant genetic contribution to the disease, because all the island groups were colonised by Vikings from Scandinavia. However, this conclusion is unjustified: the colonisations of the Faroes and Iceland were different and later than those of Shetland and Orkney. The area of Norway from which the effective colonisers of Shetland came is characterised by a much higher prevalence of multiple sclerosis than other parts, raising the possibility that the disease pattern across the islands is the result of the genes carried by the colonisers' Viking ancestors. We have no means of knowing if the disease is less or more common nowadays than when the Vikings originally arrived.

Spittlebugs

One of the best examples of selection taking place after the original founder event is in a series of experiments involving *Philaenus spumarius*, the froghopper or spittlebug (so-called because of the 'cuckoo-spit' which protects the pre-adult life of these insects) on small islands in the Baltic Sea off the coast of Finland. The spotting pattern on the wing-cases (elytra) of these bugs is highly polymorphic, different forms being determined by alleles at a single gene locus. On the Finnish mainland one form increases in frequency towards the north, whilst another form is commoner in humid areas, implying adaptation to different conditions. Olli Halkka and his colleagues found that some forms seem to be particularly hardy and survive better than others when introduced to new islands, but that the relative advantage of the forms changes as vegetation grows up, with the original colonisers being replaced by another form, which has a preference for feeding on newly dominant plants like purple loose-strife and sea mayweed.

The island races of *Philaenus* largely reflect the variability found in mainland populations. Although several elytral forms are missing on the outer islands, the same forms are absent at the northern edge of the species' range on the mainland, despite the fact that the bugs there are in breeding contact with a large southern population. In other words, the genetic structure of the island races seems to be adaptive, not merely the result of ongoing immigration. Direct proof of selection on the islands has come from an experiment in which approximately 8,000 individuals (three-quarters of the populations) were swapped between two islands with genetically different populations. After three generations, both island populations had reverted to the pre-transfer allele frequencies, although they deviated considerably from another 35 island populations in the area. In other words, the genetic makeup on the islands was not random (i.e. determined by the founder principle) and must therefore be regulated by natural selection (Halkka & Halkka, 1974; Halkka *et al.*, 1975). These Finnish island spittlebugs are one of the few cases where it has been possible to separate the founder effect from subsequent selection.

An intriguing situation exists with the species on the British islands. David Lees has surveyed the morph frequencies of spittlebugs at a number of localities. He found that the proportion of the three darker morphs (which he calls 'melanic') was somewhat higher in industrial areas of mainland Britain than in more rural areas. For example, the melanic frequency in Stockport (just outside Manchester) was 18.9%, whilst in rural Surrey (Ashurst) it was 3.4%, and at Hythe on the coast of Kent it was only 1.2%. The highest frequencies recorded (over 95%) were near a smokeless fuel factory in the Cynon Valley, south Wales. In the Isles of Scilly the frequencies were around 3% (St Mary's 3.1%, St Martin's 3.6%, Bryher 2.7%, Tresco 0%), and similar on Skokholm (3.9%). The frequencies on the Small Isles of the Inner Hebrides were somewhat higher (Rum 8.1%, Eigg 4.9% and 16.9% in two samples from different localities, Canna 6.4%, Muck 7.1%), similar to that in Arisaig on the nearby Scottish mainland (6.2%). In contrast, the frequency at Tyndrum, c.45 km inland and 300 m above sea level, was 32.0%. Lees argued from the pattern of frequencies and their constancy from year to year at the same site that they were regulated by natural selection. It would be fascinating to know the factors affecting the fitness of the different forms.

Adaptation is everywhere evident in nature, but actual studies of natural selection in operation are not common (an excellent review is that by John Endler in *Natural Selection in the Wild*, 1986). Halkka's island spittlebugs illustrate selection in action. Another island example is forceps length in the earwig *Forficula auricularia*. This is an inherited trait, although the switch

FIG 75. Large-forceps variant of male European earwig, common in British island populations. (Joseph Tomkins)

between 'short' and 'long' forceps is determined by larval nutrition. In mainland populations virtually all the males have short forceps, but on many islands up to 60% of males have long forceps, which are more effective in sexual combat. This may be related to a high density of earwigs. High frequencies have been found on Lundy, the Isles of Scilly, the Farnes and some of the Forth islands (Tomkins & Brown, 2004). Other examples of selection on islands are given in Chapter 6 (see in particular our work on house mice on Skokholm, page 158).

Founder selection affects the survival or not of individuals. It has to be distinguished from the *interactions* between individuals within a community or ecosystem, which misled ecologists in the early days of the subject into thinking of an ecological community as a 'super-organism' and seemed to lend support to the idea of a 'balance of nature', an idea living on in Jim Lovelock's Gaia hypothesis (Berry, 1989, 2003; McIntosh, 1998). The diversity and serendipities of the constitution of island populations – what Hooker in his British Association lecture called 'disharmony' – show very clearly the error of regarding a biological community as a self-regulating super-organism. Island populations are triumphs of individual adjustment, not manifestations of some master pattern (Simberloff, 1980).

ISLANDS AND NATURE RESERVES

MacArthur and Wilson's theory has led to questions being asked about the practical significance of islands at a time when ever larger parts of the globe are being affected by humans. Natural areas are increasingly becoming 'islands' in seas of developed or despoiled land. Can this sort of island be treated in the same way as a real island in terms of its biological content and diversity? Jared Diamond (1975) spelt out some of the consequences of applying 'island theory' to 'island reserves':

- A newly isolated area will temporarily hold more species than at equilibrium because it will 'gain' species from the surrounding unsuitable habitat – but the surplus will not persist;
- The rate at which equilibrium occurs will be faster for small reserves than for large ones; and
- Different species require different minimum areas to support a stable population.

In designing nature reserves, we have to bear in mind:

- A large reserve will hold more species at equilibrium than a small one;
- A reserve near other reserves will hold more species than a remote one, because they will behave like a single large one;
- A cluster of reserves will support more species than separated ones, or ones arrayed in a line;
- A round reserve will hold more species than an elongated one, because it will have a proportionately shorter boundary for 'leakage'.

Diamond's arguments led to a debate on SLOSS – is it better to aim for a *Single Large Or Several Small* reserves?

This was tested by Dan Simberloff, extending the studies on the experimental islands that he had established with Ed Wilson (page 127). He divided the original islands, cutting channels through their roots and canopy so that each island became a mini-archipelago, leaving the overall area only slightly affected. Against expectation, he found four years later that a single large island did not always harbour more species than several small ones (Simberloff & Abele, 1976).

The SLOSS argument still rumbles on (Harris, 1984a; Haila, 1990). It is an important debate, because it affects not only the biodiversity of particular islands but the survival or extinction of whole species (Lovejoy, 2000). However, it is only marginal to understanding the natural history of islands.

References and Further Reading for Chapter 5 are listed on page 342.

CHAPTER 6

British and Irish Island Forms: Differentiation

A<small>LL ISLANDS HAVE</small> *a special fascination: they can be an adventure to get to; they are liable to harbour entities that occur nowhere else; they are satisfyingly well-defined areas; above all, they pose questions about how and when their present plants and animals came to arrive, which leads to an unusually close concern with the work of specialists in other fields.*

David Allen, *Flora of the Isle of Man*, 1984

So far we have seen something of the generality of living on an island: how the British and Irish islands were formed and were colonised, and the particular pressures of island life and how this affects adaptation. We have noted a few examples of British and Irish island forms. We can now turn to looking at some of our indigenous forms in more detail.

When the Pleistocene ice sheets finally retreated, they left the British islands as a biological desert. Ten thousand years ago there were a few remnants of ice remaining in northwest Scotland, but otherwise the land was sub-Arctic tundra, with a small human population. The mean January temperature was c.1 °C but the climate was still warming: by 9000 BP, the January temperature averaged 5 °C. Ireland, Scotland, north Wales and northern England had a vegetation similar to northern Eurasia or Canada today. Thickets of willow and dwarf birch occurred where there was shelter. In midland England and south Wales there was a belt of birch woodland with some Scots pine and many familiar animals: hedgehogs, badgers, wild boar, roe and red deer, but also elk, aurochs and beavers. There were none of the rhinoceros, hippos or elephants that had occurred in earlier interglacials, nor were there lemmings, arctic fox or reindeer remaining from the full Arctic fauna.

Southeastern England was much more wooded, with birch, hazel and soon elm, oak and lime. The climate continued to warm up, producing a 'climatic optimum' between 8000 and 4500 BP, with temperatures one or two degrees higher than in recent times. Oak spread northwards at a rate of 350–500 m a year, although much slower when it reached Scotland. By 6000 BP, all of Great Britain was covered by deciduous woodland, although this was never more than stunted in the north and west of Scotland.

Throughout this period there were humans in Britain, known to us by the stone artefacts of the Late Palaeolithic and Mesolithic cultures. The earliest evidence in Ireland is from Mount Sandel in County Derry (c.9000–8800 BP). About 8500 BP, Britain finally separated from continental Europe. There had been earlier periods of isolation, but a land connection had always been re-established. This break was the final one for the time being. No doubt humans continued to cross the shallow but growing Straits of Dover, but animals and plants that could not fly would have had to depend on the chance of wind or accidental transport on logs, birds' feet or commensal accidents.

There were two or three thousand years after the Pleistocene ice disappeared when Britain was still part of continental Europe. Should we recognise pre-8000 BP inhabitants as 'native', whilst all other species are 'aliens' or 'introduced'? Perhaps we ought, but for most species we have no firm knowledge as to whether they we here in 8000 BP or not, although Godwin (1975) estimated that at least two-thirds of our present flora had arrived before we became an island.

VIKING MICE

The difficulty in distinguishing between native and alien is illustrated by long-tailed field mice (*Apodemus sylvaticus*) (the species is called 'wood mouse' over much of its range, but this can be confusing since it often lives far away from woodland; indeed it is known as the 'hill' or 'red' mouse in many places). Many authors refer to the species as 'indigenous' or 'native'. However, studies of mitochondrial DNA from field mice caught in the Mediterranean area have shown them to be much more variable than mice from northern Europe. This suggests that the southern populations are older than those in the north, and probably served as the source of recolonisation of northern Europe after the Pleistocene (Michaux *et al.*, 2003). The argument is based on the same kind of evidence as the widely accepted one that the human species spread from an origin in Africa. Assuming that *Apodemus* (Fig. 76) had to reoccupy its northern range after the retreat of the ice, can they be really regarded as 'native' in the

FIG 76. St Kilda field mouse (top) and St Kilda house mouse (bottom). (From Barrett-Hamilton, 1899)

north? How long does a species have to live in an area before it becomes 'native'? Subfossil remains of *Apodemus* have been found in many cave deposits in glacial interstadials throughout the Pleistocene. The species probably formed part of the temperate fauna of deciduous woodland before separation from continental Europe. *Apodemus* teeth have been recorded from a site near Dublin dated 7,600± 500 years ago. Does this mean that the species can be fairly described as native to the British Isles?

In 1895 de Winton described 'a sharply differentiated local form' of *Apodemus* living in the Outer Hebrides: it had a larger body but smaller ears than mainland mice, and was rather dark. He called it *Apodemus hebridensis*. Four years later Barrett-Hamilton described another species (*Apodemus hirtensis*) from St Kilda. This was 'closely allied to *Apodemus hebridensis*, from which it differs in its slightly larger size and also in the greater amount of buff or yellowish brown on the underside'. A year later, Barrett-Hamilton surveyed all the specimens of *Apodemus*

FIG 77. St Kilda field mouse. (Stewart Angus)

in the Natural History Museum and decided that *A. hirtensis* should be regarded only as a subspecies of *A. hebridensis*.

Then in 1906 six *Apodemus* specimens from Fair Isle were described as having a 'longer and narrower brain-case than typical *A. sylvaticus*' and put into a new

FIG 78. Hebridean field mouse from Mingulay. At one time Mingulay mice were distinguished as a separate subspecies, *Apodemus hebridensis nesiticus*, but they are now regarded as merely one of the distinct races of typical *Apodemus sylvaticus* that characterise virtually every Hebridean island. (Stewart Angus)

species, *A. fridariensis*. It precipitated a splitting and naming fever. Another 12 subspecies of *hebridensis* or *fridariensis* were added, making a total of 15. But, as Harrison Matthews wrote in his New Naturalist on *British Mammals* (1952),

> If we are to be scientifically honest, we must acknowledge that the evidence upon which all this is raised is not good enough. The diagnoses of many of the island forms have been drawn up after the examination of much too few specimens, so that we do not know the range of individual variation that may occur in them. Even the limits of variation in the mainland form are not defined with accuracy, nor have the skull characteristics, which are much used in diagnosis, been studied in the light of the allometric [differential] growth principle.

Clearly there was a need to examine as many specimens as possible in order to determine what variation existed in each race, and to what extent this variation was common to a number of localities.

Michael Delany began this task in the late 1950s in the Hebrides and western Highlands. He trapped mice from a range of places and habitats and made a series of measurements on each animal. He used the amount that the teeth were worn as a method of ageing the animals in his samples. This was important. Previous workers had tended to take the largest animal in their collections as a 'typical' full-grown one, ignoring the fact that there is a considerable amount of adult size variation in all rodent populations – or even that a small sample may contain no adult animals. Indeed at one time it was suggested that there was a distinct Irish field mouse: but it turned out that the small, dark mouse that was the 'type' of this was nothing more than a young adult which had not attained full size and typical coat colour.

Delany carefully 'adjusted' his samples to take into account variation in sex, age and size. He was then able to conclude with confidence (Delany, 1964) that:

> the mice from Rum are the largest, with those from North Uist, Barra and Colonsay next in size. Tail length is variable, being longest in the mice from Rum and shortest in those from Raasay ... The animals from the Outer Hebrides (except Lewis), Colonsay and Rum are lighter coloured with those from North Uist particularly pale. The more richly coloured come from Raasay and Rum and those with the least colour from North and South Uist ... The Barra and Uist mice ... are of a rather stockier build than the mice from Rum – which appear of rather similar proportions to the mice from Applecross [on the Scottish mainland].

And so on. It is obviously possible to continue this sort of descriptive comparison almost indefinitely. Every population differs to a greater or lesser extent from every other one. Delany concluded that of all the island populations he examined, only the Rum population was distinct enough to retain a subspecific name (*A. sylvaticus hamiltoni*); 'for the remainder, the differences are so small between island and mainland populations that identification of individuals becomes impracticable.'

FIG 79. Distribution of the named races (or subspecies) of small mammal species in the British Isles. With two exceptions (the Scottish Highland water vole and an Irish field mouse) they are all on small islands. This is shown particularly clearly by the races of the long-tailed field mouse (*Apodemus*) on the Scottish islands.

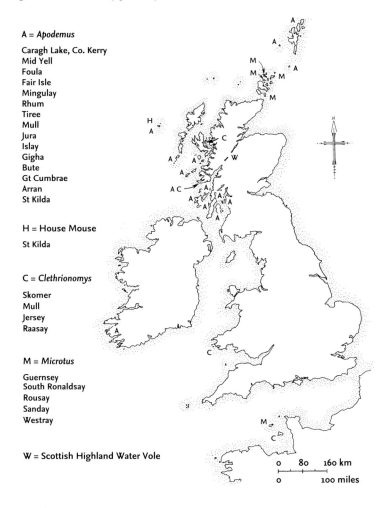

A = *Apodemus*

Caragh Lake, Co. Kerry
Mid Yell
Foula
Fair Isle
Mingulay
Rhum
Tiree
Mull
Jura
Islay
Gigha
Bute
Gt Cumbrae
Arran
St Kilda

H = House Mouse

St Kilda

C = *Clethrionomys*

Skomer
Mull
Jersey
Raasay

M = *Microtus*

Guernsey
South Ronaldsay
Rousay
Sanday
Westray

W = Scottish Highland Water Vole

0   80   160 km

0   100 miles

TABLE 24. Size of some British mice at island and mainland sites.

LONG-TAILED FIELD MOUSE, *APODEMUS SYLVATICUS*

	HEAD & BODY (mm)
ISLAND	
Foula (Shetland)	101.2
Yell (Shetland)	100.9
Fair Isle	112.9
St Kilda	114.4
Lewis	99.2
Rum	105.9
Mull	97.0
Isle of Man	95.0
St Mary's	95.5
Tresco	95.5
Sark	101
MAINLAND	
Perthshire	92.3
Surrey	87.6

HOUSE MOUSE, *MUS DOMESTICUS*

	WEIGHT (g)	HEAD & BODY (mm)
ISLAND		
Mykines (Faroes)	25.4	96.1
Foula (Shetland)	25.1	97.7
North Ronaldsay (Orkney)	17.5	85.5
Sanday (Orkney)	17.9	87.6
North Faray (Orkney)	26.2	99.0
St Kilda	—	91.5
Isle of May	19.2	88.7
Skokholm	18.0	92.6
MAINLAND		
East Fife	18.9	88.3
West Pembrokeshire	19.1	86.6
Taunton (Somerset)	13.5	86.6

Is it possible to make sense of all this? Bryan Beirne suggested that:

> Apodemus *apparently invaded the islands on three occasions. The first invasion is represented by* Apodemus fridariensis *of the Shetlands,* A. hirtensis *of St Kilda, and* A. hebridensis *of the Hebrides. They represent a population that inhabited the northern part of the Celtic Land and which later divided into three populations that developed independently of each other. Both the Shetland and Hebridean species were later divided into a number of smaller populations that in turn developed independently.*

The trouble is there is no evidence for this, nor does it fit the facts revealed by Delany's careful comparisons. Neither does Corbet's proposal (page 114) that the island races result from human introduction seem, on the face of it, to explain why there is no obvious pattern of inter-island differentiation. The islands support populations of mice of the order of several thousands, much too large for random changes ('genetic drift') to account for the differences. The answer comes from comparing each island population with every other one to get a 'genetic distance' between each, i.e. a measure of the number of genes that separate the populations.

When this is done for the Small Isles (Rum, Muck, Eigg and Canna), we find that the Eigg population is most like that of the Scottish mainland, and that the other islands are each genetically close to Eigg but unlike each other. An obvious explanation for this is that Eigg was colonised first and then mice were introduced independently to the other islands from Eigg. Because of the 'founder effect' (page 132), individual differences could be quite large but would nevertheless reflect the link between the populations concerned. This idea is supported by the human history of the Small Isles: Eigg was a political centre with Scandinavian links from the early days of modern human life in the north. In the eighth century the Vikings raided there; by the thirteenth century the island was a seat of the Lord of the Isles. Although Rum is the site of the earliest known inhabitants of Scotland, the Mesolithic and Neolithic dwellers on Rum would certainly have had only very primitive boats. The first people with proper seafaring boats to sail the northern seas were the Vikings. Although they are notorious for their pillaging raids, their early voyages were colonising ones. It is quite possible that on some of these journeys they carried mice as inadvertent stowaways with their farm animals and fodder. Such transport would certainly have been more likely than in the primitive boats of their Stone Age predecessors.

If the Vikings introduced mice into Eigg, it would have been likely also that they carried them from there to satellite settlements on the neighbouring islands. Is this supported by evidence from other Hebridean islands?

Relationships between the Outer Hebrides populations show a complicated pattern of affinities (Fig. 80). Clearly there has been no simple introduction and

FIG 80. The suggested colonisation routes of Shetland and the Hebrides by long-tailed field mice. The numbers are estimates of divergence between populations (the higher the value, the more distant the relationship), those without brackets being the 'distance' from the closest related population, and those in brackets the 'distance' from a sample trapped near Loch Sunart (taken as typifying Scottish Highland mice) (after Berry, 1969).

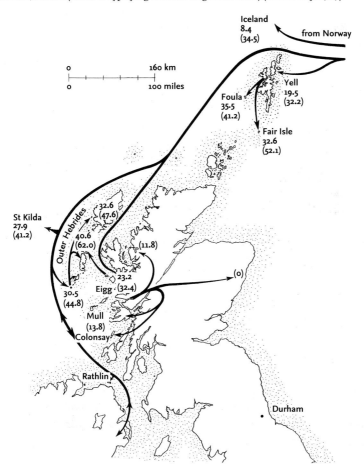

spread of field mice to the islands: Lewis/Harris is distant from every sample except South Uist, whose closest relationships are with Norway; North Uist is not at all like South Uist, and is closer to Eigg than anywhere; Barra and Mingulay are closely related to each other and to Eigg. Intriguingly, the Shetland populations are much more like Norway than the Hebridean races. The Uists became separate islands comparatively recently (perhaps as late as AD 1000), yet their mouse populations are very distinct. These relationships fit well with the probability of separately founded populations, and not at all with the likelihood that the mice are relics.

FIG 81. Underside of the skull of the house mouse. The mesopterygoid fossa (palate opening) has approximately parallel sides in most mice (see larger figure), but in mice from the Faroes the pterygoids converge anteriorly. The two upper figures are redrawn from Barrett-Hamilton and Hinton (1910–21) comparing a Faroe mouse (left) with an English animal. The trait is very variable in Shetland mice (lower figures), with different frequencies on different islands.

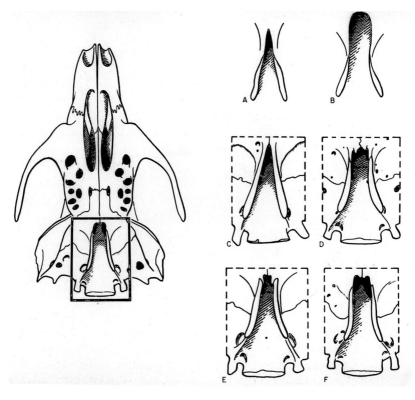

Overall, the field mouse relationships support the likelihood that the species was introduced from Norway, and hence presumably by the Vikings. Because there is no way of knowing what genes were carried by the original colonisers, we cannot know how much genetic change has taken place following the establishment of the individual island populations.

The story of the house mice (*Mus musculus*) on the Faroe Islands has similarities to that of the field mice on Shetland and the Hebrides. House mice are the only small mammals on the islands. They were originally described scientifically by Eagle Clarke in 1904, who wrote of a collection from Nólsoy (one of the smaller islands) that they were 'remarkable for their great size, indeed they are veritable giants, being considerable larger than the type and of any of its numerous geographical races'. He classified them as a new subspecies, *faeroensis*, distinguished solely by 'immense size'. On the same grounds, they were later promoted to specific rank, since the form 'differs so conspicuously from all other members of the [species] group'.

The distinctiveness of these mice is of considerable interest because there is no plausible way that they could have reached the islands, except by human transport. The earliest human inhabitants of the Faroes were apparently eighth-century Irish hermits (page 4), but the islands were not settled widely until the Norse began to arrive in the ninth century. A detailed study of the Faroese mice by Magnus Degerbøl of the Copenhagen Museum in the late 1930s suggested the existence of distinct races on at least four of the islands. Degerbøl followed the common assumption that they must have 'originated through isolation for a long space of time, while the big Nólsoy mice have then developed by adaptation to the leaping life on the bird cliffs (i.e. as a kind of ecological race)'.

This situation puzzled Julian Huxley. In his definitive exposition of the neo-Darwinian synthesis, he worked out that 'the normal minimum time for distinct sub-speciation' is 5,000 years, 'although the facts concerning rats and mice show that sub-speciation may occur much more quickly. In particular, the Faeroe house mouse, *Mus musculus faeroensis*, that was introduced to the islands not much more than 250 years ago, is now so distinct that certain modern authorities have assigned full specific status to it.' In fact, the differentiation has been even more explosive. The island of Hestur was only colonised by mice in the 1940s when an airport was being built there, but they are as distinct as those on any of the islands in the group (Fig. 82). It is difficult to explain this in any other way than that their differentiation is the chance consequence of the genes carried by the original colonisers, probably from the neighbouring island of Streymoy.

But the notion of post-colonisation changes still persists. In his comprehensive overview of *Island Populations* (1981), Mark Williamson objected to

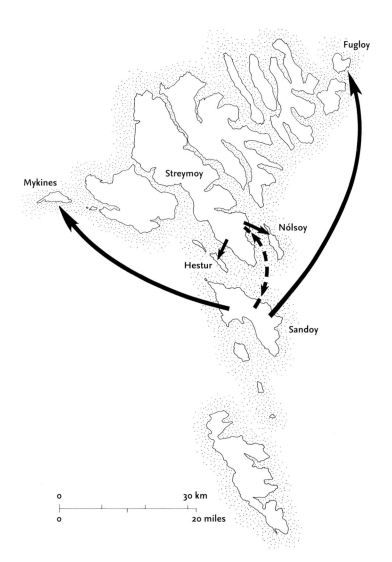

FIG 82. Spread of house mice in the Faroe Islands, based on the genetic relationships of populations on the different islands. It seems likely that mice were first established on the southern island of Sandoy and then colonised Mykines, Fugloy and Streymoy from there. They went on to spread from Streymoy to Nólsoy and Hestur. The colonisation of Hestur only occurred in the 1940s, but the Hestur mice are as distinct as those on the other islands (after Berry *et al.*, 1978).

explanations based on the uncertain chance of the founder effect on the grounds that they are entirely speculative. He suggested that the differentiation of the Faroe mice could be explained by 'adaptation to the colder and damper situation found on the islands'. To test this, Simon Davis (1983) compared mice from the mainland of Great Britain with population samples from the Orkney, Shetland and Faroe archipelagoes. His null hypothesis was that a major 'maritime effect' would result in the island populations being more similar to each other than to mainland populations. Using a statistical analysis similar to that employed by Williamson, Davis found that the island groups were very different from each other, but more like Caithness (northeast Scotland) than each other. In other words, his data showed a regional geographical influence (which one can blame on a Viking influence) rather than an island effect.

SCOTTISH VOLES AND WELSH MICE

The Orkney vole was introduced to science in 1904 by J. G. Millais, an enthusiastic mammalogist as well as an accomplished artist (he was the nephew of the famous Pre-Raphaelite, Sir John Everett Millais). Millais named it as a new species, *Microtus orcadensis*, on the grounds that it was almost twice as large as the common British vole (*Microtus agrestis*), which does not occur in the Orkney archipelago; it differed from the latter also in a number of coat-colour and skeletal traits. The Natural History Museum mammal specialist, Oldfield Thomas, confirmed it as 'a most distinct species and one of the most interesting and unexpected discoveries ever made in British mammalogy'. Within ten years, five island races had been described – from the Orkney Mainland, Sanday, Westray, Rousay and South Ronaldsay.

The nearest British vole relative of the Orkney species is on Guernsey, off the opposite end of Great Britain. This also has been described as a separate species, *Microtus sarnius*. Its namer regarded it as 'related to the vole of the Orkney Islands and to the extinct *Microtus corneri* of the British mainland; the three living species (*M. agrestis*, *M. orcadensis* and *M. sarnius*) and their fossil relative apparently belong to an older fauna than that now inhabiting Great Britain and the mainland of Europe.'

At this stage, speculation took off. Geoffrey Barrett-Hamilton argued in his magisterial *History of British Mammals* (1910–21):

> The orcadensis *group appears to have arrived in south-eastern Britain in late pleistocene times, probably from France by way of the Channel Islands, which explains*

its absence from Skandinavia. It spread through Britain, becoming specialised as it
dispersed, and eventually reached the Orkney district which was then part of the
mainland; later, on the severance of the Orkneys from the mainland, portions, probably
the northern first, became detached as separate islands. In these segregation has played
its part, and differentiation of subspecies has been the result. The persistence of M.
sarnius in an island far to the south shows that these mice owe their survival to
freedom from competition rather than to any other factor; elsewhere they have probably
succumbed to such competition, helped by the attacks of carnivora.

Leo Harrison Matthews in his New Naturalist argued similarly, albeit with a
caveat: 'It is important to remember that this is an interpretation of the available

FIG 83. Orkney voles. (From a painting by Archibald Thorburn in J. G. Millais's
Mammals of Great Britain and Ireland, 1905)

evidence. It may be the whole story, but on the other hand it may have to be modified in the future.'

In fact the story has been modified – very much. It has been shown to be wrong in five respects:

1. There is no geological evidence that climatic conditions permitting the survival of small mammals existed during the Pleistocene in or around any of the British Isles.

2. The fossil *M. corneri*, conceived as a cold-zone ancestor of both the Orkney and Guernsey species, was a palaeontologists' mistake. The lower jaws of *Microtus* are not assignable to species. All those from (subfossil) cave deposits in Britain identified as belonging to *M. corneri* are associated without exception with *M. agrestis* skulls; skulls which have been classified as *M. corneri* belong to *M. oeconomus*, a still extant tundra species, which was common in Britain during the colder interstadials of the Pleistocene.

3. There is no evidence of a land bridge between Orkney and Scotland after the retreat of the Pleistocene ice. The assumption that there was one is based on the distribution of species like *Microtus*, and is therefore a circular argument. It constantly recurs. For example, in his New Naturalist on the *Sea Coast* (1953), the geographer J. A. Steers wrote, 'there must have been a connection to account for the similarity of fauna between the islands and the mainland.'

4. *M. orcadensis* and *M. sarnius* are not distinct species, but are members of the widespread *M. arvalis* of the European mainland. The forms are morphologically very similar and crossbreed with no difficulty.

5. The claim that *M. agrestis* out-competed *M. (orcadensis) arvalis* and led to the latter's elimination from the British mainland is very unlikely, because the two species coexist over much of mainland Europe. Furthermore, *M. agrestis* extends further north in Scandinavia than *M. arvalis*, which suggests that it would have preceded *M. arvalis* in post-Pleistocene colonisation. This would have meant that it reached northern Britain (including Orkney, if the latter was still connected to Scotland) before *M. arvalis*.

It is impossible to maintain the 'classical' hypothesis of isolation followed by differentiation for the Orkney vole. The only sensible suggestion is that they were introduced by humans – probably early in the human history of the islands, because archaeologists have found subfossil voles in the Neolithic settlements of Skara Brae and Quanterness, around 6000 years BP. Comparison of Orkney voles with those from continental Europe shows that they are more closely related to animals from southern than from northern Europe. Perhaps they were carried to Orkney by early megalith builders, whose origins seem to have been from the Mediterranean area. On the other hand, the Guernsey voles may be a relict from the time that the island was still attached to what is now Brittany. They are more closely related to modern north European voles than are their Orkney cousins.

Water voles have declined in many parts of Britain but have maintained populations on some of the smaller islands, where they tend to burrow like moles and live over a wider area than their more strictly waterway-based mainland relatives. On a group of small islands in the Sound of Jura, the animals have only half the genetic variation of mainland animals, but live at ten times the density of the latter (Telfer et al., 2003). Presumably their low variability is a consequence of the small number of founders of each population.

Skokholm and its mice

So far I have emphasised the importance and persistence for island races of the genes carried by their founders, but we must remember that the island inhabitants known to us are the tip of an iceberg of all the colonising groups that reach an island but then failed to survive. Successful colonisation carries the implication that the colonisers were adapted to life in their new home or were capable of adapting to it. One of the longest genetic studies of adaptation to island life has been that of the house mouse population on the 98 ha Welsh island of Skokholm.

Unusually for an island population, its origins are apparently known. There were no mice there in 1881 when the island was last farmed intensively. Ronald Lockley lived on Skokholm in the 1930s and recorded that when its lighthouse (Fig. 84) was being built in 1913–15, mice were so abundant that special precautions had to be taken to render the building mouse-proof. They probably reached the island in the 1890s, in sacks brought across by rabbit-catchers for transporting their harvest back to the mainland.

Skokholm has an unusually well-known natural history. It has the highest density of rabbits in western Europe. When Lockley first took possession of the island he found that he could not farm conventionally because of grazing by the rabbits. He tried every means to control them, without success. One of his attempts involved introducing (with the collaboration of academic pathologists interested in exotic diseases) a few rabbits infected with an obscure South American virus called myxomatosis. On two occasions, only a handful of rabbits died as a result. The conclusion (published in the veterinary literature) was that European rabbits were resistant to the virus. Only in the 1950s, when myxomatosis was killing over 95% of British rabbits, was it realised that its failure

FIG 84. Skokholm lighthouse. According to Ronald Lockley, the lighthouse was mouse-proofed when it was built in 1908, although Trinity House cannot confirm this. (R .J. Berry)

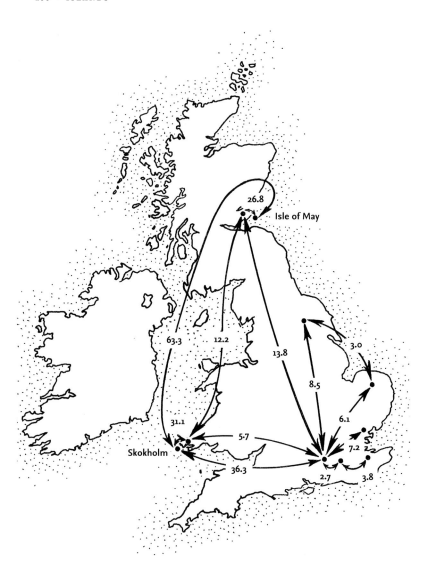

FIG 85. Relationships of some British house mouse populations. The numbers indicate degrees of resemblance, based on inherited traits. Populations on the mainland are fairly homogeneous. In contrast, animals on the Isle of May and on Skokholm are both very distinct from their nearest mainland neighbours. Although both share a similar ecology, the two island races are very different from each other. It is difficult to account for this except as a result of the genes carried to the islands by the founders of each population.

to spread on Skokholm was because the island rabbits do not have any fleas. Their lack of fleas is, of course, an example of a species 'escaping' its enemies when colonising an island.

The island mice are very peculiar in that more than half of them have a failure of fusion of some of the vertebral neural arches – in effect, a very mild form of spina bifida. This is very rarely found in wild mice (although it occurs in some laboratory strains), but it is present in just under 10% of the mice from the mainland of Wales opposite Skokholm, from where the rabbit-catchers came. This seems to be a clear case of a founder-effect trait in the island mice (Fig. 85).

The mice breed for approximately six months every year (April to September); for the winter months their chief problem is obtaining enough food to provide the energy necessary for surviving low temperatures. Studies of both skeletal and inherited biochemical variation shows that gene frequencies change one way during the summer breeding phase and the opposite way during the winter survival phase (Table 25). In other words, natural selection is operating in

TABLE 25. Percentage excess of heterozygotes (i.e. deviation from expectation) at the *Hbb* locus (the gene controlling the ß gene of haemoglobin) in mice caught in the autumn on Skokholm cliffs.

YEAR	FREQUENCY OF *Hbb*^{d}	EXCESS OF *Hbb*^{d}/*Hbb*^{s} HETEROZYGOTES (%)		FEBRUARY TEMPERATURE: DIFFERENCE FROM MEAN (°C)
		OLDER*	YOUNGER	
1968	0.438	34.8	75.0	−1.4
1969	0.464	67.8	111.0	−2.4
1971	0.271	−29.8	9.2	+1.4
1972	0.539	−11.0	31.0	+0.9
1974	0.621	40.2	31.6	+1.7
1975	0.426	−23.7	7.9	+1.1
1976	0.415	23.5	18.6	+1.4
1977	0.595	−16.7	8.3	−0.3

*aged over three months
There is an increase in the proportion of heterozygotes in younger (summer-born) animals in every year except 1974 and 1976, where the preceding winter had been unusually mild.

different directions during the two phases of the animals' lives. There is also a lesser but progressive change evident in the skeletal traits, apparently indicating that the animals are continually adapting to the island conditions. (For more details of these island mice, *see* Chapter 7 in my New Naturalist *Inheritance and Natural History*; also Berry *et al.*, 1987.) Skokholm mouse population shows two evolutionary consequences of island living:

1. Dependence and persistence of the genes present in the original colonisers; and
2. Continued adjustment to both a fluctuating environment and a new habitat.

We have found the same sort of effect in mice caught on three islands in the Antarctic (Macquarie, Marion and South Georgia). The details differ, but clearly show natural selection operating on particular genes (or more strictly, on the piece of chromosome that carries the gene). It is only when longitudinal studies (i.e. ones repeated over a period, not simple snapshots taken at a particular time) are carried out that it is possible to identify natural selection in operation.

DEER, SLUGS AND BANK VOLES

Almost wherever one searches one can find examples of differentiated island forms. One of the most extreme is the extinct 'giant Irish deer', a species noted for its enormous antlers, with a span of up to 3.6 m, although the animals had a height at the shoulder of only around 2 m. It was a relative of the red deer and was in fact not confined to Ireland, but occurred across Eurasia, although its bones are frequently found in Irish peat bogs and it seems to have been particularly common there. The species also lived on the Isle of Man. It used to be thought that the giant deer had become extinct in late Pleistocene times, about 10,000 years ago, but recent carbon-14 dating of Isle of Man fossils shows that animals were alive there 1,400 years later – perhaps the last survivors of these bizarre animals (Gonzalez *et al.*, 2000).

Races of the bank vole (*Clethrionomys glarolus alstoni* on Mull, *C. g. erica* on Raasay, *C. g. skomerensis* on Skomer and *C. g. caesarius* on Jersey) fall into the same category. Examination of any isolated island form (i.e. one not subjected to regular crossing with non-isolated relatives) suggests that it is probably unique and hence that an almost indefinite number of other local races could be recognised. The worthwhileness of naming such forms is proportional to one's determination to emphasise the attractions and importance of one's own island or island group. The original Clare Island Survey (page 100) can be regarded as being driven by such an enthusiasm. Virtually all the island small mammal forms were described in the early years of the twentieth century when taxonomic 'splitting' was fashionable.

Most of the 'special' forms of the British and Irish islands are distinct from their mainland cousins, but only to the extent that can be explained by the chance genetic constitution of their founding population and subsequent selection. Some forms have a distribution outside the island where they are found, and usually the island forms can be reasonably attributed to human introduction. The Orkney vole seems to have originated in this way; the white-toothed shrews of the Isles of Scilly are almost certainly explicable likewise. Further complication is when species differ in different parts of their range. The unusually non-migrating greylag geese of Loch Druidibeg in South Uist fall into this category.

However, there are some species which apparently fall outside a simple founder and adaptation explanation. A good example of this group is the 'Kerry slug' (Fig. 86), the only spotted British slug; it is an island form in that it occurs

FIG 86. The Kerry slug is found only in the coastal area of northern Iberia and on sandstone in west Cork and Kerry. (Paul Sterry, Nature Photographers)

on Cape Clear Island, although it is also found in west Cork and south Kerry, its only other sites in Britain and Ireland. However, it also occurs in Portugal and northwest Spain: it is a key 'Lusitanian species', which land-bridge enthusiasts suggest may have survived on a dry land between Iberia and Ireland (page 54) (Godwin, 1975, sees it as significant in his discussion of the origins of the British flora). Whilst slugs seem unlikely candidates for transport by humans and chance introduction, Noble and Jones (1996) give reasons for believing that *Arion flagellus*, another Lusitanian species, colonised Britain from Ireland in the early twentieth century, and that another slug, *Arion ater rufus*, has also only relatively recently invaded Britain (where it crosses readily with the common *A. a. ater*). Consequently, it does not seem too extravagant to suppose that the Kerry slug was brought to Ireland by some of the early human voyagers. Such considerations mean that one of the most important 'Lusitanian species' cannot be unequivocally attributed to survival as a relict.

References and Further Reading for Chapter 6 are listed on page 342.

CHAPTER 7

Islands and Species of Particular Note

I T IS A TRUISM to record that every island has its own interest and aficionados, but some have produced more for the natural historian than others. Clare Island has already been mentioned (page 100), as have the long-established bird observatories, some on mainland coasts but mostly on islands. It is impossible to be even-handed in describing the fauna and flora of our islands, simply because some have attracted more interest and publications than others.

ST KILDA: MICE, WRENS AND SHEEP

St Kilda is this: a mad, imperfect God's hoard of all the unnecessary lavish landscape luxuries he ever devised in his madness. These he has scattered at random in Atlantic isolation 100 miles from the corrupting influences of the mainland, 40 miles west of the westmost Western Isles.

Jim Crumley, in Baxter & Crumley, 1988

Probably the most famous islands in British waters are the four small, high islets lying 64 km west-north-west of the Sound of Harris, which constitute St Kilda: Hirta (430 m high), Dun (178 m), Boreray (384 m) and Soay (376 m), with their associated stacks Stac an Armin (196 m, the highest in the British Isles) and Stac Lee (172 m). They are special by any standard; in 1986 they were canonised as a World Heritage Site by UNESCO because of their vast seabird populations and indigenous mice, wrens and Soay sheep, and then in 2005 they were given rare dual status with the additional recognition of their cultural significance. They

FIG 87. Conachair (430 m), the highest point on Hirta, St Kilda. (Stewart Angus)

FIG 88. Three island wrens: (*left*) St Kilda wren (*Troglodytes troglodytes hirtensis*) (John Love); (*top right*) Faroe wren (*T. t. borealis*) – its local name is musabrodir ('brother to a mouse') (Daniel Bengtson); (*bottom right*) Fair Isle wren (*T. t. fridariensis*). (Rebecca Nason)

have been extensively chronicled: Mary Harman (1997) cites 'no less than twenty books of a general nature, nine devoted to particular aspects of the islands, four novels, innumerable articles'. One of the best accounts of a storm ever written is Hammond Innes's novel about St Kilda, *Atlantic Fury*.

There is no saint called Kilda. The name *St Kilda* first appeared on a Dutch map in 1666. Almost certainly it was applied there to the island of Haskeir, 40 km southeast of St Kilda, or possibly to the nearby Monach Islands (which are also called Heiskeir), which were known to the Vikings as *Skildir* (on the grounds that they look like domed shields floating on the surface of the sea). Probably the distant map-maker misplaced the label. Hirta is first referred to by name (*Hirtir*) in one of the Icelandic sagas.

Whatever the motive for travelling there, it is difficult for any visitor to ignore the islands' natural history. Martin Martin visited St Kilda in 1697 (he almost missed the islands in the mist, and only arrived safely by watching the flight of gannets). He found 180 people living on Hirta, a population he estimated were

FIG 89. The earliest map of St Kilda, from Martin Martin's *A Late Voyage to St Kilda* (1698), accompanied by Martin's drawings of a fulmar and an 'assilag' (storm petrel).

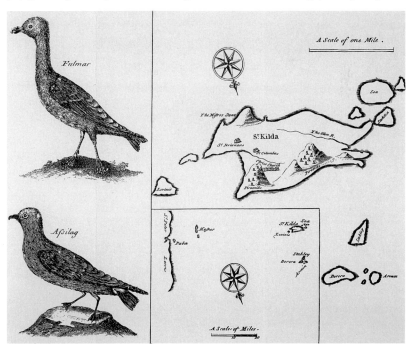

FIG 90. Dun, guarding the southern side of Village Bay, St Kilda. (Stewart Angus)

FIG 91. Boreray, St Kilda – site of the world's largest gannet colony. (Stewart Angus)

consuming 22,600 gannets each year (probably an overestimate, according to Fisher & Vevers, 1943). Martin recorded that they acquired their fishing hooks from the stomachs of gannets, presumably swallowed from lines laid by fishermen elsewhere.

The islands are the most important seabird breeding site in northwest Europe, with over a million birds. They have the oldest and biggest British colony of fulmars (67,000 pairs) and 30% of the British puffins (140,000 occupied burrows). Boreray and its adjacent stacks have the largest colony of gannets in the world (62,000 pairs; 20% of the world population). The islands have the greatest number of Leach's petrels in the eastern Atlantic, the largest colony of storm petrels in Britain and over 1% of the European kittiwakes, common guillemots and razorbills. Hirta had a human population from at least 3850 BP to AD 1930, when the inhabitants of the time asked to be taken off; they were declining in number and felt unable to cope in their isolated situation (Buchanan, 1995; Quine, 1995; Harman, 1997; Fleming, 2005).

Some of the animals are unique. The St Kilda wren (subspecies *hirtensis*) is larger and darker than its mainland relatives and not unlike the population on Fair Isle (*fridariensis*) (Williamson, 1958). In contrast, the wrens of the Outer Hebrides (*hebridensis*) and Shetland (*zetlandicus*) are greyer than the St Kilda and Fair Isle ones, although all are large forms. The Faroes and Iceland also have distinct races (*borealis* and *islandicus*, respectively), duller and redder than the Shetland form. All these races have characteristic songs. It is difficult to interpret their differentiation other than as an example of the persistence of founder-effect genes distributed differently on the different island groups.

The most distinct of the island field mouse races described in Chapter 6 is that on St Kilda. St Kilda was also the home of the only named race of the house mouse (*muralis*) in Britain and Ireland until it became extinct soon after the evacuation of the human population in 1930. Like the field mouse, the house mouse may have been of Scandinavian origin; it shares a narrowing of the mesopterygoid fossa on the underside of the skull with house mice from Shetland and the Faroes but recorded nowhere else. The last time the St Kilda house mouse was seen alive was in 1931, when an Oxford University expedition visited the islands to see what had changed since the people left in the previous year. They caught a mere 12 house mice, all of them mature adults; Robert Atkinson (1949) found only field mice when he trapped there in 1938. The 1931 expedition believed that the house mouse was an obligate commensal and would be unable to survive without humans. However, there are plenty of places where house mice live wholly independently of mankind: Skokholm is uninhabited apart from a seasonally staffed bird observatory; the human population deserted

Faray (in Orkney) in 1946 but mice still thrive there; Fraser Darling recorded mice invading his tent on the Treshnish island of Lunga, which had been uninhabited for 80 years, and we caught mice there nearly 50 years after Darling's stay. The situation seems to be that house mice do not compete successfully with field mice when they have no refuge to escape into. This refuge disappeared on St Kilda when the people departed. For some reason, this results in house mouse breeding being disrupted so that they cannot compensate loss through deaths with enough replacement young (Berry & Tricker, 1967).

However, the land animals most obvious to visitors to St Kilda are small, agile, dark-coloured sheep. These are Soay sheep, descendants of ones brought to Britain about 7,000 years ago; they are the most primitive domesticated sheep in Europe. There are a number of local races of similar sheep on British islands – in Shetland, Orkney, the Outer Hebrides (many of these with four horns), the Isle of Man (the Loghtans) – as well as the Herdwicks of the Lake District. Sheep like this have been with us for a long time – their bones have been found in the Neolithic village of Skara Brae in Orkney, dated at around 4000 BC. They are related to the sheep of Norway, the Faroes and Iceland and are very different to the heavier animals of the British mainland. Little seems to be known about their relationships or when they split from the southern breeds. There is no archaeological evidence as to when sheep were introduced to St Kilda; the earliest mention of sheep there is in the fourteenth century.

When the human inhabitants left St Kilda in 1930, they took with them their black-faced sheep from the main island of Hirta (where all the people lived), which had replaced the original animals in the 1870s. In 1932, 42 Soay rams and 65 ewes were transferred to Hirta from Soay, where they had lived as an unmanaged flock of around 200 individuals for many centuries. Feral sheep still live on Soay. There are also sheep on Boreray, which are larger and mainly white with tan faces; they are probably an early version of the blackface breed.

FIG 92. Hebridean four-horned sheep. (Scottish Natural Heritage)

FIG 93. Soay sheep on Hirta, St Kilda. (Stewart Angus)

Soay and Boreray are too remote for more than occasional visits, but the Hirta Soays have been intensively studied by veterinarians, population biologists and geneticists (Jewell *et al.*, 1974; Clutton-Brock & Pemberton, 2004). The initial interest has been in learning how population size was regulated. The flock has a three- to four-year fluctuation in numbers, varying from around 600 to 2,000 animals. Wet, windy weather in the winter is particularly hard for the sheep. It results in poor feeding and many deaths in February and March, followed by a high lamb mortality in April due to poor lactation in the mothers. Young rams are particularly prone to starvation, because they spend so much energy in the autumn in chases and copulation. In 1978–80, 72 male lambs were castrated and 68 left intact; ten years later, 38 of the castrates but only two of the intact rams survived.

The Soays are heavily infested with keds, lice, gut worms and protozoans. These parasite loads are particularly heavy in malnourished animals, pushing them to the point of death. The parasite burdens do not have the same effect on all animals: they are more deleterious in more inbred animals and in ones with genes known to be concerned with resistance (variants of the adenosine deaminase locus, the major histocompatibility complex, and gamma interferon). The flock has become a model for studying the interaction of ecology, demography and natural selection.

RUM: MICE, DEER, SHEARWATERS AND SEA EAGLES

The Inner Hebridean island of Rum is another well-chronicled island (Clutton-Brock & Ball, 1987; Magnusson, 1997; Love, 2001). It is the wettest and arguably the most mountainous island for its size in Britain. For most of the twentieth century it was known as the 'Forbidden Island', at first because of the clearance of its native Gaelic population by the Maclean of Coll – 300 evicted in 1826 and another 130 in 1828, leaving only one family. Following the reintroduction of red deer in 1845 (they had been extinct there since the 1780s), it was treated as a private sporting estate by the three families who owned the island in succession from 1857 to 1957. In 1957 the island was acquired by the (then) Nature Conservancy for £23,000, including its castle (built in 1902) and its contents, 'to be used as a nature reserve in perpetuity'. The *Daily Herald* reported 'Government-financed mouse lovers have taken over a Hebridean island – and banned the islanders from buying meat and groceries. The mouse lovers say food for sale would encourage trippers. And trippers would disturb the mice.'

The island's name may derive from the Norse *romøy*, meaning a wide or spacious island. The traditional spelling was Rum; it was changed to Rhum in

1905 by the then owner, Sir George Bullough, but reverted to its old name in 1992 when Scottish Natural Heritage took over from the Nature Conservancy Council.

Rum is a National Nature Reserve, originally envisaged as an open-air laboratory, but now managed with the aim of re-creating a habitat resembling that which existed before the native tree cover was removed. Pollen and plant remains in bogs show that in the Boreal period (10,000 to 7000 BP), there was a forest of birch, pine, willow, hazel and juniper in the more sheltered areas. This increased over the next millennia to a climatic optimum around 4500 BP, with oak, ash, alder, rowan and wych elm. At this point, Iron Age people arrived, clearing the forest for their livestock. At the same time, the climate became cooler and wetter with a sharp increase in bog moss, bracken, alder, willow and juniper and a decrease in oak and wych elm. The Viking intrusions of the eighth century AD led to the present treeless landscape, with natural scrub surviving only in steep gullies. Since 1960, half a million trees have been planted on Rum. Early days – but the island's restoration is under way.

We have already noted the distinctiveness of the island's field mice (page 147), only a little less marked than that of *Apodemus hirtensis* of St Kilda. The island also hosts pygmy shrews and, less welcome, brown rats. Rats have been on Rum since sometime after 1730; they occur in low density, but roam all over the island. A deer dying on the hills (which rise steeply to 812 m) will be found and attacked by rats within a few days. However, a ground-nesting (or, more strictly, underground-nesting) bird, which has been surprisingly little affected by the rats, is the Manx shearwater, of which there are around 100,000 pairs above the 350 m contour on the Rum mountains, probably the largest colony in the world (although only two-thirds of the combined populations of Skomer and Skokholm). The Norse-derived name of one of the mountains, Trollval (702 m), is said to come from the reaction of the Vikings to the night calls of the shearwaters, believing them to be trolls. This indicates that the colony is over 1,000 years old. There is a possibility that rats have eliminated coastal nesting birds on Rum, but only spread into the area of the existing shearwater colony in autumn each year after the shearwaters have left; there is no sign of predation during the nesting season. Rats have certainly been a problem to shearwaters on the neighbouring islands of Eigg and Canna – but they have been now eliminated on the latter (page 70).

A bird which was absent from Rum – indeed from the whole of Britain and Ireland since 1916, when the last pair nested on Skye, following widespread persecution by shepherds, gamekeepers and egg-collectors – is the white-tailed sea eagle (Fig. 94). In the Faroes there was a traditional annual 'bill-tax' (*nevtollur*) of a bird's bill that every boat owner had to pay. This was mainly aimed at controlling crows, but an eagle's beak was especially valued, and submitting one

FIG 94. White-tailed sea eagle. The species became extinct in Britain in 1916, but following a reintroduction programme it began breeding again in 1985. There are now more than 30 breeding pairs in Scotland. (John Love)

gave permanent exemption from the tax. The species is relatively common along the coast of north Norway, and it seemed a candidate for encouraging back to Britain. Attempts were made to reintroduce it from Norway with three birds in Glen Etive in 1959 and four on Fair Isle in 1968, but in 1975 a more determined programme was set up on Rum (Love, 1983). For 11 years, batches of eight-week-old birds were imported there from north Norway. In all, 82 birds were released over an 11-year period. Their establishment was slow, and another 58 birds were released in Wester Ross between 1993 and 1998. However, some of the Rum birds survived and began to breed. The first fledglings flew in 1985; in 1996 the first Scottish-born birds successfully bred. There are now over 30 pairs nesting each year, mainly in the Western Isles, annually contributing more than 20 birds to the population.

The availability of Rum as an open-air laboratory has made possible a variety of researches, most notably on the red deer. A study by Nature Conservancy scientists provided data on its reproductive cycle, feeding ecology and social behaviour, which now provide the basis for deer management throughout Scotland (Lowe, 1969). However, the most intensive biological study has been that of Tim Clutton-Brock and his colleagues (Clutton-Brock *et al.*, 1982), building on and quantifying a classic study on demography in the 1930s by Frank Fraser Darling, published as *A Herd of Wild Deer*. Darling made his observations on the

Dundonnell Estate in Wester Ross, but he had wanted to work on Rum, for he realised the advantages islands had for the long-term study he had in mind. He wrote, 'Two of the great advantages of Rum over a mainland forest are the fact that Rum is an island and the deer cannot move out, and island isolation cuts down disturbance. I'd have given all I had to have been allowed to work on Rum then.' He was refused permission by the then owner.

Reproductive behaviour has been a focus of the deer research on Rum. The island population is naturally divided into five groups by geography, with little movement of hinds between them. There has been no shooting in one of these (c.12 km²) since 1972; by 1981 the number of hinds had risen from 60 to 179, when it largely stabilised. As the numbers increased, the hinds began to have their first calf at older ages, fecundity decreased, winter calf mortality increased from 5% to 35%, and calving became later, meaning that the date of the rut was also delayed. The stags showed increasing signs of stress: their mortality increased, biasing the sex ratio in favour of females. These results can be generalised for deer management throughout Scotland: high-quality stags in large numbers are generated only in populations well below the maximum carrying capacity in any area.

A puzzling episode in the history of Rum and some of the neighbouring islands came from claims by Professor John Heslop Harrison of the University of Newcastle. For nearly 30 years, Heslop Harrison and his students contributed significantly to our knowledge of the natural history of the Hebrides. Among their records were a number of finds surprising to other experts – such as 11 sedge species (including two not otherwise known in Britain, *Carex bicolor* and *C. glacialis*), a clover (*Trifolium bocconei*, otherwise recorded only on the Lizard and in Jersey), and an Arctic-alpine willowherb (*Epilobium lactiflorum*, also not otherwise known in Britain). In addition, Heslop Harrison reported finding several arthropod species that would not normally be expected in Britain, including two water-beetles in the Outer Hebrides otherwise confined to the Canaries (*Potamononectes canariensis* and *Aulonogyrus striatus*). He fiercely defended his records, claiming that they showed clear evidence of southern (or Lusitanian) biota (*see*, for example his article in the *New Naturalist* journal in 1948). However, many of these records have never been corroborated – 11 of them from Rum alone remain unrepeated, despite diligent searching. Whilst expert opinion is divided about Heslop Harrison, a detailed investigation of his findings concluded that 'the only explanation that really fits the facts … [is that] the Professor is deliberately indulging in the most culpable dishonesty' (John Raven, author of the New Naturalist on *Mountain Flowers*, quoted by Sabbagh, 1999). Fortunately such controversy is rare. Science is driven by and is dependent upon accurate observation and recording. Considerable energy and ingenuity is employed by all biological recording schemes in validating records. Anomalies are usually fairly easy to spot and reject, but not always.

The natural history of Canna, one of Rum's nearest neighbours, has been well documented by John Lorne Campbell, who owned the island for 43 years until presenting it to the National Trust for Scotland in 1981 (Campbell, 1984).

LEPIDOPTERAN MELANISM

Dark forms of moths (the icon of these is the peppered moth) and ladybirds are best known in industrial areas, where their colour is, in part at least, cryptic on the resting surfaces. But there is also a large amount of 'geographical melanism'

Diarsia mendia

Maniola jurtina

Eupithecia venosata

Coenonympha tullia

Hadena confusa

Paradiarsia glareosa

Xestia xanothographa

Eulithis testata

Lasiocampus quercus callunae

FIG 95. Melanic moths from Shetland, and their more typical forms. (Natural History Museum)

FIG 96. Local forms of many moths are common in Orkney, although they are not as extreme as in Shetland:
1. Wood Tiger (a. Orkney, b. Wiltshire);
2. Juniper Carpet (a. Orkney, b. Scotland, c. Surrey);
3. Marbled Coronet (a. Shetland, b. Orkney, c. mainland Scotland, Argyll);
4. Ingrailed Clay (a. Shetland, b. & c. Orkney, d. Sutherland);
5. Autumnal Rustic (a. Orkney, b. mainland Scotland, Aberdeenshire);
6. Lesser Yellow Underwing (a. Orkney, b. England, Gloucestershire);
7. Oak Eggar (a. & b. Orkney, c. & d. Dorset).
(Natural History Museum)

in Lepidoptera, which can be divided into 'northern' and 'western coastal' melanism. Although this is not a specific island characteristic, it is a phenomenon that largely occurs on islands.

NORTHERN (OR HIGH LATITUDE) MELANISM

Above latitude 60° or thereabouts, short nights and extended twilight means that no prey species can rely on the protection of darkness in the summer months. At the same time, many lepidopteran species are a significant source of food for birds, both in the breeding season and during the southward migration. Melanics are particularly marked in Shetland, where 27 of the 62 native (i.e. non-migrant) species have developed local forms, of which 21 are melanic. In the Faroes only four out of 23 species are melanic, and in Iceland only two out of 21. Shetland melanics were first recorded in the 1880s. At the time, it was thought that melanism was the direct result of humidity: one author (who had never been to Shetland) declared that the melanic specimens must come from 'boggy meadows', whereas lighter individuals must have been collected on drier cliffs and hillsides.

Some of the Shetland races are composed entirely of dark individuals (e.g. ingrailed clay, netted pug, marbled coronet), while in others there is a dark form (or morph) coexisting alongside typical paler ones (autumnal rustic, square-spot rustic, northern spinach). I was involved in a four-year study of the autumnal rustic with Bernard Kettlewell, which followed his classic studies on industrial melanism. Kettlewell believed that the 'ancient', non-industrial melanics of Shetland might give a clue as to why industrial melanics spread so rapidly and in so many species in the middle of the nineteenth century (Kettlewell, 1973). Our experiments are described in New Naturalist 61 (*Inheritance and Natural History*), pages 170–5. Suffice it to say here that the situation was far more complicated than we expected. The Shetland melanic of the autumnal rustic (*Paradiarsia glareosa* f. *edda*, produced by an allele at a single gene, just like most of the other melanics) ranged in frequency from almost 100% at the north end of Shetland to around 3% at the south end of the islands. Mark–release–recapture studies showed that *edda* had a survival advantage over *typica* in the north but not in the south; there were also behavioural differences between the forms in their frequencies of flight (which could be an adaptation to reduce the chance of being blown out to sea). None of these disproved the idea that *edda* (and the other northern melanics) are the result of differential survival through bird predation, but they show the danger of making easy assumptions about the biological pressures of island life.

One of the Shetland (and Faroe) melanics is certainly not directly maintained by natural selection for camouflage on the ground. Males of the ghost moth have a 'lekking' behaviour in southern populations: they fly over their territory at dusk like 'ghosts', attracting females by their brilliant white wings. In Shetland, the males have brown or at best creamy forewings. Observation on Unst (the northernmost Shetland island) suggests that the female is attracted more by the male's pheromones than by his colour.

The likely reason for most of the northern melanics is that birds are able to see moths in flight and take them on the wing throughout the 'night'. Melanism (or melanic frequency) is a balance between crypsis when resting during the day and cryptic melanism when flying at night. Although there is no direct evidence for this in Shetland, it seems to parallel the situation in the relict old Caledonian forest outside Rannoch, where the mottled beauty is highly cryptic when at rest on lichen-covered trees, but is often disturbed by ants and flies during the day; it has a dark form, which is almost invisible in flight.

Western coastal melanism

Melanism is also found among moths and butterflies in the Hebrides and further south, apparently independent of latitude. It occurs in races found both in northwest Scotland and the islands (such as the meadow brown, large heath,

FIG 97. 'Coastal' melanics. (Natural History Museum)

Argynnis aglaia

Argynnis selene

Polyommatus icarus

Entephria caesiata

Colostygia didymata

Alcis repandata

Euphyia bilineata atlantica

Hadena caesia

Hadena barettii

Hadena perplexa capsophila

marbled coronet, oak eggar) and in forms known from the Hebrides only (dark green and pearl-bordered fritillaries, common blue, grey mountain carpet, twin-spot carpet, mottled beauty). Bird predation was suggested as the reason for this melanism by a Victorian naturalist as early as the 1880s: 'The Hebrides have certainly had the coloration of the Geometrae and other moths, which rest on the rocks in the daytime, very much affected by the grey colour of the gneiss. Those that most assimilated in colour to that of the rock would be less easily perceived by birds, and in the struggle for existence would have the best chance of preservation' (Weir, 1881) – although another proposal was that 'the exciting cause of melanism was to be looked for in certain meteorological conditions.' The truth is that still no one knows for certain how these Hebridean races have been produced.

Western coastal melanism extends all down the western seaboard. The geometrid moth *Euphyia bilineata* has a form (*atlantica*) in Shetland and the Outer Hebrides, and an even darker melanic in southwest Ireland on the Blaskets: on Tearaght (the outermost Blasket) all the population is black and large in size. Ten kilometres inland on the Irish mainland, all the moths are the typical yellow colour. The noctuid *Dianthaecia carpophaga* is another species with a black form replacing the typical on the Blaskets and other places in western Ireland; an intermediate form is found in Wales. Some melanic species are restricted to the west and southwest: the grey shears (*Hadena caesia*) is confined to the west and southwest of Ireland, the Isle of Man and Canna. Its close relative *H. barettii* is found on the shores of Devon and Cornwall, western Ireland and Wales. A black form *capsophila* of the tawny shears (*H. perplexa*) occurs in the Isle of Man, with a range of variation in Ireland. *Antitype xanthomista* is another dark, rock-sitting insect found only in north Devon and Cornwall, and on the Isle of Man. Kettlewell has pointed out that all these species feed on campion, hatch in midsummer and fly at dusk, when they are likely to be subjected to predation. Mike Majerus has added the possibility of a thermal advantage for the melanics, and a protection against wing wear through sand-blasting, but all this is speculation.

MEADOW BROWNS IN THE ISLES OF SCILLY

A situation in butterflies claimed to show the power of selection was studied for many years in the Isles of Scilly by E. B. Ford and his co-workers. The trait studied was the spots on the edge of the hind wing of the meadow brown butterfly. The number of spots in males is variable but unimodal, most individuals having two.

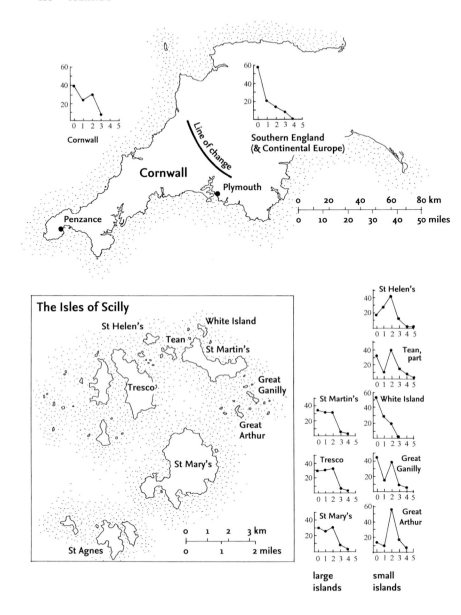

FIG 98. Distribution of spot numbers on the hind wing of female meadow brown butterflies in Devon, Cornwall and different Scilly Isles. The vertical axis of the graphs shows the percentage of moths with different spot numbers (from 0 to 5) (redrawn from Berry, 1977).

FIG 99. Underside of the hind wings of meadow brown butterflies, showing differences in spot number: left two columns, males with 0–5 spots; right two columns, females with 0–4 spots. Most males have two spots; the frequency of spot number varies in females.

Spot number in females differs in different part of the species' range: from Devon eastwards across England and in continental Europe, the females have no spots. This pattern has remained constant for many years, and on the basis of this stability Ford inferred that it must be controlled by natural selection. In Cornwall, females have a bimodal distribution, one in five having one spot but others having no or two spots. The three large islands in the Scillies have a similar pattern – albeit different to that in Cornwall, while each of the smaller islands has a different and unique pattern (Fig. 98).

The 'founder effect' expectation would suggest that the original colonisation of the smaller islands has led to their particular spot pattern, distinct from that on the large islands. Ford argued strongly against this interpretation, basing himself on the situation on the small island of Tean, which is about 1,000 m long and 14 ha in area. Before 1953, there were two distinct habitats on the island: land suitable for meadow browns at the two ends and the centre of the island, where gorse, bracken, bramble and long grass predominated; and two windswept necks of lawn-like turf, respectively 180 m and 120 m wide, where butterflies were never found (although they were frequently seen setting out to fly over the 'lawns', they always turned back after about 10 m). Ford estimated that there were around 3,000, 1,500 and 500 individuals respectively in the three favourable patches. From 1946 to 1950, the spot frequencies were similar in all three areas each year. In 1950 a small herd of cows that had been kept on Tean was removed. By 1953 the grass on the 'lawns' was long and the centre of the island had become a jungle of gorse and bracken unsuitable for the butterflies. This left two populations of meadow browns – one with the formerly existing spot pattern, one with a new one.

Ford argued that the adjustment of spotting pattern on Tean (and similar examples on two other small Scilly islands – Great Ganilly and White Island – together with a temporary change on part of the larger island of Tresco) provided 'complete evidence that it is unnecessary to appeal to "intermittent drift" or the "founder principle" '. He is only correct in this conclusion insofar as it applies to *changes* in spotting frequencies (Ford, 1975; Majerus *et al.*, 1996). Paul Brakefield (1984) has suggested a complex model for the factors affecting spot number, involving the different resting positions of male and female butterflies, activity and warning coloration. It is becoming increasingly clear also that wing spot patterns are a complex reflection of developmental processes (McMillan *et al.*, 2002). Bryan Clarke (1995) summarises Ford's work on the meadow brown as having produced 'some of the most remarkable observations ever made in evolutionary genetics. These observations can reasonably be explained by intense natural selection as Henry [Ford] argued, but the final proof must await more breeding experiments.' This is a charitable assessment; the simplest interpretation of differences between different islands (or isolated parts of a single island) still remains that different areas retain the characteristics of their original colonisers, but that subsequent selective adjustment has led to different phenotypes.

NORTH RONALDSAY SHEEP AND LUNDY CABBAGE PLUS BEETLES

Although there are plenty of examples of natural selection acting on British and Irish island populations, there are only a few where we can identify the results of the selection as adaptations to specific conditions. The western coastal melanism in moths and the reduced flight of northern populations of the autumnal rustic moth in Shetland are possible examples. Two others are the sheep on North Ronaldsay and the beetles that feed on the endemic 'Lundy cabbage'.

North Ronaldsay is the northernmost Orkney island. It is 690 ha in extent and has a 2 m high wall around the whole of its coast. The purpose of the wall is to prevent the island sheep (which are of the primitive northern race, related to the

FIG 100.
Seaweed-eating
sheep on North
Ronaldsay,
Orkney. (Richard
Welsby)

FIG 101. Lundy, the largest island in the Bristol Channel, 19 km from Devon.
(Landmark Trust)

FIG 102. Lundy 'cabbage', a primitive
brassica endemic to Lundy. (Roger Key)

FIG 104. The Lundy cabbage weevil is an
enigmatic beetle, which was originally
described from St Kilda, and then from
the Westmann islands off Iceland,
including the new volcanic island of
Surtsey. (Roger Key)

FIG 103. Lundy cabbage flea beetle, also
endemic to Lundy. (Roger Key)

Soays of St Kilda) feeding on the limited cultivated area that forms the main surface of the island. The result is that the sheep exist almost entirely on seaweed; the only time they feed on grass is after lambing, when the ewes are tethered inside the wall for a few weeks. Well-meaning animal lovers have sometimes reacted against the rather scruffy appearance of the sheep, and removed a number to good pasture. Invariably this results in a high mortality due to copper poisoning. There is only a small amount of available copper in seaweed, and the North Ronaldsay sheep have developed an inherited ability to absorb copper particularly efficiently; when they feed on grass containing 'normal' concentrations of copper, they absorb it in toxic quantities and die as a result.

There are very few animals or plants found in Britain or Ireland but nowhere else in the world. The Bristol Channel island of Lundy is unique in possessing an endemic plant (Lundy cabbage, *Coincya wrightii*, probably the only example of an outbreeding full species in Britain that is both unique and rare: Harberd, 1972). The Lundy cabbage looks rather like overgrown oilseed rape. It supports around 30 insect herbivores, including at least two indigenous forms (bronze Lundy cabbage flea beetle, *Psylliodes luridipennis*, and a weevil, *Ceutorhynchus contractus pallipes*). It is closely related to the Isle of Man cabbage (*Coincya monensis monensis*), both species apparently being spread in sea water; they are more like forms found in Iberia than in northern Britain. This raises the question as to whether the British *Coincya* species are relicts or more recent colonisers. But the relationships of the beetle are even more fascinating. *Psylliodes luridipennis* is a close relation of *P. marcida*, a beetle that feeds on another brassica, the dune-living sea rocket, which does not occur on Lundy. We do not know how the beetles got to the island, but once there they had to adapt to a new host or die. And as for the weevils, they are polymorphic for leg colour: those feeding on the cabbage are approximately equally divided between yellow-legged and black-legged forms, while those feeding on Danish scurvy grass in a part of the island where the cabbage is absent are almost all the black-legged form.

These sort of links between food and predator are probably repeated many times over on islands. We do not have the detailed studies to tell us about the nature and extent of such mutualisms.

EFFECTS OF WARS

Islands are the first landfalls of seaborne invaders, and their human dwellers are therefore at particular risk. This has produced some fascinating artefacts, ranging from the Iron Age brochs of the north of Scotland and the Northern

Isles, which seem to have been defensive havens for the residents to hide in, to the Martello Towers (Fig. 105) of the Channel Islands, southern England and Ireland (together with three in Scotland), built in 1804–12 to protect against an invasion by Napoleon and then added to in the 1830s when steam navigation and renewed international tension made invasion again possible. A German submarine fired on St Kilda in May 1918 and a couple of months later the island was 'fortified' with a four-inch cannon. In the Second World War, seven Maunsell Forts were built in the Thames Estuary as an outer line of defence; four are of them are still standing.

FIG 105. Martello tower on Hoy, one of the two built in 1813–15 to defend the entrance to Scapa Flow. About 140 Martello towers were built in many parts of the British Empire, notably along the southern English coast and on the Channel Islands. (R. J. Berry)

FIG 106. The St Kilda gun. Following 72 shells fired by a German submarine, this 4-in gun (made in 1896 and never fired in anger) was installed in October 1918, weeks before the end of the First World War. (R. J. Berry)

Security concerns have sometimes led to the removal of the indigenous population of smaller islands during wartime. A more long-lasting exclusion has been on the Essex island of Foulness, which is an explosives testing site acquired (together with the massive intertidal zone of the Maplin and Foulness Sands – over 10,000 ha in extent) in 1900–18 by the Ministry of Defence, who control access to outsiders (although there is a resident population of around 200). Because of the MOD presence, a large area of land has been taken out of arable use and has reverted to a varied grassland habitat, providing important roosting and nesting for birds. At high tide in midwinter, up to 50,000 waders roost on these grasslands (Boorman & Ranwell, 1977).

The use of Gruinard as a testing ground for germ warfare has already been described (page 73). Another military operation in Scotland began in 1957 when St Kilda became a tracking station for a missile firing range on South Uist, with a sophisticated radar installation to follow the fate of missiles launched out to sea (Williamson & Boyd, 1960). Compton Mackenzie (1957) lampooned the agreement, which allegedly safeguarded wildlife as opposed to human beings, in his novel *Rockets Galore* (subsequently made into a film). This was a sequel to *Whisky Galore*, which was based on another true event, the wrecking off Eriskay in 1941 of the SS *Politician* with a cargo of whisky bound for America (Hutchinson, 1990).

References and Further Reading for Chapter 7 are listed on page 342.

CHAPTER 8

Human History

I SLAND ROADS ARE *island roads wherever you go. They generally go uncompromisingly from one end to the other, over hills and down dips, wide enough to take one vehicle or a wandering cow, and next year they're always going to be repaired.*

Leslie Thomas, *Some Lovely Islands*, 1968

Human life on islands is sometimes described as 'clinging to the edge', although it is probably better to take this as implying 'risk-laden' rather than 'deprived'. For example, St Kilda is almost a type example of isolation but it yielded food (gannets, fulmars, puffins) for human consumption both by its native population and for export, whilst its cultivated land was sheltered from the worst storms and was more reliably productive than some of the Outer Hebridean islands. Andrew Fleming (2005) has pointed out that the successive owners of the island (whose personal finances tended to be on a knife edge) used to descend on St Kilda for several weeks every year because of the reliability of its produce, bringing with them a large retinue. Nevertheless, the perils of cliff-climbing (to harvest birds or eggs) and sea-borne invasion or piracy meant that St Kildan life was always risky.

In other cases, islands were settled just because they are as near 'the edge' as it is possible to get – by holy men who built the remarkable shelters on the Great Skellig or travelled to the Faroes or North Rona to worship better; or by those who built churches on less remote islands like the May, the Bass Rock, Inchcolm, Lindisfarne, the Aran Islands, the Calf of Man (Muir, 1885; Bradley, 1999). Then there were the pirates who found islands useful havens from which to sally forth – the May and the Bass Rock, Lundy, the Isles of Scilly, the Saltees, Valentia, and most notoriously the redoubtable Grace O'Malley (1530–1603), who ruled a whole

FIG 107. Snaring puffins on St Kilda. (From Cherry Kearton, *With Nature and a Camera*, 1897)

tract of western Ireland from her base on Clare Island. These last were the cousins of other outlaws – smugglers and wreckers tempted by long, unpoliced coasts, as well as their wholly benign relatives the beach-combers, and other scavengers.

Some of the earliest island-dwellers must have been environmental migrants escaping from land scarcity and social pressures. This was probably the spur to the early Viking voyages, as migrants flowed across Europe and displaced those living in coastal areas. Another 'overflow' into islands took place in the eighteenth and nineteenth centuries as growth in human populations again began to cause land shortage in mainland areas. Then there was a phase of artificially maintained overpopulation on many islands because landlords wanted labour, first for the kelp industry and then for fishing. But kelp prices collapsed and developments in marine technology (in both boats and fishing gear) and social pressures on island owners combined to end abruptly this phase. The result was economic hardship due to the difficulties and ever-increasing cost of transport, plus lack of opportunities for the young. This in turn led to a general movement away from island living, and the abandonment of many islands by their human inhabitants.

All this has left a vast and fascinating archaeological legacy (Rainbird, 2007). Perhaps more than any other part of our environment, islands bear the scars of their human inhabitants. The peoples who first spread north and west in the wake of the retreating ice established settlements along coasts and waterways, both for ease of travel and because there was always food to be had from the sea. They probably lived and moved in family groups, but they have left little record of their existence, beyond a few stone implements. The earliest evidence of human settlement in Scotland was at the head of Loch Scresort on Rum (8590 ± 95 BP), at about the time the last reindeer were disappearing. At that time, the entire population of Britain was probably no more than 10,000; in Scotland it may have been only a few hundred. Virtually all the early sites so far discovered were on or close to the beach, or in sea caves. These early islanders were Mesolithic hunters and gatherers. Molluscs were an important part of their diet, but they were omnivorous scavengers, eating crustaceans, fish, birds and deer. Cave middens on Jura have been dated to 8000 BP, and on Islay to 7800 BP.

Although the North Sea and the English Channel joined around 8,500 years ago, there were almost certainly islands in the North Sea that persisted long after that, and which would have been stepping stones between Britain and continental Europe. Bryony Coles (1998) has drawn on bathymetric evidence and geological surveys on both sides of the North Sea to describe a large 'Doggerland' between Denmark and northern England on the site of what is now the Dogger Bank, probably with other smaller islands off the coast of Norfolk (Fig. 108). Although archaeological testimony of life thereon is sparse, these islands may well have supported human settlements as well as terrestrial fauna and flora and thus provided ways for immigration to Britain beyond the traditional one via the Straits of Dover land bridge. There has been speculation that Scotland may have originally been peopled from northern Europe, rather than from the south. The earliest inhabitants of Ireland appear to have arrived there around 9000 BP, with the Aran Islands being occupied soon afterwards.

The vegetation of the north of Britain in 10,000 BP was dominated by the low shrubs now characteristic of the tundra of northern Canada or Scandinavia. Temperatures continued to rise, and by 8000 BP pollen studies show that most of mainland Scotland was carpeted by a hazel/birch/pine forest, which seems to have been an effective barrier to inland settlement. Further south, the dominant vegetation was closed oak woodland, although tracts of forest were beginning to show more open conditions, with signs of charcoal indicating that burning was apparently common. Six thousand years BP was an apparent climatic maximum, with temperatures declining 1 °C or 2 °C thereafter until approximately stabilising at the present level around 4000 BP.

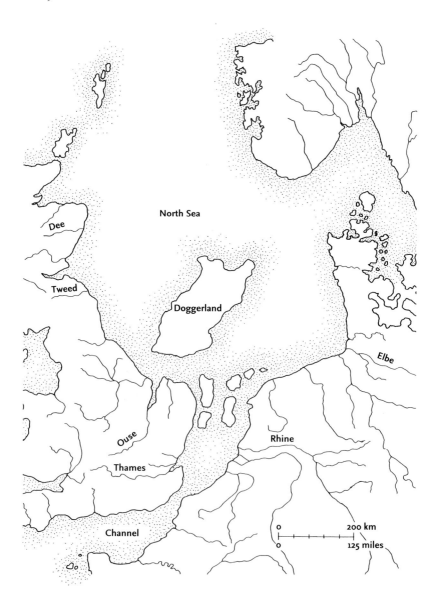

FIG 108. There would have been some sizeable islands in what is now the North Sea for some time after Britain separated from France. The largest of these has been called Doggerland. It may have been a stepping stone for immigrants to Britain from northern Europe (after Coles, 1998).

THE BEGINNING OF FARMING (c.5800 BP)

There were farmers in Orkney (at the Knap of Howar on Papa Westray) by
5500 BP. The Neolithic introduction of agriculture begins to show up generally in
the pollen record at that time, which was also the period when the climate began
to deteriorate (the *oligocratic* phase of the Flandrian). Within a short time after the
appearance of cereals in the pollen record, there was a massive decline in elms
over a wide area of northwest Europe (beginning about 5100 BP). Whether this was
the result of the change in climate or the effects of disease (a prehistoric version
of Dutch elm disease), or a consequence of the slash-and-burn techniques of the
early farmers – or a combination of all three – it certainly helped the farmers to
clear land for their crops. Regrowth would have been prevented by the
introduction and depredations of domestic sheep, goats, pigs and cows.

Ever since the Sub-Boreal period, beginning about 4000 BP, woodland in
mainland Britain and Ireland has been declining with growing agricultural and
urban land uses. The decline in forest cover coincided with an increase in cereal

FIG 109. Skara Brae, the most complete Neolithic village in Europe, occupied from
roughly 3100 to 2500 BC. Skara Brae, consisting of ten houses clustered together, is part
of the UNESCO World Heritage Site 'the Heart of Neolithic Orkney'. (R. J. Berry)

pollen – notably emmer wheat and barley – indicating agricultural activity. Whilst some of the loss of woodland must have been anthropogenic (there may have been half a million people in Britain by then), it occurred at a time when there was also a climatically driven reduction. Cooling temperatures and perhaps raised rainfall led to considerable peat formation between 4000 and 2000 BP. The incoming Iron Age people, with metal axes and ploughs, speeded up woodland clearance and the spread of cultivation. But it was a difficult time for agriculture. There seems to have been little or no farming over much of central Ireland between about 300 BC and AD 300.

The problems faced by farmers on the islands are well illustrated by the succession of events at the Scord of Brouster in the west Mainland of Shetland (Whittle *et al.*, 1986). The pollen record indicates clearance of the native vegetation from around 4700 BP, and the earliest house and fields appeared soon after. Soils under the buildings show podsolisation before 4000 BP, but the most marked changes were substantial erosion in the sloping fields around the buildings, linked to the cultivation of barley and an associated destabilisation of the slope. This led to increasing stoniness in the surface layer, and in due course abandonment of the land – perhaps linked to the difficulty of cultivation. The site is now buried under blanket bog.

Between 4000 and 1000 BP, large areas of upland soil developed into peaty podsols and then to blanket peat, leading to the landscape now characteristic of much of the north. The principal instruments for cultivation were simple wooden ploughs, often tipped with stone to penetrate the soil more efficiently. The earliest dated yoke for animal ploughing was found at the mouth of Loch Nell in Argyll, opposite Mull, dated 3430 ± 85 BP.

FIG 110.
Planti-cru on Foula, Shetland – a sheltered arrangement for growing the seeds of food or crop plants such as kale or cabbage.
(R. J. Berry)

IMMIGRATION

There must have been a steady movement of people across the North Sea and thence onto the islands from fairly early postglacial times, but signs of the earliest inhabitants are only apparent in places where there has been no later disturbance. Presumably the Channel Islands were among the places first open to settlement, but there seems to have been a break in habitation during the later Palaeolithic. La Cotte de St Brelade on Jersey was used by mammoth hunters 250,000 years ago (it is one of the most important Palaeolithic sites in Europe), but there is no archaeological evidence of human settlement on Jersey or Guernsey between 50,000 years ago and c.6000 BP, when declines in elm and lime pollen followed by a rise in pollen from herbs almost certainly indicate agricultural activity (Jee, 1982; Jones *et al.*, 1990). Bones of oxen, sheep and goats start to appear there about 5500 BP. The first people to settle on the Isles of Scilly seem to have arrived around 4000 BP. There may have been earlier visitors, but they have left no signs of their stay (Scourse, 1986).

Humans reached Ireland about 9,000 years ago. Around 8150 BP there was a major change in the type of stone tools found there, from the earlier Sandelian to the later Larnian. Whether this represents a wave of immigration or merely a new culture is unknown; we do not know where either the Sandelians or the Larnians came from. Nor do we know if the first farming activity, around 6000 BP, was carried out by the same people or another group of incomers (Mitchell & Ryan, 1997). What it seems reasonable to infer is that there was considerable movement of people across the North Channel between Ireland and southwest Scotland (Hunter, 1999).

FIG 111. The Broch on Mousa, Shetland – home to a large number of storm petrels. This is the most complete broch still standing. Brochs are found exclusively in the Northern and Western Islands and adjoining mainland. They were mainly built in the first centuries BC and AD. They seem to have been defensive structures into which a community could retreat when threatened. (R. J. Berry)

We are on more certain ground when we come to the Viking period. There was massive emigration from Scandinavia at the beginning of the ninth century, a result of the spread of Teutons through northern Europe, squeezing and effectively dispossessing the inhabitants of western Norway. The first record of their arrival in Britain was in AD 789, when, according to the *Anglo-Saxon Chronicle*, the Reeve of the King of Wessex was killed by incomers on the (then) Isle of Portland. Notoriously, the monastery on Lindisfarne was attacked in June 793, and many of the monks and nuns were slaughtered. The *Annals of Ulster* record that in 794 there was 'a laying waste by the gentiles [i.e. heathen Scandinavians] of all the islands of Britain', and the following year Skye, Iona, Rathlin and Ulster were attacked. According to *Egils Saga* (which is certainly not history as we know it), the tyranny of Harald Fairhair in Norway, after his victory at Hafrsfjord around 800 and the subsequent unification of Norway, led to major flight from the homeland and settling in 'many deserted places', including the Hebrides, Ireland, Caithness, Orkney, Shetland and the Faroes. The claim they came to 'deserted places' is overstated. Although there were probably few people living in the Faroes when the Vikings took possession, the oft-quoted statement of A. W. Brøgger (1929: 67) that the Norse settlers of Orkney and Shetland 'stepped ashore into a veritable museum' is wrong: the persistence of Celtic place names and physical characteristics show that this settlement was an assimilation into the existing populations. How welcome the incomers were we have no means of knowing.

Much sub-history is found in the sagas. The *Orkneyinga Saga* tells of Harald Fairhair setting out to punish the overseas Vikings for their raids on Norway, subduing Shetland, Orkney and the Hebrides, attacking the Isle of Man and annexing land 'farther west'. But it was only written down three centuries later than the events described, and should not be interpreted too literally. Another saga has the punitive raid being led by Kevil Flatnose, while the *Laxdaela Saga* has Kevil Flatnose on the other side, fleeing from King Harald.

Whatever the truth about the early Viking colonisers of Britain, we know that Orkney became the centre of a Viking Earldom which ruled the north and west of Britain for four or five centuries. Bo Almqvist (in Berry & Firth, 1986) describes it as a major Viking centre, 'playing a role in the North Sea similar to that played by Venice and other mighty Italian republics in the Mediterranean'. The Hebrides remained formally subject to Norway until 1266, while Orkney and Shetland only came under the Scottish crown in 1468 when King Christian I of Norway pledged them to James III of Scotland for 58,000 florins as a dowry for his daughter. Orcadians and Shetlanders have frequently spoken of themselves redeeming this pledge when rule from Edinburgh or London seems particularly irksome.

FIG 112. St Magnus Cathedral, Kirkwall, Orkney – founded by Earl Rognvald in 1137 and allegedly begun by masons from Durham Cathedral. It was originally sited on the shore, but reclamation means that it is now *c.*400 m inland. (From William Daniell's *Voyage Round Great Britain*, 1814–25)

The Western Isles were never under the control of a dynasty in the same way as Orkney under the Sinclairs, but were subject to what were effectively warlords. In 1156 Somerled, a Celtic–Norse ruler in Argyll, wrested control of all the islands south of Ardnamurchan Point from the King of (the Isle of) Man, marking a Celtic resurgence that culminated in the emergence of the Lordship of the (Western) Isles. A century later, King Haakon I of Norway led a failed attempt to re-take Bute and Kintyre from the King of the Scots. Three years after that, his son Magnus formally handed over the Kingdom of Man and the Isles to the Scottish king – in return for a payment of 4,000 marks and an annual payment of 100 marks in perpetuity. (A mark was a half-pound – or quarter-kilo – of silver.)

The twelfth and thirteenth centuries were a golden time for Orkney, with significant corn exports to Norway. This ended with the founding of the Bergen trading post (*kontor*) around 1343, when the Hanseatic merchants of Lübeck came to control and dominate Norway's trade. The trading of the Hanseatic League involved the northward transport of German grain in exchange for stockfish (dried fish). Whereas Shetland, which had fish to export and a grain deficit, profited from this arrangement, Orkney's grain exports were in competition with German cereals and faced strong opposition.

These problems were compounded by a union of the Scandinavian kingdoms and a shift of political and economic power to Copenhagen. The Orkney rental rolls at the end of the fifteenth century show that much land had passed out of cultivation and was lying tenantless.

It is not only the Northern Isles that profited from the Vikings and their voyagings. Safe and accessible harbours were always valuable. In the eighteenth century (well after the end of the classical Viking period), St Peter Port in Guernsey is recorded as trading with Russia, Sweden, Denmark, Holland, Ireland, France, Portugal, Spain and the West Indies.

KELP, FISH AND OTHER LIVELIHOODS

Many islands depended on and could rely upon harvests from the sea – either the direct harvest of fish or seals or an indirect harvest of the marine food chain through seabirds and their eggs: gannets (by far the most important), auks (mainly guillemots), fulmars and puffins (in St Kilda and the Faroes) and kittiwakes (the Bass Rock was particularly favoured for these). In 1897, it was recorded that each house on St Kilda had a 'share' of birds allotted to it of 80 young gannets, 120 adult gannets, 560 fulmars, 600 puffins, 120 guillemots and 50 razorbills – a total of 1,530 birds per share or 24,480 for the island inhabitants as a whole, between 300 and 350 birds per person. Quite apart from this, as already noted, in most years St Kilda had an excess of food, which served as rent and support for the chief's retinue. Two centuries earlier, Martin Martin listed nine items of export from Hirta: feathers, wool, butter, cheese, cows, horses, birds, oil and barley.

Notwithstanding, island life in most places was a matter of subsistence farming and chronic poverty. This changed radically on many islands with the great kelp boom at the end of the eighteenth century. Seaweed is abundant round virtually all island shores. From early times it must have been used as a fertiliser on poor land and as animal fodder; it is still commonly spread in the Channel Islands. Seaweed contains as much nitrogen as animal manure, and is even richer in potash. An additional use was for the growing glass-making and soap industry. This began first in 1684 in the Isles of Scilly, from where it was shipped to Bristol. Payments to kelp-burners in County Antrim are listed from 1711; in the northeast of England the earliest records are about 1720, in Orkney 1722, and in the Hebrides 1735. Kelp is made by burning dried weed in pits (or kilns) and collecting the ash formed. It is a source of sodium carbonate, which serves as an alkaline flux in glass manufacture, reducing the melting point of silica from 1,700 °C to 800 °C. In soap manufacture it is mixed with quick-lime and either

FIG 113. The guga harvest – young gannets collected annually from Sula Sgeir under licence by men from Ness in northern Lewis, and eaten as a delicacy. (Stewart Angus)

FIG 114. (*Left*) Stipes of seaweed exposed at low water. (Stewart Angus)
(*Below*) Burning the dried seaweed to produce kelp. (British Geological Survey)

used for bleaching or mixed with fatty substances to make soap. Later (by the early 1840s) it was also being used for iodine extraction.

Kelp-making is a very labour-intensive activity. The weed (principally *Laminaria* spp.) has to be cut and collected, then spread out to dry. The main centre in Orkney was Stronsay, to the extent that 'to the eye of a passing mariner, the smoke from the kilns distinguished Stronsay from the other islands and gave it the appearance of an active volcano' (Thomson, 1983). The kelp was shipped south, mainly to the Newcastle area. Orkney kelp was particularly valued, and during the period 1780–1830 the islands' economy was dominated by kelp manufacture, although the total output from the Hebrides was larger. Profits from kelp were double the income from rents, and estates came to be valued more for their shoreline than for the potential of their farmland. On the Clanranald estate, the biggest of the kelp-producing properties in the Western Isles, it was said that the laird was able to pocket 77% of the sale price. Every bit of shore that could produce kelp became involved in an activity that offered a sure reward. However, the boom disappeared with the removal of the salt tax in 1817 and the reduction in 1822 of tariffs on the import of Spanish *barilla*, made from the halophyte *Halogeton sativus*. Although prices increased again in the iodine years, kelp was never as profitable again. Island economies collapsed and landlords' incomes virtually disappeared, almost overnight. Effort shifted to fishing and agricultural improvement. The legacy of kelp was a higher population than could be easily supported and an abundance of over-small holdings. Nevertheless, seaweed is still harvested for alginates; the Scottish alginate industry is second only to that of the USA.

Commercial fishing was (and is) an important occupation and money-earner in (particularly) the Northern Isles and the Hebrides. The imposition of a tax on importing salt in 1712 had the effect of taking the trade from the Dutch and Hansa traders. Haaf (sea or ocean, from the Norwegian word *hav* for ocean) fishing with long lines was, like kelp-making, very labour-intensive, and the landowners who controlled the marketing of the catch exercised sanctions against their tenants to stop them leaving. However, drift-netting and trawling began to replace long-line fishing in the middle of the nineteenth century. Whereas the Orcadian kelp-makers were able to turn to agriculture, the poorer land in Shetland made this unproductive, and Shetland was considerably overpopulated towards the end of the nineteenth century.

But fishing has always been a hazardous occupation, even before the modern era of overfishing of many stocks. Rutland Island, County Donegal was conceived in the 1780s as a model fishing village by the Marquis of Conyngham; in 1784–5 around 1,200 fisherman were employed there. Then, in 1793, the herring shoals changed their migration route and deserted the coast. Only one of the planned streets was ever built, and the island is now uninhabited. The British Fisheries Society was more successful with its enterprises: around the same time (1788–90), it designed and built Ullapool on the west coast of Scotland, followed by Pulteneytown (Wick) in Caithness (1803–30). A different fate met the ports of Leverburgh at the south end of Harris and, to a lesser extent, Stornoway in Lewis. Designed by Lord Leverhulme to be a hub for a fishing fleet and distribution network, they failed to find favour with both the islanders and fishers from outwith the island, and were given to the local population (in the case of Stornoway) or sold at a massive loss.

POPULATION DECLINES

Life on an island may seem romantic to susceptible townies; in reality it is narrow; cabin'd, cribb'd, confin'd, bound in. Your shepherd who does it for a living takes a far more robust view of the supposed pleasure of trudging up the mountain again than your wet romantic. Tenants of Ailsa Craig used to pay their rent in gannet feathers. Have you ever tried to part a gannet from its feathers? I shouldn't care to have to do so for the rent.
Philip Howard, *The Times*, 1 August 1984

Involuntary emigration was – and is – a highly emotive subject in many peripheral communities. The brutal evictions in many parts of the Scottish Highlands have left an enduring scar. Notwithstanding, it is difficult to gainsay the fact that in many places the numbers of people were way above the carrying capacity of the land and there was no other intrinsic way of support. All the northern and western islands saw major declines in population in the nineteenth and twentieth centuries, with the Hebrides suffering the most. Numbers in Orkney and Shetland have stabilised since the coming of the oil industry. Further south, Jersey, Guernsey and the Isle of Man have become strongly dependent on the financial services industry. In the twenty-first century, Orkney is one of the few island groups maintaining a viable agricultural industry, building on marketing 'organic' produce. Whilst there are many practitioners of alternative or intermediate living, and obvious opportunities for jobs using electronic technology, inshore fishing

FIG 115. North Sea oil rig. (British Geological Survey)

and fish-farming remain the main sources of traditional employment in most places. Increasingly the islands depend on tourism of various sorts (such as ecotourism and archaeology) as sources of income.

For the very rich (the likes of Richard Branson, the Barclay brothers, Björn Borg, Marlon Brando), islands may be havens of peace and escape. For those who make their living as well as their homes on islands, life can be physically stressful, and shipping costs mean that it is difficult to support more than a sustenance (i.e. non-market) economy. This may attract romantics but in general has led to increasing depopulation. Many smaller islands now depend largely on subsidies (the European Union has been particularly important in this respect under its programme for rural development; one of its initiatives has been a study of 'island vulnerability', using Brownsea and Rathlin Islands as case studies), with an independent income mainly from tourists – increasingly ecotourists.

For many islands it is too late. The evacuation of St Kilda in 1930 is well known (page 334). The morale of the islanders was low following a poor harvest in 1929, but the final straw was the death of a young woman from appendicitis. Although she was taken off the island, she died soon after being admitted to hospital. On 10 May 1930, a petition signed by all the population and witnessed by the missionary (minister) and nurse was sent to the Secretary of State for Scotland, asking 'Her [sic] Majesty's Government to assist us all to leave the island this year and to find homes and occupations for us on the mainland.'

Great Blasket Island, County Kerry, is notable for the autobiographies of three islanders, which became classics of Irish literature and then more widely, following their translation into English: Thomas O'Crohan's *The Islandman* (1929), Maurice O'Sullivan's *Twenty Years A-Growing* (1929), and Peig Sayers' *Peig* (1936). In these books the islanders describe the recreations, revelries and the

FIG 116. The village on Hirta, abandoned by its human inhabitants in 1930 but now partially restored. (Andrew Berry)

FIG 117. Ruined houses on Great Blasket, County Kerry. (Steven Royle)

FIG 118. Mingulay
– deserted since
1912 (from Harvie-
Brown & Buckley,
1888).

companionships of the Blaskets' population, but all three are taken up with the
constant drain of islanders seeking a better life elsewhere. Economically and
materially, life was hard. As recently as 1938, Great Blasket had a population of 106,
but it dropped rapidly. All the young people left the island, and, more
significantly, none returned to live there. The school closed in the early 1940s. By
1953 there were 22 people remaining, and they were evacuated at their own request.

Viable island communities depend on good and affordable communications.
In 1841, 211 Irish islands had 38,138 inhabitants; in 1991, only 66 were still
populated, with 9,700 residents. Of the 19 islands with a population of over 100
and a fixed link to the mainland (i.e. a causeway or bridge), all remained inhabited
and their total population only fell from 6,640 to 5,961. In contrast, more than half
of the islands without a fixed link were totally depopulated (29 islands out of a
total of 56), with the total number of inhabitants falling from 27,821 to a mere 3,570.
The Faroes pioneered cheap and frequent ferry services between islands. It was
followed by Shetland, and then Orkney. Until it was largely superseded by ferries,
the Orkney Islands Council contracted and subsidised an inter-island air service.
The Outer Hebrides are linked by a 'spinal route' of causeways and 'ro-ro' (roll-
on/roll-off) ferries.

Island depopulation has been countered in recent decades by a trickle of
incomers seeking to escape from what they perceive as the dangers and stresses
of life elsewhere. Even Orkney, which has overall achieved a fairly stable
population, is not exempt. A fascinating social study of one of the northern
Orkney Islands by Diana Forsythe (1982) has shown the problems caused by
inward migration. In 1851, there were 937 inhabitants, but this fell steeply to 627
in 1901 and 342 in 1951. The island continued to haemorrhage its population. By
1981 there were only 186 residents, of whom 77 (41%) were incomers, all but nine
of these from outside Orkney. Forsythe writes:

Despite the incomers' expressed desire to preserve the Stormay [a fictitious name for a real island] *way of life, their very presence is helping to destroy it. Although individually the incomers are generally pleasant and well-meaning additions to the island's community, they are also contributing to a cultural evolution in which ethnic, regional and national differences are being eroded away, to be replaced by a more standardised and homogeneous way of life. In 1981, incomers were still a minority on Stormay, albeit a vocal and powerful minority. But the receiving population on Stormay is relatively old, whilst continuing in-migration from Scotland and England brings in a steady stream of young adults in their prime child-bearing years. In the face of this in-migration, its influence augmented by national radio, television and standardised education, the number of people who actually use and identify with Stormay speech and customs will inevitably diminish. There is tragedy in this situation for both islanders and incomers. The Stormay folk have welcomed the migrants as bringing new life and new ideas into their depopulated and ageing community, but they have reason to regret their generosity. The energy the incomers bring to the island is committed to a vision of the future in which local people have no active part. They have sought to attain this vision by moving to a remote island to partake of the mystique of country life. But these migrants are not countrymen, nor do they really wish to become so; instead they seek a stage on which to act out an urban conception of what rural life should be like. The coming of urban refugees may revitalise the community in a demographic sense, but it will also transform it beyond recognition, for most incomers have little understanding of the distinctiveness and value of Orkney's cultural heritage as distinct from their own. In the long run, the conflicts that have accompanied the incomers' move to the island probably will be resolved through the submergence of the way of life of the receiving community – a high price to pay for the personal fulfilment of a few.*

Forsythe concludes:

Through history the Orcadian way of life has continually changed and developed. Successive waves of in-migrants have helped to shape the course of island life, contributing to the mixture of Pictish, Norse, Scottish and English elements that make up the heritage of Orcadians today. Over time, Orkney has managed to retain an identity related to but consciously separate from those of Norway and mainland Britain. Now, once again, outsiders are coming into the archipelago, not as conquerors this time, but as refugees from the cities of the south. Like those of earlier eras, this latest wave of migration will lead to a new cultural synthesis. However because of the nature of this particular in-migration, it is doubtful that the new synthesis will retain much that is distinctively Orcadian.

References and Further Reading for Chapter 8 are listed on page 343.

CHAPTER 9

Faroe, Shetland and Orkney

T HERE ARE THREE groups of islands of approximately the same size
lying north of Great Britain, forming a chain between Scotland and
Iceland (Fig. 120):

- **Orkney** lies due north of the eastern angle of Scotland and is geologically part of
  the Caithness sandstone plateau. The capital (Kirkwall) is at 58° 59' N, 2° 58' W.

FIG 119.
Satellite image of
northern
Scotland,
showing the
Hebrides,
Orkney and
Shetland.
(Science Photo
Library)

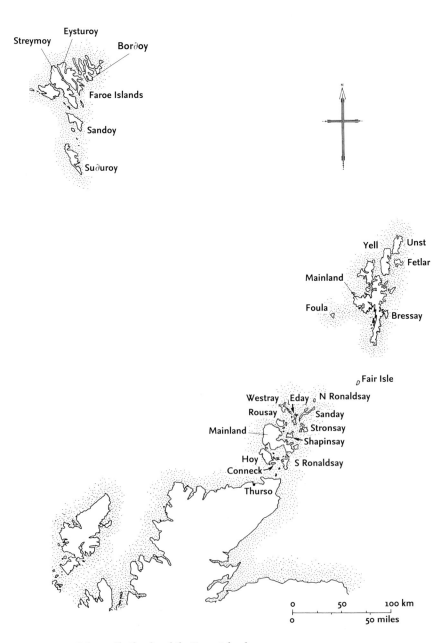

FIG 120. Orkney, Shetland and the Faroe Islands.

FIG 121. Male eider, photographed on Shetland, a common duck of northern latitudes. (Andrew Berry)

- **Shetland** is a partially drowned range of hills rising above the continental shelf, the roots of a deeply eroded mountain chain (the Caledonian Orogenic Belt) which forms much of Scotland and Norway. The capital (Lerwick) is at 60° 8' N, 1° 11' W.
- The **Faroe Islands** attained their present covering of basaltic lavas, which reach 7 km in thickness, from fissure eruptions caused by continental break-up forming the northern North Atlantic about 55 million years ago. The capital (Tórshavn) is at 62° 0' N, 6° 45' W, 782 km from Reyjavík.

The three archipelagoes lie at the centre of what has been called the north-temperate East Atlantic biotic area, including the British islands, north and west Scandinavia and Iceland.

FAROE

There are 17 inhabited islands in the Faroe archipelago, extending 113 km from south to north and 75 km from east to west in the shape of an irregularly spiked battle-axe, a total area of c.1,400 km². The main settlements are Tórshavn (population 18,800) on the largest island (Streymoy) and Klaksvík on Borðoy

FIG 122. Viðareiði at the foot of the southern slopes of the mountain Villingdalsfjall on Viðoy, the northernmost settlement of the Faroes. The church was built in 1892; its silver was a gift from the British government in gratitude for the villagers' rescue of the crew of the brig *Marwood*, shipwrecked nearby in 1847. (Sven-Axel Bengtson)

FIG 123. North end of the islands of Kunoy (*right*) and beyond, the headland of Kunoyarnakkur (819 m) on Viðoy. In the background, the mountain of Villingdalsfjall (844 m) rises above Enniberg, the northern tip of the Faroe Islands and Europe's highest vertical sea cliffs (a staggering 750 m), with extensive seabird colonies. The 'layer-cake' appearance of the rocks is clearly visible. (Daniel Bengtson)

(population 5,000). The islands are composed of layers of basalt, often separated by layers of volcanic ash (tuff), giving a 'layer-cake' appearance to the hills. The original landmass has been divided into the current archipelago by glaciation. The islands rise steeply from sea level; the highest point (Slættaratindur on Eysturoy) is 882 m. Sea-cliffs of 500 m are not uncommon; the highest is Enniberg (750 m) (Fig. 123), rising vertically at the north end of Viðoy. They comprise some of the most spectacular bird-cliffs in the world. Puffins, guillemots and fulmars are regarded as gastronomic delicacies, as is the meat and blubber of pilot whales, which are killed when they can be trapped in authorised whaling bays. (Whale hunts are graphically described by John Buchan in his novel *The Island of Sheep* and by Kenneth Williamson in *The Atlantic Islands*.) The climate is oceanic, with warm winters and little difference between summer and winter means. Rain or mist is common.

Faroese soils are generally poor. Apart from the southern island of Sandoy, there are only small patches of fertile ground. Lowland soil is largely peaty, and a mere 2% of the islands are under arable cultivation.. The commonest vegetation is grass heath. The most diverse plant families are sedges and grasses: the Cyperaceae with 26 species (19 of them *Carex*) and the Poaceae with 44 species. The islands are virtually treeless, apart from a few plantations, the oldest and most extensive being a 65 ha area on the edge of Tórshavn. The vulnerability of trees in the Faroes (and other northern islands) was shown by the extensive damage wrought by an autumn storm in 1988. Fishing is by far the most important economic activity.

FIG 124. Whale partitioning at the whale station at Áir, north of Thórshavn on the Faroe Islands. (Pehr Enckell)

FIG 125. Drying stands for hay in the Faroes. (Pehr Enckell)

FIG 126. Set of Faroese stamps issued in 1991 illustrating introduced species of meadow plants and species that eat them.

Early natural-history accounts of the islands were compiled by Peder Claussø (1632) and Tarnovius (1659), and more importantly by Jens Svabo (1782) and Jørgen Landt (1800). About 400 species of flowering plants have been recorded, of which about 60 are weeds or cultivated escapes. Most species are found also in Norway and Scotland, although a few are Arctic species with their main distribution pattern elsewhere in the Arctic and sub-Arctic (e.g. dwarf cudweed, mountain avens, trailing azalea, rooted poppy, glacier crowfoot, alpine speedwell).

FIG 127. Nólsoy, Faroe Islands. (R. J. Berry)

Perennials dominate – in many years, the cool summers mean that little seed is set. The Faroese lady's mantle is the only endemic. A comprehensive *Zoology of the Faroes* (Jensen *et al.*) was published in three volumes between 1928 and 1970. Although incomplete and outdated in many ways, it has never been replaced – although considerable additions have been made, many published in the Faroese scientific journal, *Fródskaparrit*. The terrestrial fauna is very poor (Fig. 128). There are no ants, dragonflies, mayflies or stone flies. Twenty-six species of carabids have been found, less than half that on Shetland (where there are 55 species). As in Hawaii, diptera are the main pollinators; approximately 300 species have been recorded. The only mammals are the arctic (or mountain) hare (four pairs were introduced in 1855 for hunting; they now occur on most of the islands), house mouse (page 168) and brown rat.

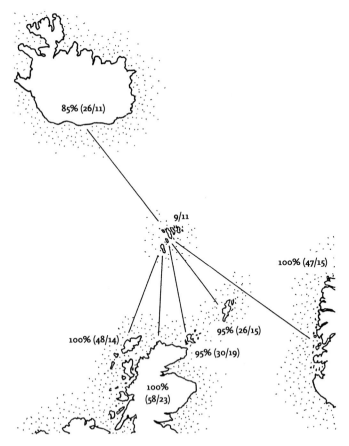

85% (26/11)

9/11

100% (47/15)

100% (48/14)

95% (26/15)

95% (30/19)

100% (58/23)

FIG 128. Faroes slug and snail fauna, and the percentage of Faroes species found in neighbouring areas. The first number in each case is the number of slug species; the second is the number of snail species (after Enckell, 1988).

In contrast to their poor terrestrial fauna and flora, the islands are home to vast numbers of breeding seabirds. Populations of 13 of the 19 breeding seabird species exceed 1% of the total European population. Probably 40% of the world population of storm petrels nest in the Faroes, with 17% of this total (around 100,000 pairs) on one island (Nólsoy) alone. Fifty-three species of birds nest regularly in the archipelago. There are local subspecies of the starling, wren, rock pipit and eider. The oystercatcher (known locally, as in Orkney and Shetland, as *tjaldur* – or shalder) is the national bird of the Faroe Islands, and is protected.

SHETLAND

Shetland (formally, but rarely in practice, Zetland – this name is said to be have been incorrectly transcribed from the Viking *Hjatland* or Yetland; it probably means 'Retreat land', from the Norwegian *halte*, but possibly *Estland* or East Land, in contrast to the Hebrides and other southern islands, which the Vikings called *Sudreyjar*), Watsonian vice-county 112, is the most northerly part of the British Isles proper, extending 109 km south from Unst (and its outlying stacks, with Muckle Flugga lighthouse 284 km east-south-east of the Faroes) to Fair Isle in the south, 39 km from Sumburgh Head at the southern end of the Shetland Mainland and 44 km from Orkney to the southwest. The area is 1429 km², very similar to the Faroes. Although there are some spectacular cliffs in Shetland (particularly on the west side), they are nowhere as high as the Faroese cliffs. Nevertheless, the highest cliff in Britain (slightly less than 400 m) is the Kame on Foula (Fig. 129). (It is often said that Conachair on St Kilda has higher cliffs, but they are not as sheer as the Kame. Another claim is that the cliffs on the seaward

FIG 129. The Kame, Foula, Shetland – the highest sea-cliff in Britain. (Mike Pennington)

side of Croaghaun Mountain, 664 m, on Achill, County Mayo, are the highest in Europe: although they are steep, they are not as sheer as those of Foula and many in the Faroes. St John's Head on Hoy in Orkney is alleged to be the highest vertical sea cliff, at 346 m.) Most of Shetland is fairly low-lying moorland; the highest point is Ronas Hill (450 m). The islands are dissected everywhere by drowned valleys; nowhere is more than 5 km from the sea.

FIG 130. Orkney is part of the Caithness plateau of Old Red Sandstone. The geology of Shetland is much more complex, with an extension of the Great Glen Fault running through the Shetland Mainland.

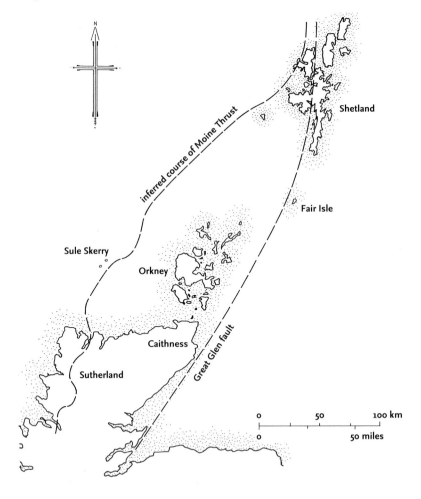

Shetland is second only to the Butt of Lewis for recorded wind; the average annual wind speed is four-fifths that experienced at the top of Ben Nevis. Relative humidity is the highest in Britain. One consequence of this is that plants that would be found growing at high levels in the Scottish mountains occur at sea level in Shetland.

The geology of Shetland is much more complicated than that of either the Faroes or Orkney. The islands are rooted on Precambrian gneisses, now partially overlain with Old Red Sandstone formed from their own erosion products. The Caledonian Mountains from which they were formed were the Himalayas of their day, extending from Norway to Scotland. The oldest exposures are in North Roe in the northern Mainland, probably more than 2,000 million years old. However, by Middle Devonian times, 350 million years ago, the chain had been eroded to such an extent that Norway, Shetland and Scotland were separated and its roots buried by the sandstone.

North–south through Shetland runs the Wall and Boundary Fault, formed during the Permo-Triassic period, a northward continuation of the Great Glen Fault which crosses mainland Scotland. It separates west and north Mainland Shetland and the outlying island of Foula from the bulk of the islands (Fig. 130). During Jurassic and Cretaceous times, 190–100 million years ago, the ditches (or *grabens*) around Shetland were subsiding and filling with mud and organic rich shales; in due course these became the source for North Sea oil. Around that time, Shetland probably became an island for the first time, when rifting occurred to the west of Shetland to create the deep-water Faroe–Shetland Trough. In the newly forming Atlantic Ocean, which arose from a split west of the Faroes around 55 million years ago, the sea floor was much deeper than the continents on the two sides, and molten lava flowed out of the rift, separating the plates bearing the island groups.

FIG 131. Tingwall Valley, a band of limestone that runs across the Mainland of Shetland and provides a fertile oasis in a generally infertile landscape. (R. J. Berry)

Throughout Upper Cretaceous and Tertiary times, the sea level rose and fell on many occasions. This was particularly important in Orkney, as we shall see. One of the greatest rises led to chalk deposits being laid down to the south and east of Shetland. These are still represented in parts of the islands, leading to much more fertile ground than exists in the Faroes. In contrast, the eastern half of Unst and much of Fetlar are composed of chromium and nickel-rich (and phosphorus-poor) ultrabasic serpentine, which supports a characteristic and species-rich flora, most notably on the Keen of Hamar (a 400 ha area in Unst), where the soil is among the oldest and poorest in Europe. *Hamar* means 'rocky outcrop on the hillside'. The rock weathers to produce small angular fragments or *debris*. Although serpentine outcrops occur elsewhere, including on Rum and Skye, in small areas of Aberdeenshire and Fife, and most notably on the Lizard peninsula in Cornwall, the Keen is one of the largest serpentine exposures in Europe. It is nationally famous for its plants; the only other similar soil is on the Lizard. An endemic species, the Shetland mouse-ear, is found only on Unst serpentine.

Postglacial times have been marked by a general rise in sea level around Shetland. At 10,000 BP the level was 65 m lower than at present; by 5000 BP it was about 10 m lower; it attained its current height only around 3000 BP. This has contributed to the existence of a host of ayres or tombolos in Shetland, many of them wholly or partially transforming arms of the sea into lochs (e.g. the Loch of Cliff on Unst, and Loch Spiggie in the south Mainland). The most perfectly formed tombolo in Britain is about 400 m long, connecting St Ninian's Isle with the Shetland Mainland. Another consequence of the rise in sea level is the common presence of submarine peat: peat formed 5,500 years ago on Whalsay is now 10 m below sea level. There are around 2,500 lochs in the islands, most of them peaty pools of half a hectare or less, three-quarters of them dystrophic or oligotrophic. All of them are affected by salt spray because of the combination of wind and spray in Shetland.

Shetland is nothing like so species-poor as the Faroes. Five hundred and forty native vascular plants have been recorded in Shetland (plus another 180 non-native species – weeds, garden escapes, etc.), 25% more than in the Faroes (300 natives), similar to the totals for Orkney (520 natives) and Skye (588 species). A factor often remarked upon in Shetland and Orkney is the brilliance of flower colour. Whether this is a feature of the plants themselves or of the air quality, no one knows.

The islands are almost treeless. A major factor in the form and composition of different communities is climate: mean summer temperatures at sea level are similar to those at 300 m in the Scottish Highlands; the growing period (temperature above 5.5 °C) is similar to that of Dalwhinnie in the central

FIG 132. Low cloud – common summer weather in Shetland. (R. J. Berry)

Highlands. There are considerable similarities between the plant communities of Shetland, Faroe and Iceland fellfield – and of the Cairngorm plateau. Peat – most of it blanket bog – covers an estimated 53% of Shetland and its vegetation is therefore an important part of the Shetland flora. *Sphagnum* species are surprisingly uncommon, while bell heather is an surprising component – it does not occur in bog vegetation elsewhere. Hair moss (*Rhacomitrium*) mixed with heather is prominent. The short growing season and exposure to wind and salt favour stock-rearing rather than arable farming; there has been considerable reclamation (or 'improvement') of hill pastures in the past few decades.

The Shetland fauna is richer than that of the Faroes, but still lacks many species found on the Scottish mainland. Arctic hares were introduced in 1907, brown hares c.1830 and hedgehogs c.1860. Rabbit warrens were first recorded in 1654. Stoats (known locally as *whitrits* – white rats) (introduced in the seventeeth century) and otters are both common. The islands' field mouse and their lepidopteran 'geographical melanism' are described on pages 151–2 and 175. Shetland is best known to naturalists for its enormous colonies of seabirds, attracted by the food in the upwelling currents at the edge of the continental shelf and the mixing of Atlantic and North Sea waters. The only regularly breeding British and Irish seabirds not found are roseate, sandwich and little terns. Shetland has nearly half the world's great skuas and more than a half of the British fulmars, arctic skuas and black guillemots. The two major gannetries on

FIG 133. The northernmost point of the British Isles – Muckle Flugga with its lighthouse as seen from Hermaness, Unst, Shetland. (Scottish Natural Heritage)

Hermaness (at the north end of Unst) and on the Noup of Noss are among the most easily approached of any in the British islands. The great skua (or *bonxie*) was first recorded in Britain from Shetland in 1774; most of the British population is still found in the islands. The fulmar (or *maalie*) bred on St Kilda from at least the seventeenth century, but began its modern spread by colonising Foula in 1878. The dark or blue phase of the fulmar is occasionally found in Shetland; it becomes much commoner further north.

As far as land birds are concerned, Shetland can be regarded as the northern apex of a triangle drawn round the Britain and Ireland and as the southern apex of a triangle drawn through Iceland and Scandinavia (Fig. 134). The western and eastern boundaries of the northern triangle are migration routes that pass through Shetland. Shetland is both isolated and yet sufficiently closer to Scandinavia than either Orkney or the Faroes to receive a greater variety of migrants and retain them as unique breeding species. It is noted for its 'northern' breeding species: red-throated divers (c.420 pairs), whooper swans, red-necked phalaropes (c.19 pairs) and black-tailed godwits. Even though Shetland has only 40 ha of woodland (mostly shelter belts; the largest true woodland, a plantation at Kergord, is only 3 ha in extent), they attract a surprising number of migrants, divided between those that breed in Iceland, Greenland, the Faroes and sometimes North America, and those that breed to the northeast – Scandinavia, Russia, Svalbard and the Arctic. Some species (such as the thrushes) regularly pass through Shetland on their way from Scandinavia to their wintering sites in Ireland or western Britain; others (pied flycatchers, redstarts, willow warblers) are en route to Africa. Typically a southeasterly wind over the North Sea will deflect birds from their direct route and produce huge 'falls' in Shetland. For such birds the islands are salvation, for otherwise they would be swept out into the Atlantic and death.

In other groups, waders and moorland birds predominate. There are 400 pairs of breeding whimbrel (another 'northern' species), c.800–1,000 pairs of ringed plover, c.1,500 pairs of golden plover, c.1,700 pairs of dunlin and around 420 pairs of red-throated divers (known as the 'rain-goose'). The species composition is always changing; almost 30% of Shetland's birds can be classified as sporadic breeders, while a further 15% have only a foothold.

FIG 134. Shetland lies at the boundary of arctic and temperate breeding birds, as well as being on the main route for many migrating birds.

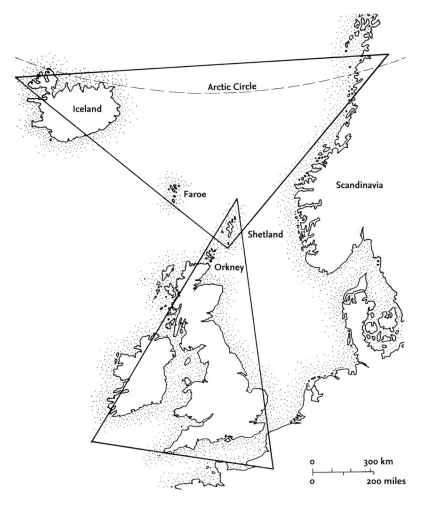

FAIR ISLE

Although part of Shetland, Fair Isle deserves a section to itself. It lies almost exactly halfway between Orkney and Shetland, 5.5 km long and 2.5 km wide. The highest point is 217 m above sea level. Despite its isolation and the turbulence of the surrounding seas, there are signs of human occupation dating back 3,000 years. The human population peaked at 380 in 1861, dropped to a low point of 42 in 1973, but has now doubled to 86 (2001 census); it is undoubtedly one of the most viable and vibrant of any of the remoter islands, internationally renowned for its patterned knitting – traditionally said to have been learnt from Spanish sailors from Armada ships wrecked on the island (although the patterns are similar to many in Scandinavia, Bulgaria and Egypt). Around 120 patterns have been recorded, many displayed in the island's museum. Notwithstanding, the basis of the economy is crofting, supplemented by inshore fishing and income from visitors, many of whom stay at the bird observatory. The southern third of the island is the crofting area, separated from the northern moorland area by the

FIG 135. East coast of Fair Isle. The tall cliff is Sheep Craig. (R. J. Berry)

Hill Dyke, which crosses the waist of the island. The rock is Old Red Sandstone, more akin to that found in Shetland than that of Orkney.

But the significance of Fair Isle for natural history is as a bird migration station. As we have already seen (page 25), William Eagle Clarke selected Fair Isle as the 'British Heligoland' on the grounds that it was isolated and therefore likely to be a welcome resting place for migrants, and that its size was such that it should be possible 'to ascertain, with some degree of accuracy what species were present daily'. Between 1905 and 1911, Eagle Clarke visited the island eight times and recorded 207 species, about half the number known ever to have occurred in the British Isles. He died in 1938 and his mantle fell on George Waterston, an Edinburgh bookseller who first set foot on Fair Isle in 1935, who returned after the Second World War and formally established the Fair Isle Bird Observatory in a group of naval huts (replaced with a purpose-built structure in 1969). During the war he had been in the same German prisoner-of-war camp as Peter Conder, a future RSPB Director; John Buxton, author of the New Naturalist monograph on *The Redstart*, who went on to establish Skomer as a National Nature Reserve and was brother-in-law to Ronald Lockley; and John Barrett, co-author with Maurice Yonge of the *Collins Guide to the Sea-Shore*. Waterston bought the island in 1948 for £3,500 and gifted it to the National Trust for Scotland in 1954.

The observatory has amply fulfilled Eagle Clarke's vision. Something like 150,000 birds have been ringed, and about 1,500 of these have been recovered elsewhere. Some of the other smaller islands in Shetland (notably Out Skerries) are almost as good as Fair Isle for seeing migrants, but they lack its isolation and

FIG 136. Dark and pale colour phases of the arctic skua on Fair Isle. (Rebecca Nason)

many birds pass over to the richer and more varied habitats of Mainland Shetland. The pattern of migration is continually changing. In 1969 and 1970 abnormally large numbers of wrynecks appeared on Fair Isle (up to 45 in one day; the previous record was 12). Some of these later turned up on the east coast of Scotland, and a few moved inland and bred in the old Caledonian pine forest. There is still a small population of wrynecks of Scandinavian origin in the Highlands, with different habitats and food from those in the almost extinct population in southern England.

Fair Isle 'migration watchers' assiduously monitor weather maps in the migration seasons. A single day in 1979 brought 1,000 willow warblers, 350 tree pipits, 140 reed buntings and more than 2,000 wheatears. Even rarities may 'bunch': totals of 31 bluethroats and 32 ortolan buntings are on record. The last of the spring migrants have barely passed through Fair Isle when the first returning birds appear: by mid July turnstones and purple sandpipers are back from their incredibly short breeding season in the Arctic. October is the month for large thrush movements, with up to 20,000 redwings liable to arrive in a morning – accompanied by predatory long-eared owls, sparrowhawks, merlins and great grey shrikes. And on top of the migration studies, the observatory staff and visitors have carried out some nationally significant long-term population studies, most importantly on the arctic skua and black guillemot.

ORKNEY

There is the Pentland Firth to cross, first of all. This is looked on as a fearsome experience by some people who are visiting Orkney for the first time. In Scrabster they sip brandy or swallow sea-sick tablets. The crossing can be rough enough – the Atlantic and the North Sea invading each other's domain twice a day, raging back and forth through the narrow channels and sounds, an eternal wrestle; and the fickle wind can be a foe or an ally. But as often as not the Firth is calm.

George Mackay Brown, *An Orkney Tapestry*, 1969

Orkney is very different to its northern neighbours. In the first place it is much more fertile; the Orcadian has been described as a farmer with a boat, while a Shetlander is said to be a fisherman with a croft. Secondly, Orkney is geographically close to Scotland, and must have had much more frequent contacts with the south over the centuries, despite the ill reputation of dangerous and rough crossings through the Pentland Firth, where the Atlantic is forced into an ungenerous 10 km wide channel.

FIG 137. Looking to the Orkney Mainland from Hoy. (Richard Welsby)

FIG 138. The tall cliffs on the west side of Hoy. St John's Head is claimed to be the highest sheer cliff in Britain (c.350 m). (From William Daniell's *Voyage Round Great Britain*, 1814–25)

FIG 139. Cliffs on the Brough of Birsay, Orkney, looking towards Marwick Head with its memorial tower to Lord Kitchener, who was drowned nearby when the ship he was travelling in was sunk by a mine. (Andrew Berry)

The Latin word for a whale is *orca*, and the islands can indeed look like whales. George Mackay Brown wrote 'The first Orkney peoples ... sailed north into the widening light ... Beyond the savage bulk of Cape Wrath there was empty ocean until in a summer dawn they saw the Orkneys like sleeping whales.' It seems unlikely, however, that the islands are named after whales. The most likely meaning is that Orkney is derived from the Celtic *Inse Orc*. The Orcs may have been the local Pictish tribe.

There are about 75 islands in Orkney, 16 of which are inhabited. The southern ones cluster round the old naval anchorage of Scapa Flow, while the northern ones form another group on the other side of the large Orkney Mainland (once called Pomona). The archipelago stretches 83 km from south to north and 37 km from west to east. It is 974 km^2 in total area, slightly less than Shetland or the Faroe Islands, but the amount of cultivated land is 51,000 ha, almost 30 times that in Shetland. The highest point of the islands is the Ward Hill on Hoy (479 m); there is no land outside Hoy higher than 300 m. There are some high cliffs on the west coast, particularly on Hoy (where the cliff-top walk round Berry Head from Rackwick past the Old Man of Hoy is one of the finest in the British islands) and on Westray. The power of Atlantic storms is shown by boulder beaches on the tops of cliffs; there is a 5 m pile of boulders at the top of 30 m cliffs at the Noup on Westray. The stack that is the Old Man of Hoy is the result of relatively recent erosion in the last 250 years; its progressive reduction (including the loss of one of its 'legs') can be seen from comparing its present state with that in old prints.

The underlying rocks of Orkney are the same granites and gneisses as in Shetland, but they are almost everywhere overlain with Devonian sandstones formed around 380 million years ago when fish were first becoming common. Although they are not particularly abundant, Orkney is an important source of primitive fish fossils, written about by Hugh Miller, the contemporary and correspondent of Charles Darwin, in the *Footprints of the Creator* (1849) – its subtitle was *The Asterolepis of Stromness* (although the fossil Miller described was not *Asterolepis*) (Saxon, 1991).

Many of the rocks are flagstones (Fig. 140), divided into thin, regular beds and used since at least the time of Skara Brae 4,000 years ago as roofing flags and field dividers (Fig. 141), as well as for paving stones. At the time they were being laid down, Britain was still part of what is now North America, and Orkney was nothing more than a depression in a vast desert, a freshwater lake, Lake Orcadie (Fig. 142). Several large rivers flowed into it, gradually filling it with sand and mud. Over 7 million years, a series of wet and dry periods led to layers of deposition 5–15 m thick, with fossil fish fragments, interrupted by softer silts,

FIG 140.
Layered
sandstone slabs
at Yesnaby,
Orkney
Mainland.
(R. J. Berry)

FIG 141. Stone slabs used as fencing in Orkney. (R. J. Berry)

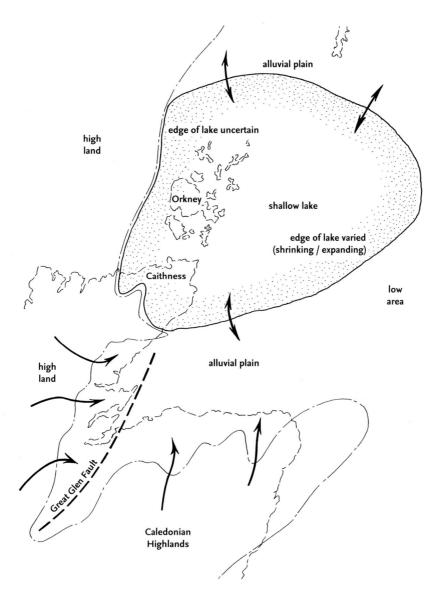

FIG 142. In Devonian times, about 380 million years ago, the area where Orkney now lies was at the lowest point of a shallow lake. Over several million years, this lake repeatedly filled and then dried out in a semi-arid and subtropical climate, forming the sedimentary rock of the Old Red Sandstone that characterises Orkney.

well seen in some of the Orkney cliffs (e.g. at Yesnaby). In the early Permian, 290 million years ago, the African continent collided with southern Europe and the Orkney region appeared above water.

The Devensian, the last advance of the Pleistocene ice, reached a maximum about 24,000 years ago, then retreated and despite a final fling (the Loch Lomond stadial, 11,000 years ago) has left a rolling, sculptured landscape. Boulder clay (or *till*) from a few centimetres to 20 m thick now covers most of the low-lying areas of Orkney, deposited from the sand, mud and rocks carried by the ice sheet. Sea levels started to rise about 8,500 years ago, increasing by 5.5 m to a maximum around 7,900 years ago.

Orkney is famous for its archaeology; it has the highest density of archaeological sites in Britain or Ireland. But its natural history is no less seductive and interesting. The hyperoceanic climate means that both summer droughts and winter frosts are uncommon; grass can grow virtually throughout the year. Linked with this, the latitude of Orkney means that there is a rapid cooling with altitude, often as much as 0.8 °C per 100 m. As in Shetland, tundra vegetation occurs at relatively low altitudes; it is possible to stand in arctic-type tundra at 300 m on Hoy and look down on lush farmland below. Orkney is one of the few places where alpine and arctic plants can be found growing alongside ones of more temperate habitats. The oyster plant (Fig. 143), a typical plant of Arctic coasts, has its most thriving British population in Orkney. One of Britain's few endemics, the Scottish primrose (Fig. 144), occurs in many places, growing mainly at the interface between communities of maritime heath and cliff-top salt-tolerant thrift.

FIG 143.
Oyster plant –
relatively
common in the
Northern Isles.
(Robert Crawford)

FIG 144. The Scottish primrose, found only in Orkney and along the coast of the adjoining Scottish mainland. (Robert Crawford)

Another climatic factor in Orkney is the relatively low total rainfall. Linked to the good drainage from the sandstone, this means that waterlogging and bog formation are less common than in either Shetland or the Hebrides.

Like all the northern isles, Orkney is virtually treeless. Up to 5000 BC, when Neolithic farming was getting under way, there was a reasonably complete cover of low woodland. The northernmost relic of such vegetation persists in Berriedale (Fig. 145) on Hoy. Although many species are absent, those present show more variation than usual. For example, the sea and buck's-horn plantains vary greatly in hairiness.

Unlike Shetland, Orkney has pygmy shrews and at least one small colony of pipistrelle bats, but the most interesting main addition to the mammal fauna when compared to Shetland is the Orkney vole, often described as 'native' or 'indigenous' but, as we have seen, an early immigrant to the islands (page 157). For the ornithological community, this is important because it attracts raptors absent from Shetland (Table 26).

TABLE 26. Breeding birds of Caithness and Sutherland, Orkney, Shetland, Faroe and Iceland.

BIRDS BREEDING REGULARLY IN CAITHNESS AND SUTHERLAND BUT NOT ORKNEY

Black-throated diver	Wood sandpiper	Grasshopper warbler
Slavonian grebe	Little tern	Whitethroat
Greylag goose	Swift	Wood warbler
Common scoter	Great spotted woodpecker	Long-tailed tit
Goosander	Sand martin	Coal tit
Sparrowhawk	House martin	Blue tit
Ptarmigan	Tree pipit	Great tit
Black grouse	Grey wagtail	Treecreeper
Partridge	Dipper	Magpie
Dotterel	Redstart	Siskin
Woodcock	Whinchat	Redpoll
Greenshank	Redwing	Bullfinch

BIRDS BREEDING REGULARLY IN ORKNEY BUT NOT SHETLAND

Little grebe	Water rail	Sedge warbler
Heron	Corncrake	Willow warbler
Mute swan	Coot	Goldcrest
Wigeon	Sandwich tern	Spotted flycatcher
Pintail	Short-eared owl	Tree sparrow
Shoveler	Dunnock	Chaffinch
Buzzard	Ring ouzel	Linnet
Golden eagle	Song thrush	Yellowhammer
Kestrel	Stonechat	

BIRDS BREEDING REGULARLY IN SHETLAND BUT NOT FAROE

Shelduck	Common tern	Rook
Peregrine	Cuckoo	Twite
Moorhen	Long-eared owl	Reed bunting
Common sandpiper	Jackdaw	Corn bunting

BIRDS BREEDING REGULARLY IN FAROE BUT NOT ICELAND

Skylark	Hooded crow	Blackbird
Swallow	Robin	

(continued)

TABLE 26. (*continued*)

BIRDS BREEDING REGULARLY IN ICELAND BUT NOT FAROE

Great northern diver	Harlequin duck	Grey phalarope
Whooper swan	Long-tailed duck	Glaucous gull
Pink-footed goose	Common scoter	Brünnich's guillemot
Shelduck	Barrow's goldeneye	Snowy owl
Wigeon	Goosander	Short-eared owl
Gadwall	Ruddy duck	Redpoll
Pintail	White-tailed eagle	Snow bunting
Shoveler	Gyrfalcon	
Scaup	Water rail	

BIRDS BREEDING REGULARLY IN FAROE BUT NOT SHETLAND

Greylag goose	Purple sandpiper	Redwing

BIRDS BREEDING REGULARLY IN SHETLAND BUT NOT ORKNEY

Common scoter	Whimbrel	Pied wagtail
Black-tailed godwit	Red-necked phalarope	

BIRDS BREEDING REGULARLY IN ORKNEY BUT NOT CAITHNESS AND SUTHERLAND

Manx shearwater	Leach's petrel	Gannet

Six species of diurnal raptors breed in Orkney, the most significant being the hen harrier: 6% of the British population nests in Orkney. The RSPB owns no fewer that 13 reserves in Orkney, 8% of the total land area, indicating the importance of the breeding birds. There is a bird observatory on North Ronaldsay. Only Shetland has more red-throated divers, and only the Hebrides have more breeding waders. One of the most obvious and evocative Orkney species is the curlew: about 5,000 pairs breed. And Orkney has its own massive seabird colonies: Copinsay (a small island which is a memorial to James Fisher) and Marwick Head both have 50,000 birds, Noup Head on Westray over 100,000.

Four hundred and twenty-four species of Lepidoptera have been recorded, only a fifth of those found in Britain as a whole, although twice as many as those found in Shetland. Probably all the Orkney species are also resident in Caithness. An interesting group is 31 species found only in the relict wood in Berriedale, five with wingless females. It would be interesting to know how long they have been isolated.

FIG 145. Berriedale Wood on Hoy – the northernmost natural woodland in the British Isles. (Robert Crawford)

Mention should also be made of the large seal colonies around Orkney: 32% of the British grey or Atlantic seals (13% of the world total) and 26% of the British common or harbour seals (13% of the European population) breed around the islands.

And finally, two 'island specialities' are the sheep on North Ronaldsay (page 185) and a herd of feral Aberdeen-Angus/Shorthorn cattle on Swona, one of the islands in the Pentland Firth. The Swona herd is listed as a distinct entity in the *World Dictionary of Livestock Breeds* (1999).

References and Further Reading for Chapter 9 are listed on page 343.

CHAPTER 10

Northwest: Rockall to Barra Head

W HERE THE LAND *is not rock it is heath, where it is not heath it is bog, where not bog it is black peaty shallow lake, and where not lake it is a sinuous arm of the sea, winding, coiling, and trailing its snake-like forms into every conceivable shape, and meeting you with all its black shiny mud in the most unexpected places.*

Alexander Carmichael, cited by Stewart Angus (1997)

Lest this seems too gloomy, William MacGillivray, a lad brought up on South Harris who rose to be Regius Professor of Natural History in Aberdeen University, wrote much more positively (in the *Northern Farmer* in 1844):

To me the wild shores of the remote Hebrides have a peculiar charm. There, in the north, extends the crowded range of the Harris mountains, partially shrouded in vapours; on the other side are seen the hills of South Uist, among which Hecla stands pre-eminent; behind you are broken crags, patches of heath, pools of brown water edged with sedges and horse tails and convered with water-lilies; on either hand are long ranges of alternating cliffs and sands; and before you is spread out the great ocean, glowing with the reflected blaze of the setting sun. Strings of gannets are passing westward in the direction of St Kilda, forty miles distant, where they will arrive in less than half an hour; the sand fords resound with the creaking cries of the terns, which are seen hovering over a shoal of fry; the shrill cries of the oyster-catcher and the loud screams of the curlew come from the distant corran; the thickets of yellow iris around give out the singular notes of the corn-crake; and at interevals comes the swelling of the ocean-murmur wafted by the gentle breezes from the rocky shore of the bleak headlands, where the grey eagle has perched his huge eyrie.

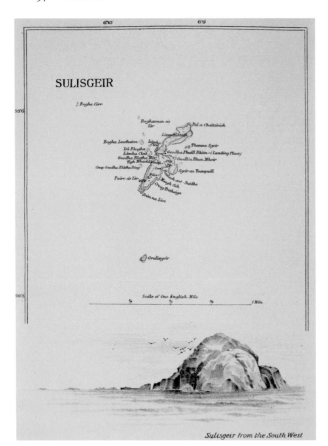

FIG 147. Ground-nesting fulmars on Sula Sgeir. (Stewart Angus)

A chain of islands shades the northwestern brow of Great Britain: a few outliers –
Sule Skerry (59° 05' N 4° 20' W, which is administratively part of Orkney), Rockall
(57° 36' N, 13° 41' W), Sula Sgeir (59° 6' N, 6° 10' W) (Figs 146 & 147) and its
neighbour North Rona (59° 7' N, 5° 49' W) (Figs 148 & 149), the islands of the St

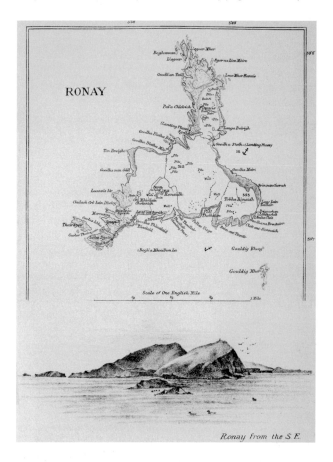

FIG 148.
North Rona. (From
*Vertebrate Fauna of
the Outer Hebrides,*
1889)

FIG 149. Seals
on North Rona.
(Stewart Angus)

Kilda group (5° 49' N, 8° 35' W) – but most prominently the Outer Hebrides, stretching 218 km from the Butt of Lewis (58° 31' N, 6° W) to Bernerary (or Barra Head) (56° 48' N, 7° 38' W). There are 119 named islands (although only 16 are now inhabited), flanked on the Atlantic side by the Monachs (or Heisker – a National Nature Reserve for its wintering geese; 57° 31' N, 7° 37' W) and the Flannan Islands (also known as the Seven Hunters; 58° 17' N, 7° 35' W) and on the inner (Minch) side by the Shiants (57° 45' W, 6° 22' W), the chain as a whole protecting the northwest of Britain from the worst fury of the Atlantic storms (Fig. 152).

FIG 150. The lighthouse on Eilean Mòr, Flannans, site of the unsolved disappearance of all three keepers in 1900. (Andrew Berry)

FIG 151. Eilean Mhuire, Shiants. (Stewart Angus)

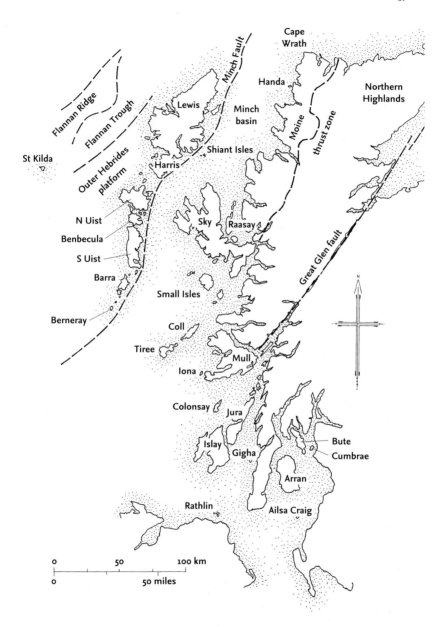

FIG 152. The Hebrides. The outer isles lie to the west of a major geological fault, which runs approximately parallel to the other fault planes in Highland Scotland.

FIG 153. Puffins on the Shiants – surprising in view of the large rat population
(Stewart Angus)

Between these outer islands and the mainland of Scotland there is a jumble of
islands, some described as Inner Hebrides (the two large islands of Skye and
Mull, only narrowly separated from the mainland; the Small Isles of Rum, Muck,
Eigg and Canna; Coll and Tiree; Colonsay; Jura and Islay), most with smaller
satellites (Raasay, Soay, Kerrera, Lismore, Iona and Staffa, Gigha plus many
smaller and mainly uninhabited islands) and others (like the spectacular bird
island of Handa, home to 180,000 seabirds) that do not fit comfortably into a neat
classification as Hebridean islands.

The Outer Hebrides formed a single island until divided by the rising
postglacial sea, probably much later than 8000 BP. Sissons (1967) calculated that
the Outer Hebrides are sinking 0.15 m every century. The Reverend John Walker
described a hurricane from the southwest at the time of high water in 1756, which
breached the isthmus connecting Benbecula and North Uist. The two Uists,
Benbecula and Eriskay are now connected by causeways with roads over them;
direct ferries link Harris with North Uist and Eriskay with Barra. The distance
from the Butt of Lewis to Barra Head is the same as from London to Sheffield.

The Outer Hebrides, together with Coll, Tiree, Iona and part of Islay, are
composed of Lewisian gneiss, formed about 2,900 million years ago and one of
the oldest rock types in the world. It does not drain well, and the spine of the
'Long Isle' (the Outer Hebrides) is almost unrelieved (and largely uninhabited)

FIG 154. Blanket peat in the Outer Hebrides. (Stewart Angus)

peat bog. The rift in the Earth's crust 55 million years ago, which split the Eurasian plate from the North American one and led to the drifting of North America from northwest Europe, was accompanied by an intense (in geological terms) burst of volcanic activity over a 5-million-year period, producing the rocks that now form Mull, the Small Isles, St Kilda and Rockall (and the Faroes). Skye is a particularly fine example of this activity: the Black Cuillin are the remains of the rocks over the original magma chamber; the Red Cuillin were formed when molten rock came into contact with the underlying crust, causing it to melt and form red granite; the Trotternish peninsula and northwest Skye were formed from lava fields that spilt from the volcano. Something like 2,000 m thickness of rocks have eroded away from the surface since their formation. Muck, Eigg and Canna are formed of plateau lavas from a volcano centred on Rum. The vertical, hexagonal columns of Fingal's Cave on Staffa and parts of Mull are the result of slow cooling of lava. The highest mountains nowadays are the Black Cuillin, rising to 993 m, and Ben More on Mull at 966 m. The highest point in the Outer Hebrides is Clisham (799 m) on Harris.

A number of the outer isles have considerable sea-cliffs and bird colonies. The birds of St Kilda are internationally important (page 75). The gannet colonies on the two massive sea-stacks off Boreray, Stac an Armin and Stac Lee, are probably the largest in the world, home to over 60,000 pairs of gannets, over

FIG 155. Puffins on the Flannans. (Andrew Berry)

FIG 156. Great Stack on Handa, Sutherland. (Stewart Angus)

FIG 157. Cliffs on Handa. (Stewart Angus)

a quarter of the British and Irish population. The bird colonies of Handa (Figs 156 & 157), a small (170 ha) island in north Sutherland, are significant: over 170 species have been recorded, with 30 regular breeders. The guillemot colony is the largest in Britain and Ireland (nearly 113,000 birds). The Flannan Islands, Sula Sgeir, North Rona, Mingulay and Berneray each hold around 30,000 pairs of seabirds, more than the total of 22,000 found in the Outer Hebrides from the Butt of Lewis to Barra. Both North Rona and the Flannans have major colonies of Leach's petrels (an estimated 1,500 pairs on each – compared to *c.*5,000 on St Kilda). Islay is especially noteworthy for overwintering wildfowl: 22,000 barnacle geese, 7,000 Greenland white-fronted geese (a third of the world population), 3,000 eider, 1,500 scaup and smaller numbers of other species. Eighty per cent of the 10,000 grey seals born each year in the Outer Hebrides occur in roughly equal proportions on the Monachs, Gasker (a small island west of Harris) and North Rona.

A feature almost unique to the Hebrides is the machair behind many west-facing shores (machair is also found on a more limited scale in northwest Ireland). *Machair* is a Gaelic word meaning an extensive, low-lying fertile plain. The machair meadows are an incidental but beneficial effect of westerly storms depositing shell-sand onshore. The result is a highly fertile strip of land stretching along much of the western fringe of the Outer Hebrides (an exception being the largely rocky coast of Lewis) and on many of the Inner Hebrides (Coll, Tiree – where a third of the land

FIG 158. Shore and machair at Ardivachar, South Uist, with Hecla (606 m) and Beinn Mhor (620 m) in the background. (Stewart Angus)

FIG 159. Croftland at Howmore, South Uist. (Stewart Angus)

surface is machair or dunes – Iona and the southern half of Colonsay). The shore itself is backed by marram grass, which binds the sand, sometime expanding into dunes. Behind this is the calcareous machair (Fig. 158), up to 3 km wide and with an average lime content of 48%; and then a strip of land where the sand is mixed with humus. The shell content distinguishes machair from the 'links' of the east coast of Scotland, which are based on more mineral-rich sand. Machair is not a truly natural habitat, because grazing – usually agricultural – is necessary to prevent it becoming rank grassland. The machair of different islands differs in its species composition, but it is consistently flower-rich. Except where they are predated (the effects of mink and hedgehogs are described on page 85), machair supports large numbers of waders: the Uists and Barra have 4,350 pairs of lapwing, 3,300 dunlin (36% of the UK breeding population), 2,650 redshank, 1,500 snipe, 2,250 ringed plover (27% of the UK population) and 2,700 oystercatchers.

The Outer Hebrides are largely treeless, but there are patches of woody scrub and areas of relict dwarf woodland in the inner isles, particularly on Skye, Raasay, Mull, Jura and Colonsay. Away from the machair, the flora is very species-poor: the majority of the bog, moorland and loch vegetation consists of only 25 species. Pollen studies show a progressive loss of species through time, at least from the outer isles. This seems to have been caused largely by soil acidification and bog development linked to loss of woodland, rather than by anthropogenic causes.

FIG 161. Kiloran Bay, Colonsay.
(Scottish Natural Heritage)

FIG 160. The northern end of Iona.
(Scottish Natural Heritage)

As usual, the more isolated islands have unexpected gaps among their residents. North Rona lacks the sea plantain, one of the most maritime of plants, despite having abundant apparently suitable habitat. The Outer Hebrides lack the Scottish primrose, cowslip, globe flower, dwarf birch, cloudberry, yellow saxifrage and arctic bearberry, all of which would be expected to occur. The fauna and flora are much richer on those islands close to the mainland: Skye and Mull can in many ways be regarded as detached pieces of the Scottish mainland. One of the best-studied islands for invertebrates is undoubtedly Rum (Fig. 162). Peter Wormell (in Clutton-Brock & Ball, 1987) notes that 2,158 insect species have been recorded there, about 10% of the total British insect fauna.

FIG 162. Rum.
(Scottish Natural
Heritage)

The distinctive animals of the Hebrides (wrens, field mice, voles, sheep, Lepidoptera) have already been discussed (pages 114, 147, 169 and 170), together with the controversies as to whether any true relicts exist. There is no need to recapitulate here in detail. Stewart Angus (2001) concludes the second volume of his study of the Outer Hebrides with a chapter on 'Enigmas and variations', which lists possibilities. The interesting questions are not usually why an endemic exists in a single locality, but why a biological process produces different results in different areas. For example, the standard catalogue of British Lepidoptera (Kloet & Hincks, 1976) lists 24 Hebridean subspecies. Some extend to other areas in northern Scotland, while others are restricted to the Hebrides (page 178). There is a melanic form (*curtisii*) of the lesser yellow underwing moth in the Hebrides and Orkney. The dark colour is produced by a single gene. E. B. Ford (1955b) crossed the dark form from Orkney with light moths from Barra and vice versa. Instead of the clear segregation into lights and darks, which he expected, he obtained a spectrum of offspring with all intermediates. He concluded that the genes modifying the appearance of the character were different at the two ends of the range; adaptation had taken place locally to local conditions.

There is a host of fascinating problems for the specialist. Unfortunately, however, some specialists get carried away with their enthusiasms. The debates raised by some of the records and claims of J. W. Heslop Harrison (page 174) have already been mentioned. Another controversial figure was Colonel Dick Meinertzhagen, a determined ornithological 'splitter'. During his lifetime (1878–1967) he amassed a collection of 20,000 bird specimens, some of them the only evidence of unique records. Sadly it later emerged that a number of these had been stolen from museum collections, and others had been labelled with fictitious information. Three birds said by him to have been caught in South Uist, and forming the only British records of American races, have been removed from the British list: subspecies of the shore lark, the snipe and the merlin. There is no indication that deceptions of this nature are common. The fact that they were once readily accepted highlights the likelihood of rare species appearing on an island at almost any time. And they do not affect the overall understanding of the lack of species on islands – and the apparently inexplicable presence or absence of particular species on particular islands.

Every island has its own biota and its own characteristics. St Kilda and Rum stand out, but each island has its own lure and excitement. Why are there no rabbits on Tiree – surely they must have been introduced in the past? But it does help to explain why hares are much commoner there than elsewhere. More or less the last foothold of the corncrake in Britain is on the western islands, particularly the southern Outer Hebrides and Tiree and Coll. (There are a few

surviving in Orkney, and many in Ireland.) Cadbury (1980) estimated that 90% of
the British population is now confined to the Outer Hebrides and Orkney.
Thanks to conservation action led by the RSPB, the species decline seems to have
been halted: 1,042 calling males were recorded in Scotland in 2004, up by 220
from the number in 2002.

John Walker, an early visitor to Tiree (in 1764), noted 'a field [of barley] having
being reaped very early in July, it was immediately ploughed and sown again with
the same grain. And from this there was a pretty good crop reaped about the
middle of October. The only instance perhaps known in Britain of two [cereal]
crops having been reaped off the same land in one season.' Another commentator
is alleged to have said that 'only the fear of paying two rents stops Tiree
producing two crops in a season.' The island claims to have as much sunshine as
any place in Britain. Its low-lying topography means that it only has a third of the
rainfall of its neighbour Mull.

FIG 163. Statue of Mary presiding over Castlebay on Barra. In the middle distance is
Vatersay, linked to Barra by a causeway completed in 1991. (R. J. Berry)

FIG 164. Gigha, 'God's island'. (Blom Aerofilms)

There are many books on the Western Isles, although most of them make only passing (or token) references to natural history. However, it is worth mentioning the relevant books in the David & Charles Islands series (currently being revised as Pevensey Island Guides): Francis Thompson on *St Kilda and other Hebridean Outliers* (1970), *Harris & Lewis* (1968) and the *Uists & Barra* (1974); F. C. Sillar & Ruth Meyler on *Skye* (1979); Noel Banks on *Six Inner Hebrides* (1977); P. A. Macnab on *Mull & Iona* (1973); Donald MacCulloch on *Staffa* (4th edition, 1975); Norman Newton on *Colonsay & Oronsay* (1990) and *Islay* (1988). But by far the most informative sources on the islands are two Royal Society of Edinburgh symposia on the *Natural Environment of the Outer Hebrides* and the *Natural Environment of the Inner Hebrides*, edited by John Morton Boyd and published in the *Proceedings* of the Society in 1979 and 1986. In 1977, the Nature Conservancy Council produced a survey of *Outer Hebrides Localities of Geological and Geomorphological Importance*. One of the early publications of Scottish Natural Heritage was a symposium volume on *The Islands of Scotland: a Living Marine Heritage*, edited by John Baxter and Michael Usher (1994). Although it deals with marine topics, which are largely outside the scope of this book, most of its contents relate to the Western Isles. Another SNH staff member, Stewart Angus, has produced two of a planned three volumes on the Outer Hebrides, *The Shaping of the Islands* (1997) and *Moor and Machair* (2001). Morton Boyd has written in collaboration with his son Ian an extensive survey of the Hebrides in an eponymous New Naturalist (1990, 1996); he also revised (1964) Frank Fraser Darling's classic New Naturalist on the *Highlands and Islands* (1947). Fraser Darling has given his own account of his stays on North Rona, the Treshnish and the Summer Isles, and Boyd gives an overview of these in *Fraser Darling's Islands* (1986). Finally, Boyd has written with Kenneth Williamson about St Kilda and some of the other islands (1960, 1963). Much has been written on St Kilda, and a great deal about Rum. A comprehensive account of the former, with an extensive bibliography, is Mary Harman's *An Isle Called Hirte* (1997), with more recent descriptions by Andrew Fleming (2005) and Michael Robson (2005); and for Rum, Magnus Magnusson's *Rum: Nature's Island* (1997) and John Love's *Rum: a Landscape without Figures* (2001). Other books with a significant natural-history content worth noting are Robert Atkinson's *Island Going* (1949) and *Shillay and the Seals* (1980); Adam Nicholson on the Shiants, *Sea Room* (2001); and three classic volumes – Seton Gordon's *The Immortal Isles* (1926), and W. H. Murray's *The Hebrides* (1966) and *The Islands of Western Scotland: the Inner and Outer Hebrides* (1973). The second number (summer 1948) of the short-lived *New Naturalist* journal was devoted to the 'Western Isles of Scotland', with articles by Arthur Geddes, Gordon Manly, J. W. Heslop Harrison, James Fisher, Robert Atkinson, Gwynne Vevers and Frank Fraser Darling.

References and Further Reading for Chapter 10 are listed on page 343.

FIG 165.
Scarista Beach,
South Harris.
(Andrew Berry)

CHAPTER 11

Between Britain and Ireland

BELOW THE HEBRIDES there is a magnificence of islands extending
south from 56° N: the Clyde islands of Bute, the Cumbraes, Arran,
Ailsa Craig; the Irish Sea islands of Man, with its satellite Calf,
Walney and Hilbre; Anglesey and Bardsey off the Lleyn peninsula of north Wales;
the Pembrokeshire islands of Ramsey, Skomer, Grassholm, Skokholm and
Caldey; and the islands in the Bristol Channel – Lundy, Steepholm and Flatholm.
It is impossible to generalise about them. They range from large islands that are
virtually mainland extensions (Bute and Anglesey), through Arran and Man,
which are mainlands in miniature, to islands like Bardsey, Skokholm and Lundy,
which reek of history, culture and mythology for naturalists.

FIG 166.
Beinn Tarsuinn,
Arran. (Geograph:
Val Vannet)

THE CLYDE ISLANDS

The geology and topography of the islands in the Firth of Clyde is as diverse as their size. The northern parts of Bute and Arran (*see* Fig. 152) are composed of Dalradian schists like much of the Highland rocks south of the Great Glen, originally laid down at the edge of the Iapetus Ocean (page 42). An old fracture (the Highland Boundary Fault), which stretches northeastwards to Stonehaven, runs across Bute and Arran; south of this are much softer sedimentary and volcanic rocks. The high ground of Goat Fell (874 m) and its associated ridges are all formed of the older rocks. Arran (43 km²) is a glorious geological jigsaw, claiming itself to be 'Scotland in miniature'. In his search for facts to support his contention that the Earth is more than a few thousand years old, and for evidence of changes since its original state (albeit for different reasons from those assumed by Thomas Burnet – *see* page 40), James Hutton regarded Arran as almost a model for the whole planet. Near Newton Point at Arran's northwestern corner, just north of Lochranza, he first discovered a particular unconformity between different rock strata, indicating movements of the Earth's crust subsequent to it being laid down. This was in 1787; it was the first recognition that, with the passage of time, layers of rock could be eroded and then fresh layers deposited over them. On Goat Fell, he was delighted to find a basalt vein (or dyke) made of glass, confirming that basalt came from a molten source of rock and had been intruded into an older rock, rather than being water-lain as assumed at the time. The following year, Hutton published his ideas as 'The Theory of the Earth; or an Investigation of the Laws Observable in the Composition, Dissolution, and Restoration of Land upon the Globe' in the first volume of the *Transactions of the Royal Society of Edinburgh*. Hutton's brief visit to Arran was a significant episode in the bringing to birth of geology as a science, and the realisation that the physical world has changed through time, a process that led inexorably to Darwin and the recognition of biological change.

Arran has two native whitebeams (*Sorbus arranensis* and *S. pseudofennica*), which grow in the deep glens of the northern half of the island. They are both hybrids between two other whitebeams, the rock whitebeam and the rowan, which coexist elsewhere without hybridising.

The year before visiting Arran, Hutton had driven down the Clyde coast through Ayr and Galloway. He remarked that the peninsula known as the Rinns of Galloway must have once been an island, in other words that sea levels had once been much higher than at present. Indeed, the number of raised beaches around the Firth of Clyde and Kintyre (very clear on Arran – for example around the mouth of Machrie Water on the west of the island) show that sea levels have at times been up to 30 m higher than nowadays, the maximum probably being at the time of the final retreat of the ice about 13,000 years ago, with the more marked 8 m level being formed about 6,000 years ago. With such sea levels, much of the current land would have been divided into islands in the past. Loch Tarbert would have linked the Sound of Jura with the Clyde estuary, isolating the Kintyre peninsula as an island. Bute would have been three islands; as it is, it is now barely an island: the narrowest point of the Kyles of Bute is only 400 m wide, although the sea is deep at this point, representing a deep ice-scoured channel.

Great Cumbrae, with its small town of Millport, was once a major holiday resort, but biologically it is best known for the Millport Marine Biological Station, the home of the Scottish Marine Biological Association from 1884 until 1970 (when it transferred to Dunstaffnage, just outside Oban) and subsequently of the Universities Marine Biological Station. The shores around Millport are among the most productive and biologically diverse of anywhere in Britain; the laboratory has a vast collection of information about the inshore waters of western Scotland.

Ailsa Craig (Fig. 167) is a volcanic plug rising abruptly 338 m from the sea intermediate between Scotland and Ireland, sometimes known as Paddy's

FIG 167.
Ailsa Craig, a volcanic plug in the middle of the Firth of Clyde, often known as Paddy's Milestone – it is halfway between Glasgow and Belfast. (British Geological Survey)

Milestone. It has the third-biggest gannetry in the British islands, home to
c.37,000 nests. Until recently, it also harboured a thriving colony of rats,
introduced in 1889 from a boat bringing supplies to the lighthouse. Prior to that
event, the island supported an extensive puffin colony (estimated at about a
quarter of a million birds). The rats have now been eradicated, thanks to the
single-minded efforts of Bernie Zonfrillo in persistently laying down poison over
the surface of the island, and puffins are beginning to return. Ailsa Craig's other
claim to fame is that it provides most of the granite for the manufacture of
curling stones.

THE ISLE OF MAN

The Irish Sea islands (Fig. 169) are as diverse as those of the Clyde. The Isle of
Man stands out, a self-governing island that is not part of the United Kingdom,
with its own legislature said to date from Viking foundations in 979, the status
of a Crown Dependency, and a 'special relationship' to the European Union
(along with Jersey and the Bailiwick of Guernsey). It lies in the middle of the
Irish Sea, a pendant below the Mull of Galloway, at the western edge of a
submarine shelf extending from Cumbria. Longitudinally, it is midway
between Cumbria and Ireland; latitudinally, the halfway point of a direct line
between John o' Groats and Land's End is said to be in Sulby Parish in the
middle of the island. The island occupies 588 km^2, about 25% larger than Arran
and 50% larger than the Isle of Wight; it stretches 48 km from 54° 25' to 54° 03'
N, and lies at about 4° 30' W. The geological evidence for the timing of the
separation of Man from England is equivocal. The fact that the only

FIG 168.
Beinn-y-Phott
and Snaefell on
the Isle of Man,
from the lower
slopes of
Carraghan.
(Geograph: Jon
Wornham)

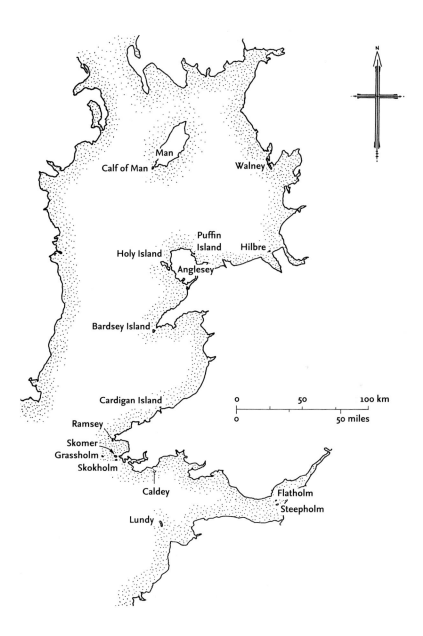

FIG 169. The principal islands of the Irish Sea and the Bristol Channel.

'indigenous' mammal is the pygmy shrew (page 42) has traditionally been taken to imply that the island was cut off before it could be colonised by terrestrial animals after the retreat of the Pleistocene ice.

Geologically, Man is a complete contrast to the complexity of Arran; the bulk of the island is composed of Manx Slates of Ordovician age, a detached portion of the English Lake District. The highest point is Snaefell (621 m). The northern coastal plain is glacial drift, with a fringe of blown sand. The Calf of Man lies like a teardrop off its southwest corner.

Man has 679 'native' plant species, approximately the same number as Arran (669 species) or Skye (663 species). David Allen (1984: 13) comments that the Isle of Man:

> has hardly any salt marsh, no true fens, virtually no natural woodland and no sizeable expanses of natural fresh water. Except for the last two, there is no reason to suppose that the situation was any different at earlier periods either. Furthermore, of particular importance botanically, Man has next to no calcareous soil. Once all these handicaps have been taken into account, its species totals are in fact not unimpressive. In every plant and animal order (except the wholly freshwater ones) that has so far been adequately worked, with a striking consistency Man proves to have two-thirds of the Irish total and two-fifths of the British.

Native plants that occur on the Isle of Man but not Ireland are rough chervil, black nightshade, common sea-lavender, yellow vetch, the Isle of Man cabbage and marsh valerian. Allen avers,

> The flora of the Island ... can boast very little in the way of the botanically spectacular. Its interest and appeal, rather, are more subtle. Because of the uniformity of so much of the Island geologically and the great range of rainfall within so small a compass, it must have few rivals as an exemplar of the influence of plant distribution when unobscured by the effects of differences in the underlying rocks.

This bears out the words of Edward Forbes, one of the most famous Manx naturalists, nearly two centuries ago: 'An insulated tract of land, such as the Isle of Man, always presents a favourable field for the observations of the naturalist, particularly when, as in this case, it furnishes a kind of commentary on the natural history of the adjoining kingdoms.'

A zoological oddity (if that is the right word) of Man is the Loghtan sheep, a primitive race related to the North Ronaldsay and Shetland breeds. It exists with white, black, grey, brown and piebald fleeces; it often has four or even six horns.

FIG 170. Chough – the Isle of Man holds 6% of the British and Irish population. (Pete Hadfield)

Like its relatives, it is small but hardy, and thrives on poor pasture. As already noted (page 63), the giant or Irish elk was apparently common on the island in earlier times. Tailless 'Manx cats' are no more than the consequence of a high frequency of a not uncommon mutation, perhaps encouraged by local selection. They are certainly not hybrids between normal tailed cats and rabbits, as was once suggested. An ornithological peculiarity is that there are few larks on the island. To more than compensate, choughs (Fig. 170) (6% of the British and Irish population) and peregrine falcons thrive, and Man hosts the highest concentration of wintering hen harriers in the British Isles.

Until its recent closure, the Marine Laboratory of the University of Liverpool was at Port Erin. One of its findings was that the sublittoral fauna round Man, and particularly round the Calf of Man, is very rich, probably as a result of the meeting of various tidal flows around the islands. The area possesses of the order of 10% more species than either the east coast of Northern Ireland or the Inner Hebrides.

The Calf of Man

The Calf of Man (249 ha) was once home to the eponymous Manx shearwater. The colony became extinct following the invasion of the island by brown rats after the grounding of a Russian ship in 1786. The Calf was given to the Manx National Trust in 1937. After the last farmer on the Calf gave up in 1958, the Trust employed an ornithologist to look after the island. In 1962 the Calf became an officially recognised bird observatory, and ornithological records have been maintained ever since. The following year, rat poisoning began. This has now eliminated the rats, and shearwaters are beginning to breed again.

FIG 171. Calf of Man, looking north to the Isle of Man itself. (Blom Aerofilms)

WALNEY

Walney is a 16 km long barrier island – a shingle and sand bar of glacial origin, which has been pushed ever closer to the mainland by tide and wind (Fig. 172). The central part of the island is a suburban overflow from the town of Barrow,

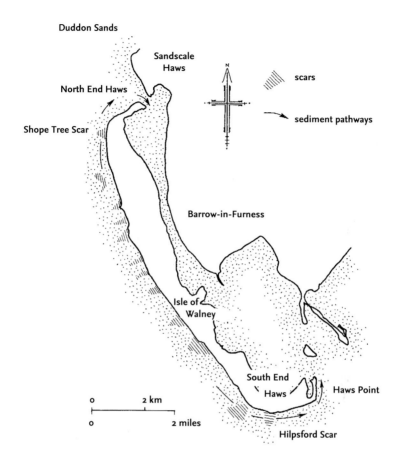

Duddon Sands

Sandscale Haws

North End Haws

Shope Tree Scar

scars

sediment pathways

Barrow-in-Furness

Isle of Walney

South End Haws

Haws Point

2 km

2 miles

Hilpsford Scar

FIG 172. Walney is a long spit, which with time has been pushed closer and closer to the Cumbrian coast.

linked to the mainland of the Furness Peninsula by a bridge; the north end is a large mobile dune system and a National Nature Reserve, while the south end is home to large flocks of waders and is a significant nesting area – and home to the Walney Bird Observatory, founded 1965. The ethologist Niko Tinbergen moved here in the mid 1960s on the completion of his studies on black-headed gulls at nearby Ravenglass in west Cumbria (after his involvement on the Farnes – page 301). In collaboration with Hugh Falkus, he made the award-winning film of lesser black-backed gull behaviour, *Signals of Survival*, on Walney.

FIG 173. North end of Walney. (Unit for Landscape Modelling, University of Cambridge)

HILBRE

The three Hilbre islands are the high points of a sandstone reef lying roughly parallel to the Wirral peninsula at the mouth of the Dee estuary, reachable at low to mid tide from the mainland. Their main natural-history interest lies in the vast flocks of waders that winter on the estuary. There may be 30,000 ducks and 100,000 waders on a typical winter's day, including more than 20,000 knots (over 10% of the British population), 30,000 dunlin (5% of the British birds) and 17,000 oystercatchers, together with large numbers of spring and autumn passage migrants (ringed plover and sanderling in particular).

THE WELSH ISLANDS

Anglesey has many features of natural-history interest, including some fine bird cliffs at the South Stack near Holyhead and an important and extensive dune system at Newborough Warren in the south of the island, but none that specifically marks it out as an island. To all intents it is a detached part of the mainland of Caernarvonshire. The small Puffin Island (27 ha) off Anglesey's east coast and (further south) Cardigan Island (16 ha), only 150 m from the mainland off the mouth of the River Teifi, are two islands that have been cleared of rats to encourage bird recolonisation.

Cardigan Island was declared free of rats by 1968–9, following a poisoning programme run by the local Wildlife Trust, assisted by the (then) Department of Agriculture. Ten years later there was no sign of birds returning, so the Trust dug artificial burrows, set out plaster puffin models, played tapes of shearwater calls and imported fledgling Manx shearwaters each year from the large colony on Skomer. Twenty-five years on, there are now indications that puffins may be seriously prospecting the island again.

The other islands of Wales (or off the Welsh coast – Lundy and Steepholm are English islands) show both similarities and differences. They are all mini-

FIG 174. Bardsey. The unusual square lighthouse dates from 1821. (Peter Hope Jones)

FIG 175. Bardsey, seen from the Lleyn Peninsula. (Peter Hope Jones)

plateaus, but geologically they trend from the oldest in the north – Bardsey (Figs
174 & 175), burial place of an alleged 20,000 saints, is largely composed of large
slabs of Precambrian siltstones and slates – while Carboniferous limestone and
mudstone make up Flatholm and Steepholm. The two last are the remnants of
out-lying folds of the Somerset Mendips. Ramsey is geologically the most
complex, with sedimentary, volcanic and igneous rocks of Cambrian and
Ordovician age and a fault arising from crustal movements in Ordovician times.
Lundy is mainly granite and is by far the youngest, being the most southerly of
the Tertiary volcanoes that also make up Skye, Rum and St Kilda.

For botanists, the main interest of these islands may be the fact that
Steepholm has one of the longest series of records in the British islands. Joseph
Banks (1743–1820) was an early visitor, and the records of his time on the island
still exist. The peony is found nowhere else but on Steepholm and Flatholm,
while the wild leek is common on Steepholm – both probably introduced by

FIG 176. Part of the gannet colony on Grassholm. (R. J. Berry)

monks in the thirteenth century. However, for most, the excitement of the
islands – particularly the Pembrokeshire ones – is in their bird populations.
Together they support more than 50% of the world's Manx shearwaters and 11%
of the world's gannets. There are bird observatories on Bardsey, Skomer and
Skokholm (the last being the oldest in Britain – set up by Ronald Lockley in 1933,
it was administered by the Field Studies Council from 1948 to 1970, and since
then by the Wildlife Trust of South & West Wales). Grassholm (Fig. 176) and
Ramsey are owned by the RSPB. In the nineteenth century, Grassholm was home
to an estimated 100,000 pairs of puffins, but the peaty soil of the island led to a
massive collapse of burrows (a situation described as a 'puffin Pompeii') and
there are no puffins there now. Ramsey has fine cliffs but relatively few birds due
to rat activity. The RSPB has begun a poisoning programme.

The Lundy Field Society was founded in 1946. Its early emphasis was on
ornithology, but it now supports and encourages a wide variety of field studies.

FIG 177. Lundy cliffs. (Roger Key)

Until they were eliminated, Lundy was one of the very few places to have both
British rat species, brown and black. The poisoning programme on Lundy
caused an outcry from ultra-conservationists, on the grounds that the black rat
is now a rare animal in Britain. This raises the question of what is a 'native'
animal, and ignores the fact that the species is extremely widespread and
common in other parts of the world. Manx shearwaters bred on Lundy in 2004,
the first time for 50 years.

Steepholm is managed as a general field station by the Kenneth Allsop
Memorial Trust. A volume edited by Tony Parsons (1996) summarises much work
by the Trust, and provides many more biological data than are available for most
islands. Flatholm is an educational natural history resource under the aegis of the
South Glamorgan County Council. Caldey is different again. Although a

FIG 178. Skokholm, with Skomer in the background. (Sid Howells)

windswept and treeless sandstone island like the other Pembrokeshire islands, it is the only one with extensive sandy beaches. It is owned and farmed by Cistercian monks: its noteworthiness is human and religious.

To return to birds: although all the islands attract migrants, their prime attraction is their breeding colonies, mainly of seabirds. As already noted, Lockley pioneered our understanding of the basic breeding biology of the Manx shearwaters in his years on Skokholm (Figs 178 & 179); this work was continued and expanded into a range of other species by the Edward Grey Institute of Oxford University when the island was administered by the Field Studies Council, and on Skomer subsequent to 1970.

The Pembrokeshire islands and Lundy were among the earliest rabbit warrens in Britain, established around the end of the twelfth century. The Bishop of St Davids put black rabbits onto Ramsey because they were worth five times the price of normal brown ones. The Skokholm rabbits, which have a very high density (page 158), were the subject of a long-term population study by the (former) Ministry of Agriculture, Fisheries & Food. One of the earliest studies on mammalian biochemical genetics was carried out on the mice on Skokholm (Berry, 1978). Long-term studies of bank voles have taken place on Skomer, where there is a named subspecies (*skomerensis*).

Islands are ideal laboratories for the sort of research on rabbits and small mammals that has been done on Skokholm and Skomer, because a discrete

FIG 179.
Skokholm cliffs.
(R. J. Berry)

population of animals can be studied, without danger of confusion by immigrants from elsewhere. The lottery of island colonisation is well illustrated by the Welsh island small mammals: there are no bank voles on Bardsey, Ramsey or Caldey; there are no field mice or shrews on Skokholm. The waters around Skomer and Lundy form the two first marine reserves in Britain.

References and Further Reading for Chapter 11 are listed on pages 343–4.

CHAPTER 12

Ireland and Her Islands

I RELAND IS AN ISLAND, and so is Great Britain. Logically both should be treated like the other islands. But to do so seems *lèse majesté* towards both of them. The natural history of Ireland has been recently and excellently described by David Cabot (1999) in New Naturalist number 84; that should be read in association with this chapter. The account here, apart from a few general remarks, is about Ireland's islands rather than Ireland as an island (Fig. 180).

Irish geology has a similar range to western Britain: the far west and northwest, from Galway to Donegal, are underlain by the same schists and gneisses as the Moinian and Dalradian rocks of the Scottish Highlands; counties Wicklow, Wexford and Waterford are composed of the same Ordovician sandstones as those of Wales. Great Britain has fewer species than continental Europe, and Ireland has fewer species than Great Britain. Both have the characteristics of islands, but neither is particularly helpful in understanding much about the natural history of islands.

The Irish islands are as resolutely romantic and fascinating as the Scottish ones – but romanticism does not support life, and the Irish islands have lost a higher proportion of their human inhabitants than their Scottish equivalents. Despite the work of the Congested Districts Board from 1891 to 1923, the Irish islands have probably suffered more from political neglect than the Hebrides. Another factor (not unconnected) is that the west-coast islands in particular have poorer communications to markets than all but the remotest Scottish islands. The potato famine of 1845–8 hit the Irish islands particularly hard because the uncertainty of ripening of cereal crops had made the islanders even more dependent on potatoes than their mainland cousins. The population of Clare

Island halved from 1,651 in the 1841 census to 845 in 1851; the population of the neighbouring island of Inishturk fell from 577 to 174 in the same decade. Many communities have now disappeared (e.g. the Inishkeas, empty since 1934; Gola, deserted from 1967; the Blaskets (Fig. 181), the most westerly land in Europe, abandoned in 1953). The account of a successful battle with a bureaucracy who

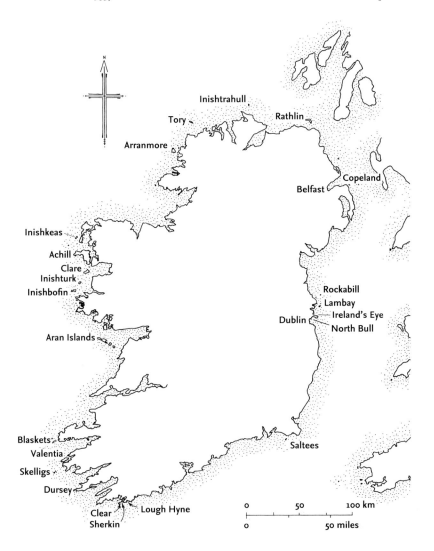

FIG 180. Ireland, showing some of the islands and island groups mentioned in this chapter.

FIG 181. Great Blasket Island. The village was abandoned in 1953. (Blom Aerofilms)

wanted to 'close' Tory island, one of the most isolated Irish islands, 12 km north of Bloody Foreland in County Donegal, has been told by Diarmuid Ó Péicin, who was the island priest at a crucial time (Ó Péicin & Nolan, 1997).

The amount of natural-history information about the Irish islands is as uneven as that about the British islands. We have already noted the massive volume of data on the plants and animals of Clare Island (page 100). There are bird observatories on Copeland (established 1954) and Cape Clear (or Clear Island) (established 1959) and detailed but not continuous observations from the Saltees. Most of the information from the other islands also relates to birds (breeding seabirds and passage migrants), and in most cases relatively little is known about other animals or plants. Several of the islands have been afforded some sort of protected status, but the establishment of a nature reserve does not necessarily mean active management, or the systematic collection of biological data.

The 136 m high bird cliffs on Rathlin (Fig. 182) (an RSPB reserve) are among the most spectacular of any of the Irish cliffs (although by no means the highest – the slopes of Croaghaun on Achill Island slope steeply from over 600 m). In the Seabird 2000 count, common guillemots on Rathlin numbered over 95,000 and razorbills nearly 21,000, more than a third of the total Irish population for both species. Unfortunately ferrets were introduced in the early 1990s and have already eliminated the herring and lesser black-backed gulls, and probably the small shearwater colony.

The northernmost and geologically oldest of the Irish islands is Inishtrahull, 7 km north of Malin Head, a mere 46 ha in area. It is composed of the same granites as Islay and Colonsay. The last families left in 1928. Most of the biological knowledge of the island comes from a lighthouse keeper, D. J. Sullivan. He collected 119 species of flowering plants and ferns, which compares favourably with the 177 species recorded on the neighbouring and much larger island of Tory (4.8 km long by 0.8 km wide) (Fig. 183).

FIG 182. Buttress at the West Lighthouse on Rathlin Island. (Thomas Bodey)

FIG 183. The Anvil, Tory Island. (Steve Royle)

FIG 184. Clew Bay, allegedly containing 365 islands – one for every day of the year. (Steve Royle)

Clare Island (*see* Fig. 60) has already been described (pages 97–101). It must be the biologically best known of any of the British and Irish islands – with the possible exceptions of St Kilda and Fair Isle. At the time of the original Clare Island Survey the human population was 460; it had declined to 140 in 1984 when Doyle and Foss repeated the botanical survey. They could find only 307 of the 413 species found 80 years earlier. They concluded that this decrease was the result of an almost complete shift in agricultural practice from a mixed arable system to sheep grazing; the greatest number of missing species were weed species associated with cereal and root crops.

The three limestone Aran Islands (Fig. 185) at the mouth of Galway Bay (Inishmore, Inishmaan and Inisheer) are perhaps the most widely known of all the Irish islands, through the writings of J. M. Synge and the wide circulation of Aran-

FIG 185. Inisheer, Aran Islands. (Steve Royle)

FIG 186. Aran fields. (Steve Royle)

FIG 187. Flowers growing on the limestone pavement, Inisheer, Aran Islands. (Steve Royle)

FIG 188. Limestone pavement on the Aran Islands. (Steve Royle)

pattern knitting. They are separated remnants of the Burren plateau (Fig. 188) of northwest County Clare, and share its extraordinary botanical richness, with arctic, Mediterranean and alpine species growing alongside each other; 437 species have been recorded on the 43 km² of the islands (for comparison, Achill is four times larger – 164 km² – but has the same number of species).

The Blasket Islands in County Kerry are probably better known for their cultural and literary history (page 202) than for their natural history. In addition to Great Blasket (459 ha, rising to 292 m) there are five islands that at one time or another had a few human inhabitants. They are the summits of the mountains that once formed a western extension of the Dingle peninsula, and are composed principally of Old Red Sandstone. The Tearaght, at 10° 39' W, is the westernmost of the Irish islands. The Blaskets hold the largest colony of storm petrels in the world (over 50,000 pairs), and substantial numbers of Manx shearwaters (20,000 pairs). Red deer were introduced to Inishvickillane in the late twentieth century.

FIG 189. Little Skellig, the largest of Ireland's gannet colonies. (Andrew Berry)

Valentia Island is a detached fragment of Old Red Sandstone off the end of the Iveragh Peninsula of County Kerry with a road bridge to the mainland. A quarry here provided the original roof slates for the Houses of Parliament in Westminster, and the paving of the platforms on many large British railway stations also came from Valentia. The island is notable for the detailed studies of its topography and human history by Frank Mitchell (1989), one of the doyens of Irish geography, although it has no greater natural history interest than the other inshore islands.

The two Skellig islands (Fig. 189) are little more than stacks rising steeply to 218 m and 136 m in height and 40 and 7 ha in area respectively, just south of Valentia and 11 km from the mainland. They are remarkable by any standards, albeit mainly for the extraordinary human history of the larger one, Skellig Michael. Between the sixth and eighth centuries, the island was home to a small community of monks, some living in beehive cells on the edge of the island's sheer cliffs. It was sacked by the Vikings and, although reoccupied, was finally deserted when the climate deteriorated in the twelfth century. Thirty-eight plant species have been recorded; rabbits and house mice and a large colony of storm petrels are also found there. The smaller Skellig has a colony of 30,000 gannets, about the same size as the one on Grassholm and by far the largest in Ireland.

The two larger islands at the mouth of Roaringwater Bay, Sherkin (Fig. 190) and Cape Clear (Fig. 191) (together with the Fastnet Rock, 7 km southwest of Cape Clear), form the southwestern tip of Ireland. They share with Clare Island the

FIG 190. Cape Clear Island from Sherkin. (Steve Royle)

FIG 191. Cape Clear. (Steve Royle)

FIG 192. Razorbill: a common auk, found on most of the islands and, because its cliff-nesting protects it from land predation, occurring also on many rocky mainland cliffs. (Andrew Berry)

FIG 193. North Bull Island, an island resulting from silting on a breakwater at the entrance to Dublin port. (Steve Royle)

distinction of being the biologically best known islands of Ireland, due to the marine station on Sherkin (founded 1975) and the bird observatory on Cape Clear (founded 1959) and the naturalists attracted thereto. The islands are the exposed remains of a submerged sandstone ridge (highest point 159 m on Cape Clear). Sherkin is only a couple of kilometres from the Cork mainland, with Cape Clear a further 5 km away. Along with the Burren and Aran Islands, they are a botanical 'hot-spot', with 12 species included in the Irish Red Data Book. Sherkin boasts 483 higher plant species as opposed to the 329 (native plus introduced species) on Clare Island, despite being only a third of the size. Nevertheless, the main interest of these islands for naturalists is probably as prime sites for observing seabird movements and migrants.

Five kilometres east of Baltimore, the embarking point for Sherkin and Cape Clear, is Ireland's first marine nature reserve: Lough Hyne (or Ine), an ice-scoured basin, which is now a small (60 ha) lake connected with the sea by a short passage. It is not an island, but is noted here because of its biological interest through the classic studies of Professor Jack Kitching on a range of littoral species, and especially the introduction of quantitative physiology into inshore biology (Kitching & Ebling, 1967; Myers et al., 1991; Norton, 2001).

The two granitic Saltee Islands (87 and 40 ha respectively) (52° 8' N, 6° 41' W) lie about 5 km off Ireland's southeastern corner. They are important bird islands, with nearly 50 breeding species, including 2,000 pairs of gannets, but there are also brown rats on the islands, reducing the ground-nesting bird species.

There are only a few small islands off the east coast of Ireland. The North Bull Island along the north side of Dublin Bay became an island about 1801; it is a 5 km long sand-dune system, which grew when harbour walls were built for the port of Dublin. In 1889 a light brown race of house mouse was described on the Bull, and a claim was made that this was the consequence of natural selection by raptors for matching the sandy background on which they lived (Jameson, 1898). However, it appears that many Dublin mice are light-coloured, and no significance should be attributed to this variation.

The birds of Ireland's Eye and Lambay are monitored routinely. Lambay is significant both because of the baseline information laid down at the time of the Lambay survey of 1905–6 (page 99) and because many of its breeding seabirds occur in nationally significant numbers: the island holds 13% of the Irish population of cormorants, along with 30% of the shags, 8% of the razorbills and 26% of the guillemots. Over 600 pairs of roseate terns (78% of the British and Irish population) and a similar number of common terns (the largest Irish colony) nest on the tiny (little more than a rock with a lighthouse) island of

Rockabill, 12 km north of Lambay. Copeland, at the entrance of Belfast Lough, was established as a bird observatory in 1954. The longest-lived wild bird ever known in the Northern Hemisphere was a Manx shearwater ringed on Copeland in 1953 and last recaptured in 2003.

David Cabot (1999: 360) has summarised the Irish islands' botany:

> *Despite fewer plant species on the islands compared with the mainland, several have found refuge away from mainland ecological pressures. One subspecies, Hart's saxifrage [found only on Arranmore], has arisen possibly through its genetic isolation and may evolve further, in the future, into a fully fledged species; many of the sometimes dramatic departures of plants from the islands are related to either the withdrawal of tillage agriculture or the intensification of sheep grazing. Overall the flora of islands is interesting because of its dynamic nature.*

This is probably a fair judgement, which can be extended to every aspect of the islands' natural history.

References and Further Reading for Chapter 12 are listed on page 344.

CHAPTER 13

The Isles of Scilly to the Channel Islands

T HE ISLANDS OFF the south coast of England range from the geologically very young Isles of Scilly (49° 56' N, 6° 18' W) to the very old (in British island terms) Channel Islands, punctuated at the halfway mark by the Isle of Wight (Fig. 195).

FIG 194.
Bishop Rock
Lighthouse –
the western
extremity of the
Isles of Scilly.
(Unit for
Landscape
Modelling,
University of
Cambridge)

THE ISLES OF SCILLY

The Isles of Scilly (never 'the Scilly Isles') are the southwest outliers of Britain, 43 km from Land's End beyond the Wolf Rock, on a line stretching 18 km out to sea. But they are much more than mere geographical markers: they have been described as 'a Lusitanian semi-oceanic archipelago'. They have conservation protection under both European and Ramsar legislation. Together the islands are 1,585 ha in extent, about the same area in total as Alderney. They are a designated Area of Outstanding Natural Beauty and a Heritage Coast site. Geologically, the islands represent a final stage in the decayed Armorican mountain chain: they are one of seven domes or cupolas on the granite of the southwest peninsula of

FIG 195. The Isles of Scilly, the Channel Islands and the Isle of Wight.

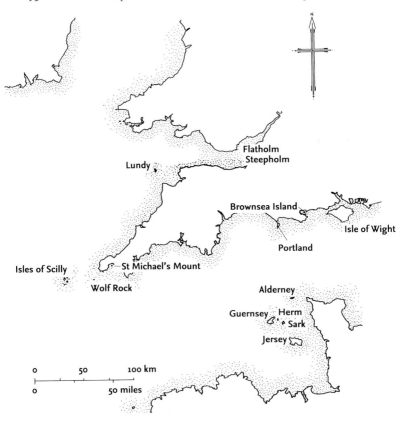

England, five of which are on the mainland, with the seventh (Haig Fras) now
wholly submerged 65 km northwest of Scilly, but with cairns suggesting it was
once inhabited. Nowhere on Scilly is more than 47 m above sea level. John Leland
wrote in 1535, 'Ther be of the Isles of Scilly 148 that bere Gresse (be syde blynd
Rokettes).' Was the sea level significantly lower in his day? Nowadays there are
around 40 islands (or islets) suitable for seabird breeding, but only five inhabited
by humans (Fig. 197). Legend, energetically encouraged by Alfred Tennyson, has it
that Scilly is the surviving remnant of Lyonesse, realm of King Arthur, the
remains of an area that once extended from present-day Cornwall. There is no
hard evidence for this, but what is certain is that mean sea levels are rising
around the present islands, and that the whole of the present archipelago was
once a single – or perhaps two – islands (Ennor or 'The Land'). The timing of the
present separation remains uncertain, but it may not have occurred until around
the end of the first millennium AD (Parslow, 2007; Robinson, 2007).

FIG 196. Aerial view of the Isles of Scilly, looking northeast from Annet and St Agnes
towards St Mary's and Tresco. (Unit for Landscape Modelling, University of Cambridge)

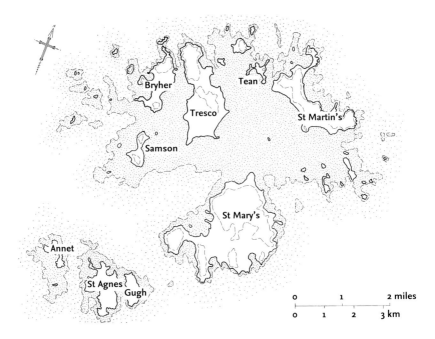

FIG 197. Map of the Isles of Scilly with the 5 m submarine contour shown. At low spring tides it is possible to walk virtually dry-shod between many of the islands. All the islands are low-lying, mostly less than 20 m above sea level (the 20 m contour is shown). The highest point is 49 m on St Mary's.

FIG 198.
St Mary's, Isles of Scilly.
(Andrew Berry)

FIG 199. Tean Island, Isles of Scilly – a major site of E. B. Ford's studies on the meadow brown butterfly. (Geograph: Chris Walpole)

Pollen analysis shows that the islands were once dominated by deciduous woodland (mainly oak and beech), but that this disappeared at the beginning of the Iron Age. Bones of dwarf red deer are relatively common in archaeological sites. Presumably these were imported by some of the early human inhabitants, although it is possible that they are true relicts. The ecology and ecological history of the islands are well described by Rosemary Parslow in her recent New Naturalist (No. 103) about the group.

Like the Channel Islands, Scilly presents an array of biogeographical puzzles. Some plants are found on Scilly and the Channel Islands but not in mainland Great Britain, including the least adder's tongue fern (Guernsey, Scilly), dwarf pansy (Jersey, Guernsey, Herm, Scilly) and orange birdsfoot (Jersey, Guernsey, Alderney, Sark, Herm, Scilly). Plants common in Scilly, which are rare on the British mainland, include early meadow grass, smaller tree-mallow, western clover, western fumitory and others. It is anomalies such as these that have led to the suggestion that they are relicts of a 'Lusitanian biota' (page 45). Another 'Lusitanian' species is the lesser white-toothed shrew. When first discovered in 1923, it was regarded as a distinct species and given the name *Crocidura cassiteridum*, but it is now classified as a subspecies of *C. suaveolens*, which is widespread on the continent of Europe (Delany & Healy, 1966). As already noted (page 129), the only other British islands on which it occurs are Jersey and Sark. The likelihood is that it has been introduced on Scilly, perhaps by early tin traders. It is obviously a candidate for a molecular phylogenetic study. The potential for accidental colonisations is well illustrated by Southern Hemisphere species, probably introduced with exotic plants: two stick-insects (*Acanthoxyla geisovii, Clitarchus hookeri*) and two flatworms (*Geoplana coxii, G. sanguinea*). Another presumed ship-borne immigrant is a cockroach (*Blatta orientalis*), first established in Britain in Scilly.

The islands are marked – like all small islands – by frequent and strong winds, but their chief climatic characteristic is the almost complete absence of winter frost. St Mary's has air frost on only four days a year on average, compared with 11 in Jersey and 18 at Penzance. This is the reason that the islands are so well known for their variety and displays of early spring flowers. But for the serious naturalist the Isles of Scilly are best known – indeed notorious – for their hosts of migrant birds, especially in the autumn. In his wide-ranging study on *The Birds of the Isles of Scilly* (2003), Peter Robinson lists an extraordinary 426 species recorded on the islands, three-quarters of all the birds on the British List. More than 50% of British 'rare birds' (i.e. those vetted by the British Birds Rarities Committee) have been found at least once in Scilly.

The earliest known inhabitants of the islands were around 2000 BC. They were Bronze Age farmers and megalithic tomb builders, probably from Spain or Brittany (or perhaps from southern Ireland), and no doubt they imported Mediterranean weeds with their crops. From Elizabeth I's days and through the Civil War, the islands were occupied by the military, who finally left in 1667. Rather soon afterwards, in 1682, a customs station was established to counter smuggling.

In 1684, kelp-making was introduced from France to the Isles of Scilly, probably the first place in Britain to be involved (the first record in the north of England was in 1720; *see page 198*). The kelp was exported to Bristol, which was an early centre for the making of lead crystal glass, and it provided a major source of income for the islanders until it finally ended in 1835 with a fall in price due to the import of plant-derived *barilla* from Spain at the end of the Napoleonic Wars, and then the introduction in 1823 of the much cheaper Leblanc process for turning sodium chloride into sodium carbonate. There was considerable poverty in Scilly after the end of the kelp industry, and the islands' recovery owed much to Augustus Smith, 'Governor' of the islands from 1834 until his death in 1872. He was a despot who did much to improve the lot of the islanders, both in education and by providing work; he has been likened to Clive or Rhodes on a small stage. His legacy lives on in the garden he established in the grounds of his house on Tresco, which ranks high in comparison with the other luxuriant gardens of western Britain. A number of the exotic plants Smith introduced into the Abbey Gardens have escaped and become naturalised. *Oxalis megalorrhiza*, for instance, an extremely frost-sensitive plant from the coasts of Chile, is now found growing on walls on Tresco and St Mary's. Smith's descendants still live on Tresco.

THE ISLE OF WIGHT

The Isle of Wight and the Isle of Purbeck were linked by a chalk ridge until the later stages of the Pleistocene. The western end of Wight was apparently connected to the mainland of Hampshire until well into the Holocene, with the rivers Avon, Stour and Yar flowing eastward. This means that most of the Hampshire biota was probably established on the island before it was separated. Wight is not remarkable for any singularities, but rather for the range of scenery and species within a relatively small area (38,100 ha, about one tenth that of Hampshire) and therefore for the density of different habitats. Hampshire is botanically the richest county in Britain, with over 1,400 species of vascular plants. Although not all of these are found on the island, the ravages of development on the mainland clearly demonstrate the importance of isolation for the protection of habitats and species. The result is that the Isle of Wight is a prime example of many archetypal southern English landscapes and their inhabitants. For example, the red squirrel is present on the island; of the 50

FIG 200. Brownsea Island, Poole Harbour. (Unit for Landscape Modelling, University of Cambridge)

species of butterflies that occur, three are Red Book species and another 11 are nationally rare; 1,985 species of beetles have been recorded, including 14 Red Book species and another 65 nationally rare; 282 of the 584 British spiders have been found on the island. And so on. Nothing characteristically 'island', but the biota is a preserved microcosm of southeast England.

One interesting feature of the Isle of Wight is that its 'ecological footprint' has been calculated (Best Foot Forward, 2000; Chambers *et al.*, 2000). This revealed that the average Wight islander had a 'footprint' of 4.47 ha, close to the UK average but two-and-a-half times their global share. (If the world's resources and area are divided by the number of people in the world with their consumption and waste, we have an average 1.9 ha available.)

Just west of the Isle of Wight is Poole Harbour (Fig. 200), with eight islands, of which the largest is Brownsea, actively managed by the Dorset Wildlife Trust. It has internationally important numbers of black-tailed godwits and avocets in the winter, and around 200 nests of both sandwich and common terns. Little egrets first nested in the UK on Brownsea (in 1996); the population is now more than 40 pairs. It was the first place in Britain where yellow-legged gulls nested. It also has a population of red squirrels.

THE CHANNEL ISLANDS

The Channel Islands (Figs 201 & 202) were described by Victor Hugo as 'fragments of France which fell into the sea to be gathered up by England'. For Leslie Thomas,

FIG 201.
Satellite image of the Channel Islands off the coast of France. (Science Photo Library)

they 'lie in the crook of the arm of France'. Geographically, they are much closer to France than to England: at 49° 13' N and 2° 8' W, Jersey is 22 km from the Cotentin peninsula in Normandy but 150 km south of Portland Bill. Alderney is less than 10 km from Cap de la Hague. The total area of the group is about half that of the Isle of Wight. The islands are composed of granite of late Precambrian and early Tertiary rocks, part of the Armorican Massif that makes up Brittany and western

FIG 202. The Channel Islands, showing major geological faults between Jersey and the other Channel Islands and also to the south of Jersey. Depths are in metres. Jersey was connected to continental Europe later than the other islands.

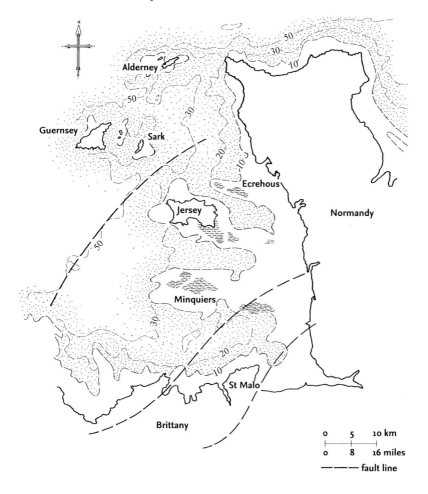

Normandy (Fig. 203). They were not glaciated in the Pleistocene and hence are the most likely of the British islands to have species that survived the Ice Ages. Their natural history is not as well known as it might be: British naturalists have tended to regard the islands as part of France, while the French have neglected them since they are part of Britain. This is a pity, because biologically they are stepping stones between the continental biodiversity of mainland Europe and the lesser diversity of Britain. It seems likely that Jersey (but probably not the other Channel Islands) was linked to the continent until the sea-level rise around 8700 BP that formed the Straits of Dover. Guernsey was two islands until 1806, when an arm of the sea (the Braye du Valle) isolating much of the northern Vale Parish was drained to allow quicker deployment of troops if faced with invaders.

The Channel Islands have much in common with the Isles of Scilly. However, they are distinguished by having many more species than most of the British islands. For example, Alderney has 11 mammals and 21 butterflies; Hirta,

FIG 203. Jersey is much more complex geologically than the other Channel Islands.

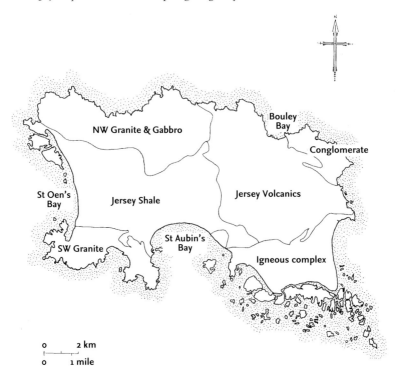

FIG 204. Sark cliffs. (Roger & Margaret Long)

half as big again, has two mammals. This does not make for predictability, as already noted, the lesser white-toothed shrew, which is found in the Isles of Scilly, also occurs in Jersey and Sark; on Jersey, the common shrew is replaced by the closely related French shrew (neither occur on Sark); but the pygmy shrew is missing from all the Channel Islands, as are the field vole, water shrew and weasel. During the last interglacial, Jersey had dwarf red deer, only about 60 cm tall. Guernsey has the water vole and the continental vole *Microtus arvalis* (the

FIG 205. Jersey, looking down from the plateau to St Ouen's Bay. (Roger & Margaret Long)

FIG 206.
Orchid meadow,
Jersey. (Roger &
Margaret Long)

same species as the Orkney vole), but no bank voles; the only vole in Jersey is a subspecies (*caesarius*) of the bank vole. The greater white-toothed shrew is confined to Guernsey, Alderney and Sark. On the continent, it lives sympatrically with the lesser white-toothed shrew, but has a rather more northern distribution.

Jersey and Guernsey are the only British sites for the agile frog and the green lizard. The wall lizard seems to be native in Jersey, although introduced colonies occur elsewhere in Britain (notably on the Isle of Wight – where the animals are of a southern European colour variety and therefore almost certainly have originated via the pet trade). Gilbert White wrote in 1769 about the green lizard, 'When some years ago, many Guernsey lizards were turned loose in Pembroke College garden in the University of Oxford, they lived a great while and seemed to enjoy themselves very well, but never bred.' Two stacks (Ortac and Les Etacs) off Alderney are home to large gannet colonies. The birds first colonised in 1940, and the two sites now hold nearly 8,000 nests. The continental short-toed treecreeper is well established in the Channel Islands whereas the common (British) treecreeper is only a rare visitor. The two species occur sympatrically in parts of continental Europe.

Both Jersey and Guernsey were once largely covered by forest dominated by pedunculate oaks, although virtually all the existing woods are planted or at best semi-natural. Holm oaks may be native in Jersey. The flora, particularly of Jersey, has a close affinity with the continent. The number of species of flowering plants is more than twice the average number found in similar areas of mainland Britain: over 1,500 species have been recorded in Jersey alone. Particularly noteworthy are orchid meadows with loose-flowered orchid and galingale. However, there are similarities as well as differences. Mary Gilham has pointed out that the flowering plant species on the shell sand of Herm Common are almost the same as on the machair of Iona – the main difference being that large areas in Herm are dominated by the burnet rose. Hedges planted on high earth banks round the many small fields are characteristic of the islands and unique in Britain; their nearest match is in west Devon and Cornwall. They date from at least the reign of the first Elizabeth (and in some cases from the early Middle Ages). In recent years, agriculture has decreased considerably in the Channel Islands, and has lost its traditional dominance. The number of holdings in Alderney has declined from 56 in the 1920s to one, while the horticultural industry of Guernsey, once the mainstay of the island's economy, is now reduced to a few specialist growers, for example propagating clematis. The consequent changes in land use will certainly be affecting the fauna and flora.

The tidal range around the Channel Islands is among the highest in the world (c.12 m at springs), exceeded within the British Isles only by the 15 m rise and fall in the Severn estuary. At low water, large tracts of sand and rock are exposed, rich in intertidal species. Of particular interest is the ormer, a

FIG 207. Herm from the air. (Blom Aerofilms)

FIG 208. Les Minquiers, a reef to the south of Jersey and former site of a large granite quarry. (Roger and Margaret Long)

FIG 209. Aerial photograph of Alderney. The two small islands are Les Etacs or Garden Rocks. They support a colony of 3,500 gannets, founded in 1940, allegedly as a result of disturbance of the Grassholm colony through gunnery practice. (Blom Aerofilms)

Mediterranean species, which reaches its northern limit in the Channel Islands. It is a local delicacy, and as a conservation measure it can only be taken from the shore at certain spring tides. In two places – Les Minquiers, 18 km south of Jersey, and Les Ecréhous, 9.5 km northeast – reefs stand above high water, and have a few houses, mainly used by fishers. The former has an area of 100 km^2 at low water but only 0.1 km^2 (10 ha) at low water. They are significant in providing feeding for passage-migrants birds, and for waders in winter. The largest British population of bottle-nosed dolphins live in the area. Les Minquiers was formerly the site of a large granite quarry, which contributed much of the stone for the Victoria Embankment in London. These reefs feature prominently in at least two novels, Victor Hugo's *Ninety-Three* and Hammond Innes's *Wreck of the Mary Deare*.

References and Further Reading for Chapter 13 are listed on page 344.

CHAPTER 14

Thanet to the Bell Rock

T HE SOUTHEASTERN CORNER of England has many unremarked
islands (Fig. 210). Some of these are large and now completely or
almost complely assimilated into their neighbouring mainland
(Thanet, Fig. 211, and Sheppey in Kent, Canvey in Essex), but there are also a
large number of other low islands, which are important for salt marshes and
wading birds – and which are almost ephemeral as tides and sea levels wax and
wane. The most notorious example of flooding was the combination of wind,
tidal surge and land-water in January 1953 that submerged 16,700 ha of farmland
in Essex alone, drowning 119 people (the conditions precipitating these are
described in an Appendix in the third edition [1962] of J. A. Steers' New
Naturalist No. 25 on *The Sea Coast*).

The North Kent Marshes around the mouth of the River Medway seem to be
almost arbitrarily divided into a patchwork of islands, which are little more than
mud banks, but which support high breeding populations of birds in the
summer and large flocks of wintering wildfowl in cold weather. Together with
the Essex coast rising above the Maplin Sands, the area is well described in an
Institute of Terrestrial Ecology report (Boorman & Ranwell, 1977):

*a predominantly 'soft' coastline of easily mobilised sediments as opposed to hard rock
… Volume and flow pattern of drainage from the land, and tidal movement from the
sea result in an intermingling of fresh and salt water which produces special ecological
conditions. In recent decades, conditions in many estuaries have been altered by
polluting matter brought down the rivers and discharged directly into the estuarine
zone. The intertidal flats and banks are rich in invertebrate animals, many of which
burrow into the substratum and feed upon detritus settling from above. Molluscs (such*

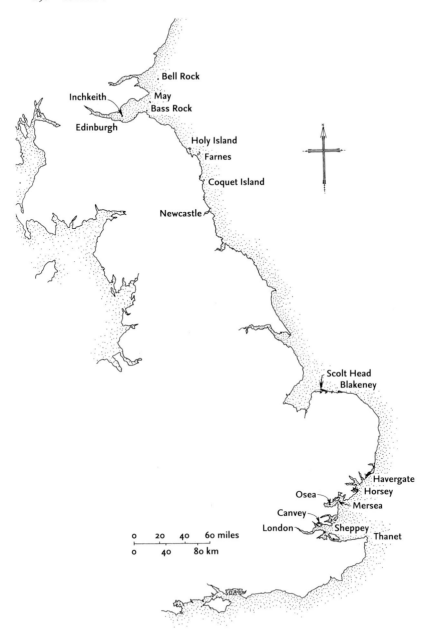

FIG 210. Main islands off the east coast of Britain.

as mussels and cockles) and worms (such as the common lugworm, Arenicola) are
abundant, together with small crustaceans. The bottom-living (or benthic) animals
form food sources for the bottom-feeding fish, and at low tide provide the staple food of
wading birds and sea birds.

The [area] provides wintering grounds for a large number of birds that migrate
north in summer to breed in the Arctic. These wintering grounds are particularly
favoured because the big tidal ranges and gently shelving shores expose large areas of
intertidal flats with abundant food in a mild oceanic situation at the western margin of
Europe, rarely frozen or ice-covered in winter. Twenty per cent of the world's 250,000
dark-bellied brent geese winter here.

Nationally, the site ranks fifth overall in importance for its winter bird flocks,
with almost 17,000 waterfowl, including (besides the brent geese)

FIG 211. Like Doggerland (page 192), Thanet was one of the islands formed when Britain
was finally cut off from continental Europe. It is unusual in that it has survived. Until
relatively recently it was separated from the rest of Kent by a tidal channel (the Wantsum
Channel). This still exists, but is now only a stream. It was only in 1485 that the first bridge
to the island was built (at Sarre). There was a ferry from Sandwich as late as the mid
eighteenth century.

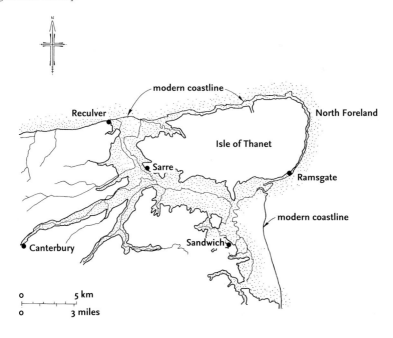

FIG 212. Causeway to Osea Island, near Maldon in the Blackwater estuary. (Geograph: Glyn Baker)

FIG 213. Havergate Island, Suffolk – an RSPB reserve famous for its breeding avocets. (Geograph: Adrian Beaumont)

internationally important concentrations of such species as oystercatcher, ringed plover, grey plover, knot, dunlin, bar-tailed and black-tailed godwit, and redshank. The 325 ha area of dwarf eel-grass is the largest continuous area of the species in Europe

Continuing further north, the Essex and Suffolk coasts are intrinsically unstable; they have been sinking 25 cm a century since Roman times. The coastline is a mosaic of habitats, from open sea, through mudflats and salt marshes, to sea wall and grazing marshes. This mosaic makes it one of the most important areas of relatively undeveloped coastline in the southern North Sea. The three biggest Essex islands (Canvey, Mersey and Foulness) all have human communities and good roads connecting them to the mainland. In contrast, there are many small islands in the estuaries, almost all protected by sea walls to convert them into grazing marshes. Does a tiny piece of raised salt marsh on a mudflat count as an island – particularly when it is connected to land by an artificial causeway?

These small islands are mostly uninhabited or have a single farmhouse. Skipper's Island in Hamford Water and Ray and Northey Islands in the Blackwater Estuary are managed as nature reserves, the first two by the Essex Wildlife Trust, the last by the National Trust. But the whole area is artificially and ever more expensively constrained by sea walls, which may be becoming too costly to maintain. It is increasingly being accepted that current sea 'defences' may have to be reduced or abandoned. The islands of southeast England are best regarded as transient features with a dynamic natural history, unlike any of the other islands round our coast.

This recognition obviously presents conservation dilemmas, as well as the uncertainty to the human inhabitants. One of the RSPB's jewels is Havergate

FIG 214. Looking across Trowland creek to Scolt Head Island, Norfolk. (Geograph: Alan Kent)

FIG 215. Coquet Island, Northumberland. (Geograph: Derek Harper)

Island (Fig. 213), a straggly 267 ha strip of land on the landward side of Orford Ness, which is a 16 km long shingle spit running south from Aldeburgh in Suffolk. Havergate achieved fame in 1947 when avocets bred there, for the first time in England for about 100 years. Until the mid 1930s, Havergate was a grazing marsh, with a surrounding sea wall.

The wall was breached in 1939, resulting in flooding from the sea and the formation of saline lagoons. This gave an unexpected bonus to the ornithological community: the island is now managed to control the salinity of its lagoons, and has attracted a variety of both breeding and wintering birds (as well as the avocets, which have fluctuated in number between 55 and 148 pairs); it also has a developing shingle flora and invertebrate fauna – a rare habitat in Britain. More flooding is likely. The RSPB's position is that while 'tidal flooding does not pose more than a temporary threat to Havergate's avocets, which can move elsewhere, special communities associated with upper salt marsh and particularly the stable vegetated shingle banks could face local extinction. These habitats are not easily protected.'

The north Norfolk coast is a complicated and changing situation. Scolt Head Island (Fig. 214) is essentially a sand and shingle ridge, growing by accretion at its western edge. Its neighbour Blakeney Point is a 5 km long spit joined to the mainland at its eastern end and not therefore a 'proper' island. However, it has all the 'boundedness' of a proper island, with extensive salt marshes on its inner margin; its ecology has been extensively studied from a field station established in 1913 by F. W. Oliver.

Going north from the sand and mud of southeastern England, the first 'hard island' is the small sandstone Coquet Island (Fig. 215), 1.5 km off the mouth of the River Amble at 55° N, notable for having 90% of the British breeding roseate

FIG 216. Farne Islands. (Blom Aerofilms)

FIG 218. Longstone Island Lighthouse in the Outer Farnes, from where Grace Darling and her father set out to rescue the crew of the *Forfarshire* in 1838. (Geograph: John Haddington)

FIG 217. Staple Island, Farnes. (Geograph: Nigel Homer)

terns, with 94 pairs in 2006 (a much bigger colony exists on Rockabill in Ireland: *see* page 277). Together with the Farne Islands, Coquet also houses half the British sandwich terns, together with common and arctic terns, eider, puffins and kittiwakes.

Forty kilometres further north is the more extensive archipelago of the Farnes (Figs 216 & 217): 15 islands at high tide, 28 at low tide, famous for one of the best-known of all British island sagas – the rescue in 1838 of the crew of the SS *Forfarshire* by Grace Darling and her father, the lighthouse keeper on Longstone Island (Fig. 218). The Farnes are the most easterly portion of the Great Whin Sill, which runs across northern England, for much of its length topped by Hadrian's Wall. Each island is a wedge shape, with a landward-facing cliff and a gentle slope northeastwards to sea level. They are treeless – and pollen analysis shows that they have always been so. They have 60,000 to 70,000 pairs of seabirds (mostly auks, terns and kittiwakes), sustained by the high productivity of the surrounding waters; they are one of the most accessible sites for viewing these birds anywhere in the British islands. Although the puffin population is increasing, significant soil erosion has led to major emigration of birds to Coquet and the Isle of May. Traditionally both eggs and adult birds were regarded as a resource to be exploited, but protection from the late nineteenth century, strictly enforced since 1925 when the National Trust acquired the islands, has resulted in increases in all the breeding species.

Niko Tinbergen, who won a Nobel Prize jointly with Konrad Lorenz for pioneering studies in ethology, worked on the behaviour of gulls and kittiwakes on the Farnes following his move from his native Holland, where he had carried out his pioneering work on herring gulls, described in his New Naturalist Monograph, *The Herring Gull's World*. Of his time on the Farnes, he wrote:

We joined that curious little guild of British island-dwelling naturalists who have all
spent some of the best years of their lives in similar isolated spots. Sometimes we
would meet other members of the guild – R. M. Lockley, Frank Fraser Darling, or
Kenneth Williamson – and, although life on the Inner Farne cannot be compared
with that on Rona, or even Skokholm or Fair Isle, we perfectly understood each other
when we were thrown together in a stuffy town: we longed to get back to our islands,
to feel the sea breeze, to see the waves breaking over the rocks, to hear the cooing of the
eiders and the kittiwakeing of the gulls echoing against the cliffs, to sniff the
invigorating salty air, loaded with the sweet scent of sea campion or with the typical,
though far from sweet, smell of the high tide mark ... Life on the islands was
delightfully uncomplicated.

The Farnes are also known for their grey seals – and for the controversies that
periodically flare up about their control. In the 1930s fewer than 100 seal pups
were born each year, but with protection the population increased enormously:
average births are now around 1,000 per year. With increased numbers,
overcrowding led to a high number of calf deaths – 20% or more of the total

FIG 219. Changes in the numbers of grey seal pups born on the Farne Islands and on the
Isle of May. Excluding seals from some of the Farnes to protect soils from erosion led to a
major dispersion of breeding animals to the Isle of May (based on Boyd, 2002).

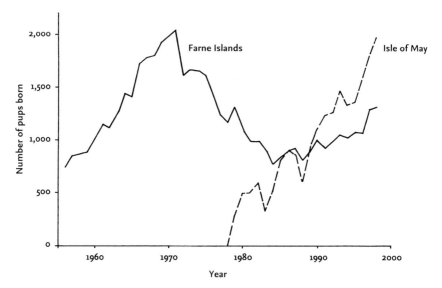

births, with 50% mortality on some crowded beaches. In the late 1970s, management was introduced to keep seals off some of the islands in order to reduce soil erosion, and this led to a significant dispersal of both breeding adults and pups to the Isle of May, the nearest breeding site to the north, where around 2,000 pups are now born annually (Fig. 219). Even so, the Farne beaches are still overcrowded. Grey seals now have no natural enemies in Britain.

A mere 5 km north of the Farnes is Lindisfarne or Holy Island, for long a place of pilgrimage because of its association with Aidan, the Apostle of Northumbria – who travelled there from Iona and founded a monastery around 635, followed a few years later by Cuthbert – and noted in part for the magnificent illuminated *Lindisfarne Gospels* produced in his memory. The island is also notorious because of its sacking by Vikings in 793 and again in 867. The natural-history interest of the island lies largely in an extensive dune system and enormous numbers of waders and wildfowl that congregate on the sheltered intertidal strait between Holy Island and the mainland, particularly in winter. It is the only regular wintering place in Britain for the pale-bellied brent geese of Svalbard.

Further north again, at the mouth of the Forth, is one of the best-chronicled of the British islands, the greenstone (a metamorphosed lava), wedge-shaped Isle

FIG 220. Lighthouse on the Isle of May – built in 1816 by Robert Stevenson. (R. J. Berry)

FIG 221. *Above:* the disused Lower Light on the Isle of May is now a bird observatory. The tower in the background is one of the fog horns. (Scottish Natural Heritage)

FIG 222. The Isle of May lies at the mouth of the Firth of Forth. (Scottish Natural Heritage)

of May (Figs 220–2) (56° 12' N, 2° 32' W), 8 km southeast of Fife and 16 km northwest of North Berwick in East Lothian (Eggeling, 1960). Like many similar islands, its earliest records are of monks – in this case dating back to the mid twelfth century. It is the site of the first Scottish lighthouse, a coal-fuelled beacon built in 1636. Two indefatigable ladies (the Misses Rintoul and Baxter) began visiting and recording birds on the May in 1907, and their observations on migrants led to a bird observatory being established in 1934, a year after that on Skokholm. The main interest of the observatory is migration, but the island also supports significant seabird colonies. The puffins have been intensively studied, and have shown a spectacular increase from 5–10 pairs in the early 1950s to an estimated 42,000 in the Seabird 2000 survey, part at least due to immigration from the Farnes (Harris, 1984b).

Further west in the estuary, the volcanic plug which is the Bass Rock (Fig. 223) is best known for its gannetry (Figs 224 & 225) – about 34,000 nests, much the same size as on Ailsa Craig, although only slightly more than half the size of that on the stacks of St Kilda. Like most of the British gannetries (the exceptions are those of Grassholm and Sule Stack), the Bass Rock colony has grown enormously in recent years (from about 8,000 in 1979), probably due to recovery from centuries of persecution. As late as 1846, gannets from the Bass were sold for food, many going to Sheffield plucked, partially cooked and wrapped in rhubarb leaves to keep them fresh. During the reign of Charles II, the island was used as a prison for covenanting ministers, then in 1691 a group

FIG 223. The Bass Rock, near North Berwick, from which the gannet has acquired its scientific name, *Morus bassanus*. (Blom Aerofilms)

FIG 224. Gannets on the Bass Rock. (R. J. Berry)

FIG 225. Gannets on the Bass Rock. (R. J. Berry)

of Jacobites claimed the rock for the abdicated monarch James II, and held it for three years. There are a number of smaller islands in the Forth, including Inchkeith and Inchcolm (Fig. 227), which are regularly monitored for their natural history, mainly their bird populations.

The final east-coast island is unlike any other in this survey: it is a rock that stands a mere 1 m above low tide. This is the Bell Rock (Fig. 228) (or Inchcape), a flat sandstone skerry 17 km southeast of Arbroath. The Bell Rock has had a 36 m high lighthouse on it since 1811 (built by the first of the 'Lighthouse Stevensons'), and it is the oldest existing rock tower in Britain. The coasts of Britain and Ireland have many such rock lighthouses, all of them now automated and unmanned, and all of them built on – and extending the surface of – small islands. Some lighthouses are on patches of ground large enough to qualify as proper islands (e.g. Flatholm, Lundy, Bardsey, the Calf of Man, Ailsa

FIG 226. Storm over the Bass Rock. (From Lockley, *Islands Round Britain* (1945), based on a drawing by J. M.W. Turner)

FIG 228. Bell Rock (or Inchcape) lighthouse, the oldest sea-washed lighthouse in existence, lying 18 km out to sea from the Firth of Tay. Designed and built by Robert Stevenson, it was completed in 1811, and has been called one of the Seven Wonders of the Industrial World. (Geograph: Derek Robertson)

FIG 227. Inchcolm Island in the Firth of Forth. (Scottish Natural Heritage)

Craig, Tory, Inishtrahull, Fair Isle), but others (like the Bell Rock, Eddystone, Skerryvore, Wolf, Fastnet, Bull Rock) are built on reefs that may be totally submerged at all but low water. The latter group are little more than homes to seaweeds and a few molluscs, and resting places for seabirds and migrants in their season. Nevertheless, they are islands, and relevant here. Many lighthouse keepers (never mind the minders of another group of mini-islands – oil and gas rigs) have kept records of their observations. The significance of the Bell Rock is that one such keeper, J. M. Campbell, was stationed there for nine years and subsequently published his *Notes* (Campbell, 1904). They can serve as a surrogate for many like him who have watched, perhaps sometimes feared, but faithfully recorded on 'non-natural' islands.

References and Further Reading for Chapter 14 are listed on page 344.

CHAPTER 15

Island Naturalists

W HO ARE THOSE who have given us knowledge about our islands? The list is long, beginning with Pytheas the Greek and his commentators, Pliny and Tacitus (page 2). It could include the Viking saga-writers and ecclesiastical historians such as Dicuil (who first described the Faroes in 825), the hagiographers and reinterpreters of the Celtic saints, especially the Venerable Bede (673–735) (Low, 1996; Bradley, 1999). All of these described islands they visited (or at least learnt about), and their accounts were used and embellished by later travellers. Of those who actually travelled to the islands, as opposed to writing down the accounts of others, most went by boat, and one of their important concerns was to note significant topographical features as navigational markers. None of these very early island-goers was a naturalist in the sense of being interested primarily in observing and recording natural history.

At the other end of the spectrum, how does one deal with the very local naturalist, who has a unique knowledge of his or her patch and often an enviable taxonomic awareness? Such people are not, of course, confined to islands, but there are many men and women of this sort. Lists of local fauna and flora are crucial datasets for later workers. Those who produce such lists provide the foundations for books like this; without their labours (and – it has to be emphasised – written as opposed to merely verbal records) we can do little more than generalise. Nowadays such local data are increasingly finding their way into local record centres and are supplemented by surveys carried out by both voluntary and statutory conservation bodies. Let us not forget these later, largely unsung John Rays, Carl Linnaeuses, Gilbert Whites. Most local natural histories list those who have contributed to them, and I can do no more here than salute them and trust that their efforts will be properly documented in appropriate places.

This chapter surveys the work of some of the more significant naturalists who have contributed to the island knowledge described in the preceding pages. Some are well known, others little celebrated outside their own area. They are part of a living tradition. Fifty years on there will be new names to be listed and celebrated – naturalists who are even now adding to our understanding of the islands and helping to protect them.

One of the most detailed accounts from an early island visitor was that of Donald Monro (1526–89), Dean of Argyll and the Isles, who made an exploratory trip through his Scottish diocese in 1549. He has given us the first account of life on St Kilda, although it was probably second-hand, provided by his steward. A much more extensive account was produced a century and a half later by a Skye man, Martin Martin (1669–1718). Martin was employed as a researcher by the Geographer Royal of Scotland, Sir Robert Sibbald (1641–1722), who had been charged by Charles II to examine 'the natural history and the geographical description of the kingdom [of Scotland]' for the Royal Society of London, which had recently been given its charter by the king (1660). Sibbald's *Scotia Illustrata* (1684) can be regarded as the foundation stone of Scottish natural history, supplemented by Martin's two books, *A Late Voyage to St Kilda* (1698), describing a visit he made to the island in 1697 with the Harris parish minister, and a more general work, *A Description of the Western Isles of Scotland* (1703).

Martin's two books stimulated considerable interest in the remoter parts of Britain, particularly the Hebrides. A century later (in 1773), Samuel Johnson and James Boswell toured the islands with Martin's *Description* in their luggage, bequeathing Boswell's memoir of the trip as probably the most widely read account of the Hebrides.

Just before Boswell and Johnson visited Scotland, a rather self-important Welsh naturalist, Thomas Pennant (1726–98) (Fig. 229), also travelled north, encouraged by Murdoch Mackenzie (page 19). Although he was amply provided for from the family estates, Pennant supplemented his income by writing somewhat upmarket travel guides, information for which he assiduously milked from his contacts. One of his correspondents was Gilbert White, from whom Pennant solicited and received a series of letters, which later formed the bulk of White's *The Natural History of Selborne* – put together and published by White after he became disenchanted with Pennant. Pennant had a good eye for scenery, and his travel books were bestsellers; his descriptions reappear time after time in the writings of later travellers. In 1769, Pennant took part in an eight-week cruise from the Clyde to Loch Broom. This was so successful that he repeated it three years later and published his journeyings as *A Tour of Scotland and Voyage to the Hebrides 1772*. This established his reputation. 'But he had no great instinct for

FIG 229.
Thomas Pennant
(1726–98).
(Linnean Society)

FIG 230. Ring of Brodgar, part of the UNESCO World Heritage site of the Heart of Neolithic Orkney. (From William Daniell's *Voyage Round Great Britain*, 1814–25)

fieldwork [being] essentially an intellectual entrepreneur, a populariser and compiler of other people's observations and ideas' (Mabey, 1986: 106). His reliance on second-hand information came close to plagiarism, and has left him with rather a tarnished reputation.

One of Pennant's correspondents was George Low (1747–95), a young clergyman who was living in Orkney and had begun work on a natural history of the islands (Fig. 231). He was recommended to Pennant by Joseph Banks (1743–1820), who met Low when he visited Orkney in 1772 (and, among other things, carried out an excavation of Skara Brae two centuries before the classic investigation by Gordon Childe). Banks was the dominant figure in British science for much of the eighteenth century; he was President of the Royal Society of London for an unprecedented 41 years. He had travelled as a botanist on the

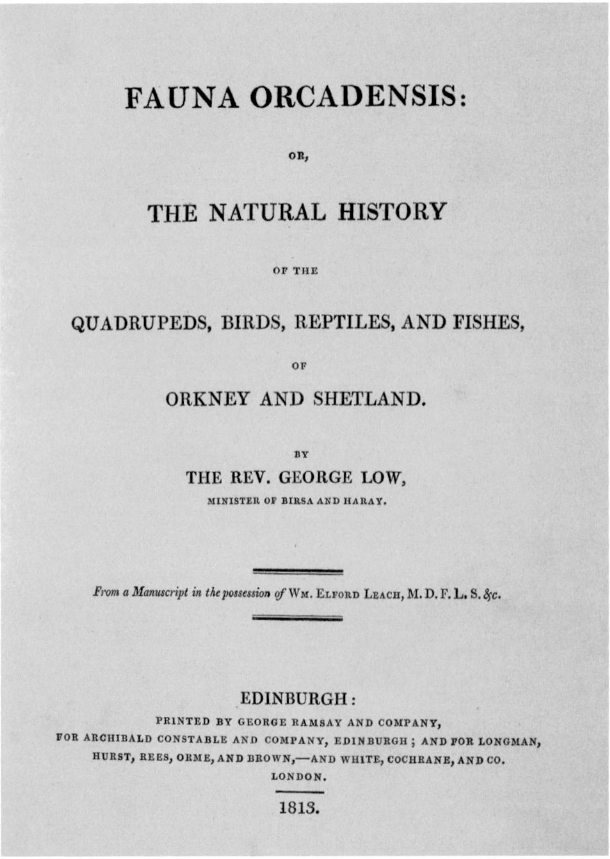

FAUNA ORCADENSIS:

OR,

THE NATURAL HISTORY

OF THE

QUADRUPEDS, BIRDS, REPTILES, AND FISHES,

OF

ORKNEY AND SHETLAND.

BY

THE REV. GEORGE LOW,

MINISTER OF BIRSA AND HARAY.

From a Manuscript in the possession of WM. ELFORD LEACH, M. D. F. L. S. &c.

EDINBURGH:

PRINTED BY GEORGE RAMSAY AND COMPANY,

FOR ARCHIBALD CONSTABLE AND COMPANY, EDINBURGH; AND FOR LONGMAN,
HURST, REES, ORME, AND BROWN,—AND WHITE, COCHRANE, AND CO.
LONDON.

1813.

FIG 231. Title page of George Low's *Fauna Orcadensis*, published 18 years after the death of the pioneering Orkney naturalist in 1813.

first ever scientific cruise in British history – the voyage of the *Endeavour* under the command of James Cook – and his collections from it formed the core of the nascent Royal Botanic Gardens at Kew, of which Banks was the first director.

Low collected information for Pennant on Orkney and Shetland for incorporating into Pennant's *Scottish Tour*, but, like Gilbert White before him, fell out with Pennant, who took all the credit for himself. In large part due to this, Low died a disappointed man, still in his forties. He can be regarded as the founding father of natural history in the Northern Isles, although his best known work, *A Tour thro' Orkney and Shetland 1774*, was not published until 1879. He also wrote a *History and Description of Orkney*, which contained lists of both the fauna and flora of the island. This was circulated in manuscript for many years, and repeatedly plagiarised by his successors (Cuthbert, 1995).

Banks's visit to Orkney took place the year after the return of the *Endeavour* from her round-the-world trip. After a disagreement with the Navy Board, Banks had chartered his own ship for an expedition to Iceland. Besides Orkney, Banks and his party spent a couple of weeks in the Hebrides, where they landed on Staffa. It was Banks who introduced the island to the world:

> *Compared to this what are the cathedrals or the palaces built by man; mere models or playthings, imitations as diminutive as his works will always be when compared with those of nature. Where is now the boast of the Architect? Regularity, the only part in which he fancied himself to exceed his mistress nature, is here found in her proportion and here it has been for ages uncounted.*

The original travellers to Staffa are lost in time. Its name is Viking, the rock pillars evoking the wooden staves used to build log cabins and Norwegian churches. But it was Banks's eulogy that thrust the Hebrides into the limelight, and made Staffa an icon of Romanticism. It inspired Mendelssohn's *Hebrides* overture; Walter Scott visited it several times, prompting him to commission J. M. W. Turner to make some illustrations for his poetic works; Wordsworth and Keats came, as did Queen Victoria, David Livingstone, Robert Louis Stevenson – the list goes on and on. Western Scotland and Staffa became part of the Grand Tour. Jules Verne simply wrote:

> *I know nothing comparable to the Hebrides ... Perhaps the sky is not so intensely blue as among the Greek Isles, but the rugged rocks and hazy horizons make it much more romantic. The Greek Archipelago gave birth to a whole society of Gods and Goddesses. That may be so! But these are very ordinary divinities ... a little too closely resembling the human beings whose weaknesses they share. It is not like that in the Hebrides.*

These islands are the retreat of supernatural beings. They are Ossian, Fingal [Fig. 232] and all the shadowy crowd escaped from the Sagas. I would not exchange this group of two hundred islands and islets washed by the Gulf Stream, these tumultuous seas, and skies loaded with mist, for all the archipelagos of eastern seas.

By the end of the eighteenth century information about the islands was beginning to reach a wide public. At much the same time that Low was travelling around Orkney and Shetland on behalf of Pennant, Sir John Sinclair of Ulbster in Caithness was collecting answers to 166 questions sent to every parish in Scotland. He published these data as *The Statistical Account of Scotland* between 1791 and 1799 (this is generally known as the *Old Statistical Account* in distinction to the *New Account* which appeared following similar enquiries in 1845). In general, the ministers were more interested in archaeology than in natural history, and answers to the natural-history questions varied enormously. For example, the minister of Northmavine (Shetland) summarised his knowledge of migratory birds very tersely: 'The Kettywakes and Thomas Norie [puffin] birds nestle in great numbers and come here in May and return in August.'

FIG 232. Staffa, showing the spectacular basalt columns and the entrance to Fingal's Cave. (Andrew Berry)

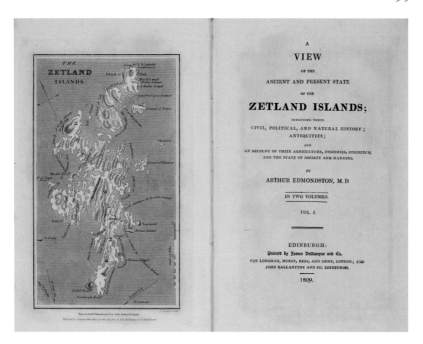

FIG 233. Title page of Arthur Edmondston's *A View of the Ancient and Present State of the Zetland Islands* (1809).

In Shetland, the remarkable Edmondston clan emerged at this time. The first was Dr Arthur Edmondston (1776–1841) of Hascosay. His two-volume *A View of the Ancient and Present State of the Zetland Islands* (1809) (Fig. 233) was the most comprehensive account of Shetland thus far, and included a complete list of the Shetland fauna as known at that time. His younger brother Laurence (1793–1879) became doctor on Unst, and planted a small plantation round his home at Halligarth, outside Baltasound. It was and is the northernmost wood in the British Isles. He was responsible for adding the glaucous, Icelandic and ivory gulls, as well as the snowy owl, to the British list.

Laurence's son-in-law Henry Saxby (1836–73) took over the Unst practice; his *Birds of Shetland* was published in 1874. Laurence's son Tom was appointed Professor of Botany in Glasgow in 1845 at the age of 20. He was accidentally shot in Peru the following year, but not before producing the first *Flora of Shetland* in 1845.

The doyen of Shetland geology was another local man, Robert Jameson (1774–1854). He went on the become Regius Professor of Natural History in the University of Edinburgh for 46 years. Charles Darwin was one of his pupils; he declared Jameson's lectures so dull that he determined never to read a book on geology (although much later he contributed significantly to the subject, and was for some years Secretary of the Geological Society). In 1797 Jameson visited Arran, and his outline of the *Mineralogy of the Shetland Islands and of the Island of Arran* appeared the following year. In 1799, he spent six weeks on Orkney and declared it the most uninteresting journey he had ever made. His *An Outline of the Mineralogy of the Scottish Isles* was published in 1800.

One of Jameson's students was an Orcadian, T. S. Traill. He became Professor of Medical Jurisprudence in Edinburgh and on a number of occasions gave Jameson's lecture course. His main contribution to natural history was an important early collection of fossil fish.

Another of Jameson's students, Ami Boué, became one of France's most eminent geologists. His *Essai Géologique sur l'Ecosse* included the first geological map of Scotland, including an attempt at correlation between the rocks of Shetland and Scotland. However, the outstanding geologists of the Northern Isles were B. N. Peach and J. Horne, two professionals with the Geological Survey. Disillusioned with the views of their superiors, which they regarded as wholly mistaken, from 1878 they began spending their summer holidays together to carry out work that they could publish in their own names. Glaciation by major ice sheets was then becoming accepted, and in 1879 they produced a geological map of Shetland, confirming that the islands had once been covered by an ice sheet from Norway. They carried on to show that Orkney and Caithness had been similarly affected. In due course their names became synonymous with solutions for the major geological problems of the Highlands and Islands of Scotland.

In Orkney, Low's death left a large gap. The *Statistical Accounts* of Birsay (Low's parish) and Shapinsay (the parish of George Barry from 1793 to 1805) contained the most information about natural history from Orkney. Barry expanded them (as well as plagiarising poor Low) in his *History of the Orkney Islands* (1805), which among other things introduced the word *vole* into English.

After Martin Martin, the major early work in the west of Scotland was Pennant's. On his 1772 tour, Pennant was accompanied by a botanist, John Lightfoot, librarian and chaplain to the Duchess of Portland. Lightfoot produced a *Flora Scotica* (1777–92), which contained many records from the Hebrides (although he probably never got there) and still remains a reference point. Other early visitors who left important records that have only recently been published are James Robertson (Henderson & Dickson, 1994) and George Atkinson (Quine, 2001). However, the most noteworthy early naturalist of the Hebrides was undoubtedly William MacGillivray (1796–1852) (Fig. 234). Although born in

FIG 234.
William MacGillivray
(1796–1852),
ornithologist, teacher
of Charles Darwin in
Edinburgh and friend
of Audubon. (Linnean
Society)

Aberdeen (where in 1841 he became Regius Professor at the University – one of
the other candidates for the post was Edward Forbes; *see* below), he spent much of
his boyhood at Northton on Harris, and it was there that he was fired with an
enthusiasm for natural history (Ralph, 1993, 1996). He was primarily an
ornithologist, but was a prodigious hard worker in the field. As a young – and
poor – man of 23 he walked the 800 km from Aberdeen to London, because he
wanted to study specimens in the Natural History Museum; as Professor in
Aberdeen it is recorded that he would walk his students 'into limp helplessness'.
The first professional zoological work about the Hebrides was his 'Account of the
series of islands usually denominated the Outer Hebrides' (1830). Although
primarily a 'closet taxonomist', MacGillivray's philosophy anticipated the next
generation of ornithologist-naturalists:

> *The man who would effectually learn from nature, must approach with affection and
> receive her instructions with a humility that would ill accord with any subsequent vain
> display of the knowledge acquired.*

The nineteenth century was a time of enormous enthusiasm for natural history in all its branches. The distinction between amateur naturalist and professional scientist was still in the future, and men and women of all sorts contributed significantly to a growing understanding of the natural world. John R. Tudor wrote a series of 'Rambling and angling notes' for the *Field*, and then in 1883 produced *Orkney and Shetland: their Past and Present State*, which contains many natural-history records, as well as a chapter on geology by Peach and Horne. Similar contributions came from all social groups (Allen, 1976; Barber, 1980), but it was disproportionately added to by those with private means who took their leisure in the rough bounds of Scotland. Some of these were naturalists – albeit often with an ambition to 'bag' as many specimens or eggs as possible (e.g. St John, 1893; Mackenzie, 1924).

Notable among the 'gentleman naturalists' was John Harvie-Brown (1844–1916) (Fig. 235), a pupil of Alfred Newton, the founding father of British ornithology. He was a zealous writer of field notes to journals and had many correspondents, but his main legacy is a series of twelve *Vertebrate Faunas* on various regions of Scotland, seven written by himself or in collaboration with

FIG 235.
John Harvie-Brown
(1844–1916). (From
*Travels of a Naturalist in
Northern Europe*, 1871)

others (*Tay Basin & Strathmore; Sutherland, Caithness & West Cromarty; Outer Hebrides; Argyll & the Inner Hebrides; Moray Basin; North-west Highlands & Skye; Orkney*), the others inspired by him (*Shetland Islands; Tweed; Dee; Dumfries; Forth*). They stand out as milestones in Scottish natural history, and are remarkably detailed and authentic, compiled from personal notes or experiences, freshly remembered. He was acutely aware how lamentably little had been documented about Scotland's wildlife, and in collaboration with J. W. H. Traill and W. Eagle Clarke he founded the journal *Annals of Scottish Natural History* (continued as the *Scottish Naturalist*) in an attempt to remedy this.

Information about other groups – vegetation, invertebrates, rocks – accumulated in much the same way as the vertebrate fauna: up to around 1830, casual but often important notes by travellers; from 1830 to about 1930, a phase of determined collecting, although frequently accompanied by poor documentation; and since 1930 an era of ecology and the study of interactions and changes. This pattern is repeated with group after group. For example, the first mention of butterflies in Scotland was in Sibbald's *Scotia Illustrata* ('Some are large, some small, some medium sized: some are adorned with one colour, some with two, some with more: some are spotted, some are without spots'). Charles Stewart's 'List of insects found in the neighbourhood of Edinburgh' (1811) seems to have been the first local list of butterflies in the United Kingdom. More systematic collecting in the nineteenth century led to suggestions being made about the origins of local races. Frank Buchanan White (1842–94), one of Scotland's greatest naturalists (and another of the begetters of the *Scottish Naturalist*), suggested that the melanic moths found in the northern and western islands were the result of 'climatic factors' (White, 1876). His contemporary F. Merrifield (1894) believed that melanism was the direct result of temperature during development. James Tutt (1899) argued that in wet areas melanic moths were better concealed, and that 'natural selection' augmented by 'hereditary tendency' favoured them; he proposed a 'differential bird predation hypothesis' for their occurrence. E. B. Ford (1937) suggested that it was the increased viability of some melanic mutants that led them to spread in areas where their cryptic advantage was compromised. Casual observations led in due course to testable hypotheses.

A similar process took place with plant collecting and recording. A major stimulus for botanical recording seems to have been a letter in 1831 from H. C. Watson in the *Magazine for Natural History* advocating an exchange of specimens on a national scale. This led to a regional network of recorders, enabling the production of distribution maps for different species. Then in the 1890s the Smith brothers at University College Dundee proposed a more systematic approach. A Central Committee for the Survey and Study of British Vegetation was established in 1904 to coordinate this; the Central Committee became the first Council of the British Ecological Society (BES) in 1913.

It would be improper to leave northern Britain without mention of one man who had an enormous influence on island natural history – and, intriguingly, one whose interest in island life was stimulated by one of the Unst Saxbys (page 315) who had come from Unst to Edinburgh to read medicine. Frank Fraser Darling (1903–79) (Fig. 236) is well known as the author of one of the classic New Naturalists, *Natural History in the Highlands and Islands* (1947), but his involvement and contributions to island biology extend far beyond that. He obtained a PhD in animal genetics from Edinburgh, but was discontented:

> *There was something wrong with my science now; it had lost the simplicity of the wondering child which I think is the approach of the greatest men of science. I did some work on animal behaviour for my own amusement but realised that if it was to be of permanent value and not just anecdotal, I must get away from the artificial atmosphere of experimentation under laboratory conditions, and not place too much weight on what I saw of the natural behaviour of wild creatures in the short periods in which I was able to watch them. I began to see that if I was constructive enough in my thinking, the goal of the island and the life of the man of science need not be incompatible.*

With a fellowship from the Leverhulme Foundation (the other Fellow appointed at the time was Charles Elton: page 26), Fraser Darling wanted to study red deer on Rum, but his request was turned down by the island's owner (page 174) and he

FIG 236. Frank Fraser Darling (1903–79). (Ian Boyd)

FIG 237. John Morton Boyd (1925–98). (Ian Boyd)

accepted as second best the chance of working with the deer on the Dundonnell Estate on the coast of Wester Ross. The result was a classic study of red deer behaviour (*A Herd of Red Deer*, 1937). He then went on to live on a succession of islands: Priest Island (Eilean a'Chlerich) in the Summer Isles, working on gulls, Lunga in the Treshnish Isles, then North Rona, studying grey seals, and finally crofting on Tanera Mor in the Summer Isles. These experiences prepared him for the task of exploring the West Highlands and Hebrides, 'to assess the factors which have led to a deterioration in social and economic conditions as a satisfying human habitat' (*West Highland Survey*, 1955). This led to Fraser Darling becoming first a national and then an international leader of biological conservation; he gave the BBC Reith Lectures in 1969 on 'Wilderness and plenty', warning of the insidious dangers of irresponsible humanity. Morton Boyd (1925–98) (Fig. 237) – reviser of Darling's *Natural History of the Highlands and Islands* and a significant player himself in island natural history (author of the New Naturalist on *The Hebrides* in collaboration with his son Ian) – wrote of Fraser Darling that 'he was as much of a mystic as of a scientist' (Boyd, 1999: 63):

> *His legacy did not include a treasure-trove of field notebooks containing the gold dust of original observation of nature. He was not a pedant devoted to minutiae. He did not appreciate the worth of numerical data in the interpretation of natural states and processes; his inclination was to let others concern themselves with numbers and probabilities, and to match statistically tested hypotheses against his own instinctive interpretation of the facts as he had observed them personally, or had them related by others whose judgment he respected.*

Fraser Darling could be regarded as a survivor of the pre-scientific era. In a review described by Peter Marren (1995) in *The New Naturalists* as 'the most bitterly disappointing book review in the history of the series', Vero Wynne-Edwards castigated the *Natural History of the Highlands and Islands* because of 'the surprising number of half-truths and errors in the book'. Notwithstanding, he 'heartily endorsed Darling's view on conservation' and 'his passionate love of his chosen land and ability to inspire it in others'.

In Ireland, a Welshman, Giraldus Cambrensis (c.1146–c.1223) produced *Topographia Hiberniae* (1185), an early and robust sketch of natural history, albeit one described as 'an amalgam, fibs and fantasy … not to be relied on without supporting evidence' (Fairley, 1975). A Dutchman who became physician to Charles I, Gerald Boate (1604–49), followed this with *Irelands Naturall History*, published posthumously in 1652 as a handbook for 'adventurers' and land speculators at the time of Oliver Cromwell.

FIG 238.
Robert Lloyd Praeger
(1865–1953).

However, by far the best-known Irish naturalist outside Ireland is much closer to modern times; it is undoubtedly Robert Lloyd Praeger (1865–1953) (Fig. 238), a librarian and the only one of the original members of the Vegetation Committee not to be a college lecturer. He was President of the British Ecological Society from 1921 to 1923. He was an indefatigable field-worker; his 'Irish Topographical Botany' (1901), published in the *Proceedings of the Royal Irish Academy*, consolidated and extended the plant geography of Ireland at a stroke, and he continued to add to its contents throughout his long life (e.g. *The Botanist in Ireland*, 1934; the *Natural History of Ireland*, 1950; and his autobiography, *The Way that I Went*, 1937). From 1903 onwards he began a series of summer visits to the islands off the west coast of Ireland; the Lambay and Clare Island Surveys have already been described in Chapter 4. Praeger was almost an archetype of a New Naturalist. In his presidential address to the BES in 1922, Praeger recognised that:

> *from the beginning of our field work the question 'why' kept intruding itself, becoming*
> *more insistent and more clamorous as time went on … So it came about that the*
> *glorious days of primary survey, when we ranged free over moor and mountain, to a*

great extent were superseded. Our campaign took on a new phase, and weapons of greater accuracy were required. Six-inch map, binoculars and pencil were replaced or at best reinforced by instruments for measuring the amount and variation of light, heat, moisture, and the whole battery of the chemical laboratory.

Frank Mitchell (1912–98) in some ways inherited Praeger's mantle, even to the extent of writing an autobiography called *The Way That I Followed* (1990). His book *Reading the Irish Landscape* (3rd edition with Michael Ryan, 1997) is essential reading for any naturalist visiting Ireland.

It is unfair to mention only two Irish naturalists. There are very many others. Bryan Beirne (1918–98) was an accomplished entomologist and doughty proponent of Ireland's fauna being a survival from the Pleistocene (page 126). Cynthia Longfield (1896–1991) was a co-author of the New Naturalist on *Dragonflies* (1960); the New Naturalist on *Ireland* (1999) by David Cabot is one of the best of recent years. And note should be taken of the Irish Biogeographical Society, which is actively collecting and publishing data on the distribution of the Irish biota, an essential preliminary to understanding the processes affecting the offshore islands.

Probably the most famous Manx naturalist was Edward Forbes (1815–54). As a student he explored the shores of Man, but most of his contributions were outwith the island. After half-heartedly studying medicine in Edinburgh (experiencing a similar disillusionment to that of Charles Darwin a few years previously – although, unlike Darwin, he eventually qualified), he dredged in the shallow seas around Shetland and then in the Aegean. He became Professor of Botany at King's College London and also Curator of the Geological Society's collections, before returning to Edinburgh in 1854 as successor to Robert Jameson (page 315), only to die within months. He is best remembered for his 1846 memoir, 'On the connexion between the distribution of the existing fauna and flora of the British Isles, and the geological changes which have affected their area' (page 112), but he was also a significant player in the intellectual revolution in biology stirred by Darwin, Lyell, Wallace and other household names.

Continuing down the west coast of England and Wales, most of the islands have active natural history and/or archaeological societies that collate and publish local data. Peter Hope Jones's *Natural History of Bardsey* (1988) is a model of what can be done at a local level. Ronald Lockley's love affair with Skokholm has already been described (page x). He described this in many books, most succinctly in *Letters from Skokholm* (1947) (largely reprised as *The Island*, 1969). Lundy has been particularly well served by its Field Society, with informative annual reports and a handsome volume of *Island Studies* (edited by Irving *et al.*, 1997) celebrating the

society's golden jubilee. The Isles of Scilly have their own recorders and
defenders (see Lousley, 1971; Thomas, 1985; Robinson, 2003), but their greatest
contributor to natural history is probably best accorded only an honorary title as
a naturalist. Augustus Smith (1803–72) became 'Lord Proprietor' of the islands in
1835 on a 99-year lease from the Duchy of Cornwall, seeing them as a
philanthropic and organisational challenge. As already noted (page 284), he
established a garden on Tresco, importing roots and seeds from Australia, New
Zealand, South Africa and Kew. He told Sir William Hooker at Kew that he had
'an insatiable appetite' for new species. By 1860 the garden was noted for growing
plants in the open for which hothouses were required at Kew. Nurture and
development of the gardens have continued under Smith's successors; by 1935
there were 153 species of Mesembryanthemum thriving there. Rosemary Parslow's
New Naturalist No. 103 The Isles of Scilly (2007) summarises the natural history of
the islands.

Along the south coast of England, it is worth pausing to note Frank Morey's
Guide to the Natural History of the Isle of Wight (1909). Although not a particularly
distinguished work in its own right, it brought together much knowledge and
data on the natural history of the island and provided a reference point for
subsequent changes, particularly important in a part of the world heavily
influenced by human activity.

At the southern extremity of the British Isles, the Channel Islands are well
served by active societies, which maintain their own archives and publications:
the Société Jersiaise (founded 1839) and the Société Guernesiaise (1882) (the
Bailiwick of Guernsey includes Sark and Herm as well as Guernsey). A useful
Natural History of Jersey was compiled by Frances Le Sueur in 1976; more
topographical accounts are provided by Jee (1982) and Jones et al. (1990).

H. J. Fleure, pioneer archaeological anthropologist and author of one of the
more significant of the early New Naturalists, Natural History of Man in Britain
(No. 18), was a Guernsey man. He spent most of his working life away from the
island, but it is said of him, 'Alone with his thoughts he explored Guernsey and
came to know his native island intimately, to become the born field naturalist,
conscious at a very early age of the wonder of the natural history of shore animals
and plants' (Alice Garnett, quoted in Marren, 1995).

The southern stretch of the east coast of England is characterised by constantly
changing mud banks and channels; its history is primarily one of human
endeavour and temporary triumph or failure. The trauma and heroism of the area
is summarised by Hilda Grieve (1959) in her account of the flood disaster of 1953.

Further north, Scolt Head and Blakeney Point have been studied in some
detail – the former by Cambridge University geographers under J. A. Steers

(author of the New Naturalist on the *Sea Coast*), the latter by biologists from University College London (Steers, 1934; Arber, 1951). Three hundred kilometres further north, the history and wildlife of the Farne Islands have been collated by Grace Watt (1951).

The islands in the Firth of Forth have a complicated history of piracy, trade, penal settlements, military defence and monasticism as well as natural history. The story of the Isle of May has been well described by Joe Eggeling, Curator of Forests in pre-independence Uganda who became Director of the Nature Conservancy in Scotland. His account of the May is a model of history, natural history and the effects of human activities (Eggeling, 1960). Knowledge of the Bass Rock was summarised by Thomas M'Crie and others in 1848; a more recent account (particularly of the island's gannetry) has been given by Bryan Nelson (1986), who lived on the Bass for three years whilst studying the birds.

But perhaps the greatest island naturalist, and the one who has had the greatest influence on our understanding of the natural history of islands, is Darwin's friend and closest scientific confidant, Joseph Hooker (Fig. 239) (page 121). The son of William Hooker, whom he was to succeed as Director of Kew Gardens, he was brought up in Glasgow, where his father was Professor of Botany. He wrote of his boyhood:

FIG 239.
Joseph Hooker
(1814–79) – the oil
painting by Hubert
Herkomer hanging in
the Linnean Society
of London. (Linnean
Society)

my father used to take me on excursions in the Highlands, where I fished a great deal,
but also botanised; and well I remember on one occasion, that, after returning home, I
built up by a heap of stones a representation of one of the mountains I had ascended,
and stuck upon it specimens of the mosses I had collected on it at heights relative to those
at which I had gathered them. This was the dawn of my love for geographical botany.

In 1839, at the age of 22, Hooker was employed by James Clark Ross as assistant
surgeon and naturalist on a cruise to the Antarctic on the ships *Erebus* and
Terror, eight years after Darwin had embarked on the *Beagle*. A parting gift from
his father's friend, Charles Lyell senior, were the proofs of Darwin's first book,
the *Journal* of the *Beagle*'s voyage. It made him despair of ever following
Darwin's footsteps, but increased his 'desire to travel and observe'. The *Erebus*
and *Terror* circumnavigated the world, largely in the Roaring Forties of the
Southern Ocean, calling at Australia, New Zealand, the Auckland and Campbell
Islands, the Falklands and Kerguelen, arriving back in Britain in 1843
(Desmond, 1999). On his return to London, Hooker began a correspondence
with Darwin. Hooker believed that the floras of many of the islands he had
visited were relics from a previous widespread landmass; Darwin thought that
they were the results of chance colonisations (Berry, in press *a* and *b*). They
argued together, and with Lyell and Forbes. They were of course both right. As
we have seen, islands can be colonised by many routes. Narrow dogmatism
always hinders good natural history.

Hooker's subsequent career does not concern us here. He went on to travel in
Sikkim, Assam and Nepal. He served as President of the Royal Society and
received the Order of Merit. But he remained a field botanist at heart. As an old
and distinguished man, he received the Royal Society's Copley Medal – and
recalled that as a small boy his determination to travel had been nurtured by
books on exploration and actually meeting some of his heroes when they visited
his father's home in Glasgow. He described Charles Darwin as the 'Pole Star and
Lode Stone' of his scientific life. And no doubt he reflected with justifiable pride
that it was his data, and his analyses of island floras, that were an important
element in establishing the credibility of Darwin's evolutionary ideas.

References and Further Reading for Chapter 15 are listed on pages 344–5.

CHAPTER 16

Facts, Fancies and Fragilities

S TANDING ON AN island cliff and watching birds expertly flirting with an importunate gale, the only element that seems impermanent is oneself. The waves hurl themselves against rocks as they have done from time immemorial and show no sign of tiring; the birds expertly ride the wind and only momentarily need to steady themselves; the vegetation crouches to the earth, allowing air and water to pass over and through it. And yet, and yet – island ecosystems are intrinsically fragile. Yes, the rocks are sturdy and seemingly unyielding, but they are in fact being irrevocably and imperceptibly

FIG 240. Road sign in North Uist. (Andrew Berry)

dissolved. Even the apparently imperishable rocks of the Outer Hebrides or northwest Ireland are all that remain of Himalayan-style mountains. The magnificent arches and stacks of Orkney and Shetland are the mere tattered remains of a former coast. And though the seemingly effortless grace of seabird flight is wonderful, we have to recognise that their long-term future is at risk: northern colonies of kittiwakes, guillemots, razorbills and arctic terns have had several disastrous breeding seasons since the beginning of the twenty-first century, with very few young fledged. The seemingly timelessness of island life is illusory.

But we should not be surprised. We have seen that all biological populations are in a state of flux, and island populations especially so: some species disappear, new ones arrive. The geology changes more slowly than the biology, but change it does. Extraordinarily, our islands have come to their present positions after an extravagant odyssey over the surface of the globe, and still face environmental onslaughts even when their days of travel, mountain building and volcanic activity are long past. Islands are concrete witnesses to biological and geological history. For the discerning naturalist, the processes that have determined this history are often clearer in the finite area of islands than in the greater extents of continents. For those with eyes to see, they are indeed living laboratories.

The notion of islands as laboratories is not new. Joseph Hooker opened Charles Darwin's eyes to the significance for science of islands. St Kilda has been a magnet and source of information for naturalists since at least the pioneering wildlife photography there by Cherry and Richard Kearton in 1896. Praeger had great ambitions that the work he initiated on Clare Island would parallel classic island studies on Hawaii, Galapagos and Easter Island. And nearer the present, when the Nature Conservancy took over Rum in 1957 it was envisaged as 'a great open-air laboratory where scientists can combine their talents for research to make a long-term examination of the vast complex of factors which has brought about the island's poverty, and out of this design and conduct experiments to revitalise the land and recover some of its lost attributes' (Williamson & Boyd, 1963: 57). Ten of the 19 observatories coordinated by the Bird Observatories Council (Bardsey, Calf of Man, Cape Clear, Copeland, Fair Isle, Isle of May, North Ronaldsay, Sanda, Skokholm and Walney) are on islands and two more are on honorary islands (Portland, Spurn) (page 23), and all of them observe much more than birds. Other islands support study centres of various sorts (e.g. Stronsay, Handa, Sherkin, Lundy). Some of the results and significance of work from these (and other) islands have been described in earlier chapters.

HUMAN IMPACTS

Ernst Mayr concluded a paper on 'the challenge of island faunas' with the warning, 'Islands are an enormously important source of information and an unparalleled testing ground for various scientific theories. But this very importance imposes an obligation on us. Their biota is vulnerable and precious. We must protect it. We have an obligation to hand over these unique faunas and floras with a minimum of loss from generation to generation' (Mayr, 1967: 374). He spoke truly. But that is only part of it. Our islands are more than biological and geological laboratories: they are also archives of human struggles. Virtually all of them have been altered by human pioneers and their ever more demanding descendants. Our earliest forebears left little legacy beyond rubbish heaps of empty shells. Later generations bequeathed us the remains of some extraordinary structures – the Neolithic villages of the Knap of Howar and Skara Brae in Orkney are now protected archaeological sites, while the megalith builders (Callanish, Brodgar, Kilmartin, the dolmens in the Channel Islands) continue to excite speculation.

FIG 241. The post office on Rum after a visit by a post-Ornithological Congress excursion. (R. J. Berry)

FIG 242. Statue of a lifeboat man at Longhope, Orkney, gazing over Scapa Flow. This commemorates one of the worst lifeboat tragedies in British waters when, in 1969, the entire crew of the Longhope boat was drowned. (R. J. Berry)

But by the middle of the first millennium after Christ, our ancestors were beginning to leave deep scars rather than surface scratches. The American historian Lynn White saw the 'historical roots of our ecologic crisis' as beginning with the invention of the ploughshare at the end of the seventh century and the consequent possibility of increasing control over the natural world (White, 1967). White's thesis has been much criticised, but his ideas drew attention to the ability of our species to dominate over the natural world – and to the fact that, like every species, humans are primarily concerned more with their own survival than with the niceties of protecting their environment. Generalities of this battle have been frighteningly documented by Jared Diamond in *Collapse: How Societies Choose to Fail or Survive* (2005), including some classic studies of the fate of island communities (such as Easter and Pitcairn Islands); more encouragingly, he contrasts reasons for the success of Orkney, Shetland and the Faeroes with those that led to the downfall of the Viking settlements in Greenland and 'Vinland'.

The marks of this struggle change as new possibilities appear, its details clearer on the northern islands than on more southern ones, or on mainland, where they tend to be erased by the impact of later populations. But we can recognise their features everywhere. Early island communities stuck to the shore, because the sea was a more reliable source of food than unimproved land away from the sea. At times, habitations crept inland but always returned to the shore in times of stress. Heaped 'lazy beds', often fertilised by seaweed, are visible on many islands. In recent years silage has almost completely replaced grain crops, because it does not require spells of fine weather before harvest. Transport is intrinsically difficult and always expensive on islands. As islanders moved from a subsistence to a more cash-based economy, this has become an increasing problem.

Another component of traditional island living is the recurrent exposure of adult males (in particular) to accidental death during fowling, fishing or seal-hunting expeditions. On St Kilda, traditional songs make it clear that the women admired good cragsman, appreciated the results of the men's labours and sang laments for victims of climbing accidents. Andrew Fleming (2001) has compared attitudes on Presbyterian St Kilda with those on the Roman Catholic Blaskets, and how the awareness of risks spilt over into assumptions of magic and the supernatural. Writing about the St Kildans at the end of the seventeenth century, Martin Martin (Fig. 243) noted that 'they have a notion that spirits are embodied, and fancy them to be locally in rocks, hills, or wherever they list, in an instant ... all events, whether good or bad, are predetermined by God.' On the Blaskets likewise, there was a fatalism that 'the world was suffused with supernatural power, and magical rites, prayers and spells' might influence it. Fleming sees

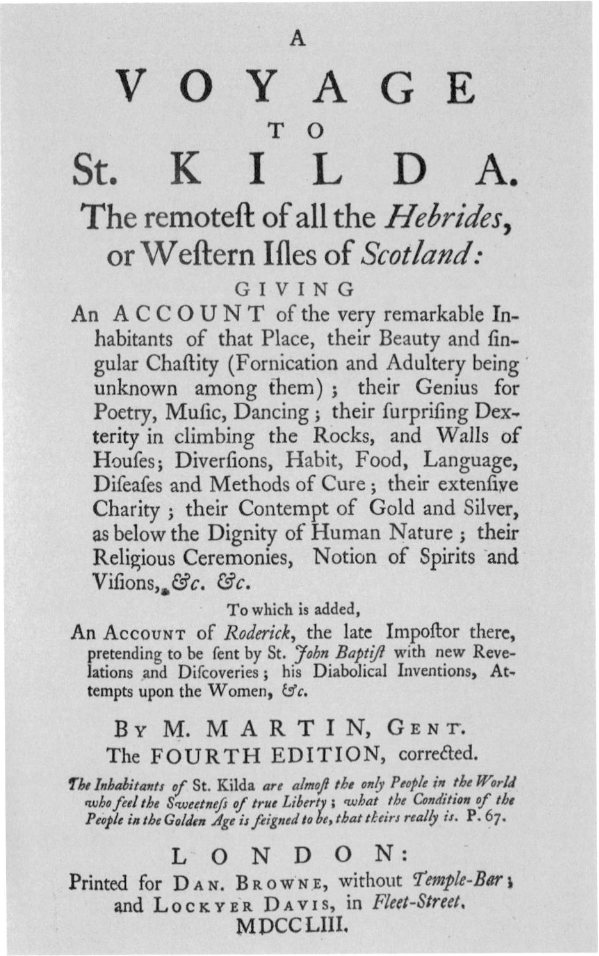

FIG 243.
Martin Martin's
account of his visit to
St Kilda in 1697, one
of the earliest written
accounts of island life.

A

V O Y A G E
T O
St. K I L D A.

The remoteſt of all the *Hebrides,*
or Weſtern Iſles of *Scotland:*

GIVING

An A C C O U N T of the very remarkable In-
habitants of that Place, their Beauty and ſin-
gular Chaſtity (Fornication and Adultery being
unknown among them) ; their Genius for
Poetry, Muſic, Dancing ; their ſurpriſing Dex-
terity in climbing the Rocks, and Walls of
Houſes; Diverſions, Habit, Food, Language,
Diſeaſes and Methods of Cure ; their extenſive
Charity ; their Contempt of Gold and Silver,
as below the Dignity of Human Nature ; their
Religious Ceremonies, Notion of Spirits and
Viſions, *&c. &c.*

To which is added,

An Account of *Roderick,* the late Impoſtor there,
pretending to be ſent by St. *John Baptiſt* with new Reve-
lations and Diſcoveries ; his Diabolical Inventions, Attempts upon the Women, *&c.*

By M. M A R T I N, Gent.

The FOURTH EDITION, correĉted.

The Inhabitants of St. Kilda *are almoſt the only People in the World
who feel the Sweetneſs of true Liberty ; what the Condition of the
People in the Golden Age is feigned to be, that theirs really is.* P. 67.

L O N D O N:

Printed for D a n. B r o w n e, without *Temple-Bar* ;
and L o c k y e r D a v i s, in *Fleet-Street.*
M DCC LIII.

'enchantment, disenchantment and Roman Catholicism collapsed into each
other over the centuries – mutual contradictions going largely unexamined'.

It is easy to romanticise island life. Seemingly the St Kildans shared the
Blasket islanders' view of the inevitability of fate: they shared out the allocation of
fowling and fishing areas by drawing lots, showing they believed in the operation
of forces outside their control. St Kilda was certainly not the Utopia portrayed by
Charles Maclean in his account of the *Island at the Edge of the World* (1972), but
even less was it the victim of a despotic socialism imposed by an externally
imposed hyper-Calvinism, as argued by John Sands (1878). Unfortunately this

FIG 244.
Sketch of John
MacKay, the
minister on St
Kilda, by George
Sands from his
bad-tempered *Out
of the World* (1878).
MacKay had
offended Sands.

oppression is the theme of one of the most widely read books about the island,
Tom Steel's *Life and Death of St Kilda*, but it is not one that has been supported by
much evidence. The religious history of the St Kildans has been analysed in
detail from the island church records by Michael Robson (2005). He concludes
that alleged repression by the island ministers (Robson, 2005: 721–2):

> *is a mistaken one, exaggerating and oversimplifying a situation in which missionary
> teaching ... certainly concentrated upon religious practice and behaviour but did not
> prevent the people from maintaining an undercurrent of traditional and probably*

ancient beliefs ... Later in the twentieth century Donald John Gillies, Donald MacDonald and Donald Ferguson were islanders who, with the encouragement of the missionaries, themselves became churchmen and who in their last years were happy to tell with sincerity about Fearchar and Dugan [shadowy figures of the distant past who allegedly murdered most of the islanders] and about the fairies that used to lurk behind the houses in which they were born.

David Quine (1982) comments simply that 'worship on St Kilda over the years reflected the Christian climate on the mainland.'

ISLANDS AND LITERARY IMAGINATION

Andrew Fleming (2005: 6) argues that Steel's account of St Kilda is really a literary myth, consciously written as a tragedy:

He picks up on two classic tragic themes. The first is the doomed struggle of the hero against his fate, an archetypal idea even older than Aeschylus, who set it at the heart of tragedy. The second features a hero who has the world at his feet, until his flawed character (or a fatal mistake), sweeps him inexorably to his doom (as in Othello, or Michael Henchard, the Mayor of Casterbridge). From an early stage in the narrative, a tragic end is foretold and foreshadowed. In history too, we know the end; particular events may have immediate causes, but for a deeper understanding we have to reach further back in time. The temptation to write history as tragedy is obvious – particularly when the 'end' involves the 'death' of a community. It is a temptation which Steel did not resist; he made use of both tragic themes.

Fleming quotes Steel's epitaph for the population of St Kilda:

There was but one solution ... The attempts of those to stave off evacuation were noble and well-intentioned, but bore the pathos and futility of working against that which must come about. St Kilda was unique. It stood in the Atlantic, the changeless amid the changed. All that could be done was to wait and allow the men and women of the Village Bay the courtesy and privilege of making for themselves the decision that would make Nature's defeat of man a reality. (Steel, 1965: 125–6)

Fleming sums up, 'Whether we take Nature or Fate to have been the ultimate cause of St Kilda's "death", Steel created a striking cosmic drama ... Tragedy is a powerful expression of the human condition, and the tragic themes of *The Life and Death* have helped to create St Kilda's iconic status.' None of this, of course, belittles the real perils and problems of life in a place like St Kilda, but it does send warning signals about interpretations written by outsiders, who bring their own attitudes and agendas. This is abundantly clear in the accounts of the holy men who committed themselves to lonely lives on isolated islands. The devotion of such people is not in doubt. What is much less certain are the facts behind the legends. For example, St Columba (521–97) was undoubtedly an important figure in history, establishing monastic communities on Oronsay and Iona, and he was a powerful evangelist to the Picts, but our understanding of him is coloured by a hagiographical and highly imaginative *Book of the Miracles of Columba*, which appeared decades after his death, followed a generation later by a classical *Vita*, including an account of Columba quelling the Loch Ness Monster (Bradley, 1999). We are properly sceptical about such accounts and tend to discount them without seeking any underlying truth, yet we uncritically accept interpretations of such as that of Tom Steel.

The truth is that islands are a rich brew for imagination. Agatha Christie exploited the effects of isolation in book after book. Richard Grove (1995: 33) describes islands as offering a contradictory set of opportunities, 'the social opportunity for redemption and newness as well as an encapsulation of problems posed by the need for physical and mental survival and health.' He develops this by examining the thoughts behind Shakespeare's *Tempest*. For Grove, while the use of an island as a dramatic context may have suggested itself to Shakespeare by a particular shipwreck in the Bermudas,

> *Italian influences, above all from Dante, may have influenced him. Thus the location of* The Tempest *provides the setting for a bewildering variety of speculation about the Edenic qualities of the island and the potential it offered for erecting an alternative Utopian society on the one hand and for starkly encountering the difficulties of sheer animal survival on the other. Reluctant simply to pour scorn on the idea of Utopia, Shakespeare seems to have chosen to highlight the contradictions between the two opposed concepts of the island as an Eden or Utopia and the island as the meeting place between indigenous inhabitant and European colonist.*

Islands certainly stimulate imagination. Does the glamour and other-worldness of islands affect our critical judgment? Is the suspension of critical reason a symptom of the disease of islomania (page 1)? Compton Mackenzie (author of *Whisky Galore* and *Rockets Galore*) was a self-professed islomaniac. He settled on Capri after service in the First World War. Forced by lack of money to leave, in 1920 he leased Herm (on which he based *Fairy Gold*). Farming losses forced him to move on to Jethou in 1923. Then in 1925 he bought the Shiants (marrying, in succession, two daughters of the tenant farmer); the Shiants were the setting for his *North Wind of Love*. In 1926 D. H. Lawrence, who knew Mackenzie in his Italian days, wrote a story, 'The man who loved islands', about a man who moved to ever smaller islands in an attempt to fill them with his personality. This enraged Mackenzie, who persuaded Lawrence's publisher to omit it from the collected edition of Lawrence's stories, although this censoring did not last long. Mackenzie's final island was Barra, where he lived for many years from 1928, and where he is buried.

Mackenzie worked out his pique by attacking the Scottish journalist Alasdair Alpin MacGregor, who had written extensively about the Hebrides ('with Patience Strong platitudes and effortless weaving of the MacTrite': Cooper, 1985: 9), parodying MacGregor's purple prose in words put into the mouth of his fictional character Hamish Hamilton Mackay (who appears in a number of Mackenzie's novels, including *The Monarch of the Glen* and *Hunting the Fairies*). MacGregor in turn vented his frustration in *The Western Isles* (1949) by vilifying the inhabitants of the Hebrides as depraved, lazy, dirty, immoral, feckless,

FIG 245. Terminal building at the airstrip on the Orkney island of Eday. It is built on a croft called London and is known locally as the fourth London airport. A short distance north is the shortest scheduled air journey in the world – from Westray to Papa Westray (2 minutes, or 1 minute 40 seconds with a following wind). (Andrew Berry)

greedy and drunken. The natives of Lewis were not pleased. They retorted that a self-professed atheist, vegetarian, anti-vivisectionist and teetotaller was not the best qualified to write about Hebrideans.

Some years earlier, MacGregor had travelled as correspondent of *The Times* on the ship which in 1930 evacuated the population of St Kilda, and produced a somewhat tedious account of the event, *A Last Voyage to St Kilda*. In 1937, Michael Powell made a film, *The Edge of the World*, based on life on the island (it was shot on Foula, because the owner of St Kilda refused permission to film there. The story of the film is well told by Powell in a book, *20,000 Feet on Foula*, 1938). MacGregor sued Powell for breach of copyright. He lost.

REAL ISLANDS AND REAL NATURE

Not all island stories and interpretations are embroidered and moulded into shape by myths like these – although one must not forget the tragicomedies of John Heslop Harrison (page 174) and Colonel Meinertzhagen (page 245). Most of those who have reported on our islands have been faithful rapporteurs. Whilst it is true that islands are excellent vehicles for fiction – like Shakespeare's *Tempest* or Aldous Huxley's *Island* or William Golding's *Lord of the Flies* – there is no reason why magic cannot inform and excite reason. Russell King (1993: 13) expounds this:

> An island is a most enticing form of land. Symbol of the eternal contest between land and water, islands are detached, self-contained entities whose boundaries are obvious; all other land divisions are more or less arbitrary. For those of artistic or poetic inclination, islands suggest mystery and adventure; they inspire and exalt. On an island, material values lose their despotic influence; one comes more directly into touch with the elemental – water, · land, fire, vegetation, and wildlife. Although each island naturally has its own personality, the unity of islands undoubtedly wields an influence over the character of the people who live upon them; life there promotes self-reliance, contentment, a sense of human scale.

Morton Boyd (1999: 236, 238) described the transfer of two islands owned by John Lorne Campbell to the National Trust for Scotland:

> I saw Canna and Sanday as an incredible gift: diverse islands of storm and tranquillity set in a fertile sea … I did not value the islands commercially as a Hebridean farm with crofts. I valued them for their spiritual and material benefits to islanders and visitors alike in the quest for health, peace and recreation. Agriculture, fishing and tree-planting ceased to be ends in themselves, but were means of contributing to the

sustainability of community life and a diverse environment ... My ethos rested on my
belief in the integrity of creation. It espoused conservation and shunned exploitation ...
I see human beings as part of the wholeness and integrity of the natural world, a credo
which through the ages has been against the will of people who place themselves above
nature and, in so doing, are collectively destructive of the world on a colossal scale.
[But] Man's quantum leap from the shadowy self-interest of today to the sunlit
selflessness of tomorrow is unlikely without the help of the Holy Spirit, which in the
beginning, 'was moving over the face of the waters'.

Boyd was born in Ayrshire of a line of stonemasons. He came to his life-long love
and work for the natural world as a reaction against industrial spoliation, and rose
to be a senior scientist and administrator in the Nature Conservancy. He wrote
widely on the Hebrides and had a house on Tiree. But he was an outsider, and as
such he might be accused of starry-eyed idealism and, no less than Tom Steel, of
putting his own spin on the facts. So let the last word be with a true islander.

Robert Rendall was born in Glasgow in 1898 of Orkney parents. But from the
age of seven, he lived in Orkney, working all his adult life in a draper's shop in
Kirkwall. He died in 1967 (Dickson, 1990). He was inspired and encouraged by a
local schoolmaster, Magnus Spence (author of the definitive, at the time, *Flora
Orcadensis*) and became a member of the local antiquarian society, where he
mixed with a range of native scholars. Rendall's particular interest was in littoral
biology, and he contributed regularly to the *Journal of Conchology*, culminating
with a major paper, 'Mollusca orcadensia', published in the *Proceedings of the
Royal Society of Edinburgh* (Rendall, 1956). He published two books of theology and
four books of poetry. In the first of his poetry collections is a poem 'Orkney
crofter', which reflects island living at its best:

Scant are the few green acres that I till,
But arched above them spreads the boundless sky,
Ripening their crops; and round them lie
Long miles of moorland hill.
Beyond the cliff-top glimmers in the sun
The far horizon's bright infinity;
And I can gaze across the sea
When my day's work is done.
The solitudes of land and sea assuage
My quenchless thirst for freedom unconfined;
With independent heart and mind
Hold I my heritage.

FIG 246. Island end: a lonely shag. (Andrew Berry)

References and Further Reading

CHAPTER 1

Earliest travellers: Bradley, 1999; Bray, 1986; Cunliffe, 2001; Marsden, 1995; Severin, 1978.
Maps: Babcock, 1922; Gauld, 1989; Owen & Pilbeam, 1992; Ramsay, 1972; Smith, 1982; Stommel, 1984.
Island lists and descriptions: Durman, 1976; Haswell-Smith, 1996; Krauskopf, 2001; McCormick, 1974a, 1974b, 1974c; Murray, 1973; Nicholson, 1995; Ritsema, 1999; Walsh, 2004.
General accounts of islands: Booth & Perrott, 1981; Higgins, 1971; Molony, 1951; Newton, 1992; Shea, 1981; Somerville, 1990; Svensson, 1955; Thomas, 1968, 1983; Williams, 1965.
General island biology: Baldacchino, 2007; Carlquist, 1965, 1974; Elton, 1958; Löve & Löve, 1963; Mueller-Dombois et al., 1981; Quammen, 1996; Southwood & Clarke, 1999; Thornton, 2007; Whittaker, 1998; Williamson, 1981.

CHAPTER 2

Baxter, 2003; Briffa & Atkinson, 1997; Craig, 1983; Cruzan & Templeton, 2000; Davis & Shaw, 2001; Davison et al., 2001; Gillen, 2003; Hewitt, 1999, 2000, 2004; Jones & Keen, 1993; Mascheretti et al., 2003; Mitchell & Ryan, 2001; Morrison, 1980; Nicolson, 1959; Preece, 1995;

Sinclair et al., 1999; Sissons, 1967; Steers, 1953, 1973; Stewart & Lister, 2001; Stringer, 2006; Stuart, 1974; Thomas, 1985; Toghill, 2000; Upton, 2004; West, 1968; Williamson, 1981; Wingfield, 1995.

CHAPTER 3

Island climates: Crawford, 2000, 2008; Conrad, 1946; Cordero Rivera et al., 2005; Vincent, 1990.
Adjustments to island life: Angerbjörn, 1986; Barrett, 1998; Berry, 1977, 1984; Carlquist, 1965, 1974; Clay, 2003; Cody & Overton, 1996; Elton, 1958; Fraser Darling, 1940; Grant, 1998b. Hengeveld, 1989; Kay & John, 1997; Lister, 1995; Royle, 2001; Whittaker, 1998; Williamson, 1981, 1984.
Introduced species: Arnold, 1993; Baskin, 2002; Bester et al., 2002; Brooke, 1990; Brooke et al., 2002; Burdick, 2005; Diamond, 2005; Fosberg, 1963; Gaskell, 2000; Genovesi, 2005; Holdgate, 1967; Jackson, 2001; Jackson & Green, 2000; Jones et al., 2003; Nordström et al., 2003; Sax et al., 2007; Southwood & Kennedy, 1983; Veitch & Clout, 2002.
Ascension: Ashmole & Ashmole, 2000.
Easter Island: Bahn & Flenley, 1992; Diamond, 2005; Hunt, 2007.

Gruinard: Stirling, 1986.
Monachs: Perring & Randall, 1972.
North Rona: Fraser Darling, 1940; Robson, 1991; Stewart, 1933.

CHAPTER 4

Turnover: Hawkesworth, 1974, 2001; Lack, 1942a, 1942b, 1969a, 1969b; Lawton & Brown, 1986; Manne et al., 1998; Myers & Giller, 1988; O'Connor, 1986; Reed, 1980, 1981; Reed et al., 1983; Reynolds & Short, 2003; Southwood, 1988; Williamson, 1981, 1983.
Stocktaking: Alford, 1975; Collins, 1999; Corbet & Harris, 1991; Dennis & Shreeve, 1996; Doyle & Foss, 1986; Fox et al., 2006; Hammond, 1983; Hirons, 1994; Lack, 1942a, 1943; Lysaght, 1998; Marshall & Haes, 1988; Merritt et al., 1996; Pimm et al., 1988; Praeger, 1907, 1915, 1923; Preston & Hill, 1997; Preston et al., 2002; Ragge, 1963; Simberloff, 1983; Smith & Smith, 1983, Thorpe, 1974.
Introductions vs. relics: Ashmole, 1979; Beirne, 1952; Coope, 1986; Corbet, 1961; Dinnin, 1996; Ford, 1955a; Fridriksson, 1975; Gaston et al., 2003; Heslop Harrison, 1956; Matthews, 1955; Tallantire & Walters, 1947; Thornton, 1996; Winchester, 2003; Yalden, 1981.

CHAPTER 5

Beirne, 1952; Brown & Kodric-Brown, 1977; Browne, 1983; Diamond, 1975; Darlington, 1957; Endler, 1986; Forbes, 1846; Gleason, 1922; Gibbons et al., 1993; Grant, 1998a; Haila, 1990; Harris, 1984a; Hayden et al., 2006; Imbrie & Imbrie, 1979; Jermy & Crabbe, 1978; Johnson & Simberloff, 1974; Lovejoy, 2000; MacArthur & Wilson, 1963, 1967; Matthews, 1955; Myers & Giller, 1988; Perring & Walters, 1962; Preston & Hill, 1997; Primack, 1993; Ritchie, 1930; Quammen, 1996; Sharrock, 1972; Simberloff, 1969, 1976; Simberloff & Abele, 1982; Simberloff & Wilson, 1969, 1970; Vincent, 1990; Wallace, 1880; Walters, 1978; Weiner,

1994; Whittaker, 1998; Williamson, 1981, 1984.
Founder genetics: Baker & Stebbins, 1965; Berry, 1977, 1989, 1997, 2003, 2004; Brakefield, 1991; Bryant et al., 1990; Clegg et al., 2002; Frankham, 1997; Gage et al., 2006; Grant, 2001; Halkka & Halkka, 1974; Halkka et al., 1975; Hewitt, 2000; Kaneshiro, 1995; McIntosh, 1998; Mayr, 1954; Provine, 1989; Simberloff, 1980; Soulé, 1983, 1987; Tomkins & Brown, 2004; Williamson, 1981.

CHAPTER 6

Allen, 1984; Barrrett-Hamilton & Hinton, 1910–21; Berry, 1977, 1978, 1996, 2004; Berry & Rose, 1975; Berry et al., 1978, 1987; Davis, 1983; Godwin, 1975; Gonzalez et al., 2000; Halkka et al., 1975; Huxley, 1942; Matthews, 1952; Michaux et al., 2003; Noble & Jones, 1996; Stuart, 1974; Telfer et al., 2003; Williamson, 1981.

CHAPTER 7

St Kilda: Berry & Tricker, 1967; Berry et al., 1992; Buchan et al., 1936; Buchanan, 1995; Clutton-Brock & Pemberton, 2004; Fisher & Vevers, 1943; Fleming, 2005; Harman, 1997; Jewell et al., 1974; St Kilda, 2003; Quine, 1995; Williamson, 1958; Williamson & Boyd, 1960.
Rum and the Small Isles: Campbell, 1984; Clutton-Brock & Ball, 1987; Clutton-Brock et al., 1982; Eggeling, 1964; Heslop Harrison, 1948; Love, 1983, 2001; Lowe, 1969; Magnusson, 1997; Pemberton et al., 1998; Sabbagh, 1999.
Lepidopteran melanism: Kettlewell, 1973; Majerus, 1998, 2002; Tutt, 1899; White, 1876.
Meadow browns: Brakefield, 1984; Clarke, 1995; Ford, 1975;
North Ronaldsay, Lundy, etc.: Compton et al., 2002; Harberd, 1972; Hutchinson, 1990; Mackenzie, 1957.

CHAPTER 8

Early settlers: Berry & Firth, 1986; Bradley, 1999; Brøgger, 1929; Coles, 1998; Crawford, 1987; Edwards & Ralston, 1997; Fleming, 1999; Hedges, 1984; Hunter, 1999; Jee, 1982; Jones *et al.*, 1990; Lacaille,1954; Low, 1996; Mitchell & Ryan, 1997; Muir, 1885; Pollard & Morrison, 1996; Rainbird, 2007; Scourse, 1986; Thomson, 2001; Whittle *et al.*, 1986; Wickham-Jones, 1994.
Fowling: Beatty, 1992; Islands Book Trust, 2005; Serjeantson, 1988.
Kelp and other livelihoods: Devine, 1994; Forsythe, 2006; Hutchinson, 2003; Macartney, 1984; Over, 1987; Smith, 1984; Thomson, 1983; Withrington, 1983.
Population: Fleming, 2001, 2005; Forsythe, 1982; Hewitson, 1996; Hunter, 1999; Richards, 2002; Stagles & Stagles, 1980; Thomson, 2001.

CHAPTER 9

Faroe: Bengtson & Bloch, 1983; Enckell, 1988; Enckell *et al.*, 1987; Jackson, 1991; Jensen *et al.*, 1928–70; Jóhansen, 1985; Rasmussen, 1952; Rutherford, 1982; Taylor & Reid, 2001; Williamson, 1948.
Shetland: Ashmole, 1979; Fenton, 1978; Goodier, 1974; Jóhansen, 1985; Johnston, 1998; Mykura, 1976; Nature Conservancy Council, 1976; Pennington *et al.*, 2004; Scott & Palmer, 1987; Senior & Swan, 1972; Spence, 1979; Thom, 1986; Tulloch, 1978; Tulloch & Hunter, 1972; Turner, 1998; Venables & Venables, 1955; Wainwright, 1962.
Fair Isle: Clarke, 1912; Dymond, 1991; Hunter, 1996; Thom, 1986, 1989; Williamson, 1965.
Orkney: Berry, 2000; Booth & Booth, 1998; Booth *et al.*, 1984; Bullard, 1995; Charter, 1995; Fenton, 1978; Goodier, 1975; Hall, 1996; Keatinge & Dickson, 1979; Lorimer, 1983, 1998; Meek, 1995; Miller, 1849; Mykura, 1976; Nature Conservancy Council, 1978; Saxon, 1991; Senior & Swan, 1972; Thom, 1986; Wainwright, 1962; Young, 1992.

CHAPTER 10

Outer Hebrides: Angus, 1997, 2001; Atkinson, 1949, 1980; Baxter & Usher, 1994; Boyd, 1979, 1986; Boyd & Boyd, 1990; Branigan & Foster, 2002; Cadbury, 1980; Ford, 1955b; Fraser Darling, 1947 [Fraser Darling & Boyd, 1964]; Gilbertson *et al.*, 1996; Gordon, 1926; Grimble, 1985; Harris, 1984b ; Haswell-Smith, 1996; Love, n.d.; Murray, 1966, 1973; MacDiarmid, 1939; Nature Conservancy Council, 1977; Nicolson, 2001; O'Dell & Walton, 1962; Pankhurst & Mullen, 1991; Robson, 2005; Thom, 1986; Thompson, 1968, 1974; Williamson & Boyd, 1963.
Rockall: Fisher, 1956.
North Rona and Sula Sgeir: Atkinson, 1949; Beatty, 1992; Fraser Darling, 1939; Haswell-Smith, 1996; Robson, 1991; Stewart, 1933; Thompson, 1970.
St Kilda: Atkinson, 1949; Buchanan, 1995; Fleming, 2005; Harman, 1997; Haswell-Smith, 1996; Maclean, 1972; Quine, 1982, 1995; Thompson, 1970; Williamson & Boyd, 1960 (*See also* the references at the end of Chapter 7).
Inner Hebrides: Atkinson, 1949; Banks, 1977; Birks, 1973; Boyd, 1983; Brooke, 1990; Campbell, 1984; Fraser Darling, 1940; Haswell-Smith, 1996; Jermy & Crabbe, 1978; Love, 2001; MacCulloch, 1819; Magnusson, 1997; Macnab, 1987; Mercer, 1974; Newton, 1988, 1990; O'Dell & Walton, 1962; Pearman & Preston, 2000; Youngson, 2001.

CHAPTER 11

Clyde Islands: Allen *et al.*, 1986; Baxter, 2003; Carmichael, 1974; Church & Smith, 2000; Lawson, 1888; Rhead & Snow, 1994; Thom, 1986.
Man: Allen, 1962, 1984; Brooke, 1990; Cullen & Jennings, 1986; Davey, 1978; Durman, 1976; Freeman *et al.*, 1966; Garrad, 1972; Gonzalez *et al.*, 2000; Marshall, 1978; Pickett, 2001; Robinson & McCarroll, 1990; Wade-Martins, 1990.

Walney: Dean, 1990; Kruuk, 2003.
Hilbre: Craggs, 1982
Anglesey: Arnold, 1989; Green, 2002; Hope Jones & Whalley, 2004; Jones, 1990; Lacey & Morgan, 1989; Rhind *et al.*, 1997.
Bardsey: Durman, 1976; Hope Jones, 1988; Rhind *et al.*, 1997.
Pembrokeshire Islands: Berry, 1978; Brooke, 1990; Buxton & Lockley, 1950; Durman, 1976; Goodman & Gillham, 1954; Green, 2002; Harris, 1984b; Howells, 1961, 1968, 1984; Lockley, 1930, 1934, 1941, 1942, 1947, 1953, 1969, 1996; Matthews, 2007; Rhind *et al.*, 1997; Saunders, 1986.
Lundy: Holbrook, 2002; Irving *et al.*, 1997; Langham & Langham, 1970.
Steepholm & Flatholm: Kenneth Allsop Memorial Trust & Fowles, 1978; Parsons, 1996.

CHAPTER 12

Akeroyd, 1996; Beattie, 1992; Cabot, 1999; Clark, 1993; Davies & Stephens, 1978; Dornan, 2000; Edwards & Warren, 1985; Fairley, 1975, 1992, 2001; Hayden & Harrington, 2000; Hayden *et al.*, 2006; Horn *et al.*, 1990; Hutchinson, 1989; Jameson, 1898; Jeffrey *et al.*, 1977; Kitching & Ebling, 1967; Lavelle, 1977; McNally, 1978; Mason, 1937; Merne & Madden, 1999; Mitchell, 1989; Mitchell & Ryan, 1997; Myers *et al.*, 1991; Norton, 2001; Ó Péicín & Nolan, 1997; Pilcher & Hall, 2001; Praeger, 1911–15, 1934, 1950; Ritsema, 1999; Roche & Merne, 1977; Royle, 1983; Ryan *et al.*, 1984; Sharrock, 1972; Sleeman *et al.*, 1986; Somerville-Large, 2000; Stagles & Stagles, 1980; Stuart & van Wijngaarden-Bakker, 1985; Waddell *et al.*, 1994.

CHAPTER 13

Isles of Scilly: Coulcher, 1999; Delany & Healey, 1966; Gibson & Murrish, n.d; Inglis-Jones, 1969; Isles of Scilly Bird Group, 2001; Llewellyn, 2005; Lousley, 1971; Over, 1987;

Parslow, 2007; Robinson, 2003; Robinson, 2007; Scourse, 1986; Spalding & Sargent, 2000; Thomas, 1985; Vyvyan, 1953.
Isle of Wight: Best Foot Forward, 2000; Brewis *et al.*, 1996; Chambers *et al.*, 2000; English Nature, 1998; Frazer, 1990; Morey, 1909.
Channel Islands: Bichard & McClintock, 1975; Day, 2004; Delany & Healey, 1966; Freeman, 1980; Jee, 1967, 1982; Jones *et al.*, 1990; Keen, 1993; Le Sueur, 1976; McClintock, 1975; Renouf & Urry, 1976; Rodwell, 1996; Veron, 1997.

CHAPTER 14

Southeast England: Beardall *et al.*, 1991; Boorman & Ranwell, 1977; Cadbury & Partridge, 2002; Corke, 1984; Gibson, 2000; Grieve, 1959; Harrison & Grant, 1976; Steers, 1934.
Coquet, Farnes and Holy Isle: Boyd, 2002; Kerr, 1992; Lunn, 2004; Morrison & Rylance, 1989; Perry, 1946; Tinbergen, 1953, 1958; Watt, 1951.
Forth Islands: Eggeling, 1960; Harris, 1984b; M'Crie *et al.*, 1848; Morris, 2003a, 2003b; Morris & Bruce, 2007; Nelson, 1986.
Bell Rock: Campbell, 1904; Nicholson, 1995.

CHAPTER 15

Allen, 1976; Arber, 1951; Barber, 1990; Barry, 1805; Berry, in press; Boyd, 1986, 1999; Bradley, 1999; Bray, 1986; Campbell, 1904; Cooper, 1979; Cuthbert, 1995; Desmond, 1999; Edmondston, 1809; Edmondston, 1843; Eggeling, 1960; Flinn, 1989; Ford, 1937; Fraser Darling, 1937, 1939, 1940, 1944, 1955, 1970; Grieve, 1959; Henderson & Dickson, 1994; Inglis-Jones, 1969; Irving *et al.*, 1997; Jee, 1982; Johnston, 2007; Jones *et al.*, 1990; Le Sueur, 1976; Llewellyn, 2005; Lockley, 1947, 1969; Lousley, 1971; Lysaght, 1974; M'Crie *et al.*, 1848; MacGillivray, 1830; Mabey, 1986; Mackenzie, 1924; Marren, 1995; Martin, 1698, 1703; Merrifield, 1894; Mitchison, 1962; Monro, 1774; Morey, 1909; Nelson, 1986; Quine, 2001;

Ralph, 1993, 1996; Rixson, 2004; Robinson, 2003; St John, 1893; Saxby, 1874; Sibbald, 1684; Steers, 1934; Thomas, 1985; Tudor, 1883; Tutt, 1899; Watt, 1951; White, 1876.

CHAPTER 16

Boyd, 1999; Cooper, 1985; Diamond, 2005; Dickson, 1990; Fleming, 2001, 2005; Grove, 1995; King, 1993; MacGregor, 1949; Maclean, 1972; Mayr, 1967; Quine, 1982; Rendall, 1956; Robson, 2005; Sands, 1878; Steel, 1965; White, 1967; Williamson & Boyd, 1963.

Bibliography

Adler, G. H. & Levins, R. (1994). The island syndrome in rodent populations. *Quarterly Review of Biology* **69**, 473–90.

Akeroyd, J. (Ed) (1996). *The Wild Plants of Sherkin, Cape Clear and Adjacent Islands of West Cork*. Sherkin Island Marine Station, Sherkin Island.

Alford, D. V. (1975). *Bumblebees*. Davis-Poynter, London.

Allen, D. E. (1962). Our knowledge of the Manx fauna and flora in 1961: a statistical summary. *Peregine* **3**, 93–5.

Allen, D. E. (1976). *The Naturalist in Britain*. Allen Lane, London.

Allen, D. E. (1984). *Flora of the Isle of Man*. Manx Museum, Douglas.

Allen, J. A., Barnett, P. R. O., Boyd, J. M., Kirkwood, R. C., Mackay, D. W. & Smyth, J. C. (Eds) (1986). The environment and the estuary of the Firth of Clyde. *Proceedings of the Royal Society of Edinburgh* **90B**.

Angerbjörn, A. (1986). Gigantism in populations of wood mice (*Apodemus*) in Europe. *Oikos* **47**, 47–56.

Angus, S. (1997). *The Outer Hebrides: the Shaping of the Islands*. White Horse Press, Cambridge.

Angus, S. (2001). *The Outer Hebrides: Moor and Machair*. White Horse Press, Cambridge.

Arber, A. (1951). Prof. F.W. Oliver, F.R.S. *Nature* **168**, 809.

Arnold, H. R. (1993). *Atlas of Mammals in Britain*. HMSO, London.

Arnold, R. N. (1989). Offshore islands and islets. In: *The Nature of North Wales* (Ed. Lacey, W. S. & Morgan, M. J.). Barracuda, Buckingham, pp.45–54.

Ashmole, N. P. (1979). The spider fauna of Shetland and its zoogeographic context. *Proceedings of the Royal Society of Edinburgh* **78B**, 63–122.

Ashmole, N. P. & Ashmole, M. (2000). *St Helena and Ascension Island: a Natural History*. Anthony Nelson, Oswestry.

Atkinson, R. (1949). *Island Going*. Collins, London.

Atkinson, R. (1980). *Shillay and the Seals*. Collins, London.

Babcock, W. H. (1922). *Legendary Islands of the Atlantic*. University Press of the Pacific, Honolulu.

Bahn, P. & Flenley, J. (1992). *Easter Island, Earth Island*. Thames & Hudson, London.

Baker, H. G. & Stebbins, G. L. (1965). *The Genetics of Colonizing Species*. Academic Press, New York.

Baldacchino, G. (Ed) (2007). *A World of Islands*. Agenda Academic, Luqa, Malta.

Banks, N. (1977). *Six Inner Hebrides*. David & Charles, Newton Abbot.

Barber, L. (1980). *The Heyday of Natural History*. Jonathan Cape, London.

Barber, L. (1990). *The Heyday of Natural History*. Jonathan Cape, London.

Barrett, S. C. H. (1998). *The reproductive biology and genetics of island plants*. In: *Evolution on Islands* (Ed. Grant, P. R.). Oxford University Press, Oxford, pp.18–34.

Barrett-Hamilton, G. E. H. (1899). On the species of *Mus* inhabiting St Kilda. *Proceedings of the Zoological Society of London for 1899*: 77–88.

Barrett-Hamilton, G. E. H. & Hinton, M. A. C. (1910–21). *History of British Mammals*. Gurney & Jackson, London.

Barry, G. (1805). *History of the Orkney Islands*. Constable, Edinburgh.

Barton, N. (1989). *Founder effect speciation*. In: *Speciation and its Consequences* (Ed. Otte, D. & Endler, J. A.). Sinauer, Sunderland, MA, pp.229–56.

Barton, N. H. (1996). Natural selection and random drift as causes of evolution on islands. *Philosophical Transactions of the Royal Society of London B* **351**, 785–95.

Baskin, Y. (2002). *A Plague of Rats and Rubbervines: the Growing Threat of Species Invasions*. Island Books, Washington DC.

Baxter, C. & Crumley, J. (1988). *St Kilda: a Portrait of Britain's Remotest Island Landscape*. Colin Baxter Photography, Lamington.

Baxter, J. M. & Usher, M. B. (Eds) (1994). *The Islands of Scotland: a Living Marine Heritage*. HMSO, London.

Baxter, S. (2003). *Revolutions in the Earth: James Hutton and the True Age of the World*. Weidenfeld & Nicolson, London.

Beardall, C. H., Dryden, R. C. & Holzer, T. J. (1991). *The Suffolk Estuaries*. Segment, Colchester.

Beattie, S. (1992). *The Book of Inistrahull*. Lighthouse Publications, Culdaff.

Beatty, J. (1992). *Sula: the Seabird-Hunters of Lewis*. Michael Joseph, London.

Beer, G. (1990). *The island and the aeroplane: the case of Virginia Woolf*. In: *Nation and Narration* (Ed. Bhabha, H.). Routledge, London, pp.265–90.

Beirne, B. P. (1952). *The Origin and History of the British Fauna*. Methuen, London.

Bengtson, S.-A. & Bloch, D. (1983). Island land bird population densities in relation to island size and habitat quality on the Faroe Islands. *Oikos* **41**, 507–22.

Bengtson, S.-A., Eliasen, K., Jacobsen, L. M. & Magnussen, E. (2004). A history of colonization and current status of the house sparrow (*Passer domesticus*) in the Faroe Islands. *Fróðskaparrit* **51**, 237–51.

Benton, T. (2006). *Bumblebees*. New Naturalist 98. Collins, London.

Berry, R. J. (1969). History in the evolution of *Apodemus sylvaticus* (Mammalia) at one edge of its range. *Journal of Zoology* **159**, 311–28.

Berry, R. J. (1977). *Inheritance and Natural History*. New Naturalist 61. Collins, London.

Berry, R. J. (1978). Genetic variation in wild house mice: where natural selection and history meet. *American Scientist* **66**, 52–60.

Berry, R. J. (Ed) (1984). *Evolution in the Galapagos Islands*. Academic Press, London.

Berry, R. J. (1989). Ecology: where genes and geography meet. *Journal of Animal Ecology* **58**, 733–59.

Berry, R. J. (1996). Small mammal differentiation on islands. *Philosophical Transactions of the Royal Society of London B* **351**, 753–64.

Berry, R. J. (1997). *The history and importance of conservation genetics: one person's perspective*. In: *The Role of Genetics in Conserving Small Populations* (Ed. Tew, T. E., Crawford, T. J., Spencer J. et al.). JNCC, Peterborough, pp.26–32.

Berry, R. J. (2000). *Orkney Nature*. Poyser, London.

Berry, R. J. (2003). *God's Book of Works: the Nature and Theology of Nature*. T. & T. Clark, London.

Berry, R. J. (2004). Island differentiation muddied by island biogeographers. *Environmental Archaeology* **9**, 117–21.

Berry, R. J. (in press a). Hooker and islands. *Biological Journal of the Linnean Society*.

Berry, R. J. (in press b). Joseph Hooker: one of Charles Darwin's best friends. *Curtis's Botanical Magazine*.

Berry, R. J. & Firth, H. N. (Eds) (1986). *The People of Orkney*. Orkney Press, Kirkwall.

Berry, R. J. & Rose, F. E. N. (1975). Islands and the evolution of *Microtus arvalis* (Microtinae). *Journal of Zoology* **177**, 385–409.

Berry, R. J. & Tricker, B. J. K. (1967). Competition and extinction: the mice of Foula, with notes on those of Fair Isle and St Kilda. *Journal of Zoology* **158**, 247–65.

Berry, R. J., Jakobson, M. E. & Peters, J. (1978). The house mouse of the Faroe Islands: a study of micro-differentiaion. *Journal of Zoology* **185**, 73–92.

Berry, R. J., Jakobson, M. E. & Peters, J. (1987). Inherited differences within an island population of the house mouse. *Journal of Zoology* **211**, 605–18.

Berry, R. J., Berry, A. J., Anderson, T. J. C. & Scriven, P. (1992). The house mice of Faray, Orkney. *Journal of Zoology* **228**, 233–46.

Best Foot Forward (2000). *Island State: an Ecological Footprint Analysis of the Isle of Wight*. Best Foot Forward, Oxford.

Bester, M. N., Bloomer, J .P., van Aarde, R. J. *et al.* (2002). A review of the successful eradication of feral cats from sub-Antarctic Marion Island, Southern Indian Ocean. *South African Journal of Wildlife Research* **32**, 65–73.

Bichard, J. D. & McClintock, D. (1975). *Wild Flowers of the Channel Islands*. Chatto & Windus, London.

Birks, H. J. B. (1973). *Past and Present Vegetation of the Isle of Skye: a Palaeoecological Study*. Cambridge University Press, Cambridge.

Boorman, L. A. & Ranwell, D. S. (1977). *Ecology of Maplin Sands and the Coastal Zones of Suffolk, Essex and North Kent*. Institute of Terrestrial Ecology, Cambridge.

Booth, C. & Booth, J. (1998). *Status and Checklist of the Vertebrate Fauna of Orkney*. C.& J. Booth, Kirkwall.

Booth, C., Cuthbert, M. & Reynolds, P. (1984). *The Birds of Orkney*. Orkney Press, Stromness.

Booth, D. & Perrott, D. (Eds) (1981). *The Shell Book of the Islands of Britain*. Guideway Windward, London.

Boyd, I. L. (2002). *The measurement of dispersal by land-bassed marine predators: implications for understanding their ecology and management*. In: *Dispersal Ecology* (Ed. Bullock, J. M., Kenwood, R. E. & Hails, R. S.). British Ecological Society Symposium 42. Blackwell, Oxford, pp.72–88.

Boyd, J. M. (Ed) (1979). The natural environment of the Outer Hebrides. *Proceedings of the Royal Society of Edinburgh* **77B**.

Boyd, J. M. (Ed) (1983). The natural environment of the Inner Hebrides. *Proceedings of the Royal Society of Edinburgh* **83B**.

Boyd, J. M. (1986). *Fraser Darling's Islands*. Edinburgh University Press, Edinburgh.

Boyd, J. M. (1999). *The Song of the Sandpiper*. Colin Baxter, Grantown-on-Spey.

Boyd, J. M. & Boyd, I. L. (1990). *The Hebrides*. New Naturalist 76. Collins, London. [Revised and reprinted (1996) in three volumes: *A Natural Tapestry, A Mosaic of Islands, A Habitable Land*. Birlinn, Edinburgh.

Bradley, I. (1999). *Celtic Christianity: Making Myths and Chasing Dreams*. Edinburgh University Press, Edinburgh.

Brakefield, P. M. (1984). *The ecological genetics of quantitative characters of* Maniola jurtina *and other butterflies*. In: *The Biology of Butterflies* (Ed. Vane-Wright, R. I. & Ackery, P. R.). Academic Press, London, pp.167–90.

Brakefield, P. M. (1991). *Genetics and the conservation of invertebrates*. In: *The Scientific Management of Temperate Communities for Conservation* (Ed. Spellerberg, I. F., Goldsmith, F. B. & Morris, M. G.). Blackwell, Oxford, pp.45–79.

Branigan, K. & Foster, P. (2002). *Barra and the Bishop's Isles*. Tempus, Stroud.

Bray, E. (1986). *The Discovery of the Hebrides: Voyagers to the Western Isles 1745–1883*. Collins, London.

Brewis, A., Bowman, P. & Rose, F. (1996). *The Flora of Hampshire*. Harley Books, Colchester.

Briffa, K. & Atkinson, T. (1997). *Reconstructing late-glacial and holocene climates*. In: *Climates of the British Isles: Present, Past and Future*

(Ed. Hulme, M. & Barrow, E.). Routledge, London, pp.84–111.

Bristowe, W. S. (1969). *A Book of Islands.* Bell, London.

Brøgger, A. W. (1929). *Ancient Emigrants.* Clarendon Press, Oxford.

Brooke, M. de L. (1990). *The Manx Shearwater.* Poyser, London.

Brooke, M. de L., Douse, A., Haysom, S., Jones, F. C. & Nicolson, A. (2002). The Atlantic Puffin population of the Shiant Islands, 2000. *Scottish Birds* **23**, 22–6.

Brown, G. M. (1969). *An Orkney Tapestry.* Gollancz, London.

Browne, J. (1983). *The Secular Ark.* Yale University Press, New Haven, CN.

Brown, J. H. & Kodric-Brown, A. (1977). Turn-over rates in island biogeography: effect of immigration or extinction. *Ecology* **58**, 445–9.

Bryant, E. H., Meffert, L. M. & McCommas, S. A. (1990). Fitness rebound in serially bottlenecked populations of the house fly. *American Naturalist* **136**, 542–9.

Buchan, J. N. S., Harrisson, T. H., Lack, D., Moy-Thomas, J. A., Petch, C. P. & Stewart, M. (1936). *St Kilda Papers.* Oxford University Press, Oxford.

Buchanan, M. (Ed) (1995). *St Kilda: the Continuing Story of the Islands.* HMSO, Edinburgh.

Bullard, E. R. (1995). *Wildflowers in Orkney: a New Checklist.* E. R. Bullard, Kirkwall.

Burdick, A. (2005). *Out of Eden: an Odyssey of Ecological Invasion.* Farrar, Srauss & Giroux, New York.

Buxton, J. & Lockley, R. M. (Eds) (1950). *Island of Skomer.* Staples, London.

Cabot, D. (1999). *Ireland.* New Naturalist 84. Collins, London.

Cadbury, C. J. (1980). The status and habitats of the corncrake in Britain 1978–79. *Bird Study* **27**, 203–18.

Cadbury, C. J. & Partridge, J. (2002). Havergate Island NNR, Suffolk. *British Wildlife* **14**, 101–5.

Campbell, J. L. (1984). *Canna: the Story of a Hebridean Island.* Oxford University Press, Oxford.

Campbell, J. M. (1904). *Notes on the Natural History of the Bell Rock.* David Douglas, Edinburgh.

Cappelen, J. & Laursen, E. V. (1998). *The Climate of the Faroe Islands – with Climatological Standard Normals, 1961–1990.* Technical Report 98-14. Danish Meteorological Istitute, Copenhagen.

Carlquist, S. (1965). *Island Life.* Natural History Press, New York.

Carlquist, S. (1974). *Island Biology.* Columbia University Press, New York.

Carmichael, A. (1974). *Kintyre.* David & Charles, Newton Abbot.

Chambers, N., Simmons, C. & Wackernagel, M. (2000). *Sharing Nature's Interest.* Earthscan, London.

Charter, E. (1995). *Farming with Wildlife in Mind.* Orkney Farming and Wildlife Advisory Group, Kirkwall.

Church, T. & Smith, T. (2000). *Arran Flora,* revised edition. Arran Natural History Society, Brodick.

Clark, W. (1993). *The Rathlin Story.* Third edition. Impact, Coleraine.

Clarke, B. C. (1995). Edmund Brisco Ford. *Biographical Memoirs of Fellows of the Royal Society* **41**, 147–68.

Clarke, W. E. (1912). *Studies in Bird Migration.* Oliver & Boyd, Edinburgh.

Clay, K. (2003). Parasites lost. *Nature* **421**, 585–6.

Clegg, S. M., Degnan, S. M., Kikkawa, J., Moritz, C., Estoup, A. & Owens, I. A. P. (2002). Genetic consequences of sequential founder events by an island-colonizing bird. *Proceedings of the National Academy of Sciences of the USA* **99**, 8127–32.

Clutton-Brock, T. & Ball, M. E. (Eds) (1987). *Rhum: the Natural History of an Island.* Edinburgh University Press, Edinburgh.

Clutton-Brock, T. & Pemberton, J. (Eds) (2004). *Soay Sheep: Dynamics and Selection in an Island Population.* Cambridge University Press, Cambridge.

Clutton-Brock, T., Guinness, F. E. & Albon, S. D. (1982). *Red Deer: Behaviour and Ecology of Two Sexes.* Edinburgh University Press, Edinburgh.

Cody, M. L. & Overton, J. McC. (1996). Short-term evolution of reduced dispersal in island plant populations. *Journal of Ecology* **84**, 53–62.

Coles, B. J. (1998). Doggerland: a speculative survey. *Proceedings of the Prehistoric Society* **64**, 45–81.

Collins, T. (1999). The Clare Island Survey of 1909–11: participants, papers and progress. *New Survey of Clare Island. I. History and Cultural Landscape* (Ed. MacCárthaigh, C. & Whelan, K.). Royal Irish Academy, Dublin, pp.1–40.

Compton, S. G., Key, R. S. & Key, R. J. D. (2002). Conserving our little Galapagos: Lundy, Lundy cabbage and its beetles. *British Wildlife* **13**, 184–90.

Conrad, V. (1946). Usual formulas of continentality and their limits. *Transactions of the American Geophysical Union* **27**, 663–4.

Coope, G. R. (1986). The invasion and colonization of the North Atlantic islands: a palaeoecological solution to a biogeographic problem. *Philosophical Transactions of the Royal Society B* **314**, 619–35.

Cooper, D. (1979). *Road to the Isles: Travellers to the Hebrides 1770–1914.* Routledge & Kegan Paul, London.

Cooper, D. (1985). *The Road to Mingulay: a View of the Western Isles.* Routledge & Kegan Paul, London.

Corbet, G. B. (1961). Origin of the British insular races of small mammals and of the 'Lusitanian' fauna. *Nature* **191**, 1037–40.

Corbet, G. B. & Harris, S. (Eds) (1991). *The Handbook of British Mammals*, 3rd edition. Blackwell, Oxford.

Corbet, P. S., Longfield, C. & Moore, N. W. (1960). *Dragonflies.* Collins, London.

Cordero Rivera, A., Lorenzo Caballa, M. O., Utzeri, C. & Vieira, V. (2005). Parthenogenetic *Ischnura hastata* (Say), widespread in the Azores (Zygoptera: Coenagrionidae). *Odonatologica* **34**, 1–9.

Corke, D. A. (1984). *The Nature of Essex.* Barracuda, Buckingham.

Coulcher, P. (1999). *The Sun Islands: a Natural History of the Isles of Scilly.* Book Guild, Lewes.

Craggs, J. (Ed) (1982). *Hilbre: the Cheshire Island.* Liverpool University Press, Liverpool.

Craig, G. Y. (Ed) (1983). *Geology of Scotland.* Scottish Academic Press, Edinburgh.

Cramp, S., Bourne, W. R. P. & Saunders, D. (1974). *The Seabirds of Britain and Ireland.* Collins, London.

Crawford, B. E. (1987). *Scandinavian Scotland.* Leicester University Press, Leicester.

Crawford, R. M. M. (2000). Ecological hazards of oceanic environments. *New Phytologist* **147**, 257–81.

Crawford, R. M. M. (2008). *Plants at the Margin.* Cambridge University Press, Cambridge.

Crookston, P. (Ed) (1981). *Island Britain.* Macdonald, London.

Cruzan, M. B. & Templeton, A. R. (2000). Paleoecology and coalescence: phylogeographic analysis of hypotheses from the fossil record. *Trends in Ecology and Evolution* **15**, 491–6.

Cullen, J. P. & Jennings, P. P. (1986). *Birds of the Isle of Man.* Bridgreen, Douglas.

Cunliffe, B. (2001). *The Extraordinary Voyage of Pytheas the Greek: the Man who Discovered Britain.* Allen Lane, London.

Cuthbert, O. D. (1995). *The Life and Letters of an Orkney Naturalist.* Orkney Press, Kirkwall.

Darlington, P. J. (1957). *Zoogeography.* Wiley, New York.

Davenport, J. L., Sleeman, D. P. & Woodman, P. C. (2008). *Mind the Gap. Postglacial Colonization of Ireland.* Irish Naturalists' Journal, Special Supplement.

Davey, P. (Ed) (1978). Man and environment in the Isle of Man. *British Archaeological Report: British Series* **54**.

Davies, G. L. H. & Stephens, N. (1978). *The Geomorphology of the British Isles: Ireland.* Methuen, London.

Davis, M. B. & Shaw, R. G. (2001). Range shifts and adaptive responses to Quaternary climate change. *Science* **292**, 675–9.

Davis, S. J. M. (1983). Morphometric variation of populations of house mice, *Mus domesticus* in Britain and Faroe. *Journal of Zoology* **199**, 521–34.

Davison, A., Birks, J. D. S., Brookes, R. C., Messenger, J. E. & Griffiths, H. I. (2001). Mitochondrial phylogeography and population history of pine *martens Martes martes* compared with polecats *Mustela putorius*. *Molecular Ecology* **10**, 2479–88.

Day, S. (2004). *Wildlife of the Channel Islands*. Seaflower Books, Bradford-on-Avon.

Dean, T. (1990). *The Natural History of Walney Island*. Faust, Burnley.

Delany, M. J. (1964). Variation in the long-tailed field-mouse (*Apodemus sylvaticus* (L)) in north-west Scotland. I. Comparison of individual characters. *Proceedings of the Royal Society of London B* **161**, 191–9.

Delany, M. J. & Healey, M. J. R. (1966). Variation in the white-toothed shrews (*Crocidura* spp.) in the British Isles. *Proceedings of the Royal Society of London B* **164**, 63–74.

Dennis, R. & Shreeve, T. (1996). *Butterflies on British and Irish Offshore Islands*. Gem, Wallingford.

Desmond, R. (1999). *Sir Joseph Dalton Hooker: Traveller and Plant Collector*. Antique Collectors' Club, Woodbridge.

Devine, T. M. (1994). *Clanship to Crofters' War. The Social Transformation of the Scottish Highlands*. Manchester University Press, Manchester.

Devoy, R. J. N. (1995). Deglaciation, earth crustal behaviour and sea-level changes in the determination of insularity: a perspective from Ireland. *Geological Society Special Publication* **96**, 181–208.

Diamond, J. M. (1975). Assembly of species communities. In: *Ecology and Evolution of Communities* (Ed. Cody, M. L. & Diamond, J. M.). Harvard Univesity Press, Cambridge, MA, pp.324–444.

Diamond, J. M. (2005). *Collapse: How Societies Choose to Fail or Survive*. Allen Lane, London.

Dickson, N. (1990). *An Island Shore: the Life and Work of Robert Rendall*. Orkney Press, Kirkwall.

Dinnin, M. (1996). The development of the Outer Hebridean entomofauna: a fossil perspective. In: *The Outer Hebrides: the Last 40,000 Years* (Ed. Gilbertson, D., Kent, M. & Grattan, J.). Sheffield University Press, Sheffield, pp.163–83.

Dornan, B. (2000). *The Inishkeas*. Four Courts Press, Dublin.

Doyle, G. J. & Foss, P. J. (1986). A resurvey of the Clare Island flora. *Irish Naturalists' Journal* **22**, 85–9.

Drower, G. (2002). *Heligoland*. Sutton, Stroud.

Durman, R. (Ed) (1976). *Bird Observatories in Britain and Ireland*. Poyser, Berkhamsted.

Dymond, J. N. (1991). *The Birds of Fair Isle*. Privately printed, Edinburgh.

Edmondston, A. (1809). *A View of the Ancient and Present State of the Zetland Isles*. James Ballantyne, Edinburgh.

Edmondston, T. (1843). *A Flora of Shetland*. Aberdeen.

Edwards, K. J. & Ralston, I. B. M. (Eds) (1997). *Scotland: Environment and Archaeology, 8000 BC – AD 1000*. Wiley, Chichester.

Edwards, K. J. & Warren, W. P. (Eds) (1985). *The Quaternary History of Ireland*. Academic Press, London.

Eggeling, W. J. (1960). *The Isle of May*. Oliver & Boyd, Edinburgh.

Eggeling, W. J. (1964). A nature reserve management plan for the Isle of Rhum. *Journal of Applied Ecology* **1**, 405–19.

Elton, C. S. (1927). *Animal Ecology*. Sidgwick & Jackson, London.

Elton, C. S. (1958). *The Ecology of Invasions by Animals and Plants*. Methuen, London.

Enckell, P. H. (1988). When, how and whence? *Fródskaparrit* **34**, 50–67.

Enckell, P. H., Bengtson, S.-A. & Wiman, B. (1987). Serf and waif colonization: distribution and dispersal of invertebrate species in Faroe Island settlement areas. *Journal of Biogeography* **14**, 89–104.

Endler, J. A. (1986). *Natural Selection in the Wild*. Princeton University Press, Princeton, NJ.

English Nature (1998). *Isle of Wight: Natural Area Profile*. English Nature, Lyndhurst.

Fairley, J. S. (1975). *An Irish Beast Book.* Blackstaff, Belfast.

Fairley, J. S. (1992). *Irish Wild Mammals: a Guide to the Literature.* James Fairley, Galway.

Fairley, J. S. (2001). *A Basket of Weasels.* Privately printed, Belfast.

Fairnell, E. H. & Barrett, J. H. (2007). Fur-bearing species and Scottish islands. *Journal of Archaeological Science* 34, 463–84.

Fenton, A. (1978). *The Northern Isles: Orkney and Shetland.* John Donald, Edinburgh.

Fisher, J. (1952). *The Fulmar.* Collins, London.

Fisher, J. (1956). *Rockall.* Geoffrey Bles, London.

Fisher, J. & Vevers, H. G. (1943). The breeding distribution, history and population of the North Atlantic Gannet (*Sula bassana*). *Journal of Animal Ecology* 10, 204–72.

Fleming, A. (1999). Human ecology and the early history of St Kilda, Scotland. *Journal of Historical Geography* 25, 183–200.

Fleming, A. (2001). Dangerous islands: fate, faith and cosmology. *Landscapes* 2, 4–21.

Fleming, A. (2005). *St Kilda and the Wider World.* Windgather Press, Macclesfield.

Flinn, D. (1989). *Travellers in a Bygone Shetland.* Scottish Academic Press, Edinburgh.

Flux, J. (1993). Relative effects of cats, myxomatosis, traditional control or competitors in removing rabbits from islands. *New Zealand Journal of Zoology* 20, 13–18.

Flux, J. & Fullagar, P. (1992). World distribution of the rabbit *Oryctolagus cuniculus* on islands. *Mammal Review* 22, 151–205.

Forbes, E. (1846). On the connexion between the distribution of the existing fauna and flora of the British Isles, and the geological changes which have affected their area, especially during the epoch of the northern drift. *Memoirs of the Geological Survey of Great Britain* 1, 336–432.

Ford, E. B. (1937). Problems of heredity in the Lepidoptera. *Biological Reviews* 12, 461–503.

Ford, E. B. (1955a). *Moths.* New Naturalist 30. Collins, London.

Ford, E. B. (1955b). Polymorphism and taxonomy. *Heredity* 9, 255–64.

Ford, E. B. (1975). *Ecological Genetics.* Third edition. Chapman & Hall, London.

Forsythe, D. (1982). *Urban–Rural Migration, Change and Conflict in an Orkney Island Community.* North Sea Oil Panel Occcasional Paper 14. Social Science Research Council, London.

Forsythe, W. (2006). The archaeology of the kelp industry in the northern islands of Ireland. *International Journal of Nautical Archaeology* 35, 218–29.

Fosberg, F. R. (Ed) (1963). *Man's Place in the Island Ecosystem.* Bishop Museum Press, Honolulu.

Foster, J. B. (1964). Evolution of mammals on islands. *Nature* 202, 234–5.

Fox, R., Asher, J., Brereton, T., Roy, D. & Warren, M. (2006). *The State of Butterflies in Brtain and Ireland.* Pisces, Newbury.

Frankham, R. (1997). Do island populations have less genetic variation than mainland populations? *Heredity* 78, 311–27.

Fraser Darling, F. (1937). *A Herd of Red Deer.* Oxford University Press, Oxford.

Fraser Darling, F. (1939). *A Naturalist on Rona.* Clarendon Press, Oxford.

Fraser Darling, F. (1940). *Island Years.* Bell, London.

Fraser Darling, F. (1944). *Island Farm.* Bell, London.

Fraser Darling, F. (1947). *Natural History in the Highlands and Islands.* New Naturalist 6. Collins, London. [Revised in collaboration with J. M. Boyd, 1964.]

Fraser Darling, F. (1955). *West Highland Survey: an Essay in Human Ecology.* Oxford University Press, London.

Fraser Darling, F. (1970). *Wilderness and Plenty: the Reith Lectures for 1969.* BBC, London.

Frazer, O. (1990). *The Natural History of the Isle of Wight.* Dovecote Press, Wimborne.

Freeman, R. B. (1980). *Notes on the Fauna of Alderney.* Alderney Society, Alderney.

Freeman, T. W., Rodgers, H. B. & Kinvig, R. H. (1966). *Lancashire, Cheshire and the Isle of Man.* Nelson, London.

Fridriksson, S. (1975). *Surtsey: Evolution of Life on a Volcanic Island.* Butterworth, London.

Fridriksson, S. (2005). *Surtsey: Ecosystems Formed.* University of Iceland Press, Reykjavik.

Gage, M. J. G., Surridge, A. K., Tomkins, J. L. et al. (2006). Reduced heterozygosity depresses sperm quality in wild rabbits, *Oryctolagus cuniculus*. *Current Biology* 16, 612–17.

Garrad, L. S. (1972). *The Naturalist in the Isle of Man*. David & Charles, Newton Abbot.

Gaskell, J. (2000). *Who Killed the Great Auk?* Oxford University Press, Oxford.

Gaston, K. J., Jones, A. G., Hänel, C. & Chown, S. L. (2003). Rates of species introduction to a remote oceanic island. *Proceedings of the Royal Society of London B* 270, 1091–8.

Gätke, H. (1895). *Heligoland as an Ornithological Observatory*. David Douglas, Edinburgh.

Gauld, W. (1989). In the lee of Rockall. *Northern Studies* 26, 43–55.

Genovesi, P. (2005). Eradication of invasive species in Europe: a review. *Biological Invasions* 7, 127–33.

Gibbons, D. W., Reid, J. B. & Chapman, R. A. (Eds) (1993). *The New Atlas of Breeding Birds in Britain and Ireland: 1988–1991*. Poyser, London.

Gibson, C. (2000). *The Essex Coast: Beyond 2000*. English Nature, Colchester.

Gibson, F. & Murrish, P. (n.d.). *A Precious Heritage*. Isles of Scilly Environmental Trust, St Mary's.

Gilbertson, D., Kent, M. & Grattan, J. (Eds) (1996). *The Outer Hebrides: the Last 14,000 years*. Sheffield University Press, Sheffield.

Gillen, C. (2003). *Geology and Landscapes of Scotland*. Terra, Harpenden.

Gillis, J. R. (2003). *Taking history offshore*. In: *Islands in History and Representation* (Ed. Edmond, R. & Smith, V.). Routledge, London, pp.19–31.

Gleason, H. A. (1922). On the relation between species and area. *Ecology* 3, 158–62.

Godwin, H. (1975). *The History of the British Flora*. Second edition. Cambridge University Press, Cambridge.

Gonzalez, S., Kitchener, A. C. & Lister, A. M. (2000). Survival of the Irish elk into the Holocene. *Nature* 405, 753–4.

Goodier, R. (Ed) (1974). *The Natural Environment of Shetland*. Nature Conservancy Council, Edinburgh.

Goodier, R. (Ed) (1975). *The Natural Environment of Orkney*. Nature Conservancy Council, Edinburgh.

Goodman, G. T. & Gillham, M. E. (1954). Ecology of the Pembrokeshire Islands. II. Skokholm, environment and vegetation. *Journal of Ecology* 42, 296–327.

Gordon, S. (1926). *The Immortal Isles*. Williams & Norgate, London.

Grant, P. R. (Ed) (1998a). *Evolution on Islands*. Oxford University Press, Oxford.

Grant, P. R. (1998b). Patterns on islands and microevolution. In: *Evolution on Islands* (Ed. Grant, P. R.). Oxford University Press, Oxford, pp.1–17.

Grant, P. R. (2001). Reconstructing the evolution of birds on islands: 100 years of research. *Oikos* 92, 385–403.

Green, J. (2002). *Birds in Wales 1992–2000*. Welsh Ornithological Society, Cardigan.

Grieve, H. (1959). *The Great Tide: the Story of the 1953 Flood Disaster in Essex*. Essex County Council, Chelmsford.

Grimble, I. (1985). *Scottish Islands*. BBC, London.

Grove, R. (1995). *Green Imperialism: Colonial Expansion, Tropical Island Edens, and the Origins of Environmentalism*. Cambridge University Press, Cambridge.

Haag, C. R., Riek, M., Hottinger, J. W., Pajunen, V. J. & Ebert, D. (2006). Founder effects as determinants of within-island and among-island genetic structure of *Daphnia* metapopulations. *Heredity* 96, 150–8.

Haila, Y. (1990). Towards an ecological definition of an island: a northwest European perspective. *Journal of Biogeography* 17, 561–8.

Halkka, O. & Halkka, L. (1974). Partial population transfers as a means of estimating the effectiveness of natural selection. *Hereditas* 78, 314–15.

Halkka, O., Halkka, L. & Raatikainen, M. (1975). Transfer of individuals as a means of investigating natural selection in operation. *Hereditas* 80, 27–34.

Hall, A. M. (Ed) (1996). *The Quaternary of Orkney: Field Guide*. Quaternary Research Association, Cambridge.

Hamill, R. M., Doyle, D. & Duke, E. J. (2006). Spatial patterns of genetic diversity across European subspecies of the mountain hare, *Lepus timidus* L. *Heredity* **97**, 355–65.

Hammond, C. O. (1983). *The Dragonflies of Great Britain and Ireland.* Second edition. Harley Books, Colchester.

Harberd, D. J. (1972). A contribution to the cytotaxonomy of *Brassica* (cruciferae) and its allies. *Botanical Journal of the Linnean Society* **65**, 1–23.

Harman, M. (1997). *An Isle Called Hirte.* Maclean Press, Waternish.

Harris, H. (1966). Enzyme polymorphisms in man. *Proceedings of the Royal Society of London B* **164**, 298–310.

Harris, L. D. (1984a). *The Fragmented Forest: Island Biogeography Theory and the Preservation of Biotic Diversity.* Chicago University Press, Chicago.

Harris, M. P. (1984b). *The Puffin.* Poyser, Calton.

Harrison, J. & Grant, P. (1976). *The Thames Transformed.* Andre Deutsch, London.

Harvie-Brown, J. A. & Buckley, T. E. (1888). *Vertebrate Fauna of the Outer Hebrides.* Douglas, Edinburgh.

Haswell-Smith, H. (1996). *The Scottish Islands: a Comprehensive Guide to Every Scottish Island.* Canongate, Edinburgh.

Hawkesworth, D. L. (Ed) (1974). *The Changing Flora and Fauna of Britain.* Academic Press, London.

Hawkesworth, D. L. (Ed) (2001). *The Changing Wildlife of Great Britain and Ireland.* Taylor & Francis, London.

Hayden, T. & Harrington, R. (2000). *Exploring Irish Mammals.* Town House, Dublin.

Hayden, T. J., Murray, D. A. & O'Connor, J. P. (2006). *Fauna and Flora of Atlantic Islands.* Occasional Publication of the Irish Biogeographical Society 9. Irish Biogeographical Society, Dublin.

Hedges, J. W. (1984). *Tomb of the Eagles: a Window on Stone Age Tribal Britain.* John Murray, London.

Henderson, D. M. & Dickson, J. H. (Eds) (1994). *A Naturalist in the Highlands. James Robertson – His Life and Travels in Scotland 1767–1771.* Scottish Academic Press, Edinburgh.

Hengeveld, R. (1989). *Dynamics of Biological Invasions.* Chapman & Hall, London.

Heslop Harrison, J. W. (1948). The passing of the Ice Age and its effect on the plant and animal life of the Scottish Western Isles. *New Naturalist*, 83–90.

Heslop-Harrison, J. W. (1956). On field studies of the plants and animals of the Scottish Western Isles. *Proceedings of the Linnean Society of London* **167**, 103–6.

Hewitson, J. (1996). *Clinging to the Edge: Journals from an Orkney Island.* Mainstream, Edinburgh.

Hewitt, G. M. (1999). Post-glacial recolonization of European biota. *Biological Journal of the Linnean Society* **68**, 87–112.

Hewitt, G. M. (2000). The genetic legacy of the Quaternary ice ages. *Nature* **405**, 907–13.

Hewitt, G. M. (2004). Genetic consequences of climatic oscillations in the Quaternary. *Philosophical Transactions of the Royal Society of London B* **359**, 183–95.

Higgins, L. R. (1971). *A Tangle of Islands.* Robert Hale, London.

Hirons, M. J. D. (1994). The flora of the Farne Islands. *Transactions of the Natural History Society of Northumberland* **57**, 69–114. [Republished in booklet form by the National Trust.]

Holbrook, A. (2002). *Lundy Island: a Bibliography.* University of Bath Press, Bath.

Holdgate, M. W. (1967). The influence of introduced species on the ecosystems of temperate oceanic islands. *Proceedings of the IUCN 10th Technical Meeting (Lucerne, 1966)* **3** (11), 151–76.

Hope Jones, P. J. (1988). *The Natural History of Bardsey.* National Museum of Wales, Cardiff.

Hope Jones, P. J. & Whalley, P. (2004). *Birds of Anglesey.* Mentes Mon, Llangefni.

Horn, W., Marshall, J. W. & Rourke, G. D. (1990). *The Forgotten Hermitage of Skellig Michael.* University of California Press, Berkeley, CA.

Howells, R. (1961). *Cliffs of Freedom*. Gomerian Press, Llandysul.

Howells, R. (1968). *The Sounds Between*. Gomerian Press, Llandysul.

Howells, R. (1984). *Caldey*. Gomer Press, Llandysul.

Hunt, T. L. (2007). Rethinking Easter Island's ecological catastrophe. *Journal of Archaeological Science* **34**, 485–502.

Hunter, J. (1999). *Last of the Free*. Mainstream, Edinburgh.

Hunter, J. R. (1996). *Fair Isle: the Archaeology of an Island Community*. HMSO, Edinburgh.

Hutchinson, C. D. (1989). *Birds in Ireland*. Poyser, Calton.

Hutchinson, R. (1990). *Polly*. Mainstream, Edinburgh.

Hutchinson, R. (2003). *The Soap Man: Lewis, Harris and Lord Leverhulme*. Birlinn, Edinburgh.

Huxley, J. S. (1942). *Evolution: the Modern Synthesis*. George Allen & Unwin, London.

Imbrie, J. & Imbrie, K. P. (1979). *Ice Ages: Solving the Mystery*. Harvard University Press, Cambridge, MA.

Inglis-Jones, E. (1969). *Augustus Smith of Scilly*. Faber & Faber, London.

Innes, J. B., Chiverrell, R. C., Blackford, J. J. *et al.* (2004). Earliest Holocene vegetation history and island biogeography of the Isle of Man, British Isles. *Journal of Biogeography* **31**, 761–72.

Irving, R. A., Schofield, A. J. & Webster, C. J. (1997). *Island Studies: Fifty Years of the Lundy Field Society*. Lundy Field Society, Bideford.

Islands Book Trust (2005). *Traditions of Sea-Bird Fowling in the North Atlantic Region*. Islands Book Trust, Port of Ness.

Isles of Scilly Bird Group (2001). *Isles of Scilly Bird and Natural History Review 2000*. Isles of Scilly Bird Group, St Mary's.

Jackson, A. (1991). *The Faroes: the Faraway Islands*. Robert Hale, London.

Jackson, D. B. (2001). Experimental removal of introduced hedgehogs improves wader nest success in the Western Isles, Scotland. *Journal of Applied Ecology* **38**, 802–12.

Jackson, D. B. & Green, R. E. (2000). The importance of the introduced hedgehog (*Erinaceus europaeus*) as a predator of the eggs of waders (Charadrii) on the machair in South Uist, Scotland. *Biological Conservation* **93**, 333–48.

Jameson, H. L. (1898). On the probable case of protective coloration in the house mouse (*Mus musculus* Linn.). *Journal of the Linnean Society (Zoology)* **26**, 456–73.

Jee, N. (1967). *Guernsey's Natural History*. Guernsey Press, Guernsey.

Jee, N. (1982). *Landscapes of the Channel Islands*. Phillimore, Chichester.

Jensen, A. S., Lundbeck, W., Mortensen, T. & Spärck, R. (Eds) (1928–70). *The Zoology of the Faroes*. A. F. Høst, Copenhagen.

Jeffrey, D. W., Goodwillie, R. N., Healy, B. *et al.* (1977). *North Bull Island, Dublin Bay: a Modern Coastal Natural History*. Royal Dublin Society, Dublin.

Jermy, A. C. & Crabbe, J. A. (Eds) (1978). *The Island of Mull: a Survey of its Flora and Environment*. British Museum (Natural History), London.

Jewell, P. A., Milner, C. & Boyd, J. M. (1974). *Island Survivors: the Ecology of the Soay Sheep of St Kilda*. Athlone Press, London.

Jóhansen, J. (1985). *Studies in the Vegetational History of the Faroe and Shetland Islands*. Foroya Frodskaperfelag, Tórshavn.

Johnson, M. P. & Simberloff, D. S. (1974). Environmental determinants of island species numbers in the British Isles. *Journal of Biogeography* **1**, 149–54.

Johnston, J. L. (1998). *A Naturalist's Shetland*. Poyser, London.

Johnston, J. L. (2007). *Victorians 60° North*. Shetland Times, Lerwick.

Jones, A. G., Chown, S. L., Ryan, P. G., Gremmen, N. J. M. & Gaston, K. J. (2003). A review of conservation threats on Gough Island: a case study for terrestrial conservation in the Southern Oceans. *Biological Conservation* **113**, 75–87.

Jones, R. L. & Keen, D. H. (1993). *Pleistocene Environments in the British Isles*. Chapman & Hall, London.

Jones, R., Keen, D., Birnie, J. & Waton, P. (1990). *Past Landscapes of Jersey.* Société Jersiaise, St Helier.

Jones, W. E. (Ed) (1990). *A Natural History of Anglesey.* Anglesey Antiquarian Society, Llangefni.

Kaeuffer, R., Coltman, D. W., Chapuis, J.-L., Pontier, D. & Réale, D. (2007). Unexpected heterozygosity in an island mouflon population founded by a single pair of individuals. *Proceedings of the Royal Society of London B* **274**, 527–33.

Kaneshiro, K. Y. (1995). *Evolution, speciation and the genetic structure of island populations.* In: *Islands: Biological Diversity and Ecosystem Function* (Ed. Vitousek, P. M., Loope, L. L. & Adsersen, H.). Springer, Berlin, pp.22–33.

Kay, Q. & John, R. (1997). *Patterns of variation in relation to the conservation of rare and declining plant species.* In: *The Role of Genetics in Conserving Small Populations* (Ed. Tew, T. E., Crawford, T. J., Spencer, J. W. *et al.*). JNCC, Peterborough, pp.41–55.

Keatinge, T. H. & Dickson, J. H. (1979). Mid-Flandrian changes in the vegetation on Mainland Orkney. *New Phytologist* **82**, 585–612.

Keen, D. H. (Ed) (1993). *Quaternary of Jersey: Field Guide.* Quaternary Research Association, London.

Keller, L. F. & Waller, D. M. (2002). Inbreeding effects in wild populations. *Trends in Ecology and Evolution* **17**, 230–41.

Kenneth Allsop Memorial Trust & Fowles, J. (Eds) (1978). *Steepholm: a Case Study in the Study of Evolution.* Kenneth Allsop Memorial Trust, Sherborn.

Kerr, I. (1992). *Lindisfarne's Birds.* Revised edition. Northumberland & Tyneside Bird Club, Newcastle.

Kettlewell, H. B. D. (1973). *The Evolution of Melanism.* Clarendon Press, Oxford.

King, R. (1993). *The geographical fascination of islands.* In: *The Development Process in Small Island States* (Ed. Lockhart, D. G., Drakakis-Smith, D. & Schembri, J.). Routledge, London, pp.13–37.

Kitching, J. A. & Ebling, F. J. (1967). The ecology of Lough Ine. *Advances in Ecological Research* **4**, 198–292.

Kloet, G. S. & Hincks, D. (1976). *A Check List of British Insects.* Second edition. Royal Entomological Society, London.

Krauskopf, S. (2001). *Irish Lighthouses.* Appletree Press, Belfast.

Kruuk, H. (2003). *Niko's Nature.* Oxford University Press, Oxford.

Lacaille, A. D. (1954). *The Stone Age in Scotland.* Oxford University Press, London.

Lacey, W. S. & Morgan, M. J. (1989). *The Nature of North Wales.* Barracuda, Buckingham.

Lack, D. (1942a). The breeding birds of Orkney. *Ibis* **84**, 461–84.

Lack, D. (1942b). Ecological features of the bird faunas of British small islands. *Journal of Animal Ecology* **11**, 9–36.

Lack, D. (1943). The breeding birds of Orkney. *Ibis* **85**, 1–27.

Lack, D. (1969a). The numbers of bird species on islands. *Bird Study* **16**, 193–209.

Lack, D. (1969b). Population changes in the land birds of a small island. *Journal of Animal Ecology* **38**, 211–18.

Lambeck, K. & Purcell, A. P. (2001). Sea-level change in the Irish Sea since the last glacial maximum: constraints from isostatic modeling. *Journal of Quaternary Science* **16**, 497–506.

Langham, A. & Langham, M. (1970). *Lundy.* David & Charles, Newton Abbot.

Lavelle, D. (1977). *Skellig: Island Outpost of Europe.* Second edition. O'Brien, Dublin.

Lawson, R. (1888). *Ailsa Craig: its History and Natural History.* J.& R. Parlane, Paisley.

Lawton, J. H. & Brown, K. C. (1986). The population and community ecology of invading insects. *Philosophical Transactions of the Royal Society B* **314**, 607–17.

Le Sueur, F. (1976). *A Natural History of Jersey.* Phillimore, Chichester.

Lewontin, R. C. & Hubby, J. L. (1966). A molecular approach to the study of genic heterozygosity in natural populations of *Drosophila pseudoobscura. Genetics* **54**, 595–609.

Lister, A. M. (1995). *Sea-levels and the evolution of island endemics: the dwarf red deer of Jersey.* In: *Island Britain: a Quaternary Perspective* (Ed. Preece, R. C.). Geological Society, London, pp.151–72.

Llewellyn, S. (2005). *Emperor Smith: the Man Who Built Scilly.* Dovecote Press, Wimborne.

Lloyd, C., Tasker, M. L. & Partridge, K. (1991). *The Status of Seabirds in Britain and Ireland.* Poyser, London.

Lockley, R. M. (1938). *I Know an Island.* Harrap, London.

Lockley, R. M. (1945). *Islands Round Britain.* Collins, London.

Lockley, R. M. (1947). *Letters from Skokholm.* Dent, London. [This book contains much of the 'meat' from Lockley's earlier autobiographical writings on Skokholm: *Dream Island* (Witherby, 1930); *Island Days* (Witherby, 1934); *The Way to an Island* (Dent, 1941); and his later reprises *The Island* (Deutsch, 1969) and *Dear Islandman* (Gomer Press, 1996); also his pioneering studies of *Shearwaters* (Dent, 1942) and *Puffins* (Dent (1953).]

Lorimer, R. I. (1983). *The Lepidoptera of Orkney.* Classey, Faringdon.

Lorimer, R. I. (1998). *Unfinished Business.* Hedera, Faringdon.

Lousley, J. E. (1971). *The Flora of the Isles of Scilly.* David & Charles, Newton Abbot.

Löve, A. & Löve, D. (Eds) (1963). *North Atlantic Biota and their History.* Pergamon, Oxford.

Love, J. (n.d.). *Scotland's Living Landscapes: Machair.* Scottish Natural Heritage, Battleby.

Love, J. A. (1983). *Return of the Sea-Eagle.* Cambridge University Press, Cambridge.

Love, J. A. (2001). *Rum: a Landscape without Figures.* Birlinn, Edinburgh.

Lovejoy, T. (2000). *Biodiversity.* In: *Respect for the Earth* (Prince of Wales *et al*). Profile, London, pp.22–35.

Low, M. (1996). *Celtic Christianity and Nature.* Edinburgh University Press, Edinburgh.

Lowe, V. P. W. (1969). Population dynamics of the red deer (*Cervas elephus* L.) on Rhum. *Journal of Animal Ecology* **38**, 425–57.

Lunn, A. (2004). *Northumberland.* New Naturalist 95. Collins, London.

Lysaght, A. M. (1974). Joseph Banks at Skara brae and Stennis, Orkney, 1772. *Notes and Records of the Royal Society of London* **28**, 221–34.

Lysaght, S. (1998). *Robert Lloyd Praeger: the Life of a Naturalist.* Four Courts Press, Dublin.

Mabey, R. (1986). *Gilbert White.* Century, London

MacArthur, R. H. & Wilson, E. O. (1963). An equilibrium theory of island biogeography. *Evolution* **17**, 373–87.

MacArthur, R. H. & Wilson, E. O. (1967). *The Theory of Island Biogeography.* Princeton University Press, Princeton, NJ.

Macartney, A. (Ed) (1984). *Islands of Europe.* Unit for the Study of Government in Scotland, Edinburgh.

McClintock, D. (1975). *The Wild Flowers of Guernsey.* Collins, London.

McCormick, D. (1974a). *Islands of England & Wales.* Osprey, London.

McCormick, D. (1974b). *Islands of Scotland.* Osprey, London.

McCormick, D. (1974c). *Islands of Ireland.* Osprey, London.

M'Crie, T., Miller, H., Anderson, J., Fleming, J. & Balfour, J. H. (1848). *The Bass Rock.* John Greig, Edinburgh.

MacCulloch, J. (1819). *A Description of the Western Isles of Scotland.* London.

MacDiarmid, H. (1939). *The Islands of Scotland.* Batsford, London.

MacGillivray, W. (1830). Account of the series of islands usually denominated the Outer Hebrides. *Edinburgh Journal of Natural and Geographical Science* **1**, 245–50, 40l–11; **2**, 87–95, 160–5, 321–34.

MacGregor, A. A. (1931). *A Last Voyage to St Kilda.* Cassell, London.

MacGregor, A. A. (1949). *The Western Isles.* Robert Hale, London.

McIntosh, R. P. (1998). The myth of community as organism. *Perspectives in Biology and Medicine* **41**, 426–38.

Mackenzie, C. (1957). *Rockets Galore.* Chatto & Windus, London.

Mackenzie, O. H. (1924). *A Hundred Years in the Highlands.* Edward Arnold, London.

Maclean, C. (1972). *Island on the Edge of the World: Utopian St Kilda and its Passing.* Tom Stacey, London.

McMillan, W. O., Monteiro, A. & Kapan, D. D. (2002). Development and evolution on the wing. *Trends in Ecology and Evolution* **17**, 125–33.

Macnab, P. A. (1987). *Mull & Iona.* Second edition. David & Charles, Newton Abbot.

McNally, K. (1978). *The Islands of Ireland.* Batsford, London.

Magnusson, M. (1997). *Rum: Nature's Island.* Luath Press, Edinburgh.

Majerus, M. E. N. (1998). *Melanism.* Oxford University Press, Oxford.

Majerus, M. E. N. (2002). *Moths.* New Naturalist 90. Collins, London.

Majerus, M., Amos, W. & Hurst, G. (1996). *Evolution: the Four Billion Year War.* Longman, London.

Manchester, S. & Bullock, J. (2000). The impacts of non-native species on UK biodiversity and the effectiveness of control. *Journal of Applied Ecology* **37**, 845–64.

Manne, L. L., Pimm, S. L., Diamond, J. M. & Reed, T. M. (1998). The form of the curves: a direct evaluation of MacArthur & Wilson's classical theory. *Journal of Animal Ecology* **67**, 784–94.

Marren, P. (1995). *The New Naturalists.* New Naturalist 82. Collins, London.

Marsden, J. (1995). *Sea-Road of the Saints: Celtic Holy Men of the Hebrides.* Floris Books, Edinburgh.

Marshall, J. A. & Haes, E. C. M. (1988). *Grasshoppers and Allied Insects of Great Britain and Ireland.* Harley Books, Colchester.

Marshall, W. L. (1978). *The Calf of Man.* Shearwater Press, Ramsey.

Martin, M. (1698). *A Late Voyage to St Kilda, the Remotest of All the Hebrides.* London.

Martin, M. (1703). *A Description of the Western Islands of Scotland.* London [Annotated and illustrated edition edited by M. Robson issued in 2003 by the Islands Book Trust, Port of Ness.]

Martínková, N., McDonald, R. A. & Searle, J. B. (2007). Stoats (*Mustela erminea*) provide evidence of natural overland colonization of Ireland. *Proceedings of the Royal Society of London B* **274**, 1387–93.

Mascheretti, S., Rogatcheva, M. B., Guduz, I., Fredga, K. & Searle, J. B. (2003). How did pygmy shrews colonize Ireland? Clues from a phylogenetic analysis of mitochondrial cytochrome b sequences. *Proceedings of the Royal Society of London B* **270**, 1593–9.

Mason, T. H. (1937). *The Islands of Ireland.* Batsford, London.

Matthews, J. (2007). *Skomer Island.* Graffeg, Cardiff.

Matthews, J. R. (1955). *Origin and Distribution of the British Flora.* Hutchinson, London.

Matthews, L. H. (1952). *British Mammals.* New Naturalist 21. Collins, London.

Mayr, E. (1942). *Systematics and the Origin of Species.* Columbia University Press, New York.

Mayr, E. (1954). *Change of genetic environment and evolution.* In: *Evolution as a Process* (Ed. Huxley, J. S., Hardy, A. C. & Ford, E. B.). Allen & Unwin, London, pp.157–80.

Mayr, E. (1967). The challenge of island faunas. *Australian Natural History* **15**, 359–74.

Macnab. P. A. (1973). *Mull and Iona.* David & Charles, Newton Abbott.

Mason, I. L. (1996). *A World Dictionary of Livestock Breed Types and Varieties,* 2nd revised ed. Commonwealth Agriculture Bureaux, Farnham Royal.

Meek, E. R. (1995). *Islands of Birds.* RSPB, Lerwick.

Mercer, J. (1974). *Hebridean Islands: Colonsay, Gigha, Jura.* Blackie, Glasgow.

Merne, O. J. & Madden, B. (1999). Breeding seabirds of Lambay, County Dublin. *Irish Birds* **6**, 345–58.

Merrifield, F. (1894). Temperature experiments in 1893 on several species of *Vanessa* and other Lepidoptera. *Transactions of the Entomological Society of London* **1894**, 425–38.

Merritt, R., Moore, M. W. & Eversham, B. C. (1996). *Atlas of the Dragonflies of Britain and Ireland.* HMSO, London.

Michaux, J. R., Magnanou, E., Paradis, E., Nieberding, C. & Libois, R. (2003). Mitochondrial phylogeny of the woodmouse (*Apodemus sylvaticus*) in the western Palearctic Region. *Molecular Ecology* **12**, 685–97.

Miller, H. (1849). *Footprints of the Creator.* Nimmo, Edinburgh.

Miller, H. (1858). *The Cruise of the Betsey.* Thomas Constable, Edinburgh.

Mitchell, F. (1989). *Man and Environment in Valencia Island.* Royal Irish Academy, Dublin.

Mitchell, F. (1990). *The Way I Followed.* Country House, Dublin.

Mitchell, F. & Ryan, M. (1997). *Reading the Irish Landscape.* Third edition. Town House, Dublin.

Mitchell, P. I., Newton, S. F., Ratcliffe, N. & Dunn, T. E. (Eds) (2004). *Seabird Populations of Britain and Ireland: Results of the Seabird 2000 Census (1998–2002).* Poyser, London.

Mitchison, R. (1962). *Agricultural Sir John: the Life of Sir John Sinclair of Ulbster, 1745–1835.* Geoffrey Bles, London.

Molony, E. (Ed) (1951). *Portraits of Islands.* Denis Dobson, London.

Monro, D. (1774). *Description of the Western Isles of Scotland.* Thomas D. Morrison, Glasgow.

Morey, F. (Ed) (1909). *A Guide to the Natural History of the Isle of Wight.* William Wesley, London.

Morris, R. (2003a). *The Wildlife of Inchcolm.* Hillside, Leven.

Morris, R. (2003b). *The Wildlife of Inchkeith.* Privately published.

Morris, R. & Bruce, B. (2007). *The East Lothian Emeralds.* Save Wemyss Ancient Caves Society, Dysart.

Morrison, A. (1980). *Early Man in Britain and Ireland.* Croom Helm, London.

Morrison, P. G. & Rylance, T. (1989). *Coquet Island.* Belfry Publicity, Newcastle.

Mueller-Dombois, D., Bridges, K. W. & Carson, H. L. (Eds) (1981). *Island Ecosystems.* Hutchinson Ross, Stroudsburg, PA.

Muir, T. S. (1885). *Ecclesiological Notes on Some of the Islands of Scotland.* David Douglas, Edinburgh.

Murray, W. H. (1966). *The Hebrides.* Heinemann, London.

Murray, W. H. (1973). *The Islands of Western Scotland.* Eyre Methuen, London.

Myers, A. A. & Giller, P. S. (Eds) (1988). *Analytical Biogeography.* Chapman & Hall, London.

Myers, A. A., Little, C., Costello, M. J. & Partridge, J. C. (Eds) (1991). *The Ecology of Loch Hyne. Proceedings of a Conference, 4–5 September 1990.* Royal Irish Academy, Dublin.

Mykura, W. (1976). *British Regional Geology: Orkney and Shetland.* HMSO, Edinburgh.

Nature Conservancy Concil (1976). *Shetland: Localities of Geological and Geomorphological Importance.* NCC, Newbury.

Nature Conservancy Council (1977). *Outer Hebrides: Localities of Geological and Geomorphological Importance.* NCC, Newbury.

Nature Conservancy Council (1978). *Orkney: Localities of Geological and Geomorphoilogical Importance.* NCC, Newbury.

Nelson, J. B. (1986). *Living with Seabrds.* Edinburgh University Press, Edinburgh.

Newton, N. (1992). *The Shell Guide to the Islands of Britain.* David & Charles, Newton Abbot.

Newton, N. S. (1988). *Islay.* David & Charles, Newton Abbot.

Newton, N. S. (1990). *Colonsay & Oronsay.* David & Charles, Newton Abbot.

Nicholson, C. (1995). *Rock Lighthouses of Britain: the End of an Era?* Whittles, Latheronwheel.

Nicolson, A. (2001). *Sea-Room.* HarperCollins, London.

Nicolson, M. H. (1959). *Mountain Gloom and Mountain Glory.* Cornell University Press, Ithaca, NY.

Noble, L. R. & Jones, C. S. (1996). *A molecular and ecological investigation of the large arionid slugs of north west Europe: the potential for new pests.* In: *The Ecology of Agricultural Pests* (Ed. Symondson, W. O. C. & Liddell, J. E.). Chapman & Hall, London, pp.93–131.

Nordström, M., Högmander, J., Laine, J., Nummelin, J., Laanetu, N. & Korpimäki, E. (2003). Effects of feral mink removal on seabirds, waders and passerines on small islands in the Baltic Sea. *Biological Conservation* **109**, 359–68.

Norton, T. (2001). *Reflections on a Summer Sea.* Random House, London.

O'Connor, R. J. (1986). Biological characteristics of invaders among bird species in Britain. *Philosophical Transactions of the Royal Society of London B* **314**, 583–98.

O'Dell, A. C. & Walton, K. (1962). *The Highlands & Islands of Scotland.* Nelson, Edinburgh.

Ó Péicin, D. & Nolan, L. (1997). *Islanders: the True Story of One Man's Fight to Save a Way of Life.* HarperCollins, London.

Over, L. (1987). *The Kelp Industry in Scilly.* Isles of Scilly Museum Publication 14. St Mary's.

Owen, T. & Pilbeam, E. (1992). *Ordnance Survey: Map Makers to Britain since 1791.* HMSO, London.

Paine, R. T. (1980). Food webs, linkage interaction strength and community infrastructure. *Journal of Animal Ecology* **49**, 667–85.

Pankhurst, R. J. & Mullen, J. M. (1991). *Flora of the Outer Hebrides.* Natural History Museum, London.

Parslow, R. (2007). *The Isles of Scilly.* New Naturalist 103. Collins, London.

Parsons, T. (Ed) (1996). *The Invertebrates of the Island of Steep Holm in the Bristol Channel.* Kenneth Allsop Memorial Trust, Wincanton.

Pearman, D. A. & Preston, C. D. (2000). *A Flora of Tiree, Gunna and Coll.* Privately published.

Pemberton, J. M., Smith, J. A., Coulson, T. N. *et al.* (1998). The maintenance of genetic polymorphism in small island populations: large mammals in the Hebrides. In: *Evolution on Islands* (Ed. Grant, P. R.). Oxford University Press, Oxford, pp.51–66.

Pennant, T. (1761–6). *British Zoology.* London: J&J March.

Pennington, P., Osborn, K., Harvey, P. *et al.*

(2004). *The Birds of Shetland.* Christopher Helm, London.

Perring, F. H. & Randall, R. E. (1972). An annotated flora of the Monach Isles NNR, Outer Hebrides. *Transactions of the Botanical Society of Edinburgh* **41**, 431–44.

Perring, F. H. & Walters, S. M. (Eds) (1962). *Atlas of the British Flora.* Nelson, London.

Perry, R. (1946). *A Naturalist on Lindisfarne.* Lindsay Drummond, London.

Pickett, E. (2001). *Isle of Man: Foundations of a Landscape.* British Geological Survey, Swindon.

Piertney, S. B., Stewart, W. A., Lambin, X., Telfer, S., Aars, J. & Dallas, J. F. (2005). Phylogeographic history of water voles (*Arvicola terrestris*) in the United Kingdom. *Molecular Biology* **14**, 1435–44.

Pilcher, J. & Hall, V. (2001). *Flora Hibernica.* Collins Press, Wilton.

Pimm, S. L., Jones, H. L. & Diamond, J. (1988). On the risk of extinction. *American Naturalist* **132**, 757–85.

Pollard, T. & Morrison, A. (Eds) (1996). *The Early Prehistory of Scotland.* Edinburgh University Press, Edinburgh.

Powell, M. (1938). *20,000 Feet on Foula.* Faber & Faber, London.

Praeger, R. L. (1901). Irish topographical botany. *Proceedings of the Royal Irish Academy*, **7**, 1–410.

Praeger, R. L. (1907). Contributions to the natural history of Lambay Island, County Dublin. *Irish Naturalist* **16**, 1–112.

Praeger, R.L. (Eds) (1911–15). Biological survey of Clare Island in the County of Mayo, Ireland, and of the adjoining district. *Proceedings of the Royal Irish Academy* **31B**, sections I, II and III.

Praeger, R. L. (1915). A biological survey of Clare Island in the County of Mayo, Ireland and of the adjoining district. Part 68. General Summary. *Proceedings of the Royal Irish Academy* **31**.

Praeger, R. L. (1923). Dispersal and distribution. *Journal of Ecology* **11**, 114–23.

Praeger, R. L. (1934). *The Botanist in Ireland.* Hodges Figgis, Dublin.

Praeger, R. L. (1937). *The Way That I Went.* Methuen, London, and Hodges, Figgis & Co., Dublin.

Praeger, R. L. (1950). *Natural History of Ireland: a Sketch of its Flora and Fauna.* Collins, London.

Preece, R. C. (Eds) (1995). *Island Britain: a Quaternary Perspective.* Geological Society Special Publication 96. Geological Society, London.

Preston, C. D. & Hill, M. O. (1997). The geographical relationships of British and Irish vascular plants. *Botanical Journal of the Linnean Society* **124**, 1–120.

Preston, C. D., Pearman, D. A. & Dines, T. D. (2002). *New Atlas of the British & Irish Flora.* Oxford University Press, Oxford.

Primack, R. B. (1993). *Essentials of Conservation Biology.* Sinauer, Sunderland, MA.

Provine, W. B. (1989). *Founder effects and genetic revolutions in microevolution and speciation: an historical perspective.* In: *Genetics, Speciation and the Founder Principle* (Eds Giddings, L. V., Kaneshiro, K. Y. & Anderson, W. W.). Oxford University Press, New York, pp.43–76.

Quammen, D. (1996). *The Song of the Dodo: Island Biogeography in an Age of Extinctions.* Hutchinson, London.

Quine, D. A. (1982). *St Kilda Revisited.* Downland Press, Frome.

Quine, D. A. (1995). *St Kilda.* Colin Baxter, Grantown-on-Spey.

Quine, D. A. (Ed) (2001). *Expeditions to the Hebrides by George Clayton Atkinson in 1831 and 1833.* Maclean Press, Waternish.

Ragge, D. R. (1963). First record of the grasshopper *Stenobothrus stigmaticus* (Rambur) (Acridae) in the British Isles, with other new distribution records and notes on the origin of the British Orthoptera. *Entomologist* **96**, 211–17.

Rainbird, P. (2007). *The Archaeology of Islands.* Cambridge University Press, Cambridge.

Ralph, R. (1993). *William MacGillivray.* HMSO, London.

Ralph, R. (Ed) (1996). *William MacGillivray.* Acair, Stornoway.

Ramsay, R. H. (1972). *No Longer on the Map.* Viking, New York.

Rasmussen, R. (1952). *Foroya Flora.* Thomsen, Tórshavn.

Reed, T. M. (1980). Turnover frequency in island birds. *Journal of Biogeography* **7**, 329–35.

Reed, T. M. (1981). The number of breeding landbird species on British islands. *Journal of Animal Ecology* **50**, 613–24.

Reed, T. M., Currie, A. & Love, J. A. (1983). Birds of the Inner Hebrides. *Proceedings of the Royal Society of Edinburgh* **83B**, 449–72.

Rendall, R. (1956). Mollusca orcadensia. *Proceedings of the Royal Society of Edinburgh* **66B**, 131–201.

Renouf, J. & Urry, J. (1976). *The First Farmers in the Channel Islands.* Education Committee, St Helier.

Reynolds, J. C. & Short, M. J. (2003). The status of foxes *Vulpes vulpes* on the Isle of Man in 1999. *Mammal Review* **33**, 69–76.

Rhead, J. & Snow, P. (1994). *Birds of Arran.* Saker Press, Islay.

Rhind, P. M., Blackstock, T. H. & Parr, S. J. (Eds) (1997). *Welsh Islands: Ecology, Conservation and Land Use.* Countryside Council for Wales, Bangor.

Richards, E. (2002). *The Highland Clearances.* Birlinn. Edinburgh.

Ritchie, J. (1930). Scotland's testimony to the march of evolution. *Scottish Naturalist for 1930*, 161–9.

Ritsema, A. (1999). *Discover the Islands of Ireland.* Collins Press, Wilton.

Rixson, D. (2004). *The Hebridean Traveller.* Birlinn, Edinburgh.

Robinson, G. (2007). *The Prehistoric Island Landscape of Scilly.* British Archaeological Report 447.

Robinson, P. (2003). *The Birds of the Isles of Scilly.* Christopher Helm, London.

Robinson, V. & McCarroll, D. (Eds) (1990). *The Isle of Man.* Liverpool University Press, Liverpool.

Robson, M. (1991). *Rona: the Distant Island.* Acair, Stornoway.

Robson, M. (2005). *St Kilda: Church, Visitors and 'Natives'.* Islands Book Trust, Point of Ness.

Roche, R. & Merne, O. (1977). *Saltees: Islands of Birds and Legends*. O'Brien, Dublin.

Rodwell, W. (1996). *Les Ecréhous, Jersey*. Société Jersiaise, St Helier.

Royle, S .A. (1983). The economy and society of the Aran Islands, County Galway, in the early nineteenth century. *Irish Geography* 16, 36–54.

Royle, S. A. (2001). *A Geography of Islands: Small Island Insularity*. Routledge, London.

Russell, G. J., Diamond, J. M., Reed, T. M. & Pimm, S. L. (2006). Breeding birds on small islands: island biogeography or optimal foraging? *Journal of Animal Ecology* 75, 324–39.

Rutherford, G. K. (Ed) (1982). *The Physical Environment of the Faeroe Islands*. Junk, The Hague.

Ryan, J. G., O'Connor, J. P. & Beirne, B. P. (1984). *A Bibliography of Irish Entomology*. Flyleaf Press, Glenageary.

Sabbagh, K. (1999). *A Rum Affair: How Botany's Piltdown Man was Unmasked*. Allen Lane, London.

Saccheri, I., Kuussaari, M., Kankare, M., Vikman, P., Fortelius, W. & Hanski, I. (1998). Inbreeding and extinction in a butterfly metapopulation. *Nature* 392, 491–4.

St John, C. (1893). *Short Sketches of the Wild Sports and Natural History of the Highlands*. John Murray, London.

St Kilda (2003). *Revised Nomination for Inclusion in the World Heritage Site List*. Scottish Executive, Edinburgh.

Sands, J. (1878). *Out of the World, or Life in St Kilda*. MacLachlan & Stewart, Edinburgh.

Saunders, D. (1986). *The Nature of West Wales*. Barracuda, Buckingham.

Sax, D. F., Stachowicz, J. J., Brown, J. H. *et al.* (2007). Ecological and evolutionary insights from species invasions. *Trends in Ecology and Evolution* 22, 465–71.

Saxby, H. (1874). *The Birds of Shetland*. Maclaren & Stewart, Edinburgh.

Saxon, J. (1991). *The Fossil Fishes of the North of Scotland*. Third edition. Humphries, Thurso.

Schoener, A. (1988). Experimental island biogeography. In: *Analytical Biogeography* (Ed. Myers, A. A. & Giller, P. S.). Chapman & Hall, London, pp.483–512.

Scott, W. & Palmer, R. (1987). *The Flowering Plants and Ferns of the Shetland Islands*. Shetland Times, Lerwick.

Scourse, J. D. (1986). *The Isles of Scilly: Field Guide*. Quaternary Research Association, Coventry.

Senior, W. H. & Swan, W. B. (1972). *Survey of Agriculture in Caithness, Orkney and Shetland*. Highland Development Board Special Report 8. Highland Development Board, Inverness.

Serjeantson, D. (1988). Archaeological and ethnographic evidence for seabird exploitation in Scotland. *Archaeozoologia* 2, 209–22.

Severin, T. (1978). *The Brendan Voyage*. Hutchinson, London.

Sharrock, J. T. R. (Ed) (1972). *The Natural History of Cape Clear Island*. Poyser, Berkhamsted.

Shea, M. (1981). *Britain's Offshore Islands*. Country Life, Richmond upon Thames.

Sibbald, R. (1684). *Scotia Illustrata*. Edinburgh.

Sillar, F. C. & Meyler, R. (1979). *Skye*. David & Charles, Newton Abbott.

Simberloff, D. (1969). Experimental zoogeography of islands: a model for insular colonization. *Ecology* 50, 296–314.

Simberloff, D. (1976). Species turnover and equilibrium island biogeography. *Science* 194, 572–8.

Simberloff, D. (1980). A succession of paradigms in ecology: essentialism to materialism and probabilism. *Synthese* 43, 3–39.

Simberloff, D. (1983). When is an island community at equilibrium? *Science* 220, 1275–7.

Simberloff, D. & Abele, L. G. (1976). Island biogeography theory and conservation practice. *Science* 191, 285–6.

Simberloff, D. & Abele, L. G. (1982). Refuge design and island biogeographic theory: effects of fragmentation. *American Naturalist* 120, 41–50.

Simberloff, D. & Wilson, E. O. (1969). Experimental zoogeography of islands. The colonisation of empty islands. *Ecology* **50**, 278–96.

Simberloff, D. & Wilson, E. O. (1970). Experimental zoogeography of islands. A two year record of colonization. *Ecology* **51**, 934–7.

Sinclair, W. T., Morman, J. D. & Ennos, R. A. (1999). The postglacial history of Scots pine (*Pinus sylvestris* L.) in western Europe: evidence from mitochondrial DNA variation. *Molecular Ecology* **8**, 83–8.

Sissons, J. B. (1967). *The Evolution of Scotland's Scenery*. Oliver & Boyd, Edinburgh.

Sleeman, D. P., Devoy, R. J. & Woodman, P. C. (Eds) (1986). Proceedings of the Postglacial Colonization Conference. *Occasional Publication of the Irish Biogeographical Society* **1**.

Smith, D. (1982). *Antique Maps of the British Isles*. Batsford, London.

Smith, H. D. (1984). *Shetland Life and Trade 1550–1914*. John Donald, Edinburgh.

Smith, K. & Smith, V. (1983). *A Bibliography of the Entomology of the Smaller British Offshore Islands*. Classey, Faringdon.

Somerville, C. (1990). *The Other British Isles*. Grafton, London.

Somerville-Large, P. (2000). *Ireland's Islands*. Gill & Macmillan, Dublin.

Soulé, M. E. (1983). *What do we really know about extinction?* In: *Genetics and Conservation* (Ed. Schonewald-Cox, C. M., Chambers, S. M., MacBryde, B. & Thomas, W. L.). Benjamin/Cummings, Menlo Park, CA, pp.111–24.

Soulé, M. E. (Ed) (1987). *Viable Populations for Conservation*. Cambridge University Press, Cambridge.

Southwood, T. R. E. (1988). Tactics, stategies and templets. *Oikos* **52**, 3–18.

Southwood, T. R. E. & Clarke, J. R. (1999). Charles Sutherland Elton. *Biographical Memoirs of Fellows of the Royal Society of London* **45**, 129–46.

Southwood, T. R. E. & Kennedy, C. E. J. (1983). Trees as islands. *Oikos* **41**, 359–71.

Spalding, A. & Sargent, P. (2000). *Scilly's Wildlife Heritage*. Twelveheads Press, Truro.

Spence, D. H. N. (1979). *Shetland's Living Landscape: a Study in Island Plant Ecology*. Thuleprint, Sandwick.

Stagles, J. & Stagles, R. (1980). *The Blasket Islands: Next Parish America*. O'Brien, Dublin.

Steel, T. (1965). *The Life and Death of St Kilda*. National Trust for Scotland, Edinburgh.

Steers, J. A. (Ed) (1934). *Scolt Head Island*. Heffer, Cambridge.

Steers, J. A. (1953). *The Sea Coast*. New Naturalist 25. Collins, London.

Steers, J. A. (1973). *The Coastline of Scotland*. Cambridge University Press, Cambridge.

Stewart, J. R. & Lister, A. M. (2001). Cryptic northern refugia and the origins of the modern biota. *Trends in Ecology and Evolution* **16**, 608–13.

Stewart, M. (1933). *Ronay*. Oxford University Press, London.

Stirling, A. (1986). Anthrax island clean-up. *Geographical Magazine* **58**, 493–4.

Stommel, H. (1984). *Lost Islands*. University of British Columbia Press, Victoria, BC.

Stringer, C. (2006). *Homo Britannicus*. Allen Lane, London.

Stuart, A. J. (1974). Pleistocene history of the British vertebrate fauna. *Biological Reviews* **49**, 225–66.

Stuart, A. J. & Wijngaarden-Bakker, L. H. (1985). Quaternary vertebrates. In: *The Quaternary History of Ireland* (Ed. Edwards, K. J. & Warren, W. P.). Academic Press, London, pp.221–409.

Svensson, R. (1955). *Lonely Isles*. Batsford, London.

Tallantire, P. & Walters, S. M. (1947). The late-glacial period. *Nature* **159**, 556–9.

Taylor, S. J. & Reid, J. B. (2001). *The Distribution of Seabirds and Cetaceans around the Faroe Islands*. JNCC, Peterborough.

Telfer, S., Dallas, J. F., Aars, J., Piertney, S. B., Stewart, W. A. & Lambin, X. (2003). Demographic and genetic structure of fossoial water voles (*Arvicola terrestris*) on Scottish islands. *Journal of Zoology* **259**, 23–9.

Thom, V. M. (1986). *Birds in Scotland.* Poyser, Calton.

Thom, V. M. (1989). *Fair Isle. An Island Saga.* John Donald, Edinburgh.

Thomas, C. (1985). *Explorations of a Drowned Landscape: Archaeology and History of the Isles of Scilly.* Batsford, London.

Thomas, L. (1968). *Some Lovely Islands.* Arlington Books, London.

Thomas, L. (1983). *A World of Islands.* Michael Joseph, London.

Thompson, F. (1968). *Harris and Lewis.* David & Charles, Newton Abbot.

Thompson, F. (1970). *St Kilda and other Hebridean Outliers.* David & Charles, Newton Abbot.

Thompson, F. (1974). *The Uists and Barra.* David & Charles, Newton Abbot.

Thomson, W. P. L. (1983). *Kelp-Making in Orkney.* Orkney Press, Kirkwall.

Thomson, W. P. L. (2001). *The New History of Orkney.* Mercat, Edinburgh.

Thornton, I. (1996). *Krakatau: the Destruction and Reassembly of an Island Ecosystem.* Harvard University Press, Cambridge, MA.

Thornton, I. (2007). *Island Colonization.* Cambridge University Press, Cambridge.

Thorpe, W. H. (1974). David Lambert Lack, 1910–1973. *Biographical Memoirs of Fellows of the Royal Society* **20**, 271–93.

Tinbergen, N. (1953). *The Herring Gull's World.* New Naturalist Monographs. Collins, London.

Tinbergen, N. (1958). *Curious Naturalists.* Country Life, London.

Toghill, P. (2000). *The Geology of Britain: an Introduction.* Swan Hill Press, Shrewsbury.

Tomkins, J. L. & Brown, G. S. (2004). Population density drives the local evolution of a threshold dimorphism. *Nature* **431**, 1099–103.

Tosh, D. G., Lusby, L., Montgomery, W. I. & O'Halloran, J. (2008). First record of a greater white-toothed shrew *Crocidura russula* in Ireland. *Mammal Review*, **38**, 321–6.

Tudor, J. R. (1883). *The Orkneys and Shetland: their Past and Present State.* Edward Stanford, London.

Tulloch, R. (1978). *A Guide to Shetland Mammals.* Shetland Times, Lerwick.

Tulloch, R. & Hunter, F. (1972). *Guide to Shetland Birds.* Shetland Times, Lerwick.

Turner, V. (1998). *Ancient Shetland.* Batsford, London.

Tutt, J. W. (1899). *A Natural History of the British Lepidoptera.* Swann Sonnenschein, London.

Upton, B. (2004). *Volcanoes and the Making of Scotland.* Dundin Academic Press, Edinburgh.

Veitch, C. & Clout, M. (Eds) (2002). *Turning the Tide: the Eradication of Invasive Species.* IUCN, Gland.

Venables, L. S. V. & Venables, U. M. (1955). *Birds and Mammals of Shetland.* Oliver & Boyd, Edinburgh.

Veron, P. K. (Ed) (1997). *Important Sites for Birds in the Channel Isles.* La Société Guernesiaise, Guernsey.

Vincent, P. (1990). *The Biogeography of the British Isles: an Introduction.* Routledge, London.

Vyvyan, C. C. (1953). *The Scilly Isles.* Robert Hale, London.

Waddell, J., O'Connell, J. W. & Korff, A. (Eds) (1994). *The Book of Aran.* Tir Eolas, Kinvara.

Wade-Martins, P. (1990). *The Manx Loghtan Story.* Geerings, Ashford.

Wainwright, F. T. (Ed) (1962). *The Northern Isles.* Nelson, Edinburgh.

Wallace, A. R. (1880). *Island Life.* Macmillan, London.

Walsh, D. (2004). *Oileáin.* Pesda Press, Bangor.

Walters, S. M. (1978). British endemics. In: *Essays in Plant Taxonomy* (Ed. Street, H. E.). Academic Press, London, pp.263–74.

Watson, H. C. (1835). *Outlines of the Geographical Distribution of British Plants.* Edinburgh (privately printed).

Watson, H. C. (1847–59). *Cybele Britannica.* Longman, London.

Watt, G. (1951). *The Farne Islands: their History and Wild Life.* Country Life, London. [Later editions are published under Grace Watt's married name of Hickling].

Weiner, J. (1994). *The Beak of the Finch.* Jonathan Cape, London.

Weir, J. J. (1881). Notes on the Lepidoptera of the Outer Hebrides. *Entomologist* **14**, 218–23.

West, R. G. (1968). *Pleistocene Geology and Biology with particular reference to the British Isles.* Longmans, Green, London.

White, D. F. B. (1876). On melanochroism and leucochroism. *Entomologist's Monthly Magazine* **13**, 145–9.

White, L. (1967). The historical roots of our ecologic crisis. *Science* **155**, 1203–7.

Whittaker, R. J. (1998). *Island Biogeography.* Oxford University Press, Oxford.

Whittle, A., Keith-Lucas, M., Milles, A., Noddle, B., Rees, S. & Romans, J. (1986). *Scord of Brouster: an Early Agricultural Settlement on Shetland.* Oxford University Committee for Archaeology, Oxford.

Wickham-Jones, C. R. (1994). *Scotland's First Settlers.* Batsford, London.

Williams, M. & Harper, D. (1999). *The Making of Ireland.* Immel, London

Williams, R. (1965). *Where the World is Quiet.* Witherby, London.

Williamson, K. (1948). *The Atlantic Islands.* Collins, London.

Williamson, K. (1958). Population and breeding environment of the St Kilda and Fair Isle wrens. *British Birds* **51**, 369–93.

Williamson, K. (1965). *Fair Isle and Its Birds.* Oliver & Boyd, Edinburgh.

Williamson, K. & Boyd, J. M. (1960). *St Kilda Summer.* Hutchinson, London.

Williamson, K. & Boyd, J. M. (1963). *A Mosaic of Islands.* Oliver & Boyd, Edinburgh.

Williamson, M. H. (1981). *Island Populations.* Oxford University Press, Oxford.

Williamson, M. H. (1983). The land-bird community of Skokholm: ordination and turnover. *Oikos* **41**, 378–84

Williamson, M. H. (1984). Sir Joseph Hooker's Lecture on Insular Floras. *Biological Journal of the Linnean Society* **22**, 55–77.

Willis, K. J. & van Andel, T. H. (2004). Trees or no trees? The environments of central and eastern Europe during the Last Glaciation. *Quaternary Science Reviews* **23**, 2369–87.

Winchester, S. (2003). *Krakatoa: the Day the World Exploded.* Viking, London.

Wingfield, R. T. R. (1995). *A model of sea-levels in the Irish and Celtic Seas during the end-Pleistocene to Holocene transition.* In: *Island Britain: a Quaternary Perspective* (Ed. Preece, R. C.). Geological Society, London, pp.209–42.

Withrington, D. J. (Ed) (1983). *Shetland and the Outside World 1469–1969.* Oxford University Press, Oxford.

Woodman, P., McCarthy, M. & Monaghan, N. (1997). The Irish Quaternary Fauna Project. *Quaternary Science Reviews* **16**, 129–59.

Yalden, D. W. (1981). The occurrence of the pygmy shrew *Sorex minutus* on moorland and the implications for its presence in Ireland. *Journal of Zoology* **195**, 147–56.

Yalden, D. W. (1999). *The History of British Mammals.* Poyser, London.

Young, D. (Ed) (1992). *Stroma.* North of Scotland Newspapers, Wick.

Youngson, P. (2001). *Jura: Island of Deer.* Birlinn, Edinburgh.

Index

The New Naturalist Library

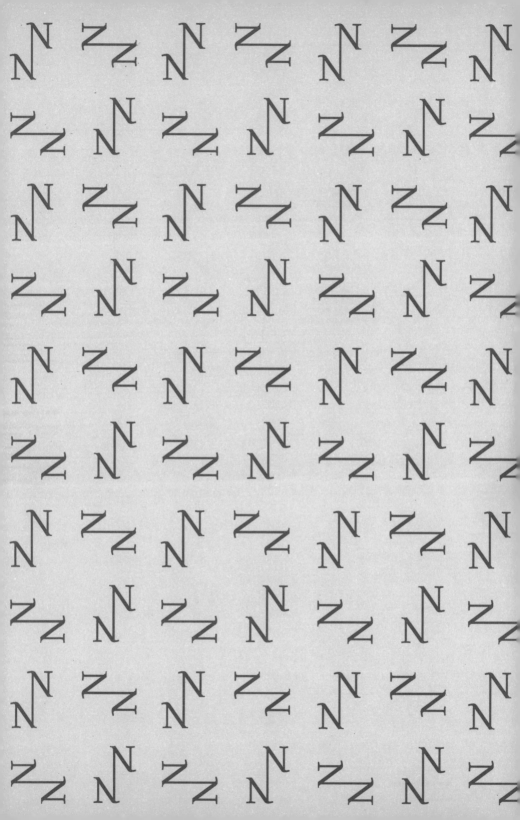